SLEEPWALKING
TO SURRENDER

SLEEPWALKING TO SURRENDER

DEALING WITH TERRORISM IN PAKISTAN

KHALED AHMED

PENGUIN
VIKING

An imprint of Penguin Random House

VIKING

USA | Canada | UK | Ireland | Australia
New Zealand | India | South Africa | China | Singapore

Viking is part of the Penguin Random House group of companies
whose addresses can be found at global.penguinrandomhouse.com

Published by Penguin Random House India Pvt. Ltd
4th Floor, Capital Tower 1, MG Road,
Gurugram 122 002, Haryana, India

Penguin
Random House
India

First published in Viking by Penguin Random House India 2016

ISBN 9780670088966

Typeset in Adobe Garamond by Manipal Digital Systems, Manipal
Printed at Replika Press Pvt. Ltd, India

www.penguin.co.in

For Fasih Ahmed,
editor of AG Publications' Newsweek Pakistan,
who made it possible for me to write with freedom
and made my writings readable with his first-rate professional editing

Contents

1

Introduction

Terrorism, Ideology and the Crumbling State

In October 2013, after the Taliban killed a major general of the Pakistan army in Dir and blew up eighty Christians in Peshawar, Pakistan was busy rationalizing the situation in favour of 'peace talks' with them. A judge in Peshawar, in an effort to ingratiate himself into the Taliban's good books, helpfully questioned: 'Why is modern banking still allowed in Pakistan?' He was within his rights because the sharia Appellate Bench of Pakistan's Supreme Court had indeed banned it. Banking, as we know it today, is banned in Islam, so is insurance and the state lottery, but Pakistan is still carrying on with them. Nor is the judge the only one questioning such practices; al-Qaeda's Ayman al-Zawahiri condemns Pakistan for not banning modern banking.

The religious parties, unable to win elections, have always drawn their strength, not from the elected assemblies, but from al-Qaeda and the Taliban, as the latter kill in the name of Islam. (The exceptions among religious groups are the Shi'ites and Barelvi Sunnis, who are routinely butchered by the Taliban as deviants from the faith.) In unison, they defended dialogue with the killers who didn't want to be distracted from terrorism as they prepared for talks with the Nawaz Sharif government, fortified by an all-party consensus on peace talks instead of 'war against terrorism'. The National University of Science and Technology (NUST) at Islamabad prophylactically started fining girl students who wore jeans on campus.

The Council of Islamic Ideology (CII), constitutionally mandated to 'guide' the legislature, refused to award death to those who make wrongful accusations under the blasphemy law, which gives death as minimum punishment to those who insult the Holy Prophet (PBUH). It also piously deemed DNA evidence as secondary, not primary, proof in cases of rape, where the perpetrator simply cannot be punished because of the conditionality of four eyewitnesses to the forcible sexual assault. It recommended that earlier legislation under *hudood* (Quranic punishments) correcting this legal irrationality, be rolled back.

Muslims produce their best men when they are not ruling the state they live in. The most gifted intellectuals, like Muhammad Iqbal and Muhammad Abduh, survived only under the British Empire because their works were too 'groundbreaking' for their co-religionists. When Muslims acquire a state they go into a kind of recidivist trance: 'give us utopia or nothing'. They make noises about the 'modern Islamic' state but the moment such a state is created, they start squabbling over it. Despite their denial of 'theology', this is all they have when thinking of the state. They deny the presence of a clergy in Islam but their society is crawling with clergy, and despite avowals to the contrary, they slavishly follow their frozen-in-time medieval doctrines, savagely discriminatory to women and non-Muslims.

The other thing that has Muslims in a tizzy is education. If you want to educate yourself, never ask a Muslim what to do. He will accept modern education, saying the Quran is for all times, including modern times, and therefore allows modern education. But he baulks the moment you say 'secular' education. The age of reason, which gave us modern education, is not his cup of tea because what he understands by 'reason' is 'deductive logic'. He accepts the discipline of economics while ideologically rejecting the concepts of banking and savings. He is 'literalist', therefore he can be a banker without accepting the institution he serves.

In physics too, Pakistan's most gifted, UK-educated nuclear scientist, Sultan Bashiruddin Mahmood, for instance, believed in the existence of jinns. He actually read a paper to General Zia, which said he could produce electricity for all of Pakistan from one 'tamed' jinn. The nuclear physicist, Pervez Hoodbhoy, who is consistently criticized by Pakistan's religious establishment, says Muslims avoid soiling their faith by staying away from the theory of science and learn it as mere 'technology'. They 'steal' science to make nuclear weapons in Pakistan and Iran. When Hoodbhoy condemned a Muslim 'scientist' who claimed he was running his car on water, for being a crook, no one really believed him.

The world thinks Muslims are poor and crazy because their states have abysmal records in education. If you think you can improve a Muslim through education, then take a look at the curricula in Pakistan. Any attempt to tone down references to war as a way of life by the provincial authority is attacked by the clergy, after which the media starts growling, sending the education minister scurrying back to texts mandating jihad for all Muslims. This is a state that has defamed itself through proxy wars it used to call jihad.

Any change in the ideological content of textbooks is criticized, amid naked threats, till the removed lessons are reinstated. This happened, for instance, in the province of Khyber Pakhtunkhwa in Pakistan, as if in preparation for the rule of the Taliban. Muslim youth are not iconoclastic because they are born in modern times; their aggression is regressive because they are iconoclasts of modernity. 'Radical' in Islam is the act of going back; the same goes for 'revolution'. In Arabic, 'modern' (*jadeed*) is derived from *jadd* meaning 'grandfather'. The more educated a Muslim is, the more dangerous he is for his country and the rest of the world. Because of the content of indoctrination in syllabi, the French writer, Olivier Roy, is less dismissive of Muslims as they come to grips with the modern state and its current system of governance, which is democracy. He says Islamists are no longer able to brush aside the democratic process simply because it is not a caliphate as they envisage it. Looking at the Muslim Brotherhood in Egypt, he says they have to accept the premier institution of democracy—the elections— to retain support among the people. He mentions the Ikhwan in Egypt, the Ennahda in Tunisia and the Islah in Yemen. He thinks the acceptance of democracy by Islamists is a new phenomenon which should inspire hope.[1]

But the Egyptians got scared of the elected Brotherhood president, Mohammed Morsi, and his sharia which the Ikhwan pledged on placards saying '*Na'amlil Sharia*' (yes to sharia!), and staged the biggest rally in human history against him to force the army to intervene. In Turkey, the modern Kemalist state is being rolled back because Prime Minister Erdogan is keener than even Fethullah Gulen, the expat genius whose shadow presides over Turkey's retrogression, to enforce sharia. Iran has democracy if elections denote democracy; and it is now thirty years since clerical rule started making the people think they are hardly living under a democracy. And sharia keeps getting more stringent: signs are Pakistan's sharia could have had to be beefed up had the peace-talks with the Taliban gone ahead.

For now, in Olivier Roy's words, Muslims are busy creating chaos. Presumably, after this chaos ends, there will be an order that gives the Muslim common man a life that he can live. What we have now is described by Abu Bakr Naji, the founding philosopher of the al-Qaeda-linked group, al-Shabab, in the title of his book,

The Management of Savagery. As it moved to peace talks, Pakistan was, in my view, in the grip of this 'management of savagery' by the Taliban, pulling the 'modern' state down through the killing of innocent people—with the Muslim population indoctrinated in favour of savagery by the 'defective' (in the eyes of the Taliban) sharia currently in force.

Bangladesh was created 'secular' in reaction to Pakistan, but soon enough the military decided to listen to the 'genius' of Bengali Muslims and make it Islamic. Shockingly for Muslims of the world, not long ago, the Supreme Court of Bangladesh rejected the Islamic amendments and reverted the constitution to its secular shape. But the government of Prime Minister Sheikh Hasina Wajed, with its three-fourths majority in Parliament, dared not legislate accordingly for fear of polarizing the state and inviting mujahideen from all over the Islamic world to 'set things right'.

Politics of Surrender

The process of capitulation in 2014 called peace talks was preceded by an All Parties Conference (APC) in Islamabad in September unanimously recommending the initiation of dialogue with 'all the stakeholders to curb terrorism', meaning 'white-flag' talks with the Taliban. Two APCs before this had tried anti-Americanism to woo the terrorists, thinking the Taliban would be satisfied, but failed and also ended up doing nothing against America. After the army announced it was getting out of Malakand (Swat-Dir) in 2009, the Taliban killed a major general and a lieutenant colonel there, and killed four additional troops in North Waziristan, on 15 September.

The army had already tried its populist anti-Americanism under General Kayani in deference to its internal emotion, but could not do without the $60 million a month it received from the US-led Coalition Support Fund for deployment in the Federally Administered Tribal Areas (FATA), while needlessly tormenting a government it thought was pro-American and pro-India. The APC line was: fighting the Taliban was part of the big mistake of becoming America's ally after 9/11. Rumour was that Imran Khan whose party is ruling in strategic Khyber Pakhtunkhwa abutting on FATA had convinced Army Chief General Kayani to take the army out of FATA gradually as an earnest of sincerity to the Taliban who were fighting Pakistan 'because of its slavishly pro-America policy'.

The APC attached no conditions to its offer of talks, except for self-mortifyingly vowing to go to the UN against American drones killing the Taliban in FATA; which led to the Taliban discussing with their seventy-eight splinters how best to respond to the offer after the Tehreek-e-Taliban Pakistan (TTP) welcomed it through a spokesman. On 15 September, they proclaimed the freeing of TTP prisoners as their precondition for talks. Pakistan's politics looked like bringing it humiliation and no peace.

Significantly, in the Urdu language press, the APC was hailed as supreme wisdom; in the English media, serious doubts were expressed about talking to terrorists from a position of weakness. A clash of linguistic narratives took place pointedly on talk shows carried by the well-known Pakistani channel GEO TV where 'English-medium' former Pakistan ambassador to the US and head of Islamabad's NGO Jinnah Institute, Sherry Rehman, was pitted against the 'Urdu-medium', recently-'outed' super-non-state actor, former chief of 'defunct' Harkat-ul-Mujahideen and front-row member of Defence of Pakistan Council which vowed to fight India till the bitter end, Fazlur Rehman Khalil. As for the charge that Pakistan was getting ready to talk to the Taliban from prostration, Khalil's answer was stock: if the superpower can talk peace with the Taliban 'strangers' why can't Pakistan with its own 'misguided sons'? Ms Rehman's rebuttal was easy: the Americans are leaving a country they had occupied; Pakistan was not leaving Pakistan. Then came a more complicated issue: if Pakistan can be ready to talk to the Baloch insurgents taking the terrorism path in Balochistan, why can't it talk to the Taliban? Ms Rehman said:

because the Taliban had come from outside while the Baloch were Pakistanis. She carefully suppressed the comment that, while both were terrorists, the Taliban had to be fought because they were ideologically more threatening.

The Taliban and hundreds of international warriors wanted to create a state according to the tenets of Islam listed in al-Qaeda chief al-Zawahiri's treatise 'The Morning and the Lamp'. In this, he denigrates Jinnah's vision of Pakistan and destroys the Pakistani constitution article by article with Islamic argument. (Pakistan has taken pains to knock it out of the Internet but the 'alternative constitution' was translated into Urdu and widely distributed by madrasas in Pakistan.)[2]

The truth on the ground was that the Pakistan army was fighting the Taliban openly and Baloch insurgents deniably because both were engaging in terrorism, and the Baloch Liberation Front (BLF) was learning new tricks from the Taliban, enjoying a kind of terror condominium in Balochistan. There could be no difference of approach: both were terrorists; both funded from abroad and challenged a state that not long ago was doing the same sort of thing in other states. Then how was the BLF different from the TTP?

The answer is: because the TTP was ideologically driven and the BLF secular. The Taliban had the same ideology as Pakistan's, and its claims were 'corrective' of a 'misguided state'; while the BLF didn't resonate with the Muslim mind in Pakistan, the TTP did. The TTP could take over the state with people's consent and dispose of its nuclear weapons, the BLF couldn't. The Taliban thought themselves destined to rule Pakistan; the Baloch wanted only to secede. And why should the Taliban version of sharia be more persuasive than the sharia proclaimed by the Constitution of the Islamic Republic of Pakistan? Because the Taliban sharia was more 'authentic'. The constitutional sharia didn't enforce Islamic punishments under the doctrine of deterrence ('munkirat' or doing bad things) and had no provision of punishment under the doctrine of approval (for not doing 'marufat' or good things).

The new extremist Muslim mind favours Islamic punishments (hudood) without 'due process' and wants to punish people for not doing good things like saying namaz. (The modern state punishes crimes listed in the penal code; it doesn't punish anyone for not doing good deeds.) The biggest complaint from madrasa purists in Pakistan is against bank interest which their jurisprudence consensually condemns as prohibited usury (*riba*). Therefore, Pakistan was well-advised not to talk peace with the Taliban without first 'softening' them with punitive action with the help of other 'threatened' nations of the world, including India.

Pakistan was therefore more endangered by the Taliban than by Baloch separatists. (Note the 'absorptive' nature of the first and 'recessive' nature of the second.) India is not endangered by the Naxalite-Maoist insurgency in many of its states because the ideology of the state of India is not the same as that of the rebels. Although Prime Minister Manmohan Singh expressed his concern over the spread of this rebellion, there were no signs that India would ever 'talk peace' with them from a position of weakness. India was also not holding APCs recommending unconditional peace offers in the northeastern corner of the country.

In the northeast of India, a cluster of small states (Manipur, Assam, Nagaland, Tripura, Meghalaya) have been convulsed with 'freedom movements' that have become violent. Out of the five, the first three were still giving trouble in 2007 and violence there had actually increased after a ceasefire agreed by the Indian army in 1997. If Pakistan had been watching, it would have learned that ceasefires with terrorists only give them time to regroup and form bigger armies. Also, there are some other lessons that Pakistan and Afghanistan should have learned from India's experience with terrorism since the 1950s.

One big lesson was not to glamorize the misfortunes of tribal communities gone wrong for lack of normal evolution. Pakistanis are guilty of fabricating the myth that the Pakhtun never give up fighting and have never been conquered. They often mouth this obscenity standing in front of camps where countless Pakhtun women and children suffer history's worst brutalization. India has deployed its army against the warriors of the northeast without parlaying with them from either a position of weakness or ideological vulnerability. But as noted above, India is lucky it is not an ideological state and its masses are not given to extremism like the Muslims of the world, thus legitimizing the terrorist creed of al-Qaeda.

Talking to the Taliban

Prime Minister Nawaz Sharif seemed poised in the middle of January 2004 to get the army to attack the Taliban stronghold of North Waziristan. A retaliatory military sally there had already killed dozens of them and probably 'softened' the pathologically violent new Taliban chief, Mullah Fazlullah. But the end of January, Sharif was probably told of this 'softening' which persuaded him to change tack radically to switch to the 'talk' mode with the 'softened' Taliban still killing innocent Pakistanis all over the country.

What proved that he was actually in the 'attack' mode earlier was the way he treated a 'teacher of the Taliban' cleric Maulana Sami ul-Haq of Akora Khattak madrasa near Peshawar where the assassins of ex-premier Benazir Bhutto had stayed before coming to Rawalpindi in 2008 to complete their job. Haq was suddenly 'dropped' and had to slink back to his seminary complaining Sharif had not deigned to grant him audience. Now the 'talks' mode was back and Sharif nominated four individuals to a team, who would talk to a panel likewise chosen by the Taliban.

The four members of the Sharif team were: Rustam Shah Mohmand, Irfan Siddiqi, Rahimullah Yusufzai and Major Muhammad Amir (retd). Rustam Shah Mohmand was an old member of the Civil Service of Pakistan who served as political agent in the tribal areas, rose to the office of chief secretary of the Frontier Province before getting charge of the Afghan refugee camps in Pakistan, finally landing up as ambassador in Kabul. He was linked to Imran Khan's Tehreek-e-Insaf and hence spastic about the United States, opposed to military operations in the tribal areas, balanced only by his equally intense desire to get Pakistan to normalize ties with India, swearing that the Indian presence in Afghanistan would not destabilize Pakistan. He was Nawaz Sharif's appointee to the committee charged in the 1990s with normalizing Pakistan's relations with what is today the Northern Alliance in Afghanistan.

Irfan Siddiqi was adviser to the prime minister and had been media consultant to him when the latter languished out of power in Lahore. He was the only non-Pashtun in the team and wanted the Taliban to agree to a bilateral ceasefire before the two sides engaged. Journalist Yousafzai was a veteran Taliban-watcher with credibility in the global media and was sure that his team would end up being a sounding board from where to glean the agenda of actual talks.

Major Amir (retd), an ex-ISI officer, aroused comment, but his background was firmly pro-Sharif by reason of his training inside the army, fearing the PPP as a liberal party soft on India and Pakistan's nuclear programme. Patently non-intellectual, he represented the ideological nature of the army where no intellect is required to become an intelligence officer. In 1989, he tried, together with another ISI officer, Brigadier Imtiaz Billa, to persuade some PPP members of the National Assembly to 'defect' in order to topple the government of Benazir Bhutto. One can gauge the moronic level of the planning from the fact that the operation Midnight Jackals turned out to be a reverse sting in which the PPP politicians filmed them *in flagrante delicto*. Both were fired from service.

Unlike Egypt, Pakistan has a 'political middle' that can mediate between Islamists and liberals, and that is represented by Nawaz Sharif's Muslim League. It has a nexus with an intensely right-wing army and will lend ear to the plaints of the religious parties aspiring to a premodern utopia with an umbilical connection with the Taliban and al-Qaeda. The ISI loved him and Major Amir was counted among officers who leaned in his favour when he was challenging the army chiefs. Major Amir had come on TV in the past to confess that he did stage the Midnight Jackals plot to subvert Benazir Bhutto. He hailed from Swabi in Khyber Pakhtunkhwa where his brother Tayyab ran the famous Panjpir madrasa where Taliban chief Fazlullah picked up his ultra-radical anti-democracy Islam on the basis of which he captured the valley of Swat in 2007. The madrasa earned a bad reputation as a jihadi nursery. After Major Amir was retired from the army, the PPP tried to besiege the Panjpir madrasa with a police force but was unsuccessful in bringing it to heel, probably because of a hidden abetting hand from the ISI.

Expelled from Islamabad, both Brigadier Imtiaz Billa and Major Amir were given sanctuary by Nawaz Sharif in Punjab which was fighting a province-centre war with Bhutto. Both the intelligence officers served the cause of this war. After the PPP government fell in 1990, the next government under Nawaz Sharif actually reinstated the Panjpir seminary by taking a procession of trucks to Swabi led by media adviser Mushahid Hussain and ex-ISI chief General Hamid Gul who too had since been retired by Army Chief General Asif Nawaz for insubordination. Nawaz Sharif was then loaded with anti-American baggage, intellectually chaperoned by Mushahid Hussain and spiritually aided by a brainwashed nation convinced that the US was egging India on to destroy Pakistan. This is still the case, but Nawaz Sharif is now a mature politician, no longer interested in the rhetoric of his advisers.

There was still clearer evidence of the ISI nexus with terrorism. In April 2010, two ex-ISI officers, ex-air-force officer Khalid Khwaja and Col Imam, with their loyalties clearly on the side of al-Qaeda and the Taliban, were captured by the Asian Tigers faction of the Taliban in Waziristan. Before being executed, Khalid Khwaja confessed on the Internet that he was working for the pro-al-Qaeda and Taliban faction of the ISI. The video on the Internet had him saying: 'The top jihadi commanders are the ISI's proxies and are given a free hand to collect funds. The leaders include Maulana Fazlur Rehman Khalil (who laid the foundations of the International Islamic Front with bin Laden in 1998), and Maulana Masood Azhar (chief of Jaish-e-Mohammad).'

Some voices of criticism were raised about Major Amir in the Pakistani press because of his murky past, but there was still some sense in taking on board people like him when talking to the Taliban. The Taliban said they were willing to talk and, for the first time, they also declared their confidence in the team chosen by Sharif. The 'crunch' person was the Taliban chief Mullah Fazlullah. Did Sharif's team have traction with him because of Major Amir? Would he allow a ceasefire? What would he demand in return? Were the Taliban 'softened' enough to change policy? If they were divided on policy would any decision to cease fire actually hold? Would the Taliban resile from their demand for the imposition of their kind of horribly punitive sharia? Most analysts thought nothing would come of the talks; but the perceptive among them thought the meetings would reveal the mind of the Taliban leadership to some extent, after which the Pakistan army could invade the Taliban hideout in North Waziristan.

Peace Pipe or Pipe Dream?

In February 2014, the peace pipe Pakistan wished to smoke with the Taliban was turned into a pipe dream after the banned organization issued, on 9 February, the following 'to do' list for Islamabad before it could think of ceasefire:

1) stop drone attacks; 2) introduce sharia law in courts; 3) introduce an Islamic system of education in public and private institutions; 4) release Pakistani and foreign Taliban prisoners; 5) restore property damaged by drone attacks and pay compensation; 6) hand over control of tribal areas to local forces; 7) withdraw

the army from tribal areas and close down checkposts; 8) drop all criminal charges against the Taliban; 9) release prisoners from both sides; 10) grant equal rights for all—poor and rich; 11) offer jobs to families of drone attack victims; 12) end interest-based system; 13) end support for the US 'war on terror'; 14) replace the democratic system of governance with the Islamic system; and, 15) end all relations with the US.

Responding to Pakistan's nomination of its negotiating team, the Taliban named a five-member equally 'pro-Taliban' team without consultation with them: Maulana Sami ul-Haq (JUI-S), Imran Khan of Pakistan Tehreek-e-Insaf (PTI), Kifaetullah (JUI-F), Maulana Abdul Aziz of Red Mosque of Islamabad, and Professor Mohammad Ibrahim of Jamaat-e-Islami (JI). None of them was a member of the Tehreek-e-Taliban Pakistan (TTP), which was a banned organization. The new Taliban leader Mullah Fazlullah seemed to thumb his nose at the state of Pakistan by choosing his team from the politico-religious mainstream. The five members represent a Talibanized section of the country boasting old connections with the Afghan Taliban and Tehreek Taliban Pakistan (TTP). The irony was crushing: Prime Minister Nawaz Sharif's own team contained people with pro-Taliban and anti-American leanings. The idea was to win the confidence of the Taliban, but Mullah Fazlullah didn't bite. The talks wouldn't commit the TTP to anything.

Another irony was that Fazlullah had named Imran Khan in his panel, thus creating a situation where PTI would be talking to itself while pretending to talk to the TTP. Mercifully, Khan begged off from this absurd scenario. After that Kifaetullah of JUI-F too bowed out. JUI-F is more vulnerable to the Taliban because of its location in Dera Ismail Khan closer to North Waziristan than Sami ul-Haq whose seminary is close to Peshawar. Fazlur Rehman had escaped attacks from the terrorists, which meant North Waziristan thought him soft on the state of Pakistan. Maulana Abdul Aziz, frontman of al-Qaeda's policy of Islamic vigilantism in Islamabad, whom the judiciary is too scared to convict in scores of cases of terrorism, held a separate press conference in the capital surrounded by scary-looking armed guards to say: 'nothing short of removal of democracy and the constitution itself would be acceptable as a condition for peace'. Aziz's Red Mosque was attacked by commando troops in 2007 after he staged a number of vigilante incidents to force Islamabad to become an Islamic city the way the TTP thinks it should be. He symbolized Pakistan's trajectory of Islamization since 1947 and causes the Pakistani mind to split over what should be the next phase of state identity. By voting right-wing in 2013 against the ever-dwindling liberal elements, the people of Pakistan joined the issue on the side of the Taliban. Intimidation wasa persuader more than was realized.

After Imran Khan and JUI-F opted out, Fazlullah showed his erect middle finger from his upturned palm, so to speak, to Islamabad once again by proposing two replacements: chief reporter of a leading English-language newspaper, Ansar Abbasi, whose reports read like sermonizing opinion pieces; and a serving senior bureaucrat Oria Maqbul Jan whose crazy advocacy of the Taliban has upset all kinds of Pakistanis. Both begged off although their worldviews in TV talk shows had presaged the next mutation of the Islamic state.

A debate was raging on TV about sharia. Almost all the religious organizations—most of them with street muscle and some clearly aligned with the TTP—were convinced that sharia was not in force and that therefore the Taliban demand for the dismantling of the modern state was justified. An important presence in the negotiating panel appointed by the Taliban, Jamaat-e-Islami, however decided not to support the Taliban's rejection of the current constitution. But the Jamaat clerics insisted that Pakistan's Islamic Constitution had not been acted upon. They had in the past rejected the modern state's punishment of 'bad' conduct (munkirat) under a penal code and neglect of 'good' conduct (marufat) as pieties enforceable through punitive legislation.

The drive to get the arrested Taliban out of state custody remained fiercely on top of the Taliban agenda. They had already broken into two big jails under the administered jurisdiction of the state and gotten their killers out—most of them returning piously to their job of killing innocent people. The Shia remained in their crosshairs and they didn't mind lying when it suited them to keep the common Pakistani deluded into thinking that the Shia were in fact being killed by America and India. They denied the killing of Shias in a Peshawar restaurant earlier in February 2014.

One reason the TTP had more credibility than the state is the former's intimidatory hold over the media. Most opinion-makers in Urdu were already on their side because of Urdu's more unbuttoned ideological message against the modern state. But the English-language newspapers are actually threatened into censoring themselves by removing the more convincing liberal-secular voices from their opinion pages. The 'popular consensus' was thus against the state and in favour of the terrorists. Of course peace had to prevail, but would the state accept its death that easily? As the farce of peace talks unfolded, one thought Prime Minister Sharif would have to intervene at some stage to put an end to it. It took a change of command in the army to do that and the prime minister was actually rescued from playing his Russian roulette with peace talks.

In the first week of February, Finance Minister Ishaq Dar had to go to Dubai to meet the IMF team because the multilateral financial institution was scared of coming to Islamabad after being painted by the media as an enemy of Islam and an instrument of America's diabolical plots against Pakistan. Dar was asking the IMF for another loan of half a billion dollars while the Taliban had made a billion dollars from Karachi alone in the year 2013. One reason the Taliban couldn't think of peace was the money they were extracting in Pakistan with almost zero loss of manpower, setting themselves apart from the terror franchises in Yemen, Somalia and Mali—dying states that don't have financial teats for terrorists to suck on. Pakistanis wondered who was financing the Taliban, often blaming Saudi Arabia, America and India. The fact was that the Taliban were in the process of emptying Karachi of its cash after leaching the city of Peshawar dry. Out of the four billion dollars the Afghan Taliban made from heroin, at least one billion fell to the TTP's share as the 'southern funnel'. Moreover, news of shakedowns from Islamabad and Lahore were being suppressed because the well-heeled victims wanted to keep it hush-hush.

The Ideology Trap

Pakistan said by talking to a Pakistani panel of negotiators the Taliban had recognized the Constitution of Pakistan; the Taliban said Pakistan had de facto lifted its ban on the TTP by officially talking to its panel. The peace negotiators hadn't yet stopped high-fiving over their achievement of peace when the talks collapsed. In February 2014, a Taliban-owned attack killed thirteen policemen in Karachi.

As if to rebut the Pakistani assumption, the Taliban spokesperson ShahidullahShahid says the Taliban aspires to making its chief Mullah Fazlullah the caliph of Pakistan under a suzerain in Afghanistan, Mullah Omar, the *amirul-momineen* of a universal state that will come into being after the Taliban's triumphal return to the throne of Kabul.

While the two sides talked and constantly 'broke' news to the TV channels that both were on track with bright chances of success, terrorist attacks continued at the rate of one a day, human casualty being steadily eight innocent Pakistanis dead a day. Of course, the Taliban denied they were killing while talking despite their signature on every incident. But they broke the Pakistani heart by actually owning up to the death of thirteen police commandos employed at Rs 14,000 per month. But instead of questioning the TTP on its double-dealing, pro-talks politicians accepted that the terrorists could not kill after they had given their pious word, and blamed the 'foreign hand' that didn't want peace breaking out in the country. An official dutifully announced that Islamabad was crawling with Khad (the Afghan Secret Service) and Mossad spies; another allegedly arrested an Indian spy near the saintly shrine of Data Darbar of Lahore. Politicians fulminated against Black Water, the private company to which the task was outsourced and other elements to whom America has outsourced the job of scuttling the peace talks. So while peace-loving Pakistan and the TTP engage in talks, Israel, India and the Karzai government, led by the United States, were killing innocent Pakistanis, including, ironically, Christians. Clerics, wielding clout by reason of their well-funded madrasas, rejected the Taliban's recourse to terror but felt empowered by their challenge to the 'pagan' state and were breathing fire against the 'obscenity of culture' and 'nudity of women'—the latter reference being to unveiled women out shopping among men.

The world may have felt faint with disbelief but in Pakistan there was a consensus over this galloping narrative of the 'wrong war' which the peace talks must end. The consensus was so strong that even those who knew better would go on TV saying General Musharraf committed a blunder accepting UN Security resolution 1373 under Article 7 and joining the war on terrorism. Only they omitted mentioning the unanimous resolution un-vetoed by China refusing which an already economically challenged Pakistan would have suffered sanctions, including invasion. There was an unconscionable conflation, in this consensus, of the 2001 America-led invasion of Afghanistan under a UN resolution, which Pakistan accepted, with the 2003 America-led invasion of Iraq without a UN resolution, which Turkey refused to join, to whip the populace into self-flagellation over how Turkey was more of a 'man' than Pakistan led by chicken-hearted Musharraf who must now be hanged post-haste by an itching judiciary.

Prime Minister Sharif had good credentials in the eyes of the Taliban. Compared to the PPP, whose May 2013 election was booby-trapped by them with threats, Sharif had moved against the pet hate of the Taliban and ISI-linked jihadi organizations,

General Musharraf (retd), whom he aimed to try for treason. The state was ready to hang General Musharraf as a trophy to the Taliban, subliminally bending the knee to their decree of death against him. A little girl from Swat, Malala Yousafzai, shot in the head by the Taliban, had been rejected even by girls who perceived an insult to the Holy Prophet (PBUH) in her book, which was banned in the Khyber Pakhtunkhwa province. In Nigeria, Boko Haram destroyed schools and colleges just like the Taliban and beheaded Nigerian troops together with innocent Muslim civilians, a copycat action received from Pakistan.

Writing in *Dawn* of 2 April 2014, Zahid Hussain mused: 'What is most disturbing, however, is that the government's policy of appeasement has divided the country on provincial, ethnic and sectarian lines. The much-touted consensus among the political parties on talks with the Taliban is all but broken. The militants have cleverly exploited this divide and selectively target only those political parties that are actively resisting them. The TTP has refused to release the sons of late governor Salmaan Taseer and former prime minister Yousaf Raza Gilani because the PPP government in Sindh is cracking down on the group. Legitimizing the TTP has, in fact, increased the sense of insecurity not only among the minority sects, but is also of concern to the majority Sunni Muslims who believe in a more tolerant Islam. Any deal on the TTP's terms will plunge the country into civil strife destroying its social fabric.'

~

Talibanization

On 20 April, the new army chief General Raheel Sharif could not take the farce anymore and while observing the Martyrs' Day for 6000 soldiers killed by the Taliban, told the Taliban what the Sharif government couldn't: accept the writ of the state or be prepared to face attack. This came after the peace talks were fizzling out but against the mindset often called Talibanization. The government was getting ready for 'real' Islam after a Taliban takeover. Islamabad was promising Islamic banking and no 'usury' in state schemes. Interior minister Chaudhry Nisar Ali Khan said the 3 March murder of a 'liberal' additional sessions judge in Islamabad was in fact the work of his own security guard gone trigger-happy 'in panic', and not the Taliban assailants who had broken into his court. The Taliban denied they had killed the judge.

Soon enough, the reader of the court of the slain judge Rafaqat Ahmed Khan Awan accused police of coercing him into backing interior minister Khan's claim that the judge had been killed by his own guard. As icing on the cake, the guard too denied before a special judge of the anti-terrorism court that he had killed the judge. This was not the only act of sucking up to the killers. The Council of Islamic Ideology (CII) which 'advises' the state on how to implement true Islam dropped a new 'anticipatory' bombshell on 10 March, declaring Section 6 of the Muslim Family Law Ordinance (1961) as violating the sharia. The CII decreed that a husband did not require permission from the first wife for his second marriage. As the law stood, if you married again without the permission of your first wife, you went to jail for a year after paying Rs 5000 as fine. But was the law ever enforced? People marry again and again with the consent of the clergy who insist that Islam doesn't stand in the way of the right to polygamy. The same is true of marrying under-age girls. The law stands aside in bemusement, but now the CII said child marriage was Islamic. Facilitating rapists, it said DNA evidence was not permissible as decisive in Islam. The message for raped women was: bring four male eyewitnesses or be whipped for *qazf* (wrongful accusation).

The CII, aggressive under Talibanization, bent before the capacity of the Tehreek-e-Taliban Pakistan (PTI) to target-kill people supporting modern or 'liberal' views that most Pakistanis despise anyway. Now it said more laws must be enacted to allow child marriage. The CII became toxic after the induction, done by the outgoing 'liberal' PPP government and extended by Nawaz Sharif, of Maulana Muhammad Khan Sheerani from the hardline friendly-to-Taliban Deobandi religious party, Jamiat Ulema-e-Pakistan. Women's rights' NGO, Aurat Foundation, led by Justice Nasira Javid Iqbal (retd), daughter-in-law of the national poet Muhammad Iqbal—who cares?—demanded in Lahore that the order appointing JUI's Maulana Sheerani as chairman of the Council of Islamic Ideology be revoked. The women were already suffering the past appointment by the ruling Muslim League, of misogynist Justice Nazir Akhtar (retd) as head of charity treasury (BaitulMaal) in Punjab. A champion of Blasphemy Law, he was definitely not a champion of the unveiled women's rights. Prostration before Islamist terror was not of recent vintage.

Isolationism: Getting Ready for Surrender

Pakistan's foreign policy remained isolationist with the approval of the national elite and the masses addicted to a vernacular media. This was a kind of 'beauty parlour' touch to the bride of the state who was to be 'prepared' for ritual consummation with the Taliban. The army stands guard over this isolationism and diplomats of the country's Foreign Office stand squarely behind the army and, pointedly, not behind the elected government and its unexpected statesmanlike 'innovations'.

For the first time however a book that hit the market in 2011 presented a deviant voice from within the Foreign Office that may have presaged diplomacy coming into its own in Pakistan. Ex-foreign secretary Riaz Muhammad Khan published *Afghanistan and Pakistan: Conflict, Extremism and Resistance to Modernity*[3] and at least put things on record that no other diplomat had dared talk about. The book was not only about foreign policy but also the nature of the state shaping it. The reference to extremism and resistance to modernity in the title of the book was significant, which most Pakistani bureaucrats and retired generals would take as digression from the 'pure art' of describing foreign affairs as practised amorally by governments in the pursuit of their national interests.

Khan's book threatened to expose the unfolding of Pakistan's foreign policy as a negative factor in the evolution of the state, something that no one serving Pakistan in whatever official capacity thinks of doing. The reason is loyalty to the employer and attachment to nationalism where no impartial judgements are allowed. It challenged opinion-making in Pakistan with the following observation: 'On regional and global issues, Pakistani reactions and commentaries often betray a besieged mentality verging on a persecution complex. In addition to an appetite for outlandish conspiracy theories, the political culture of the country shows a proclivity to look for extraordinary explanations, in particular for failures. Political changes in the country have often been attributed to foreign machinations rather than to mistakes committed at home.'

Extremism based on religion springs from a condition of certitude. And no certitude is possible without reductionism. When collective certitude wells up, it leads to violence. Individuals backed by groups become fascistic in their effort to impose their creed on others. People who are fired by conviction can be opposed at the risk of attracting the label of heresy. Liberals are less impressive because they find fault with creeds and are singularly lacking in the symbolism of power. The state in Pakistan, to the extent it is religious, is an extremist state. The author states: 'Militant groups such as Sipah-e-Sahaba and Jaish-e-Mohammad commonly resort to threats to browbeat opponents. A perverse form of religious vigilantism is evident in the violence directed against individuals and religious minorities over alleged incidents of blasphemy. Low-level police officials and even lower court judges feel harassed and/or have dealt with cases under pressure from fanatical religious groups'.[4]

The book contains a tonic passage about the doctrinal noose strangulating rational policy: 'Pursuit of dubious and impractical doctrines and ideas would only give rise to misgivings and distrust.

Ideas such as "strategic depth" only reflected confused and warped thinking that sometimes clouded Pakistan's policy and approach to Afghanistan.' The 'instruments of Pakistan's foreign policy'—the mujahideen—were not really controlled by the state; in fact there is growing evidence that it was the other way around. Khan tells us about how Prime Minister Nawaz Sharif's effort in 1992, through Jamaat-e-Islami chief Qazi Hussain Ahmad, to get the mujahideen to agree to his policy, came to grief. In 2012, Qazi Hussain Ahmad possibly died from the stress he suffered from an unsuccessful suicide-bomber attack from the very elements he had supported as an instrument of Pakistan's foreign policy.

Khan knew that ISI's support of the 'charismatic' mujahideen was based not on any strategic analyses but on 'reverse indoctrination', something that haunts the GHQ in Rawalpindi where the army chief may at times be scared of his own officers. Soon, the army chiefs of Pakistan became convinced that if they tried to get rid of the non state actors-turned terrorists they could get killed. Khan writes what must rate as the most significant paragraph in the book: 'In April 2000, I had occasion to raise the issue of support to jihadi groups with General Pervez Musharraf, then chief executive, on the occasion of the Havana G-77 summit, in the company of Foreign Secretary Shamshad Ahmed and National Security Adviser Tariq Aziz. I argued that Musharraf could not realize his economic agenda for development without giving up support for jihadist groups, who were spawning an environment hostile to foreign investment and economic growth. Musharraf disagreed and placed the blame for economic ills on corruption. When I persisted, he literally closed the argument with a remark that what I was suggesting could bring an end to his government.'

Pakistani policymakers would find it difficult to stomach the following paragraph even after Prime Minister Sharif may himself be convinced of it: 'Pakistan's ambition to become a hub of economic activity would be difficult to realize without the opening of transit routes to India. When Pakistan initiated the idea of activating the Karakoram Highway for commerce with Kazakhstan and Kyrgyzstan in early 1993, the two countries were enthusiastic. The Kazakh minister for transportation convened a meeting and invited both the Pakistani and Indian ambassadors based in Alma Ata. He was disappointed to learn that India could not be included at that time, in view of tensions in relations between the two South Asian neighbours.'

2

A War Waiting to Be Waged

On 20 April 2014, amid rumblings of failed 'peace talks' with the Taliban, Pakistan's powerful chief of the Army Staff (COAS), General Raheel Sharif, issued a warning to all terrorist groups: 'you must accept the writ of the state, failing which, the army was more than capable of dealing with threats from insurgents'. He was speaking on the occasion of the army's Martyrs' Day in Rawalpindi commemorating the 5000 men fallen to terrorist attacks.

Three days later, Defence Minister Chaudhry Nisar Ali Khan confessed the peace talks were derailed and the committees chosen by both sides had either grown impotent through resignations or become too empowered with Taliban backing and started to politick for their own hidden agenda for change. Meanwhile, the intelligence report on 7 May was that sixty-nine Taliban groups were opposed to peace talks!

Earlier, on 24 April, fighter jets had carried out a large-scale attack on eleven militant hideouts in the Khyber Agency and strategically crucial Tirah Valley, killing scores of terrorists. This was a repeat of the February strikes on the same targets which had accounted for thirty-five militants dead and the destruction of an improvised explosives device (IEDs)-making factory and a huge cache of arms, ammunition and explosives.

In January, the army received public acclamation when its jets and helicopter gunships attacked several villages of the North Waziristan agency killing at least forty militants. This was the first use of fighter jets in North Waziristan since 2007, when a ceasefire agreement was reached with the agency's tribal chiefs. This time, no one bothered about the collateral damage the media had moaned about when the CIA drones attacked the same targets. The reason was clear enough: the Tehreek-e-Taliban Pakistan (TTP) talked peace with the government while committing 'deniable' murders and robberies, laying claim to the state which it would convert into a caliphate of divinely ordained pieties.

TTP Splits

Pakistan is slowly turning away from the politicians' 'all-parties' consensus to conduct talks with 'misled brothers' after America's war against terrorism 'which was not Pakistan's war'. It now appears that Pakistan is about to start its own war against terrorism. The signs are auspicious too. The TTP has developed a split between the Mehsud successor of late chief Hakimullah, led by Shehrayar Mehsud and a rival Mehsud gang led by Khan Said (pronounced 'Sad') Sajna. The Mehsuds are a powerful tribal clan based in North and South Waziristan, famous for their war of defiance against the British. The battleground for this internal mayhem is both North and South Waziristan where more than fifty TTP warriors were killed in April. On 6 May in Tank, South Waziristan, six more died in a rival ambush; on 7 May, the battle was raging in Shawal, North Waziristan.

Considered within the framework of strategy, the first sign of a weakening enemy may be at hand. It is up to Pakistan to pursue the policy started by the targeted air-force operations and push the TTP towards a conclusion aimed at reviving the writ of the state in affected areas and retrieving the constitution from its slow demise while the state sleepwalks into peace talks with the enemy.

During 2013, when Prime Minister Sharif's government was convinced by the state agitprop about 'it's not our war', more than 1025 civilians and 475 security forces personnel were killed in terrorist attacks. The people suffering these attacks became quickly disabused and started agreeing with the international view that the country was faced with terrorist groups like al-Qaeda, Tehreek-e-Taliban Pakistan, the Punjabi Taliban, and Lashkar-e-Jhangvi. The earlier brainwash that pushed Pakistan into appeasement and gradual surrender was evaporating under conditions of widespread carnage and extraction: the TTP had reportedly squeezed half a billion dollars from Karachi alone in one year. In Lahore, most of the *bhatta* (protection money) calls made to businessmen were traced to North Waziristan from where orders were given to local operators to kill in case of 'default'.

The TTP didn't take kindly to the attacks and, though handicapped with an internal split, retaliated in Miramshah in North Waziristan on 3 May. It killed Malik Qadir Khan, a tribal chief of Waziristan and a member of the peace committee who had signed a peace agreement between the government and the local Taliban in 2007. His mistake was to express dissatisfaction with the on-going peace talks. This was a signal for Pakistan: unless you act, the TTP split will be repaired through further bloodshed.

It looked as if Army Chief General Sharif had the right military instinct: the time may have come to fight Pakistan's own war against terrorism before it was too late. And the big change in Afghanistan might be one of the signs presaging it. Even as he spoke on Martyrs' Day, Afghan troops backed by ISAF air power killed at least sixty militants out of the 300 belonging to the Haqqani Network trying to cross the Pak-Afghan border from their safe haven in North Waziristan.

After a long time, Pakistan and the international community seemed to coincide on the terror incubating on Pakistan's territory and the biggest terrorist group Pakistan was hosting on its soil was the Haqqani Network about whom a harassed US Chairman of the Joint Chiefs of Staff, Admiral Michael Mullen, had said in 2011: 'It is one of several extremist organizations serving as proxies of the government of Pakistan.'

Ditching of the Haqqani Network

There were rumours afloat in Pakistan that the Pakistan army was about to ditch the Haqqanis, the first sign of which came when in November 2013, Dr Nasiruddin Haqqani, the top fundraiser and organizer of the Haqqani Network as well as its liaison man with the Pakistani security establishment, was mysteriously murdered in Islamabad. The TTP, Haqqani's partner inside al-Qaeda's large umbrella, blamed the ISI.

If the this report was correct, some irony would be rubbed off the statement Prime Minister Nawaz Sharif made at 10 Downing Street on 30 April to his British counterpart, David Cameron: 'Pakistan will not allow its land to be used against any country.' He got back a very subliminal answer from Mr Cameron: 'The enemies of Pakistan are my enemies too because we want to defeat the extremism, the terrorism that threatens your country and so many others in the region.' Appropriately, in the background, in the typically rowdy British parliamentary style, lawmakers demanded that British aid to Pakistan 'be cut unless there is proof the funds help stop Islamic extremism'. Pakistan was the largest recipient of bilateral British aid, with Islamabad set to receive £446 million ($750 million) of assistance in 2014. The UK was giving funds to Pakistan not only for not exporting terrorism, which it was blamed for doing through the Haqqani Network, but also for stamping out extremism in Pakistan.

Pakistan was in dire economic straits and that could be a blessing as there was hardly any other internal persuasion to end extremism and act against the TTP and the Haqqani Network. But some Pakistani legislations, like the Blasphemy Law, were so extreme in religious discrimination that the State might not be able to find a conceptual basis for opposing extremism.

Triangle of Error

Vahid Brown and Don Lassler place the Haqqani Network (HN) in a four-cornered relation with the Pakistani Taliban, the Pakistani military, and al-Qaeda: 'All the latter three groups rely on the Haqqanis for their unparalleled capacity to deliver anti-regime and anti-Coalition violence in Afghanistan—a capacity that, again, is itself built partly on the Haqqanis' relations with these groups. Pakistan is determined to limit the influence of its arch-rival India in Afghanistan, and the Haqqanis have proven willing to direct their violence toward this end.'[1]

The Haqqani Network reportedly gave satisfaction to Islamabad by bombing the Indian embassy in 2008. That satisfaction may have worn off, as signalled by the murder of Nasiruddin Haqqani, but to chart a new course Pakistan may additionally need a new attitude towards the region. The book says: 'So long as Pakistan's army remains committed to unilaterally shaping the post-American future of Afghanistan in its perceived interests, HN will continue to be a valuable asset of the military.'[2]

However, if statements emanating from Islamabad were to be credited, Pakistan was now neutral on Afghanistan, accepted the results of the latest election there as its results became clear in June, and was no longer obsessed with India 'and its consulates'.

According to Amir Mir—brother of journalist and TV anchor Hamid Mir who escaped an assassination attempt in

Karachi on 19 April 2014—observed in the *News* of 17 April: 'The Pakistani establishment has made it clear to the Afghan Taliban and the Haqqani Network that the time has come for them to choose between the Tehreek-e-Taliban Pakistan and the state of Pakistan, if they want to stay friends with Islamabad.' As this assessment made it into print the 'peace talks' had entered a crucial stage, with the TTP demanding the release of 800 of their warriors from Pakistani jails. Will Pakistan declare the Network terrorist, following in the footsteps of Washington which dubbed it a Foreign Terrorist Organization (FTO) under the existing laws in 2012?

However, it was a bit naive to presume that the Afghan Taliban and the Haqqani Network would choose to 'stay friends' with Pakistan indefinitely. The TTP was a non-friend because it had killed a lot of good Pakistani soldiers and officers, including GOC Swat, Major General Sanaullah Niazi, in an ambush by the TTP's new chief Mullah Fazlullah. Far from favouring a friend, the Afghan Taliban—or possibly the Afghan National Army as a tit for tat—was providing the killer a safe haven in the Kunar province across the border. Pakistan only had enemies in various gradations, hardly any friends, because its strategic vision didn't allow real friends to get near it without getting hurt.

If, as the world claimed, Osama bin Laden was being kept in a safe house in Abbottabad, he was hardly a friend of Pakistan by any stretch of the imagination. If, as journalist Carlotta Gall alleges, Mullah Omar too is being kept in a safe house in Balochistan, he may likewise not be overcome by too much affection for his hosts.

Matt Waldman of Carr Center for Human Rights Policy, Kennedy School of Government, Harvard University, wrote in a report based on interviews with Afghan Taliban commanders, in 2010: 'Although many informed Afghans interviewed argue that the ISI is controlling the Taliban leadership, this is probably an exaggeration, given the powerful internal force and dynamics of the movement. The Taliban leadership also has a record of resisting Pakistani pressure (for instance, the refusal of the Taliban regime to recognize the Durand Line or to hand over Osama bin Laden to the US).'[3]

Extremism of the Victim

The Pakistan army was in for a lot of surprises as it followed up on its warning to the Afghan Taliban and the Haqqani Network. It had waited too long in the wings and mulled too long the security situation only in light of 'external enemies' to note that Pakistan's population has submitted more completely to indigenous terror networks than it could imagine.

In Islamabad, emblematically, the al-Qaeda affiliated cleric Abdul Aziz of the infamous Red Mosque had renamed the library of his girls' seminary Jamia Hafza after Osama bin Laden. And the lawyers of the capital city, as reported by the *Guardian* of 30 April 2014, had named a mosque in Faizabad after Mumtaz Qadri, the policeman who killed the Punjab governor Salmaan Taseer in 2011. Governor Taseer's fault was that he had publicly supported reform of Pakistan's controversial blasphemy laws targeting Pakistan's poverty-stricken Christian community in the name of the Holy Prophet although often the objective of the plaintiff is to dispossess the victims of their land through vigilante action. Tragically, lawyer Rashid Rehman defending the victim community of Christians as a representative of the Human Rights Commission in Multan, was assassinated on 7 May for challenging the Blasphemy Law.

American diplomacy got activated after the rumoured breakup of the 'triangle of error' now that Islamabad had stubbed its toe talking peace with the TTP. US Special Representative for Afghanistan and Pakistan James Dobbins, in Islamabad in April, complained that Pakistan was not taking appropriate measures to curb terrorism in the country 'as the religious seminaries in the tribal areas and Balochistan were the cause of attacks inside Afghanistan and India'.

The Network's Deeds in Afghanistan

The biggest problem will of course be the Network ensconced in North Waziristan. A roster of cross-border horrors inflicted by it on Afghanistan read like this:

It was responsible for the storming of the Serena Hotel in Kabul during a visit by Norwegian officials in January 2008; it carried out a suicide attack against the Indian embassy in Kabul in July 2008 that killed two senior Indian officials and over fifty others; it similarly attacked a CIA base in Khost province in December 2009 'that marked the most deadly attack on the CIA in twenty-five years'; it assaulted the US Bagram Airfield in mid-May 2010, was behind a long siege of the US embassy in Kabul in September 2011, and a complex and coordinated attack on US Base Camp Salerno in Khost province in 2012.

America released to the public the documents it collected from Osama bin Laden's compound after its 2 May 2011 raid in Abbottabad. They revealed Mullah Omar as the central figure in the storm gathering simultaneously on its borders and in its major cities. Haqqani swears allegiance to him, so does the current al-Qaeda leader, Ayman-al-Zawahiri.

If the decision to cleanse North Waziristan of terrorists that attack not only across the Durand Line but also southwards in the four provinces of Pakistan, were to be finally taken, it would have the blessings and possible assistance from the threatened states around the globe. In the immediate neighbourhood, Iran, Uzbekistan, India and China would be greatly relieved. Russia and India would be less inclined to gang up in Afghanistan if they were assured that Pakistan would help encircle and round up the Chechens and Uzbeks straddling the Pak-Afghan border. The Chinese, who had a big stake in mineral and hydrocarbon projects in Afghanistan, would return to the camps they had fled. Saudi Arabia, fighting al-Qaeda and its Afghan–Chechen warriors in Yemen, would pay big money for the roll-back of the 'strategic depth' by Pakistan.

Pakistan's 'Strategic Pivot'

The change, of course, was necessitated by the contradictions of policy of the past. If the Haqqani Network had served to add enough spine to the TTP to enable it to spread its tentacles southwards, and if the Afghan Taliban, led by Mullah Omar, would not stand by Pakistan in its battle against the TTP, then this 'triangle of error' had to be dismantled. The army fights external enemies, but what should it do if the external enemy—the Haqqani Network, Uzbeks, Chechens and Uighurs—is drawn in and made to benefit from such 'internal bounties' as safe havens and untold sums of money extracted from the national economy?

If the Pakistan army helped target-kill TTP leaders, Baitullah and Hakimullah, through drone attacks; and got rid, similarly, of that very dangerous Uzbek warlord Tahir Yuldashev, it had acted in the interest of its own survival and the survival of Pakistan. If a strategic shift in military thinking actually took place, it would be of great benefit, even if a bit late in the day. The army had already proved it could tackle the TTP in Swat and the federally-run tribal agencies barring North Waziristan. Its efforts ran aground when the old GHQ under General Ashfaq Kayani decided to take on India in the region and America and its powerful allies at the global level at the same time.

The obsessive 'India strategy', which harmed democratically elected governments inside Pakistan more than in India, was frequently marvelled at by friendly analysts. Anatol Lieven presents a sympathetic view of the Pakistan army as it copes with terrorism, but nonetheless states his critique of its obsessive behaviour:

'A common definition of tragedy is that of a noble figure betrayed and destroyed by some inner flaw. The Pakistani military is in some ways an admirable institution, but it suffers from one tragic feature which has been with it from the beginning, which has defined its whole character and worldview, which has done terrible damage to Pakistan and which could in some circumstances destroy Pakistan and its armed forces altogether.

This is the military's obsession with India in general, and Kashmir in particular . . . Pakistani politicians share responsibility for encouraging ordinary Pakistanis to see jihad in Kashmir as legitimate.'[4]

The non-state actors of Punjab, who spearhead Pakistan's India strategy and challenge elected governments with 'long marches' every time they move to initiate free trade with India, have become empowered over time by reason of their status of semi-combatants within civilian populations. Their operational plans may be in sync with the 'national agenda' but their ideological interface with the 'triangle of error'—the TTP, Afghan Taliban and Haqqani Network—may have been difficult to contend with. Since these non-state actors were backed by a vast network of madrasas, it would not be wise to challenge the illegal quantum of influence they had won over time.

Dangers of Heroic Isolation

The weakened state could easily busy itself in internal bickering and infighting, further competitively tightening the noose of international isolation by stakeholders accusing one another of following a 'foreign agenda' or being collaborative with a 'foreign hand'. Pakistan couldn't take this for very long without dying of internal combustion. But it could regain strength by pulling down the castle of 'magnificent solitude' it had constructed around the 'national purpose'. Get the scared world outside to help you deal with the 'triangle of error' in the mountains first; then build up the policing capacity of the state with outside assistance—not only with money, which can drain away through bureaucratic cracks, but also direct participation in induction and training—to confront the 'enemy within'.

Iran stonewalled itself heroically against the world, which it first interpreted as its enemy. The state grew as a deity in the eyes of Iranians 'drunk with the wine of nationalism'. However, after nearly half a century of magnificent isolation, the system that heavily tilted towards the clergy has been forced by a languishing economy to relent and tell the world Iran was no longer interested in acts of derring-do. The Great Leader Ali Khamenei called the volte-face 'heroic flexibility' (*narmishqaharmanan*). Pakistan's military strategy too must embrace this heroic flexibility and come out of its isolation to save the state from self-destructing.

In 2014, the moment may have arrived to look inside. The population was hardly divided in its extremism: opinion survey polls said the nation was united against India and the United States and preferred 'heroic isolation' to 'slavery', with its emblem, the 'begging bowl', and the accompanying shame of 'fighting America's war'. Also revealed, equally loudly, was the verdict of the national economy ambushed by the breakdown of law and order after years of globalization, making its trading partners and investors sensitive to lack of security in Pakistan.

The other introspection could focus on whether the army was on the same page from the inside, that is, it was no longer at risk from revolutionary-Islamist officers who openly announced their credentials, as was done by General Shahid Aziz (retd) in his 2013 nationally acclaimed biographical account *Yeh Khamoshi Kahan Tak* (How Long This Silence?), with a telltale subtitle *Ek Sipahi ki Dastan-e-Ishq-o-Junoon* (The Story of Passion and Madness of a Soldier).

The internal fracture was disclosed by American Republican politician Pat Buchanan who wrote in 2009 against the American decision to ditch Pakistan after the discovery of Osama bin Laden in Abbottabad: 'If Pakistan's intelligence services, army and government all knew the exact location of bin Laden, we would know it. For we have people inside sympathetic to us, just as some are sympathetic to al-Qaeda. And if people inside discovered the exact location of bin Laden or al-Qaeda, they would leak it to us, if only because the money on the table for such intelligence is irresistible.

'That the Pakistani intelligence services are shot through with elements loyal to a Taliban they helped bring to power in Kabul, that there are Pakistani army officers who believe they should be defending their country against India, not fighting America's war in Waziristan, is also undeniable. But what does it avail us to insult these people who have cast their lot with us, many of whom will, with families and friends, pay a far more terrible price than we if we lose these wars.'[5]

Overfed on an Ideological Diet

Is Pakistan ideologically driven in its foreign policy which manipulates and moulds internal policy as well? Many 'nationalist' analysts link the state ideology not only to Islam but India too with which Pakistan must resolve the outstanding dispute of Kashmir before embarking on a 'normal' economy-driven foreign policy.

The past decade has seen Pakistan gradually weaning itself from this ideological diet—even when it was ruled by a general after the overthrow of an elected 'pro-India' government in 1999. Unfortunately, after the end of this 'mixed' military regime, the elected government of the Pakistan People's Party found it impossible to pursue an India policy frontloaded with an already agreed regime of free trade under the aegis of the World Trade Organization. This happened after the 2013 election too, under the new government of the Pakistan Muslim League (Nawaz).

On 6 May, speaking to a group of Pakistani ambassadors serving in Saudi Arabia and the Gulf, Prime Minister Nawaz Sharif articulated a frank deviation from ideology when he made it clear that his 'foreign policy is driven by economic considerations'. Most Pakistanis, analysing the foreign policies of other nations, accuse them of pursuing economic objectives, little realizing that they are actually defying a norm and thus revealing their own intellectual misdirection.

If Pakistan's strategy is 'geopolitical', predicated on not trading with India as a pressure to bend it to agreeing to a solution for Kashmir, it will not work, as India's economy is not heavily dependent on Pakistan. Nor is India too hurt by Pakistan's policy of not allowing it a trade corridor to Afghanistan and Central Asia, especially after its construction, on the Iranian coast of the Arabian Sea, of the port of Chabahar, linking Afghanistan to India with a broad highway. This development has given the lie to the much bandied permanence of the 'geopolitical factor'.

Trade versus Terror

Since the ouster of General Musharraf from government in 2008, Pakistan has not been able to 'open up' with India mainly because of the pressure applied by the non-state actors of the not-so-covert proxy war. The political argument advanced against free trade with India will find no takers outside Pakistan.

Today, Pakistan trades 2000 items with India through 'official exchange' where no rules exist because of the abeyance of the bilateral free trade treaty, which means India is free to use non-tariff barriers to protect its market. For instance, it blocks Pakistan's three-times-cheaper cement with arbitrary duties. Under free trade and its negative list, it may still trade 2000 items with Pakistan but will be bound by the conditions of the free-trade treaty. Trade and transit facilities will defuse the tensions and remove application of hostile anti-economic measures in mutual conduct. Needless to say, the new bilateral trade will be followed by adjustments on both sides—more on the side of Pakistan—and will settle down, like everyone else in the world, to an unsteady equilibrium of mutual advantage constantly under the review of trade talks.

Former World Bank economist Ijaz Nabi wrote recently in *Newsweek* Pakistan: 'WTO consistent (Most-Favoured Nation) trade with India will require re-orienting the supply chains to potentially more profitable Indian sources. This necessitates unfettered access to each other's markets to identify opportunities and strike business deals. Disruptions caused by travel bans and suspension of trade routes would do little to encourage Pakistani firms to develop supply lines with India.

'The curtailment of economic transactions following the Mumbai attacks was costly and some businesses that were beginning to tap into Indian technical and management expertise were badly burnt. The potential gains from bilateral trade in terms of regional economic vibrancy, strengthening of economic growth in India and Pakistan, creating much needed productive jobs and peace and stability are too large to be disrupted for short-term non-economic gains.'[6]

The solution to the problem of terrorism driving investors away from Pakistan and causing its own capital to flee abroad is not peace talks with terrorists but a resolute use of force to recapture the writ of the state. This resolute force will have punch, if not distracted by the 'geopolitical' factor in foreign policy, dividing the army between 'two fronts'. Pakistan may be at a crossroads today; and it looks as if it is going to make the right policy choice in 2015. A reversal of the India-centric worldview will make Afghanistan safe for Pakistan, and the opening up of trade corridors—both north-south and east-west—will transform the landscape of terror into economic engagement through massive infrastructural development.

3

Owning the War against Terrorism

On 21 June 2014, the Pakistan army told the people of Pakistan that its action in North Waziristan was proceeding according to plan. The Inter-Services Public Relations website declared that between 15 and 21 June more than 250 terrorists had been killed including Uzbek and other Central Asian foreign elements fighting the al-Qaeda jihad against Pakistan. By 30 June, the army claimed nearly 350 militants killed in North Waziristan during Operation Zarb-e-Azb and that the army was now carrying out a ground offensive with tanks and armored vehicles.

The North Waziristan base of the Tehreek-e-Taliban Pakistan (TTP) was attacked with helicopters gunships, attack aircraft and ground troops, forcing the Afghan Taliban, including the Haqqani Network, to flee into Afghanistan together with their friends. According to the website, only on 15 June, up to 140 terrorists—most of them Uzbeks—were killed without any collateral damage.

The Pakistani press has reported the military version without details relating to such formerly 'friendly' Pakistani elements as the warriors of Hafiz Gul Bahadur.

However the tragedy of the 'internally displaced people' of the affected area will inevitably recall the earlier evacuation of the Swat IDPs before it was cleansed of the Taliban five years ago. The IDPs of North Waziristan numbering half a million have come down to Bannu in the Khyber Pakhtunkhwa province, and the initial reports simply repeat the litany of the inability of the state to roll with the blow of the operation's consequences. The mostly derelict federal and provincial governments were expected to get their act together before the refugees suffered the pain of being homeless for too long. In the region, populations once displaced seldom completely returned home.

The Fallout of Zarb-e-Azb

Did the government grasp what impact the operation in North Waziristan would have on the internal and external security doctrines of Pakistan? Chances were that it did not have much of a clue because representative governments have neither ever formulated them nor changed them in the past. The notorious 'strategic depth', often laid at the door of ex-army chief General Aslam Beg but announced to a gathering of editors in Islamabad by ex-army chief General Ashfaq Pervaiz Kayani, was apparently at an end. General Kayani had stated in 2010: 'If Afghanistan is peaceful, stable and friendly, we have our strategic depth, because our western border is secure. You (the Pakistani army) are not looking both ways.'

Internationally abominated, the interventionist doctrine of the 'depth' is a thing of the past after the army, led by General Raheel Sharif and supported by the ruling party in Islamabad, attacked the Taliban in North Waziristan. Mullah Omar, on whose government the doctrine was predicated, was ensconced somewhere in Pakistan; but he must have been devastated by what

Pakistan had done to the people who called him their amirul-momineen (Leader of the Faithful).

Needless to say, Ayman-al-Zawahiri, also hiding somewhere in Pakistan or Afghanistan, was in a state of rage after seeing his international warriors mowed down by Pakistan army fire. A bad, low-IQ, doctrine had come to an end and would have consequences for Pakistan just as its application had consequences for the world. This is what ex-foreign secretary of Pakistan, Riaz Muhammad Khan, says about the flawed doctrine:

'Political analysts often point out that two considerations preoccupied the Pakistani army's strategic thinking regarding its support of various Afghan Mujahedin groups: first, its view of Afghanistan as providing strategic depth to Pakistan; and second, its interest in having a friendly government in Afghanistan. While the concept of a friendly government was flawed, the aspiration of strategic depth in Afghanistan defied reason from the point of view of the traditional interpretation of the concept. "Friendly government" is a highly subjective concept that encourages patronage and interference and spawns suspicion and provocation.

'Later a more benign interpretation was constructed to suggest that the concept only meant that Pakistan should feel secure along its western border in times of tension with India . . . the seduction of these fanciful ideas and the dynamics of the Pashtun population of the two countries' bordering regions sucked Pakistan deeper into the Afghanistan quagmire, especially when its intelligence establishment saw an opportunity in the gathering of a new unexpected force, the Taliban, in southwestern Afghanistan.'[1]

Had the internal security policy changed too? Brigadier Asad Munir (retd), a former ISI officer, said this to the daily *Dawn* on 22 June 2014: 'The internal security doctrine has changed as well. Gone are the days when you could brand someone a traitor simply because they didn't agree with your policies. Among political leaders, victimization has all but faded away.' But this also meant that the army would not object to tackling the 'internal enemy' (read Taliban) instead of saying that terrorism has to be dealt with by the police or a special civilian force. Let's have a look at the international crisis two other armies have precipitated by not facing up to terrorism.

The Armies That Ran Away: Iraq

Two states in the Muslim world have turned tail and run in the face of terrorism in recent times. In Iraq, the Islamic State of Iraq and al-Sham (ISIS) attacked across the Syrian border and occupied Mosul. The Iraqi army was not able to withstand the onslaught. Surrounded, it tore off its uniform and ran away from the battlefield on 10 June 2014. Then ISIS attacked and took hold of Tikrit, a town in the north of Baghdad and once home to Iraqi dictator Saddam Hussein. Once again attempts by the Iraqi army to retake the territory failed and ISIS declared the 'conquered' area as the Caliphate of Islam headed by Abu Bakr Baghdadi, on 30 June. The new 'state' extended from Aleppo in Syria to Mosul and Tikrit in Iraq, with favourable resonance in Iraq's Sunni province of Anbar.

Iraq has been misruled under democracy after the fall of Saddam Hussein as the state turned from a secular to a religious identity. Unlike Pakistan, Shia-majority Iraq is communally divided and ghettoized; and the government of Shia prime minister Maliki has actually used its majority to persecute the Sunnis, which doesn't happen in Pakistan where the census doesn't count the Shia as a separate identity. Other developments in Iraq too have differed from Pakistan, except that the Taliban in Pakistan are Sunni like the majority population and threaten the state with their 'superior' sharia practices and render it vulnerable. The Sunni ISIS is opposed by the majority Shia population in Iraq.

Maliki has sought to remove Sunnis from important representative positions and has purged the US-trained army after almost a decade of pluralist nation-building starting 2003. Sectarian tensions have since hindered state-building processes and destabilized the country. But the Iraqi government has not made a clear attempt to overcome these divides and build a common national identity. In fact, many actions taken to-date have only served to further fragment the struggling state.

ISIS has developed differences with al-Qaeda that remote-controls the war in the region from its base in Pakistan-Afghanistan; but this goes back to the progenitor of the sectarian Sunni terror, Abu Musab al-Zarqawi, who ironically went to Iraq from the early bastion of al-Qaeda in Peshawar to fight the Americans, thus connecting Pakistan with what is happening in Iraq today.

ISIS and Pakistan

The founder of ISIS was a Jordanian named Abu Musab al-Zarqawi. The Washington Post wrote on 14 June 2014: 'On the eve of the US invasion of Iraq in 2003, a thirty-six-year-old Jordanian who called himself 'the Stranger' slipped into the suburbs of Baghdad armed with a few weapons, bags of cash and an audacious plan for starting a war he hoped would unite Sunni Muslims across the Middle East.'

A Jordanian street bully, Zarqawi went to Peshawar in 1989 inspired by the lectures of al-Qaeda's Arab 'founder' Abdullah Azzam, then teaching at the International Islamic University of Islamabad. Patronized by Afghan warlords AbdurRabRasul Sayyaf and Jalaluddin Haqqani, he fought the Russian troops at Tora Bora together with Osama bin Laden. In 1999, he was imprisoned for six months in Peshawar 'on Arab request' but was let off on the order of 'influential friends'.

He returned to the battlefield in Kandahar where he was wounded and was treated in Karachi—by two al-Qaeda doctors who later fled to North Waziristan—after which he planned to fight the Americans in Iraq and made his way to Kurdistan in northern Iraq through the tribal areas of Pakistan where he reportedly also had time to sire children on two newly-wed wives in the tradition of Osama bin Laden and Ayman-al-Zawahiri.

Ironically Iran helped him pass through its territory on the request of another Afghan warlord, GulbuddinHekmatyar. After he started killing Shias in Iraq instead of Americans, al-Qaeda tried to ditch him but couldn't because of the support and funding he was receiving from the Muslims of the United Kingdom. He was killed in an American bombing raid in Baghdad in 2006. Today ISIS is once again at odds with al-Qaeda, but once again all the auguries point to a reconciliation which may see al-Zawahiri taking a backseat to ISIS in the Middle East.

As reported in the daily *Jang* (10 June 2006) Jamaatud Dawa (old Lashkar-e-Taiba) carried out a funeral prayer in absentia for Zarqawi in Lahore and condemned the Foreign Office for saying that the death of the Shia-killer in Iraq was an achievement in the war against terrorism. The congregation that blessed Zarqawi kept weeping loudly for the great shaheed. In the National Assembly, the clerical alliance MMA demanded fateha prayer for Zarqawi but was denied by the speaker. Reported in the daily *Nawa-e-Waqt,* a Jamaat-e-Islami leader, Syed Munawwar Hasan, said Pakistan was reluctant to call Zarqawi shaheed as that would offend Washington.

The Armies That Ran Away: Nigeria

Unlike Pakistan, which is broke, the Organization of Islamic Conference member Nigeria is the largest economy of Africa, growing at the rate of 7 per cent. It has thirty-six provinces and has a majority Muslim population, 50 per cent as against 40 per cent Christians. It is vulnerable to an al-Qaeda affiliate Boko Haram the same way as Pakistan because of the Sunni-Maliki faith of the Nigerian Muslims. Boko Haram declares it is going to bring strict sharia to Nigeria just like the Taliban in Pakistan.

In Nigeria, sharia has been instituted as the main body of civil and criminal law in nine Muslim-majority and in some parts of three Muslim-plurality states since 1999. The enforcement of the sharia on Christians has frequently led to violence, killing hundreds of Christians who are then forced to flee the state. Like

Pakistan, terrorist Boko Haram is active in the tribal north but, again like Pakistan, attacks southern states including the capital, Abuja.

Boko Haram created a global stir when it kidnapped over 200 school-going girls from the northeastern state of Chibok saying it would sell them to pious Muslims. The Nigerian army watched from a distance. In all, about 3 million of the 168 million Nigerians have been affected physically and economically by the unhampered rise of Boko Haram. Nigerians openly expressed loss of faith in their army on the BBC. On 29 June 2014, Boko Haram once again attacked Chibok, resisted by the local population with bows and arrows before it succumbed to superior arms. The army was called for help but it refused to show up.

The Nigerian army's reluctance to fight terrorism is comparable to Pakistan's unwillingness to take on the 'unfriendly' Taliban of North Waziristan spreading their 'persuasion through fear' in the Tribal Areas and the rest of Pakistan. This happened particularly during the tenure of Army Chief General Kayani who instead turned anti-American and began harassing American diplomats in Pakistan, likely pandering to the Taliban demand that Pakistan break with the United States' war against terrorism.

If and when the dust settles on the debate over terrorism, General Kayani will become an interesting study for an investigation into Pakistan's delay in tackling the problem of the Taliban at the right time. Former army spokesperson Major General Athar Abbas (retd) disclosed (BBC, 30 June 2014) that the army was on the brink of launching a military offensive in North Waziristan three years ago but, because of General Kayani's reluctance, was unable to go ahead. He said: 'He was very reluctant when it came to the North Waziristan operation. Kayani thought the decision to launch the operation would reflect on his personality and people would take it as his personal decision, which is why he kept delaying the operation.'

More pointedly, in a formal briefing to the media on Operation Zarb-e-Azb on 26 June, Inter-Services Public Relations Director

General, Major General Asim Bajwa told reporters the ongoing military operation in North Waziristan was a 'war of survival' and will pave the way for the dawn of permanent peace in the country.

Military Sphinx: General Kayani

General Kayani was second-in-command to Army Chief Pervez Musharraf when the Pakistan army decided—after toppling the elected government of Nawaz Sharif—to join the global war under the UN-granted tutelage of the United States in 2001. He was personally involved in the America-backed plan to bring the Pakistan People's Party leader Benazir Bhutto back from exile; and if he felt that the deal was a villainous trick played on Pakistan by the US, he did not say it.

But perhaps somewhere deep inside Kayani there was a feeling that Pakistan was taking a wrong direction—or there was simply a realization that the al-Qaeda–Taliban combine was too strong to challenge, given its extension into Pakistan's vast madrasa network, producing cannon-fodder for jihad and into the religious parties hankering for power they could not win electorally. The attack on his office in the General Headquarters in Rawalpindi in 2009 by a gang of terrorists led by an officer from inside the army, made him realize the limits of his decision-making.

Kayani was not a 'modern' man in the Pakistani sense despite his training courses in the US. After Musharraf, he was chief of the Army Staff from 2007 to 2013, including a three-year extension by the PPP government he had tamed as he rode the anti-American wave created by a Talibanized media not least encouraged by him. General Kayani had also served as the director general of the Inter-Services Intelligence (ISI) which qualified him as the top brain in the army shaping Pakistan's foreign policy and deciding how the elected government would rule.

In 2011, he interpreted the killing of Osama bin Laden by the Americans in Abbottabad as being against the interests of Pakistan, reacting against the ruling PPP when it welcomed the assassination. He even went to the Supreme Court seeking to prove that a PPP-appointed ambassador to Washington had treasonably asked the Americans to 'tame the Pakistan army'. The power he wielded by blinking the challenge of terrorism was immense among a nation 84 per cent of whom hated America. In 2011, *Forbes* named him the thirty-fourth most powerful person in the world. In 2012, *Forbes* named him the twenty-eighth most powerful person in the world.

In September 2012, just months before his final retirement, General Kayani accomplished a somersault at the Pakistan Military Academy in Abbottabad near where bin Laden was shot dead a year earlier by American SEALs. He told the PMA cadets: 'Any person who believes his opinion to be the final verdict is an extremist . . . If this is the correct definition of extremism and terrorism, then the war against it is our own war, and a just war too.'[2]

Course-correction by General Sharif

General Kayani left Pakistan in suicidal but heroic isolation, internally self-congratulatory but externally without friends unless you count states too scared of its nuclear arsenal falling into the hands of al-Qaeda. As the former military spokesman, quoted above, indicated, he will be finally held responsible for the delay in facing up to the challenge of terrorism, not imposed on Pakistan by India and America, but the Pakistani state itself through policies of proxy wars.

It is remarkable how the decision to change course by the new army chief, General Raheel Sharif, has been welcomed immediately by the entire nation despite noises of protest from elements empowered by the Taliban–al-Qaeda combine. The political parties, not long ago basking in a criminally optimistic all-parties consensus on holding peace talks with the Taliban while they went on killing innocent Pakistani citizens, began to line up behind General Sharif and his corps commanders. The new war may be a long haul but at least it has begun and it is going to be different from the challenge faced by the armies in Nigeria and Iraq if and when they decide to stop running away from the enemy.

The Iraqi army was rated highly under Saddam Hussein but was scattered by the American invasion of Iraq in 2003. After the American exit, however, the Iraqi army was purged once again and made sectarian by a short-sighted prime minister who exploited democracy's majoritarian vice. Iraq is sitting on the world's second largest oil reserves but it is too intellectually disadvantaged to think straight on internal security. In contrast, the Pakistan army is not polarized on religious and sectarian grounds and remains a monolith, if you exclude the damage done by past policies of Islamization and the consequent de-professionalization.

The Pakistan army is recognized internationally as a disciplined force unlike any in the Arab world and has steadily served under the UN flag with distinction. Unlike the armies of Iraq and Nigeria, it knows its terrorists closely after dealing with them under five well-known 'agreements': 1) Shakai (24 March 2004) Nek Muhammad and General Safdar Hussain only with Ahmadzai Wazir tribe of South Waziristan; 2) Sararogha (22 February 2005) with Baitullah Mehsud only with Mehsud tribe; 3) Khyber (21 June 2008) with only Mangal Bagh and his Afridi Lashkar Islam; 4) North Waziristan (5 September 2006) by Governor General Ali Muhammad Jan Aurakzai only with tribes of North Waziristan; 5) South Waziristan (2007) only with Maulvi Nazir and his Ahmadzai Wazir tribe followers; 6) Swat (2009) with Sufi Muhammad while the dominant warlord was Fazlullah.

It was on the basis of the poor quality of observance of these agreements by the Taliban that General Sharif decided in 2014 to initiate Operation Zarb-e-Azb that General Kayani had fought shy of. The postponement of the decision to act in Nigeria and Iraq will have unanticipated results, including the American advice to Baghdad to postpone democracy because it has postponed facing up to the ISIS.

A Council of Intimidation

Commentators who rate Pakistan unequal to the task of taking on terrorism point to the near impossibility of defeating the Taliban–al-Qaeda affiliates in Punjab and Karachi. While the Karachi nettle will have to be firmly grasped, the apparently impregnable fort of terrorism in Punjab is supposed to exceed the capacity of the army to fight it. What is not realized is the nature of Punjab terrorism mainly in the shape of al-Qaeda allies, Lashkar-e-Taiba, and the mother of all militants, Sipah-e-Sahaba.

The militancy in Punjab is the result of the interface of the ISI and the proxy warriors it garnered from the south of the province. Former ISI chief General Ahmad Shuja Pasha (retd) used non-state actors and madrasas to 'soften' the PPP government's resolve to 'flirt with India'. He unleashed the Defence of Pakistan Council and its 'long marches' to Islamabad. The council might have driven the country's political parties to despair about fighting terrorism and instead succumb to a policy of appeasement of terror through 'peace talks' with the Taliban.

Therefore it was General Kayani's policy of magnificent passivity that triggered the all-parties consensus behind these talks that ended up merely making the task of General Raheel Sharif more difficult by empowering the jihadi elements aligned with the Taliban. The Defence of Pakistan Council came in handy to do some America-bashing close to the heart of General Kayani.

Columnist Tazeen Javed, writing in the daily *Express Tribune* of 3 February 2012, expressed the following apprehension: 'One cannot be faulted for assuming that the Defence of Pakistan Council may perhaps comprise officials of the defence ministry, four-star generals and decorated admirals who wish to ponder the defence needs of the country and make major strategic decisions.' Of course America took note of the gallery of rogues in the long-marching council with funding from the fabulously rich but banned-at-the-UN Jamaatud Dawa of Hafiz Saeed, himself carrying a bounty of $10 million on his head. Some of the rogues in the gallery were described like this:

Maulana Sami ul-Haq, known as the spiritual father of the Taliban because of his position as director of a madrasa in Khyber Pakhtunkhwa that counts key militant leaders among its alumni. Maulana Fazlur Rehman Khalil, who was once leader of Harkat-ul-Mujahideen, a banned Islamist group with links to al-Qaeda, often called the post office of Osama bin Laden because he handled his correspondence from Islamabad. He was among the signatories to Osama bin Laden's 1998 fatwa that declared war against the West. Hafiz Abdur Rehman Makki, the deputy leader of Jamaatud Dawa, a UN-blacklisted group believed to be a front for Lashkar-e-Taiba, blamed for the 2008 attacks on Mumbai, who roused an angry audience to chants of 'Death to America.

Also present in the 'long march' was the former chief of the ISI, riding in a flashy SUV as the council proceeded from Lahore to Islamabad, General Hamid Gul. His son, Abdullah Gul, arisen in status because of the ISI-arranged campaign, said: 'We will fight to the last drop of our blood. Pakistan cannot be taken for granted.' The politicians who joined the council included Sheikh Rashid, leader of a nondescript party who is the darling of talk shows because of his unbuttoned rhetoric; and Imran Khan's Tehreek-e-Insaf Pakistan party whose representative figured in one 'long march'.

Tinderbox or Tame Kennel?

Terrorism in Punjab, present or potential, can be switched off if the army chief wants because of the close nexus Punjabi terrorism has with the ISI. The entire world knows this every time Pakistan officially declares that internationally wanted terrorists of Punjab are not in Pakistan; and journalists trying to reach them in south Punjab are harassed and driven away. The mother of all terrorist organizations Sipah-e-Sahaba is based in south Punjab but is spreading its wings over Sindh. It has been let off the hook and allowed to go under a changed name by a tame and unprotected judiciary, just like Jamaatud Dawa was after it morphed away from the earlier name of Lashkar-e-Taiba.

In south Punjab, the Khanpur Madrasa's Abdullah bin Masud controls the region's Sipah-e-Sahaba. Leader of the Sipah offshoot, Jaish-e-Mohammad, Masood Azhar, an internationally wanted terrorist, is said to be located in Cholistan in south Punjab where he runs a training camp for his warriors for which he receives financial aid from al-Qaeda. He was protected by the ISI as he acquired five acres for his 'centre' in Bahawalpur City. Thousands of Jaish militants are living in Bahawalpur where Azhar too secretly resides. He frequently visits the Taliban and al-Qaeda leaders on the Afghan border. Malik Ishaq, once in jail in Lahore for killing hundreds of Shia Muslims, belongs to Rahimyar Khan and is leader of another Sipah offshoot, Lashkar-e-Jhangvi. He ruled the territory when in jail, even talking from his cell to political leaders of Punjab. He was acquitted of charges of Shia-killing because the witnesses ran away'.Jaish has twenty madrasas in Multan from where jihadi warriors can be picked up at any time. These warriors also help out Lashkar-e-Jhangvi if and when required. Lashkar gets the bulk of its funding from Faisalabad; but after Faisalabad the biggest source is Multan. Lashkar's camps at Muridke and ChehlaBandi in Azad Kashmir draw most of their Kashmir proxy warriors from Multan Division.

Over the Long Haul

General Raheel Sharif's initiative against the Taliban will please the world as it has pleased the people of Pakistan. He has already lessened the intensity of the 'heroic isolation' that General Kayani favoured. These two factors will help Pakistan fight the long-haul war against elements that its earlier policies spawned. Operation Zarb-e-Azb has revealed that some of the misgivings of General Kayani were misplaced. In Punjab the battle will not be as tough because of the control the army has enjoyed over terrorists and the habit of obedience it has drilled into them.

It is Karachi where the battle will be tough and of long duration. One insight that we have drawn from the terror in Iraq and Nigeria is that the police simply can't take on these highly trained, well-armed and better educated militants dying for Paradise. Induction into the police at the lower levels is not merit-based and equipped with no filter against men already converted to the enemy worldview. The war against terrorism is the army's to fight. Egypt's failure to revive democracy has revealed another lesson that Pakistan must take to heart: don't let Islamist organizations usurp the turf of social services properly belonging to the state. In the ripeness of time, after taking over education, health services and employment sectors, these organizations will start winning elections just like the Muslim Brotherhood. Normal parties winning elections is exactly what the indirect participatory role democracy needs; but Islamist organizations reject democracy after coming to power and want to transform it into a system of perpetual power through a new, 'better' constitution.

The war is going to look dangerous because of the gradual weakening of a covertly jihadi state. Sixty per cent of the territory is without government writ whose functionaries are shrinking from duty or are liaising with terrorists. This scenario will make the taming of the Taliban devil seem hard if not impossible. To offset this internal weakness Pakistan needs to tweak its isolationist external policy. Among the neighbours it must court, India is the most important state with whom cooperation in Afghanistan will carry dividends for Pakistan's internal war. On 1 July 2014, Michael Kugelman of the Woodrow Wilson Center in Washington did the following double take on Pakistan army's course-correction: 'Last week, Pakistan's chief military spokesman said something extraordinary—something that could signal a sea change in the country's security policy—which makes it all the more perplexing that the international media has given scant coverage to what the spokesman General Asim Bajwa had to say: "There is no discrimination among different Tehreek-e-Taliban Pakistan groups or the Haqqani Network, the army will crush them all." If this is in fact true, then it is great news.'

4

A Revolution against Democracy

Into the last week of August 2014, 'revolutions' unleashed by two political parties and their charismatic, God-connected leaders—some would say army-connected—hamstrung Pakistan's already troubled economy and sent out to the world another ominous signal from a perennially unstable nuclear-equipped state. Imran Khan's Pakistan Tehreek-e-Insaf (PTI) and Tahir ul-Qadri's Pakistan AwamiTehreek (PAT) amassed their supporters side by side on the Constitution Avenue in front of the Parliament House in Islamabad, asking Prime Minister Nawaz Sharif to bow out of office 'because the 2013 election was rigged'.

On 19 August, Imran Khan broke into the Red Zone, protecting important state institutions and the diplomatic enclave—where he had earlier pledged not to go—and took his party in front of the Parliament House saying if Prime Minister Nawaz Sharif didn't resign he would take his several thousand followers to the prime minister's house and drag him out 'by his neck'.

His increasing low-discourse agitation was hinged on his accusation that the 2013 election which brought Sharif's party to power had been rigged. First he had wanted the tainted constituencies investigated; now he wanted the prime minister to go. He also probably knew that Sharif had fallen out with the army on three much-discussed scores: refusal by Prime Minister Sharif to stop prosecuting ex-army chief Pervez Musharraf on charges of treason; not punishing the Geo TV enough after it accused the Inter-Services Intelligence (ISI) of attacking and nearly killing its ace anchor, Hamid Mir; and getting too cosy with India in the name of normalization through expanded trade under a WTO blueprint.

The daily *Dawn* quoted Imran Khan, 'We will free Pakistan of Pharaohs' and went on to say: 'The image of a righteous Prophet Moses (Musa) dethroning a wicked *Faraun* (Pharaoh) has often been employed before. It was perfectly effective during Iran's Islamic Revolution. A poster of Ayatollah Khomeini, in the role of Musa dethroning Mohammad Reza, the last Shah of Iran, cast in the role of Pharaoh. Hosni Mubarak, the erstwhile strongman of Egypt, was also termed by his opponents as a modern Pharaoh.'

Tahir ul-Qadri, leading another crowd of mixed male and female disciples that penetrated Islamabad, was more detailed, given his religious scholarship. He quoted the Quran in Arabic and then translated the divine message as ordering two prophet-brothers Aaron (Haroon) and Moses to attack the palace of the Egyptian Pharaoh. So far remaining strictly separated, the two cult leaders had brooked no dilution of their charisma. Now they became 'brothers' challenging Nawaz Sharif, the Pharaoh of Pakistan. Nursing an old feud with him, dual-nationality Qadri may have been woken from his restless sleep in Canada to realize that Sharif's tiff with the army had crossed into a dangerous new territory.

People versus the Pharaoh

Khan was more amateur in his scriptural expertise. He quoted Ali the Fourth Caliph of Islam on how an infidel but just state would survive but an unjust Islamic state would not. The third Caliph Umar could be collared in the street by a commoner questioning his acquisition of a new shirt while he was without one. The ideal (city) state where the caliphs walked was the Athens of Islam with utopian 'participatory democracy' in place, 'justice coming to the citizen's doorstep'. Khan's unguarded moment came when he said he was influenced by 'Mahatma Gandhi'; but a more canny Tahir ul-Qadri couldn't have said it. Instead of the shower of praise he expected, Khan got a heavy dose of textbook nationalism by the media which looked at Gandhi as the villainous, half-naked man who dared oppose Jinnah, the father of the nation. Qadri was ideologically correct and stayed away from Khan's next 'extra-Islamic' reference to Civil Disobedience too.

The irony was that whereas Khan's party was represented in Parliament, Qadri was an outsider to democracy, a scholar with a cult following who had 'written five hundred books with five hundred more ready for printing'. Both leaders boasted about themselves like amateur politicians pushed on to a stage they hardly deserved. Khan's reference to his muscle power which could cause Muslim Leaguers to 'wet their shalwars' was hardly couth. Both avoided the intellectual fallout from this reference by claiming that democracy had been overthrown by Sharif's pharaonic conduct. The palace they were attacking was democracy; but the constitution was against them. By rejecting all overtures for 'consultation' for 'electoral reform' which was Khan's main plank of agitation, the great cricketer signalled war. The PTI's Independence March and PAT's Revolution March were both rejecting the courts of law and their interpretation of the agitation as an illegitimate act. Qadri used political science in his rhetoric but was probably sure that his obsolete reference to 'direct' and 'participatory' democracy would not be challenged by a population steeped in the 'participatory' city-state utopia of Islam.

A Utopia of Welfare

What man achieved in the twentieth century is democracy that lasts, an order secure against mob attacks. Athens was superseded by

Rome; and Europe today harks back to 'direct democracy' of city-state Athens only when it holds referendums and suffers their negative fallout. Pakistan too has rued all the referendums it has held so far. Today, people choose their representatives and send them to Parliament to enact laws on their behalf. If you don't like them, defeat them in the next election but till then you must hold your peace. An ex-World Bank economist Deepak Lal has clarified the reference to direct democracy: 'The underlying theory behind the NGOs' claims, and the source of their popular appeal, is the wholly illiberal theory of participatory democracy. The Western notion of a liberal democracy is based on representative democracy. From the founding fathers of the American republic to liberal thinkers like Immanuel Kant, direct or participatory democracy on the model of the Greek city-states has been held to be deeply illiberal. Subject to populist pressures and the changing passions of the majority, it can oppress minorities. Greater popular participation does not necessarily subserve liberty. The great liberal thinkers have therefore been keen to have indirect representative democracy hedged by various checks and balances which could prevent the majority from oppressing the minority.'[1]

Today's economist, who sees the germ of the 'welfare state' and its infamous budget deficits in 'participatory' democracy, gets predictably jittery. He knows that the early clauses of the constitution pledging equality and security of livelihood to all are only hortatory in nature and the state merely needs to 'aspire' to them. It appears that when the fathers of the constitution sit down to discuss the document they consign the 'hot air' of their misplaced early enthusiasm to early articles. But if you are a Muslim trying to avoid the obsolete caliphate of history by grabbing its utopia through 'welfare' you are indulging in a rhetoric no economist following the market mantra will be able to implement. Qadri and his Awami Tehreek want to revive the forty 'rights'-related opening articles of the constitution to cause the economist to freeze in his tracks. Khan too refers to *falahi* (welfare) state in his speeches as his answer to the difficult questions about how a terror-stricken state can survive. Khan is clearly 'confiscatory' in his welfare pledge—like Bhutto in the 1970s—while Qadri only hints at it but wants to replace the present political order with a welfare state.

Men of Predestiny

Khan has made his 'divine' journey from unfairly maligned 'playboy' bachelorhood to a God-inspired 'servant of the poor' phase in his sixties through revelations made by clairvoyants. In his autobiography, *Pakistan: A Personal History*, he talks about a strong sense of personal destiny and recalled:[2] 'Pirji from Sahiwal said I would be very famous and make my mother a household name.'[3] Imran had announced his first retirement when he met another clairvoyant: 'Baba Chala lived in a little village just a few miles from the Indian border. He certainly had not heard about my retirement . . . the man looked at me and said I had not left my profession . . . It is the will of Allah; you are still in the game.'[4] But the man who stood by him as his spiritual mentor was Mian Bashir (d. 2005) who shocked him by naming the Quranic *ayat* his mother used to read to baby Imran and predicted that Allah had turned the tables in his favour in the Lamb–Botham libel suit whose reparations would have pauperized Khan.[5] Mian Bashir also disarmed a sceptical Jemima by accurately guessing her three secret wishes.[6] On 1 September 2014, however, his latest spiritual guide and clairvoyant, Ahmad Rafeeq Akhtar, came on TV from his home in Gujjar Khan in Punjab to denounce his disciple saying he had become misguided and was following a conspiracy hatched by 'hidden powers'. Fellow disciple and well-known columnist Haroon ul Rasheed had already parted ways with him predicting doom for Khan in his columns and on TV.

On the other hand, Tahir ul-Qadri is a man of God. He communicates with Him in his dreams which he gets in a routine manner; and when he gives his order of the day in the Red Zone of Islamabad, his crowd takes it as divine message. In a famous dream which his detractors use to blacken his name without denting the faith of his disciples, the Prophet of Islam (Peace be upon Him) 'chose' him as his deputy after rejecting all the other schools of thought in Pakistan's religious hierarchy. As a Barelvi he was a potential target of the Taliban and al-Qaeda, which was confirmed by Ahmad Ludhianvi, leader of the banned-and-renamed Sipah-e-Sahaba when he denounced the 'ecstatic' singing and dancing by the PAT and PTI in the Red Zone as 'obscenity', even as the Inter-Services Intelligence told the Sharif government that the Taliban had dispatched a dynamite-laden suicide van to Islamabad to kill the offending protesters.

The Model Town Massacre

Pakistan was jolted out of its political hinges by an event in Lahore on 17 June when the Lahore police lost its head and killed fourteen and injured almost a hundred of a PAT gathering in front of Qadri's house in Model Town. The saintly leader was to arrive from Canada and lead a 'revolution' against a political order he thought neither democratic nor Islamic under the current constitution. The media, attracted to the sensation of violence, tilted into a coverage-race and regaled the highly politicized people of Pakistan to scenes of violence that quickly divested the ruling Muslim League of its legitimacy in their eyes unless some recompense was offered. If someone was behind Qadri's plan to hit Pakistan with a 'revolution' he had surely not counted on the Lahore police handing him victory on a platter. The 17 June 'massacre' provided Qadri and his rumoured backers from within the deep state with a casus belli. Prime Minister Sharif was to pay for it with his head, Qadri said, and from there on handled the situation with inflammatory oratory, big money, and strategic skill.

Meanwhile, Imran Khan, thwarted by a thicket of electoral regulations from satisfaction on the 'rigging of four constituencies' against his party during the 2013 general election, locked on to the negative image of the Sharif government created by the Lahore Massacre and announced that his party workers would target Islamabad on 14 August, Pakistan's Independence Day, and appropriately called his campaign *Azadi* (Independence) March after Qadri had announced his Revolution March earlier. Unfortunately for Sharif, during the Independence Day ceremony in Islamabad the body language of the army chief General Raheel Sharif was read by many as a signal of 'disapproval' and must have given heart to the two Khan–Qadri 'long marches' starting from Model Town and Zaman Park in Lahore.

The 'revolution', obviated by democracy and hitherto in the hands of the Taliban, was back, strangely justified by the media and the country's knee-jerk politicians. It was a desired revolution because 'democracy has gone astray' and the ruling party controlled by the authoritarian Sharif clan had 'become a tool in the extraction of illegitimate wealth from the political system'. As August drew to its close, people remembered the divinely revealed deadline of 31 August for the fall of the government by Qadri, while Khan actually felt the premonition that 'something will happen' on 23 August to force the government to succumb to his six-point charter of demands 'discussable' only after Sharif's resignation.

Political science teaches that 'revolution' is different from 'change', but the parties on the warpath seemed to conflate the two. Change was democracy with its inbuilt period of 'change of government'; and revolution was a sanguinary uprooting that came after a long period of authoritarian oppression. However, in Pakistan most politicians prefer to name their parties *tehreek* meaning 'movement', rather than a party because tehreek implies a spontaneous massing of people intent on following an objective— which is what a revolution looks like in history when it starts. The half-hidden intent behind each tehreek is violent change while also implying inspiration of a higher 'cause' preferably mixed with religion.

The Six-point Challenge

The Parliament has passed a resolution rejecting the 'revolution' and joined the Supreme Court of Pakistan to ask the leaders of the revolution to vacate the Red Zone and let the law take its course on their demands. The response from Qadri was foretold in his roadmap for the state: to change itself into a 'welfare' entity after getting rid of the current government and parliament.

Khan's Six Points echoed his inflexibility: Negotiations with the government after Sharif has resigned; another election to be held under new electoral reforms; a caretaker out of 'independent' people; all election commissioners who 'rigged' the 2013 election be made to resign; and those guilty of rigging be punished. The 'something will happen on 23 August' statement by Imran Khan also contained a 'cricket' simile that pointed to what the daily *Dawn* called a 'déjà vu'. He said, 'On Saturday the finger of the umpire will be raised' ordering the Sharif government to quit the field. A *Dawn* editorial on 21 August echoed: 'Without a doubt, the army leadership has grabbed with both hands the opportunity that the political leadership has created for it—perhaps even steered events from behind the scenes to the present impasse.'

Khan may once have been the army's 'candidate' for coronation as an anointed ruler of the country through familiar interruption of a 'corrupt' democratic order; he may not be as 'anointed' today: he has opposed—and half-heartedly recanted—the new army chief General Raheel Sharif's war against the Taliban who have a soft corner for Khan whose province Khyber Pakhtunkhwa they have nevertheless laid waste through bombings and extractions. Why should the GHQ lend a hand if Khan is soft on the Taliban? But the army–Sharif relations were strained starting with the Musharraf case mentioned above. Relations with India have always been controlled by the army and any overture by a civilian leader for realistic 'normalization' with New Delhi has tended to destabilize Pakistan, as it did under the PPP government for five years. Why should Sharif fly off to India to flatter the new

Indian prime minister, Narendra Modi, after he accused Pakistan of proxy war inside Indian-administered Kashmir?

A probable tell-tale challenge from Imran Khan may have improved his standing vis-à-vis the army: he responded to an American routine statement of backing the legal order in Pakistan and not supporting Khan's 'long march'. In his typically unbuttoned style, which many comedians imitate on TV, he called Sharif a 'slave of America' and added 'slave of India' for good measure. He had earlier announced that upon coming to power he would renege on all 'foreign aid' taken by Pakistan with the help of America 'from this day on'. He repeated his confiscatory intent once again by saying, 'Why should I go to the IMF when I can bring back the $200 billion concealed abroad by our corrupt politicians?'

Swaying to the Military Tune?

There was more tell-tale stuff coming from Khan that prompted some opinion-writers to predict a military-backed change of government in Pakistan. Khan denounced the media house called Jang-Geo Group for badmouthing him and his party but did not refer to the quarrel that Geo had picked with the army by airing an accusation of prompted attack after its ace anchor Hamid Mir was nearly killed by terrorists earlier in the year. Khan knew that Geo TV transmission through cable had been forced out of the market, leading to default on the network's salaries. And 'mysterious' but effective phone-calls in Lahore were asking cables to 'take Geo off' even as he spoke.

The Paris-based International Crisis Group (ICG) in its statement of 21 August encapsulated what the world thought was happening in Pakistan as it also implied the isolation Pakistanis were willing to endure by accepting what was happening as 'democratic':

'The protests rocking Islamabad threaten to upend the constitutional order, set back rule of law and open the possibility of a soft coup, with the military ruling through the backdoor. Renewed political instability at the centre would imperil any progress that has been made in addressing grievous economic, development and security challenges. The government's moves, supported by the parliamentary opposition, to accommodate some of the protestors' demands—particularly as regards electoral reform—are welcome. It is worrying, however, that protest leaders appear adamant in rejecting such outreach. Crisis Group calls on the political and military leadership to continue adherence to the constitution and enforcement of the rule of law, while permitting the right to peaceful protest.'

Pakistan collapsed materially in the face of Taliban terror; it also collapsed intellectually if you examine the political intent of the Khan–Qadri duo. Both relied on statements of great exaggeration, the insults carried in them qualifying as 'hate speech'. Why does Pakistan behave the way it does? If it is a generic Muslim angst, it started in Pakistan much before it infected the Arabs. The 1999 toppling of the Sharif government happened after Army Chief General Musharraf tried to deliver to the nation the 'much-deserved' trophy of Kargil but was unfortunately defeated by India and by international isolation. There are many cult figures in Pakistan who manifest a non-intellectual tendency to excess. This excess is often expressed in hate speech.

In history, the strongman fades after overreaching himself. This is the fate of the cult leader too, his lack of realism reinforced by his worshipping flock. The cult leaders of Pakistan are threatened by a flaw of miscalculation that compels them to overreach. In the prototype, the death of the cult leader leads to the death of his flock. But in the present case, the state itself can die or graduate to a 'failed' status from the current dysfunctional one.

Attrition Sets In?

On 17 August, Khan gave two days to Sharif to resign as prime minister; on 21 August, he gave him another two days. Meanwhile, both houses of the parliament passed unanimous resolutions calling the *dharna* (sit-in) by the PTI and PAT as being in violation of the Constitution since there was no way a prime minister could be forced to resign. All the parties more or less cleaved to the position taken by the ruling Muslim League–Nawaz that it would be ultra vires of the Constitution if Sharif was cashiered from his job by force.

Other symptoms of attrition of the PTI–PAT 'long march' were in evidence by 22 August. Lawyers all over Pakistan got together and issued a warning to the two that any effort at removing Sharif by force would be physically opposed. Religious parties belonging to the anti-Barelvi consensus, rallied around the ruling party. Leader of the formerly banned terrorist party Sipah-e-Sahaba, Ahmad Ludhianvi, condemned the 'ecstatic' song-and-dance routine started by the two protesting parties, followed by another condemnation by chief of the powerful Jamaatud Dawa, Hafiz Saeed.

A crescendo was reached when the head cleric of Islamabad's notorious pro-al-Qaeda Red Mosque, Maulana Abdul Aziz, too abominated the obscene 'heresy' in the Parliament Square called D-Chowk. Aziz was nominated to its negotiating team by the Taliban, together with Imran Khan, for the peace talks that went nowhere earlier in the year. Expectedly, the foremost rival cleric of Imran Khan, Maulana Fazlur Rehman, retaliated against Khan's frequent defamations directed at him by joining the chorus. In Balochistan, the government participated in a meeting held by Baloch politicians to condemn the 'long march'.

Standing atop his shipping container in Islamabad, Khan responded by asking his partymen to resign from the central and provincial legislatures. Some of his forty members of the National Assembly were said to have deposited their resignations with the Speaker, but a large group didn't and decided to form a separate rebels' group called 'forward bloc'. His government in Khyber Pakhtunkhwa did not resign either probably because it thought that its performance was good, as reported in a survey made by Christine Fair in the August 2014 issue of the Karachi monthly magazine *Herald*. A no-confidence move effectively prevented dissolution of the house under law. Not only was Khan's chief minister reluctant to resign but his coalition partner, the Jamaat-e-Islami, too was strongly opposed to it, its leader Sirajul Haq posing as a mediator between Khan and Sharif. The Khyber Pakhtunkhwa government was supposed to despise the latter leader.

Nature Strikes Too

Add to this the attrition of nature, the sun that beat down relentlessly on the two side-by-side gatherings not well-provided with any defence against the elements. Food was well-organized on the PAT side but there was a shortage of washrooms which forced men, women and children—including infants—to defecate in the open while the remnants of food thrown around on the square became a health hazard. Disease broke out, but PAT had a team of doctors with a supply of medicines to look after them; on the other hand, PTI was not organized for this emergency. As dysentery and flu spread and an unpleasant stench conquered the air, PTI protesters from outside Islamabad started complaining. PAT accused the government of mixing the water supplied to the crowd with poison.

Desperation set in. PAT leader Tahir ul-Qadri, seeing that no 'finger' of Sharif's dismissal had been raised by the 'umpire' mentioned by Khan, asked his followers to give the call to prayer (*azan*), loudly, seven times, which is normally perceived as a desperate appeal to God for intervention in case of natural calamities. He strengthened this gesture by making a reference to his own death if his followers abandoned him. Khan too referred to his own death if his followers deserted him: 'Sharif's resignation or my death!' Khan employed other bizarre methods to prevent his crowd from breaking: he promised to get married if they remained steadfast and achieved the ouster of the prime minister. (When that attracted sarcastic comment in the media, he added to his many rescinded earlier statements by saying he meant 'happiness' when he said 'marriage'.)

He asked the people of Pakistan not to deposit their savings in state-owned banks and told expat Pakistanis to use the illegal havala channel to transfer funds to Pakistan instead of the banks. By the time the week drew to a close on 24 August, the economy had reacted negatively and the media reported a loss of Rs 490 billion at the stock exchange; trade minister Khurram Dastgir Khan put the over-all loss at Rs 800,000–300 billion on the capital market and 500 billion because of the rupee's depreciation.

The press calculated the expenses borne by the two parties conducting the agitation: 'On the basis of about 200 big pots (*degs*) of food of Rs 5000 per day, two cranes available to move the containers, a few dozen trucks mounted with generators and fitted with floodlights, two containers with twenty-four mobile toilets, some AC-fitted luxury containers for the leaders, they paid Rs 20 million a day.' Starting 14 August, the protest was still on after a fortnight although Khan's party seemed to wilt a little under these factors of attrition.

As these signs of attrition became pronounced, a former secretary of the Election Commission of Pakistan, Kanwar Dilshad, was quoted by Khan as saying that ex-chief justice of Pakistan and the chief election commissioner Justice Fakhruddin G. Ebrahim (retd) were in cahoots when they conspired to allow the election of 2013 to be supervised by judicial officers rather than the school-teachers normally employed by the Election Commission. Dilshad later denied some details of this allegation but still maintained that Chief Justice Iftikhar Chaudhry was not constitutionally empowered to address the judicial officers supervising the election which he had done.

Then the bombshell came from his junior, the former additional secretary of the Election Commission, Afzal Khan, who went on an openly anti-Sharif and pro-army ARY TV channel to accuse Justice Ebrahim (retd), Chief Justice Chaudhry, former appointee judge of the Commission, Justice Riaz Kayani (retd), and former

Justice Tassadaq Husain Jilani, in charge of the Commission after Justice Ebrahim had departed, of being guilty of rigging the 2013 election. Suiting his style to the high-tension atmosphere and debased rhetoric in Islamabad, Afzal Khan said, asserting he had no proof to back his charges: 'They should all be tried under Article 6 of the Constitution and hanged for treason.' He did not say that he had joined Khan's campaign but was seen standing next to him on the container stage at Constitution Avenue. The PTI, whose committee, led by vice-chairman of the party Shah Mehmood Qureshi, had just deadlocked a meeting with the ruling party on PTI's 'six points', went ballistic after Afzal Khan's allegations. Leader Khan immediately gave another twenty-four hours before he would unleash his mob on the prime minister's house to throw Sharif physically out of office.

Army as 'Third Umpire'?

The civil–military equation was already wobbly when Qadri in Canada and Khan in Bani Gala in Islamabad decided to take their parties into the 'long march'. The last time Qadri thought of doing this, it was appropriately winter and the disciple families holding on to their infants in Islamabad were well-equipped to handle the weather. This time, the timing, it would seem, was not of his choosing: no one can do street politics in the middle of the hot and humid climate of the plains in Pakistan. The PTI seemed to silently coordinate its own 'long march' with that of PAT.

It is unlikely the army persuaded the two party leaders to brave the hot weather in Islamabad to teach Nawaz Sharif a lesson. Had it done so, it would have intervened by the beginning of the third week of August when the media and public opinion were clearly tilting in their favour. It is quite possible that, even if it had planned the 'long march', its lack of action after 14 August swung the political reaction in favour of the ruling party. Yet, no one missed the angry references by PAT and PTI leaders to the same issues that had alienated the army from Nawaz Sharif.

London-based Pakistani journalist Abbas Nasir writing in *Dawn* of 23 August, disclosed: 'In a report earlier this week, Reuters' well-informed reporter in Islamabad, quoting unnamed military sources, reported that the prime minister had been assured by the military his government will survive but will have to "share space with the army".' If the army had obtained satisfaction on the issues it had with Sharif and finally 'settled' its dispute with him over Geo TV and the fate of its ex-chief Musharraf, then the two parties sweating it out in front of the Parliament House in Islamabad were short-changed and the country destabilized for nothing.

It is true that Khan and Qadri could never really be favourites with the GHQ: Khan was a known loose cannon and had opposed General Raheel Sharif's invasion of North Waziristan and was still making such obliquely tilted remarks as 'we will hand over Gullu Butt [a violent Muslim League worker] to the Taliban'. And Qadri was anathema to a Deobandi underworld of jihadi outfits held on leash by the army while some of his fellow-Barelvis thought he had betrayed them over the Blasphemy Law issue to the West. Whatever the role of the army behind the 'long march' of 2014, the political system was seriously destabilized. While Sharif's opposition in Parliament rallied around him, their attitude was ambivalent, to say the least. The PPP leader Asif Ali Zardari took pains to call on the beleaguered Sharifs at their sprawling residence at Jati Umrain in Lahore and assured them that his party would not allow the elected government to fall or the prime minister himself to be toppled through the blackmail of long marches. Much of the protective rhetoric by the pro-Sharif opposition too carried a concealed reference to 'an intrusive army', but the ambiance in Pakistan was no longer good for democracy.

Even as Zardari offered assurances to Sharif, a number of PPP stalwarts on the media thought he could 'retreat' a little in the face of the Khan–Qadri duo. Some hinted at his accepting the dubious PTI proposal that he leave the scene temporarily and let someone else from his party take his job before setting up an agreed-by-all caretaker government who would then hold fresh elections. Meanwhile, Imran Khan's case-building against 'sons of politicians', being 'prepared' to take over after their fathers have quit, is gaining traction. As news of ex-ISI chief General Ahmad Shuja Pasha (retd) visiting Pakistan and meeting PTI leaders circulated, his personal vendetta with the 'political system' as noted by editor, Bob Dietz, on the website of the Committee to Protect of Journalists, was revived in the following extract:

'Hamid Mir spoke about his meeting with Pasha: 'After the May 2011 US raid on Abbottabad, as the TV anchors pounded the military for being incompetent, Hamid Mir, one of the most popular personalities on Geo TV, got a call from a brigadier that the director general of intelligence at the time, Shuja Pasha, wanted to see him. Here's how the conversation with Pasha proceeded, according to Mir:

"Mr Mir, this system and Pakistan cannot co-exist."
"What system?" asked Mir.
"The parliamentary form of democracy and Pakistan."
"Do you want a presidential form?" asked Mir.
"Yes."
"This is not your job. It's the job of Parliament to change the constitution."

'Pasha then spoke abusively about the son of the Punjab chief minister, the son of the president, the sons of other chief ministers. "Do you want your children ruled by these sons?" he asked Mir.

"We had a very bad meeting," Mir told me when we met in Islamabad. "He is talking politics the whole time." After that meeting, parliamentary democracy and the sons of different politicians began taking a critical beating from talk-show hosts and columnists. And suddenly they were all promoting Imran Khan, the popular cricketer-turned-populist-politician who led the Pakistan Tehreek-e-Insaf party, or PTI, in the May 2013 elections.

'Pasha had decided Khan was the man to back. Politicians called me, "Mir, Mir, I want advice. Should I join Imran Khan? Pasha is putting pressure on us."'[7]

In the middle of August 2014, as violent demonstrations in Islamabad unfolded under the direction of Imran Khan and Tahir ul-Qadri, the president of the PTI, Javed Hashmi, broke ranks and accused Imran Khan of acting on the 'advice' of elements that left 'no space' between the party programme and plans afoot for military rule, hinting that Khan was acting on the advice of the army.

A rumour likewise circulated about the shifting of ex-ISI officer Brigadier Ejaz Shah (retd) from his residence in Lahore Defence Society to a guesthouse in Islamabad to plan the assault strategy of the Khan–Qadri duo. Brigadier Shah was being connected to an earlier rumour that ex-ISI chief Pasha had visited Lahore. Pasha was also connected with the earlier 'visit' of Tahir ul-Qadri to Pakistan and his party's sit-in protest against the PPP government in January 2013. This was finally confirmed by Hashmi who disclosed to a TV channel that Shah had prepared the entire 'script' of the party's action-plan and had got PTI chief Khan to go to London to meet PAT chief Qadri secretly in the first week of June 2014.

The Army Stays Clear?

After having designated Saturday, 30 August, as D-day, leaders of the twin sit-ins declared a day earlier that they had been invited by the army chief General Raheel Sharif for talks. Qadri declared before going to the meeting that the army had agreed to be the arbiter and used the Urdu words *salis* and *zaamin*, an agreed third-party judge whose verdict the two disputing parties normally pledge to accept. Qadri also stated that the arbitration had been sought by Prime Minister Sharif. This was vehemently denied by the prime minister after an uproar of protest and condemnation from a supportive opposition in the National Assembly. The army cleared up the confusion by saying through its public relations department that the government had asked the army chief to 'facilitate' resumption of the deadlocked talks with the Khan–Qadri duo, not 'arbitrate' between them.

The media gave full coverage to this development which appeared like an extra-constitutional scandal to most politicians and some of the media, including the hitherto pro-government MQM chief Altaf Hussain, who now asked the army to take over the government by unseating Sharif. On 20 August, the press reported the polarized view on whether the army had 'intervened', portraying the Khan–Qadri duo as approaching General Sharif for intervention. Qadri, after an apparently infructuous meeting with the army chief, told his audience to 'wait beyond the deadline of Saturday' because he had seen 'the spark of sincerity in the eye of the general'.

By Saturday, as the two rebel leaders called off their D-day, the army appeared to be steadfast in its determination not to step into the crisis and resolve it one way or another. Public expectation of 'intervention', honed by a jurisprudence of military takeovers, was belied. But the crisis of a state made wobbly by years of instability went on.

'Edict from the Army'

Soon enough, the very next day, the called-off D-Day was on again. Brushing aside protests from the president of the party, chairman PTI Imran Khan ordered his mob to move ahead and surround the prime minister's house beyond the Red Line manned by the police. As clashes between the PAT–PTI demonstrators and the government became violent on Sunday, 31 August, the army chief General Sharif held an emergency meeting of his corps commanders and issued what was called by the daily *Dawn* 'an edict of the army'. It stated:

'While reaffirming support to democracy, the conference reviewed with serious concern, the existing political crisis and the violent turn it has taken, resulting in large scale injuries and loss of lives. Further use of force will only aggravate the problem. It was once again reiterated that the situation should be resolved politically without wasting any time and without recourse to violent means. The army remains committed to playing its part in ensuring security of the state and will never fall short of meeting national aspirations.'

A polarized media interpreted the message from the army to suit their points of view. The Jang Group of newspapers, on the wrong side of the army and suffering what it considered illegal closure of its GEO TV on the cable network, printed a front-page analysis in its Urdu daily portraying the message as being loaded against the government as it appeared to give a time-bound deadline for 'political solution' forbidding 'violence' without discriminating between violence of the mob and violence of the state against those acting against the law.

Predictions, that after the message from the army, violent protest would die down were belied. A more intense escalation of mob attacks in Islamabad was backed by well-organized PTI–PAT demonstrations in Lahore and Karachi, forcing the 'now non-violent police' into retreat. It was clear that the Khan–Qadri duo had interpreted the message as a go-ahead signal.

Endgame: Three Scenarios

In a polarized state, opinion is formed through prejudgement. TV channels and the print media presented three scenarios about how the crisis, triggered by the agitation in Islamabad by Imran Khan's Pakistan Tehreek-e-Insaf (PTI) and Tahir ul-Qadri's Pakistan Awami Tehreek (PAT), will come to an end. The first scenario embraced by those opposed to Nawaz Sharif's Pakistan Muslim League government had Prime Minister Sharif resigning his office to allow a fair audit of the 2013 general election. The second scenario put forward by the government and its supporters required the government to stand firm against agitation and allow a judicial commission to decide whether the election was tainted enough to require a mid-term election. The third scenario is predicated on the assumption that civil-military relations had hit bottom and, climaxing the steady signs of mutual rivalry, a takeover was possible, resulting in a caretaker phase of governance before the next election was allowed to take place.

Scenario One: Resign or Go on Leave!

The most widespread opinion, thanks to a GEO-versus-the-Rest split in the media and mild rebellion within the political parties arrayed behind Prime Minister Sharif in Parliament, was that he should resign and let a judicial commission audit the 2013 election, after which he would somehow be returned to office if the commission was found in his favour. The Sharif cabinet maintained that it couldn't be held responsible for the rigging if Sharif was not in power as, under the constitution elections are conducted by an agreed caretaker government, and not the government in power. In 2013 Pakistan People's Party (PPP) was in power and not Muslim League. Bending to the aggrieved parties agitating on the Constitution Avenue, TV anchors and politicians sought quasi-constitutional measures to make indictment of the PML possible.

As the constitution didn't allow removal of the prime minister except through a successful vote of no-confidence in Parliament, the scenario was made to include the 'option' of voluntary resignation by Sharif, which added to the thrust of the Khan–Qadri duo's stance that their agitation has delegitimized him and he should resign under moral pressure. As the agitating parties failed, through several rounds of talks, to persuade the government in power to vacate, a palliative was offered through yet another extra-constitutional device: that the prime minister should go 'on leave', allowing scope for the speculation that he would be able to return to office after the judicial commission on the 2013 polls found that the polls were not widely rigged.

The Sharif-should-resign slogan gelled while speculations were rife that the army was opposed to him remaining in power after confrontation with it over former army chief General Musharraf's trial for treason, the accusations levelled by a GEO TV anchor against the army of colluding with terrorists, and less clearly, over Sharif's excessive enthusiasm for normalizing relations with India through trade. The PPP, a major presence in Parliament and ruling in the province of Sindh, was supportive of Sharif at the level of its de facto leader and co-chairman, Asif Ali Zardari, but in Punjab its second-echelon leaders still chafed under the memory of PML's hounding of the PPP when the latter ruled in Islamabad from 2008 to 2013. The MQM, remote-controlled from London by its leader Altaf Hussain, formally adopted the policy of supporting the 'constitutional' right of PTI and PAT to protest and demanding the resignation of the prime minister. The 'big leader' Altaf Hussain first miscalculated the chances of the success of the agitation and called for a military takeover, then recanted soon enough to join the anti-agitation consensus in Parliament.

Jamaat-e-Islami, strengthened by its presence in the Khyber Pakhtunkhwa coalition along with the ruling PTI, decided to adopt neutrality rather than partisanship on the issue of PTI's agitation. Its new leader Sirajul Haq adroitly placed himself in the position of peacemaker, opposing Khan's policy of resignations in the provincial assembly but being ambivalent and occasionally soft on the PM's resignation. TV anchors displayed postures of neutrality but tended to support the resignation call, based on the moral pressure on Sharif to correct the blunder of killing a number of PAT supporters in Lahore on 17 June. Most were united on the position that Sharif's younger brother, Punjab chief minister Shahbaz Sharif, should resign. More stridently, the TV channels opposed to the Sharif-supported GEO channel, saw Sharif's hand in the Lahore killings too, and backed the PTI–PAT stance that the prime minister should resign or 'go on leave'. GEO TV, under pressure from the army on the closure 'through threatening phone calls' of its news channel on TV cable network across Pakistan, occasionally allowed removal of Shahbaz Sharif while defending Nawaz.

The army unintendedly strengthened the 'resignation' chorus by repeatedly describing its position on the crisis through the ISPR. It emphasized that the political impasse should be resolved politically through 'talks' and that force should not be used even as the 'last option'. Since the army was already deployed under a constitutional provision to protect important state properties in the capital, this total exclusion of 'force' was interpreted as the army's refusal to defend the government against the Khan–Qadri agitation.

This scenario fluctuated in its practicability with the vicissitudes of the agitation itself. The agitation fed off three factors and in turn the three factors fed off the intensity of the agitation: 1) the stance of the army perceived as offended with the government; 2) the stance of the opposition parties in Parliament; and 3) the ongoing competitive tussle between GEO TV, on the one hand, and the other TV channels struggling for their share of the market, on the other.

Scenario Two: Government Survives

The force behind this thesis was derived from the parliament, which defended the right of the prime minister to resist the agitation and lean on the constitution to maintain his right to rule. Parliamentary support to Nawaz Sharif came from two parties that felt they were maltreated in the past by the army and the elements that benefited from the army's policies. In the lead of this support was the PPP whose leader, Asif Ali Zardari, as President of Pakistan, was opposed by the army high command for his party's entire tenure of five years in power. The second tier of support came from the Awami National Party (ANP) which ruled in Khyber Pakhtunkhwa and felt aggrieved because it was opposed to the GHQ's handling of the Taliban as instruments of policy in Afghanistan. The third element in Parliament was the MQM, which had been in and out of favour with the army but tended to be pragmatic and changeable in its stance to the constitutional status of the government in power.

There were other factors supporting the prime minister. The business community of Pakistan was worried by the negative effect of the agitation and wanted it brought to closure. The professions, led by the lawyers, were likewise upset by the obstructive nature of the strategy being pursued by the agitating parties. Less visible but no less decisive was the thinking of the 'non-state actors' of Punjab enjoying interface with the army but clearly opposed to the rising Tahir ul-Qadri phenomenon behind the less threatening Imran Khan. The condemnation of the 'song and dance' routine of the sit-in rejected Khan equally with Qadri who was condemned for his heretic religious beliefs. Since these jihadi elements boasted private armies their opposition to the agitation couldn't be ignored by the army if it became the final arbiter.

There may be some stragglers in parliamentary support for Prime Minister Sharif—as in the case of some Punjabi leaders of the PPP and the 'volte face tactics' used by the MQM leader, Altaf Hussain—but the retreat of the army in its tacit or implied support to the agitation was most crucial in deciding the fate of the unfolding crisis on Constitution Avenue. On 31 August, president of the PTI Javed Hashmi, decided to go public on what he alleged was his party's secret connection with some elements of the army and its secret service the ISI acting in concert to overthrow the elected government.

Deluded by his senior status into believing that Imran Khan's cult would brook variant advice, Hashmi accused the big leader of arbitrarily changing agreed party positions after receiving signals from his concealed minders. Khan and his party read as positive the formal but vague signals emanating from the army chief through the ISPR and looked to him to decide the crisis in their favour. Hashmi's public 'revelations' shocked many supporters into changing their loyalty to the PTI.

Last but not least, Prime Minister Sharif was buttressed by the statements issued on the crisis by foreign governments, including Pakistan's largest trading partners, the United States and the European Union, including the United Kingdom, clearly supporting the constitutionally elected government and refusing to accept the position of the agitating parties. The army may be limited in its worldview to national security but it couldn't ignore the international opinion threatening to isolate Pakistan before punishing it economically.

The one benefit to the state of Pakistan that this scenario would bring was the systemic evolution of democracy through reform of its electoral system. The cutting down to size of the Sharif government through several weeks of political turmoil would be beneficial for the survival of the state as more modest but meaningful behavioural change would be made possible through restrictive lawmaking.

Scenario Three: The Army Takes Over

Any direct takeover by the army was never in the works, but after twenty days of the unfolding of the crisis in Islamabad it may have become impossible for the military high command to deviate from its formal commitment to democracy. Any 'indirect' change of government at this point may also have become impossible because of the way its pronouncement of this commitment had been interpreted in the country. Its announcement through the ISPR that the government should engage with the agitation politically and not use force was commented upon by an editorial in *Dawn* of 2 September.

'The carefully constructed veneer of neutrality that the army leadership had constructed through much of the national political crisis instigated by Imran Khan and Tahir ul-Qadri has been torn apart. First, [by advising non-use of force] came the army's statement on Sunday, the third in a series of statements in recent days on the political crisis, which quite astonishingly elevated the legitimacy and credibility of the demands of Imran Khan, Tahir ul-Qadri and their violent protesters above that of the choices and actions of an elected government dealing with a political crisis.'

The stance taken by the army high command on non-use of force caused a PAT–PTI mob to assault the compound of the Parliament House and occupy its lawn. The police—aware of its low rank in the hierarchy of state force—got thrashed by the mob, then simply allowed the occupation while the military troops stood aside and did nothing. A number of police commanders, sensing the real backing the PAT–PTI adventure had, got themselves transferred after refusal to act.

Most damaging of all were the revelations made by Javed Hashmi who made public facts that the Urdu print media understandably refused to digest and print. The conspiracy to get rid of Prime Minister Sharif was hatched at least a year earlier by some retired army officers reviving old contacts with PAT–PTI leaders. These contacts went back to when the ISI was headed by General Ahmad Shuja Pasha. Pasha had initiated the policy of recalling retired ISI officers like Brigadier Ejaz Shah to service and giving them offices at Aabpara, the headquarters of the ISI.

Shah was Intelligence Bureau chief and home secretary Punjab during the General Musharraf regime. While home secretary, Shah had provided shelter to an al-Qaeda agent, Omar Sheikh, accused of taking part in the murder of American journalist Daniel Pearl in Karachi. He also ended up featuring in Benazir Bhutto's famous letter forecasting her assassination. The UN Commission Report on her assassination had this to say about him in April 2010 in its paragraph 218:

'Ms Bhutto's own concerns about threats to her by al-Qaeda and other militants resulted in part from her knowledge of their links with people who had worked with or been assets of the ISI. She feared that the authorities could activate these connections, using radical Islamists to harm her, while hiding their own role in any attack. This was the basis for her allegations against Lt General Hamid Gul (retd) and Brigadier Ejaz Shah (retd), in her 16 October letter to General Musharraf . . .

'Brigadier Ejaz Shah, Director General of the Intelligence Bureau in 2007 and a former ISI officer, was a member of General

Musharraf's inner circle. When Omar Saeed Sheikh, the main accused in the Daniel Pearl murder case, was cornered in 2002, he requested to surrender to Brigadier Shah. Some believe this was because of Brigadier Shah's reported intelligence connections with Mr Sheikh; Brigadier Shah vigorously denied this and told the Commission that the surrender was facilitated through family ties in their home community.'

After the killing of Osama bin Laden in Abbottabad, a number of revelations about renegade ISI contacts with al-Qaeda were made. One significant detail of this 'connection' was a statement by ex-ISI chief General Ziauddin Butt (retd)—which he later recanted because of its serious nature—that Ejaz Shah was one of the contacts enjoyed by bin Laden within the military establishment. In February 2012, Bruce Riedel, a senior adviser in the Obama administration, stated in an article in the *Daily Beast*:

'Now there is an explosive new charge. The former head of Pakistan's Inter-Services Intelligence Directorate (ISI) says former President Pervez Musharraf knew bin Laden was in Abbottabad. General Ziauddin Khwaja, also known as Ziauddin Butt, was head of ISI from 1997 to 1999 . . . Ziauddin says that the safe house in Abbottabad was made to order for bin Laden by another Pakistani intelligence officer, Brigadier General Ijaz Shah . . . who was responsible for setting up bin Laden in Abbottabad, ensuring his safety and keeping him hidden from the outside.'

It became almost certain that in 2014 the Pasha–Shah duo and possibly others were 'handling' the agitation from Lahore to Islamabad after having laid plans for it at least a year earlier probably without the knowledge of the General Raheel Sharif command. They wanted to present the 'fait accompli' of a breakdown of the democratic order to the army already unhappy with the Sharif government. They talked to the PAT–PTI leadership on behalf of the army high command without telling them the truth. This became apparent when the army chief invited them for talks after having been asked to do so by Prime Minister Sharif. Both

Khan and Qadri were puzzled by what transpired at the meeting. It clearly did not meet their expectations of the 'guarantees' that Qadri actually mentioned before leaving for the meeting.

Javed Hashmi provided further clues in a TV interview on 2 September. He said that Ejaz Shah often rebuked the PAT–PTI leaders for not gathering the promised numbers of agitators in Islamabad which might become the 'trigger' Shah thought for 'army action'. Shah also insisted that the agitation should start and end within the month of August despite protests from the client leaders that the month of August would be too hot for the mobs. He also reprimanded the leaders of the agitation for not getting the mob to attack the Parliament House. Hashmi claimed that a lot of retired army officers were lined up behind the anti-democracy campaign, who appeared on TV channels regularly.

On the same day, Interior Minister Chaudhry Nisar Ali, known for his contacts in the 'deep state', announced in a joint session of Parliament that the mobs assaulting the state institutions were not an ordinary crowd but a trained army of men prepared to wound and kill. This statement tended to revive the debate about the raising of private armies in south Punjab under the leadership of religious leaders which led to the weakening of the writ of the state in the country. It is axiomatic since the times of Machiavelli—who talked of private armies—that states crumble when they make use of mercenary soldiers.

Astoundingly, journalist and TV anchor Talat Husain, who has an effective finger on the institutional pulse of Islamabad, 'predicted' in the monthly journal *Newsline* of June 2014:

'As the pressure mounts, with Aabpara and Imran working together, events will be pushed to ensure that the civilian government leans on the Pindiwalas for support. At that point, Nawaz Sharif may have no option but to either call for re-elections or stand belittled and cut down to size before the establishment. If re-elections are held, massive rigging in favour of Imran Khan will take place and he will become an elected prime minister before the end of the year.'

The Pasha–Shah initiative actually made the chances of removal of the Sharif government by the army almost impossible. Pasha had used the 'other' armies against the PPP—which had refused to give him his third extension as ISI chief—against the government by bringing them on the road as 'Defence of Pakistan Council'. The PAT–PTI agitation had been publicly opposed by most of the south Punjab non-state actor jihadi leaders which the army cannot have failed to notice. The stage was simply not set for a midstream change of government.

Finally, did the army under General Raheel Sharif at any time consider overthrowing the government? A *Reuters'* report by reporter Mehreen Zahra-Malik, dated 5 September, cleared up the mystery:

'Weeks of mounting anti-government protests in Pakistan was enough to convince five of the powerful army's eleven Corps Commanders that it was time for them to step in and force embattled Prime Minister Nawaz Sharif to resign. But Army Chief General Raheel Sharif decided the time was not right to overthrow the civilian leadership, and moved to quell any disagreement in his ranks by overruling the hawks and declaring the crisis must be solved through politics, not force.'

Another nugget produced by *Newsweek* Pakistan (6–13 September) was even more chastening: 'After the prime minister's meeting with the army chief the same day, ISPR denied breaking-news reports claiming that General Sharif had asked Prime Minister Sharif to resign or go on leave as baseless. (In fact, according to a party source, the general said that he served at the pleasure of the prime minister and would resign if asked.)'

Another London Plan and Electoral 'Punctures'?

Rumours had started circulating in mid-August that the Khan–Qadri protest had actually been planned in London by an old contact of the 'Chaudhrys of Gujrat', Shujaat Hussain and PervaizElahi, who got them to meet two other persons in London in May 2014, Imran Khan and Tahir ul-Qadri, disclosing to them the 'plan' that would get them rid of the Nawaz Sharif government on the question of rigging. As disclosed by the *News* in its issue of 10 September 2014, the linchpin of the plan was one Dr Ejaz Hussain, 'a UK-based former adviser to Chaudhry Pervaiz Elahi, who was able to convince Dr Tahir ul-Qadri that the 'establishment' had decided a role for him; he also spread a conspiracy in the chattering circles of Islamabad that Najam Sethi [caretaker chief minister of Punjab during the 2013 election] had fixed 'punctures' on thirty-five seats to give edge to PMLN over its rival parties.'

Dr Hussain was supposed to be an expert on computers and had lectured previously at the army's prestigious institution The National Defence University in Islamabad on'Pakistan's Cyber Security and Outer Space Challenges'. He had relied on 'the revelations made by Edward Snowden on the snooping done by the US on Pakistan' and claimed that 'he had come across more than a thousand sources' to build his case. America's 'cyber-invasion' of Pakistan was supposed to have caught caretaker chief minister Sethi talking on the phone to the Sharifs: 'phone chat/SMS were recorded as Sethi assured both Nawaz and Shahbaz (in Punjabi): "Mian Saab—*aye tee/pentiseetan da rola aye, purtusik'abraonaeen—main tiyari karlai aye keaena tee/ pentiseetanwich main dus-tu-pundra hazaar votaan da pancharla diyanga.'* (I have made preparation and I will fix punctures of about 10,000–15,000 votes in fifteen constituencies.)

Dr Hussain went on to implicate then army chief General Ashfaq Pervaiz Kayani in the rigging plot, a charge repeated by Chaudhry Shujaat after he and Pervaiz Elahi had joined the Khan–Qadri agitation. He also involved the American National Security Authority (NSA) reading the snooped message from Pakistan and wondering what *painchar* meant. It approached, he alleged, its British counterpart for the word's actual meaning and was told that it was actually a changed form of word 'puncture'.

The *News* article ends the story by saying: 'When approached by the *News*, the UK defence and diplomatic sources laughed off the allegations presented as facts to the mainstream Pakistan media by Imran Khan and a few anchors. They said there was no truth in this story and Ejaz Hussain failed to tell how he came to know this story.' Dr Ejaz Hussain was ferreted out of the TV footage of the Qadri camp in Islamabad by Geo TV. He was found sitting at the edge of what appeared to be the cleric's 'container' cabinet and seemed more at home with them than with the more 'upper-crust' crowd surrounding Imran Khan.

5

Ground Zero Karachi

On 9 June 2014, Pakistan's largest international airport at Karachi was attacked by ten terrorists who ended up killing eighteen security personnel before dying through suicide and bullets from their victims. Whatever their objective, the terrorists clearly failed to achieve it, if you compare it to similar attacks in the past. The total damage was estimated at $5 million. The reaction of the administration, which failed to protect the airport, was the same as in the past: India did it!

The TV channels, dizzy from the marsh gas of ideology, picked up the 'India did it' refrain and churned it endlessly for days to come while its written version appeared mostly in the Urdu press which expresses Pakistan's nationalist passions more effectively. The TV anchors declared that the terrorists were carrying blood-clotting injections on them to stop bleeding the same way Indian soldiers did, thereby seeking to prove that India was behind the terrorist operation. But when an injection pack was shown close up on TV the importer's address clearly indicated a shop in Karachi. Later on, the newspapers disclosed that the cell phone SIMs the terrorists used had been bought from a retailer in Nawabshah in Sindh and not Afghanistan. An Urdu daily also reported that the government had ordered scrutiny of the passport records of Indians who had visited Pakistan in the past three years.

The weapons used by the terrorists were likewise 'discovered' to have come from India despite Indian High Commissioner Raghavan's assertion that India had nothing to do with the unsuccessful terrorist operation. The 'India factor' persisted even after the Rangers commandant came on TV and announced that the weapons were still being investigated and no final decision about provenance had been made. The newspapers however insisted India was somehow involved because a number of sharp-tongued retired Pakistani military officers who frequent talk shows insisted that 'India had done it again'. Information Minister Pervaiz Rasheed was persuaded by this flurry of accusations to state that the 'foreign hand cannot be ruled out'.

Urdu-reading Pakistanis reeled under the orchestrated frog chorus of 'India did it' as retired Air Marshal Shahid Latif, retired General Rahat Latif and retired ISI chief Ziauddin Butt were quoted in the daily *Dunya* as asserting that 'foreign agencies (read India and the United States) were funding and training the Taliban terrorists and their affiliates and equipping them with Indian weapons'. Linking these statements to the rage drummed up by anti-government politicians, further reportage implicated Prime Minister Nawaz Sharif in the Karachi attack, saying his soft approach to the newly elected anti-Pakistan Indian prime minister was responsible for the latest 'foreign hand' incident. Fire-breathing politician Sheikh Rashid, aligned informally with Imran Khan's Tehreek-e-Insaf party, predicted that 'very soon' an attack on Parliament in Islamabad was on the cards. He said: 'Had Pakistan done something like this in India, India under Modi would have attacked Pakistan on the border.' The message was: attack India now and teach it a lesson! But the real objective clearly was to immolate the Nawaz Sharif government on the collective ritual dance of the 'foreign hand'.

The TTP and IMU Own Attack

Then on 10 May the Taliban spokesman Shahidullah Shahid owned the airport attack: 'The airport assault was an act of revenge for the 2013 killing of TTP chief Hakimullah Mehsud in a US drone attack. Pakistan used the peace talks as a tool of war. We have yet to take revenge for the deaths of hundreds of innocent tribal women and children in Pakistani air strikes. It's just the beginning, we have taken revenge for one (Mehsud); we have to take revenge for hundreds.'

Oddly, this was followed by a message from Usman Ghazi, the emir of the Islamic Movement of Uzbekistan (IMU) on its website, saying: 'Yesterday 9 June 2014, at midnight, ten brave martyrdom-seeking mujahideen of Islamic Movement of Uzbekistan wearing their explosive-filled vests attacked a very special section of Karachi International Airport of Pakistan which is not visible to the common folk visiting the Airport.' The website carried the photographs of ten Uzbeks chosen from several thousand Uzbeks sheltering in North Waziristan for at least two decades and routinely attacking Indian installations in Afghanistan under the tutelage of the Haqqani Network. All ten terrorists were therefore Pakistani-born. Ghazi added ominously: 'The Karachi airport attack was executed to avenge the latest full-scale bombardments and night attacks with fighter jets by the Pakistan Apostate Army which started on 21 May 2014, in Waziristan.' Who cares if there is a discrepancy in the post-attack statements of TTP's Shahidullah Shahid and IMU's chief? But there was something to ponder for the 'India hand' partisans in the latest attack.

When the smoke settled on the airport disaster on 15 June, the Pakistan army struck back: fighter jets struck nearly eight militant hideouts in North Waziristan tribal region, killing over fifty foreign militants. Its public relations unit said those killed were 'mostly Uzbek' and that 'on the directions of the government, the Armed Forces of Pakistan have launched a comprehensive operation against foreign and local terrorists who are hiding in sanctuaries in North Waziristan'. The operation was significantly named Zarb-e-Azb, which is the name of the sword of the Holy Prophet (Peace Be Upon Him). And the prime minister was quoted by the media as exhorting the army to confront the TTP and its foreign adjuncts till they are all removed from the scene. The opposition comprising the PPP, ANP, MQM, the Shia alliance and the Barelvi-Sunni leaders targeted by the terrorists, welcomed the operation while the others kept their fire under the bushel, choosing to postpone decision over a popular military initiative clearly enlisting the support of the man in the street.

~

Drones Fly Again

After a lapse of six months, which interregnum the Americans clearly said was allowed to let Pakistan's effort at 'peace talks' with the Taliban unfold unhindered, the US drone attacks resumed on 10 June, targeting a village in the Taliban-controlled tribal agency of North Waziristan and killing four Uzbeks of IMU and two members of the Movement of the Taliban in Punjab. On 12 June, reports came in that two more drone strikes had killed commander Haji Gul of the Haqqani Network in North Waziristan and two commanders of the Afghan Taliban, Mufti Sufyan and Abu Bakar while heading towards Afghanistan with a truck laden with explosives.

Pakistan had similarly reacted with an 'India did it' diagnosis to a Taliban attack on the Mehran air base belonging to the Pakistan navy in 2011, accusing India and the United States of having prompted the attack even though the damage sustained included two expensive American surveillance aircraft. The attack happened days after the death of Osama bin Laden in Abbottabad at the hands of helicopter-borne American SEALs. While accusing India, the administration in Karachi couldn't believe that the Taliban could attack Karachi, interpreting the incident in line with the thinking of the Pakistan army deeply offended by the American 'drone' trespass. And the attack took place 'from within the army', as reported by Saleem Shahzad in *Asia Times* online, for which he paid with his life.

Saleem Shahzad wrote: 'The brazen al-Qaeda-linked attack on the Pakistan navy's Mehran airbase in the southern port city of Karachi on a Sunday night in May 2011 marks the violent beginning of an internal ideological struggle between Islamist elements in the Pakistani armed forces and their secular and liberal top brass. More than 10 heavily armed militants attacked the base from three sides, [blowing up two P-3C Orion surveillance aircraft while damaging another]. At least twenty security personnel are known to have been killed.'[1]

He wrote this when the attack was still in progress. On 1 June, the *Guardian* correspondent Declan Walsh reported that Saleem Shahzad had been killed by unknown persons. Walsh himself was expelled from Pakistan in May 2013, allegedly for his reporting on Balochistan.

Ideological Cracks within

Why did Shahzad refer to 'an internal ideological struggle between Islamist elements in the Pakistani armed forces and their secular and liberal top brass' in what might have been one of his last reports? He had found that an al-Qaeda operative formerly associated with Pakistan army in connection with jihad in Indian-administered Kashmir, Ilyas Kashmiri, had attacked the Mehran naval base after challenging the naval chief to release from captivity scores of naval personnel found to have joined al-Qaeda.

The trend goes back to the beginning of the rule of General Pervez Musharraf. The flag of rebellion was first raised by Maulana Akram Awan in his seminary at Manara in Chakwal in the second week of December 2000, which subsided only after federal religion minister Mahmood Ghazi visited him and said his prayers behind him on 22 December, making him postpone his 'revolution'. Maulana Awan had vowed that his thousands of disciples of Tanzim ul Ikhwan training at Manara would lay siege to Islamabad and compel General Musharraf to 'enforce' Islam in Pakistan.His threat was that if General Musharraf failed to carry out this 'enforcement', his followers 'will offer their throats to be cut' in the name of Islam.

Soon however, someone in the Islamabad establishment prompted Maulana Awan to go back on his word and resume his threat. This behaviour pattern pointed to 'inside' elements guiding the radicals: Maulana Awan was made to say that Minister Ghazi had resiled from his pledges. However, on 24 December Maulana Awan, after interior minister Moinuddin Haider announced his government's determination to stop the procession, postponed his 'long march' indefinitely. As if on cue, Maulana Awan's vigil at Manara was visited by Jamaat-e-Islami's Qazi Hussain Ahmad, Sipah-e-Sahaba's Maulana Azam Tariq, coup-maker-to-be Major General Zaheerul Islam Abbasi and the most belligerent Taliban-supporting Sufi Muhammad of Malakand. It was safe to go there because Awan was supposed to get all his 'signals' from within the establishment.[2]

Qazi Hussain Ahmad thought that it was actually a clear call from the army to get rid of a secular Ataturk-loving General Pervez Musharraf because he 'did not sit well' with an army which was predominantly Islamist. Of course, General Musharraf was not the first army chief to be found wanting in Islamic credentials. Before him, Army Chief General Jehangir Karamat was subjected to the same harassment by the subordinates who surrounded him.

Even the ISPR's journal *Hilal* had written against him as the incumbent chief.

Coming back to Ilyas Kashmiri, some sources had designated him a member of the SSG commando regiment of the Pakistan army, a charge denied by Pakistan. What was not denied however was that General Musharraf had presented Kashmiri with monetary reward after the latter brought back from one of his forays into Indian-administered Kashmir the severed head of an Indian officer. After deserting to al-Qaeda, Ilyas Kashmiri was able to use army officers like Captain Haroon Ashiq to also defect and kill fellow-officers. Captain Ashiq killed Major General Feisal Alavi (retd) in 2008 as punishment for having led a commando operation in Waziristan against the Taliban. Caught after the murder, Captain Ashiq was acquitted by a court in 2011.

In 2010, the son of a senior retired air force officer Faisal Shahzad came from the US where he was resident, visited Waziristan and planned with TTP chief Hakimullah Mehsud to blow up New York's Times Square with a car bomb. The bomb didn't go off and Shahzad was captured. His video together with Hakimullah gave Washington the basis on which to kill him with a drone strike. In 2013, another son of a senior army officer, Umar Abdullah, killed the chief prosecutor of the Federal Investigation Agency (FIA) Chaudhry Zulfiqar Ali but was wounded during his al-Qaeda-ordered hit. Ali was close to indicting important madrasa clerics and deep-state elements who had facilitated the killing of ex-prime minister Benazir Bhutto in 2008 (ostensibly by TTP chief Baitullah Mehsud) at the behest of al-Qaeda. It developed that the son of Lieutenant-Colonel Khalid Mahmood Abbasi had joined al-Qaeda because his father was found implicated in the attempt on the life of General Musharraf in 2003 and forcibly retired from the army. As reported in the *News*, 'Col Abbasi, who was posted in Kohat at the time of his arrest, was a religious-minded person who used to deliver daily lessons from the Quran to his junior officers.'

Enter IMU

This question of 'ideological struggle' has cropped up again after the Karachi airport attack. Terrorism analyst Amir Mir wrote in the *News* of 13 June that the Uzbeks who attacked the airport were part of Ansarul Aseer run by an air-force officer who had defected to al-Qaeda, Adnan Rasheed, arrested in connection with an abortive attack on the army chief General Pervez Musharraf in 2003 but sprung from a prison in Bannu in 2012. According to Mir, based on the videos released by IMU, the jailbreak was accomplished by a force mostly constituted of Uzbeks. Mir observes:

'The TTP and IMU have long been working in tandem and conducting joint terrorist attacks, especially targeting Pakistani security forces. However, the 15 April 2012 Bannu Jail operation was perhaps the only event filmed and marketed by IMU. The 25-minute Uzbek-language video, released on 14 June, 2012, showed over 200 militants armed with guns, grenades and rockets, attacking the Bannu Central Jail of Khyber Pakhtunkhwa and releasing 384 prisoners, including Adnan Rasheed, an ex-PAF officer who is the suspected mastermind of the Karachi airport attack in 2014. If the contents of the video are to be believed, the jailbreak was planned after Adnan Rasheed wrote to the emir of the Uzbek jihadis, Usman Ghazi, seeking his help to escape from Bannu prison. The jailbreak plot was subsequently orchestrated with the support of the Tehreek-e-Taliban.'

Adnan Rasheed's own diary on the Internet tells the story of his conversion to terrorism in the name of religion under the persuasion of a senior air force officer who sent him to a training camp run by 'non-state actor' Jaish-e-Mohammad in Mansehra near Abbottabad. In 2013, a hired killer working for the TTP for Rs 1400 per month in Karachi confessed on TV that he had been likewise trained at Mansehra in 2012.

There have been steady reports about Islamists inside Pakistan who believed in the cause of al-Qaeda more than their oath of loyalty to Pakistan. In his book, *Duty: Memoirs of a Secretary at War*, Robert M. Gates wrote: 'In every instance when we had provided a heads-up to the Pakistani military or intelligence services, the target was forewarned and fled, or the Pakistanis went after the target unilaterally, prematurely, and unsuccessfully.'

After his retirement General Shahid Aziz, a corps commander who had earlier served in the ISI, wrote his passionate memoir titled *Yeh Khamoshi Kahan Tak* (How Long This Silence?), with a telltale subtitle *Ek Sipahi ki Dastan-e-Ishq-o-Junoon* (The Story of Passion and Madness of a Soldier). His worldview comes to the fore in the following sentence: 'The bombs that kill innocent Pakistanis in bazaars and mosques are planted by friends of America, and this terrorism is done to persuade Pakistan to embrace America more closely, allow the government to pursue pro-America policies and to alienate Pakistan from the mujahideen [sic]. But this trend of support to the killers of Muslims is open rebellion against Allah'.

The Karachi airport attack was carried out very much on the pattern of the earlier Mehran base attack by Ilyas Kashmiri. The late Saleem Shahzad had found similarities in earlier attacks too with an 'internal stamp': Mumbai on 26 November 2008, ten militants went on a three-day rampage; Police Academy in Lahore in 2009, at least twenty-three people dead and hundreds injured; the Sri Lankan cricket team in Lahore in 2009, six policemen killed and several injured; General Headquarters Rawalpindi in 2009, several hostages taken and then released; Parade Lane Mosque in Rawalpindi in 2009, at least forty killed. He wrote:

'Pakistani security forces confirmed that at least three of these attacks were carried out by 313 Brigade led by Ilyas Kashmiri while the others were blamed on Pakistani militants trained by Kashmiri. After the 11 September 2001, attacks on the US, Pakistan's top brass took a policy turn and joined America's "war on terror", but a large chunk of officers took retirement and, with serving colleagues, helped the Taliban. This changed the dynamics of the Afghan war theatre. This collection of former and serving officers was responsible for a number of attacks on the military, including the military headquarters in 2009 and against ex-president General Pervez Musharraf.'

Karachi as Mega-ghetto

Today Karachi is a battlefield where al-Qaeda and its affiliated terrorists must wage a successful war if they have to survive as a global movement. This is the city that yields a billion dollars annually through extractions made by the various Taliban through force of arms. This sum doesn't include the extortions made by the criminal elements who have adopted the methods of intimidation of the Taliban. Karachi has thus been Talibanized, not only in the way the people think but also the way criminals operate.

In 1947, Karachi was a model city, self-consciously built by its Gujarati-speaking elite comprising Memons, Bohras, Agha Khanis, Parsis and Hindus. It had an evolved sense of commercial ethic, called 'trust' by Fukuyama, which the rest of Pakistan, populated by 'warrior' races, never learned. It had a population of 45,000 and a local government idealized by the rest of India for its civic virtue. After sixty-six years, after pell-mell external and internal migration, it is a sprawling megapolis bursting at the seams with a population inhabiting mostly illegal shantytowns with 'no-go' areas.

If the 2011 pre-census house count of Karachi is to be believed, then Karachi's population increased from 9.8 million to 21.2 million between 1998 and 2011, growing at the rate of 4.8 per cent—the national growth rate being 2.9 per cent—out of which nearly half is produced by migration. The city contributes 25 per cent of the country's GDP while its bank accounts are 50 per cent of the country's total bank accounts; it issues 72 per cent of the total capital in the country.

In 1947, 600,000 refugees hit Karachi and made it a problem city. Some idea of the Karachi crisis can be formed from the fact that, between 1951 and 1972, it grew by 217 per cent! This happened after the government established an industrial estate attracting migration from the hinterland. Karachi was subjected to regional diasporas: from 1972 to 1978, it received 35,000 refugees from Bangladesh; from 1977 to 1986, about 300,000 people came in from Iran and Afghanistan. Illegal immigrants from Sri Lanka, Bangladesh and the Philippines, working as domestic help are estimated to be 200,000. A city whose infrastructure was meant to serve only 400,000 people is being made to serve over 20 million.

According to the last census in 1998, 50 per cent of the city's population is Urdu-speaking, 14 per cent Punjabi-speaking, 12 per cent Pashto-speaking and about 9 per cent Sindhi-speaking. (Pashtun leader Shahi Syed claims 4 million Pashtuns in the city.) Today, rough estimates put the population of Pashtuns higher than the Punjabis, making Karachi the largest Pashtun city in the world. The other community crucial to Karachi's peace is the Shia, not counted as such by the census. Karachi is estimated to be the largest Shia city in the country, which means it is capable of hitting back when attacked by sectarian elements encouraged by the largest concentration of madrasas in the city and the Taliban who empower them through violence. Reports from Karachi suggest that out of the average of ten people killed in Karachi daily at least two are always Shia; also, Karachi is the only city where retaliatory Shia attacks on carefully targeted Deobandi clerics are in evidence.

Says architect Arif Hasan, a founding member of the Asian Coalition of Housing Rights, 'Almost 75 per cent of the city's population lives in settlements or neighbourhoods segregated on the basis of ethnicity. This is not just true of low-income settlements but also of lower-middle-income and some middle-income settlements as well. As such, the city is physically divided along ethnic lines and, in an increasing number of cases, along religious lines as well. Crossing from one ethnically defined neighbourhood to the other is, in many cases, no longer possible.'

Ideology Heads for Karachi

Some leaders like Imran Khan claim that there was no terrorism in Pakistan before 9/11 and that it began only after Musharraf decided to fight 'the American war'. The argument is therefore developed that if Pakistan gets out of this American war, terrorism will subside too. The truth however is that terrorism began after certain ideological choices made by General Zia vis-a-vis Afghanistan and the Gulf. In 1987, terror spread in Kurram and Gilgit where the Shia were ruthlessly targeted. Zia had a bad personal equation with Imam Khomeini who knew Zia's real relationship with the Gulf Sunni states.

Targeted assassinations thought to be carried out by jihadi groups actually predate 9/11 and the US-led war against the Taliban and al-Qaeda in Afghanistan. Militant Sunni organizations Sipah-e-Sahaba Pakistan (SSP) and Lashkar-e-Jhangvi, inspired by such seminaries of Karachi as Jamia Banuria, are known to have had close ideological and operational links with jihadi groups such as Jaish-e-Mohammad in Punjab known for doing jihad in India-administered Kashmir.

Pakistani journalist Zia Ur Rehman, writing in CIA's Counter Terrorism Center journal in July 2012, says: 'Karachi is considered an attractive hideout for al-Qaeda and Taliban groups because the sheer size of the city, combined with its assortment of ethnic and linguistic groups, makes it easy to live and operate unseen. Al-Qaeda and Taliban groups can also rely on logistical and other support from Karachi's assortment of militant, religious and sectarian groups. The capture of several high-profile al-Qaeda and Taliban leaders from Karachi shows that both organizations are operating in the city. Security experts argue that al-Qaeda has successfully merged with Karachi-based local militant groups in Pakistan, and is in the process of shifting its base from the tribal areas to urban areas, especially Karachi, to avoid drone strikes.'

The Mangho Pir Sanctuary

The violence in Karachi spiked since the end of 2012, and Taliban and al-Qaeda groups established a firm foothold by 2014. There are twenty-five Taliban and al-Qaeda-linked groups operating in the city, some, like the Badr Mansoor group, directly affiliated according to one document seized at Osama bin Laden's compound in Abbottabad. The Qari Zafar group is another such al-Qaeda company.

The groups doing terrorism of one sort or another in Karachi are: Lashkar-e-Jhangvi (LeJ)—Lashkar-e-Jhangvi Al Alami, Qari Zafar group, Qari Shakeel group, Akram Lahori group and Farooq Bengali group. Then there are three factions of the Tehreek-e-Taliban Pakistan (TTP): Commander Waliur Rehman group (from South Waziristan), Badr Mansoor group (from North Waziristan) and Mullah Fazlullah group (from Swat). The remaining jihadi-cum-sectarian groups in Karachi include Sipah-e-Sahaba Pakistan (SSP), Sipah-e-Muhammad Pakistan (SMP), Sunni Tehreek (ST), Dawat-e-Islami (DeI), Harkat-ul-Mujahideen (HuM), Harkat-ul-Mujahideen al-Alami (HUMA), Jaish-e-Mohammad (JeM), Jamaatul Furqan (JuF), Harkatul Jihad-e-Islami (HuJI), Tehrik-e-Nifaz-e-Shariat-e-Mohammadi (TNSM), Jandullah, Tehreek-e-Islami Lashkar-e-Muhammadi (TILM), Lashkar-e-Islami (LeI), Mehdi Militia (MM), Hezbollah, Kharooj, Tawheed Brigade (TB), Al Mukhtar group, Punjabi Mujahideen etc.

Eleven areas of Karachi are 'no-go', currently controlled by these groups. Some of the localities in Karachi under Taliban control include Sohrab Goth, Baldia Town, Quaid Abad, Shireen Jinnah Colony, New Karachi Industrial Area, Sultanabad, Mangho Pir, Sarjani Town, Qasba Colony, Shah Faisal Colony, Shah Latif Town and Peer Abad. The most well-known centre of Taliban activity is the Mangho Pir colony, which was once sparsely but diversely populated but is now the exclusive stronghold of such

Taliban groups as have direct links to the TTP and al-Qaeda. The police and Rangers can't go there because they still lack the preparedness to challenge these groups. Mangho Pir is where the Mehsuds of Waziristan have landed after being ousted by military operations in the tribal areas. The attackers of the Karachi airport did not actually have to trudge from North Waziristan laden with ammunition. Mangho Pir can provide men and material from its own resource-base.

Setting Things Right

After the Karachi Airport attack, the ideological tide seemed to turn despite the noises about India and its rascalities in Balochistan. Even the popular Tehreek-e-Insaf no longer spoke with one voice about our 'brethren' Taliban and seemed ready to support the land and air operations against them ordered by the new army General Raheel Sharif. This development came late, giving almost one year in which to persuade the Pakistani mind in favour of holding 'peace talks' talks with the Taliban. The peace talks, held by Islamabad from a position of weakness—which galled the army—needlessly empowered the religious parties and provided terrorism with the rhetoric of righteousness. The 'peace talks' interregnum may have done more damage than Pakistan can compute: not only did the religious parties become unapologetic about terrorism but the country's 20,000 seminaries were emboldened in their covert recruitment of fresh warriors of Talibanization.

It was certainly not enough to simply launch attacks on the TTP and destroy its sanctuaries. The 'national security state' which spawned the terrorists must also be revisited and rationalized. Lahore-based the *Friday Times* editorialized on 13 June, giving three things that Pakistan must roll back to halt the state's slow-burning implosion:

'One, [Pakistan] has accorded primacy to the military over the civilian order. This has had adverse consequences for the rule of law, political stability and democracy. Two, it has justified the military's doctrine of 'asymmetric warfare' based on first-strike nuclear weapons and armed non-state actors for external meddling in the region to redress conventional military imbalances. This in turn has led to the growth of cancerous sectarian, jihadi and Taliban groups. Three, it has sanctioned a disastrous love-hate relationship with the United States which has stunted economic and political development.'

6

Solitude of the Sheikh

Before the historic dharna of Imran Khan and Dr TahiurlQadri in 2014, there was a kind of rehearsal for it in 2013, by Dr Qadri. Dr Tahir ul-Qadri's 'long march' in 2013 was impressive but its aftermath was a bit of an anticlimax as no one actually believed that the 'declaration' between him and the ruling PPP coalition was constitutionally enforceable. Some went to the extent of saying the signatures affixed on the declaration by the PPP leaders were faked. The Islamabad sit-in of 14 January was unprecedented and demonstrated Qadri's organizational genius. But why did he fail to achieve his goal of cleansing the country's political system?

In December 2012, Tahir ul-Qadri launched himself as a deliverer against a state almost dismantled by terrorism. Hence Qadri's slogan: 'save the state before politics'. He was in politics in the 1990s and then again in the Musharraf era with his Pakistan Awami Tehreek (PAT) but cut no electoral ice and decided to leave Pakistan. When he was in Europe, his Barelvi-Sunni sect gravitated to him because of their feeling that they had become the 'forgotten children of Islam' in the face of Saudi-backed, dollar-leveraged takeover of their mosques. In 2005 he shifted to Canada and acquired Canadian nationality.

He was threatening in posture while announcing his challenge of a 'long march' to Islamabad and claimed a great following among the masses, which he proved by gathering a 'mammoth' crowd in Lahore on 24 December, estimating it to be 'one million', but which was big enough nevertheless to convince everyone that he could take his 'long march' to Islamabad of 'four million followers'. The demands or ultimatums which he flung at the government were: 1) immediately dissolve the incumbent government plus provincial governments; 2) scrap the Election Commission of Pakistan because it was powerless and faulty in composition; 3) announce a caretaker government with the assent of the army and the Supreme Court; and 4) enforce Articles 62 and 63 setting standards of Muslim piety to clean up the political landscape before holding elections.

Tahir ul-Qadri made public his dislike of PPP and PMLN, which sentiment was close to what the army is supposed to feel too. Imran Khan's party Pakistan Tehreek-e-Insaf too embraced this view against the more or less settled bipartisan system familiar under democracy in Pakistan and elsewhere. Like Imran Khan, he sought to delegitimize the system on the basis of a dubious idea and was therefore immediately linked by many to the army. The mainstream parties PPP and PMLN—stabbed in the back by the army by turns with overthrows—thought Qadri was being prompted by the army, which in turn, made two more putatively army-supported parties PTI and MQM rally behind him. The religious parties needless to say linked him to the United States. As *The Economist* described the 'long march': 'Just before setting off for their "long march" to Islamabad, on 13 January, supporters of Tahir ul-Qadri, a populist cleric who has burst onto Pakistan's political scene, cut the throat of a bull that lay trussed in the back of a lorry. A quartet of bleating goats was similarly dispatched.'

Solitude of the Sheikh

Qadri described himself as Sheikh ul Islam, a status probably stemming from a dream he once saw in which the Prophet of Islam (Peace be upon Him) 'chose' him as his deputy after rejecting all the other schools of thought in Pakistan's religious hierarchy. Since he was a Barelvi and therefore in the crosshairs of the Taliban and al-Qaeda, and since Sunni Tehreek had gone radical and was no longer a Barelvi adjunct of MQM, Qadri's movement Tehreek-e-Minhajul Quran could be the substitute partner of the army and a gateway to Punjab, his treasury.

In Lahore, the Barelvi clerics, wedded to the anti-blasphemy law that routinely victimized non-Muslims, cursed him for having told the West that Christians did not attract the mischief of the law 'meant only to punish the Muslims'. They thronged the Governor's House on the Mall and challenged him to debate— Qadri of course did not turn up. But he had impressive external credentials: Qadri founded Minhajul Quran in October 1981 and extended its network to over ninety countries and has been given a consultative status in the United Nations Economic and Social Council. His 'monumental 600-page fatwa against Suicide Bombings' made the West take notice of him. He became Adviser on Counter-Radicalism to the Government of the UK Pakistanis may have been unaware of his scholarship which the West couldn't ignore: according to his devotees, he has authored close to 1000 books, on Sufism, Islamic law, social systems, science, evolution, human rights, philosophy, translation and *tafseer* (exegesis) of Quran (fourteen volumes), Hadith and science of Hadith (twenty-four volumes), the life of the Holy Prophet Peace be Upon Him (fourteen volumes), and History of Islamic Constitutional Theory.

Qadri's 'long march' was expensive. The transport charges reportedly soaked up half a billion rupees from Qadri's purse, which he denies. His statement in Islamabad was that the 'four million'—the most optimistic estimate pegged it at 50,000— paid their own way to Islamabad and also paid for the food they consumed for four days before the sit-in was called off after a Qadri-coalition 'declaration' accepted all his demands. Qadri kept changing his position.

At one moment he wanted the government to 'go home'; at another he wanted President Zardari to quit. The Supreme Court, ordering, in an unrelated case, the arrest of the sitting prime minister in the middle of Qadri's aggressive speech, seemed to give a nod. Imran Khan chimed in with Qadri, announcing his own conditionality of dismissal of Zardari before the elections, once again signalled vaguely in a Lahore High Court notice of contempt to the President.

It is the solitude of the vatic leader that is dangerous for the state. Possessed of godlike powers, they are deceived by their own 'unconsulting' wisdom into involving them in situations of deadlock that Qadri finally faced in Islamabad as his followers shivered in the cold, experiencing Pakistan's most severe winter in a quarter century. The charismatic leader brings about his downfall through his 'divine isolation' which attracts friend and foe alike in the beginning but finally dooms him to failure.

Nawaz Sharif's Finesse

PMLN chief Nawaz Sharif was furious. He announced that Qadri had paid each woman Rs 2000 to come to the Islamabad sit-in. According to a column in the Urdu daily *Jang,* there was a time when Sharif thought Qadri was Imam Mehdi, but after a falling out, mostly attributed to Qadri's hubris, the Sharif family despised the spiritually self-centred cleric, owing his rise to their Model Town residential mosque. The PPP for its part unleashed two federal stalwarts on Qadri, ministers of the interior and of information, lampooning their easy-to-mimic victim.

If Qadri was a firebrand orator, his detractors were almost abusive in their less talented outbursts. A careless reference to Qadri as 'Pope' because of his bizarre headgear angered the Christians. When everyone feared that hot words would unleash violence—

which could be followed by an army clampdown—Zardari stepped in with his familiar political poultice of reconciliation. The Islamabad Declaration people said meant nothing because it was not constitutionally protected and the government didn't have the kind of majority in Parliament to act on what Qadri wanted.

In Lahore, Nawaz Sharif gathered all the extra-parliamentary opposition leaders in a tour de force of strategy against Imran Khan who was relying on these very leaders earlier to somehow overthrow the bipartisan system which Nawaz Sharif had benefited from. Scared of Qadri because of his acceptable-to-the-West, 'soft Islam', and financial power, they rallied behind the slogan of 'elections on time'. Khan suffered because of the grand entry but dubious promise of Qadri which he thought was the winning card. An erring Islamic-ideological state, under terminal threat from a more stringent brand of Islam of al-Qaeda, is supposed to be challenged by another Islamic prescription offered by a man whose credentials were under challenge from the radical orthodoxy that embraced jihad and indirectly supported the Taliban and al-Qaeda.

The majority population in Pakistan is supposed to be Barelvi, but the state has chosen since 1949 to give its imprimatur to the Deobandi-Wahhabi madrasas who supply cannon-fodder to its asymmetrical jihad. This has shifted power to the non-Barelvi parties and left the non-aggressive Barelvis on the margins of Pakistan's political order. The marginalized Barelvi leader, aware that he had a larger following than the state-patronized jihadi schools of thought, introverted himself and concentrated on organization and accumulation of resources on the basis of rituals connected with the celebration of saints. He had the spiritual power of cure and prediction; he related to the masses more intimately because of his epiphanic encounters with the holy Prophet (Peace Be Upon Him) through a chain of Islamic mystics.

But the power came from organization and his ability to extract wealth from his mass following. There are two kinds of 'big leaders' in the religious community: those who accumulate wealth on the basis of intimidation through jihad and foreign funding, and those who do it with organizational skill and contact with the masses. The jihad-related leaders are all more or less well-heeled. Money—and mobilization among trained youths—are the tools they employ to pressure the patron state.

One among them, Hafiz Saeed, is more 'resourceful', able to spend billions during a natural calamity as a means of projection of power. Because of jihad, he has a $10 million US bounty riding on his head. His wealth stems from the hides of sacrificial animals, and partly from expat Pakistanis living on social security in the EU and in the US. He not only threatens Pakistan with the dare of jihad; he can fling cross-border threats too.

On the non-jihadi Barelvi side, there are two leaders with legendary wealth: IlyasQadri of Dawat-e-Islami and Tahir-ul-Qadri of Tehree-e-Minhajul Quran. The mode of show of strength for Ilyas Qadri is his congregation of 'millions' of 'green turban' devotees in Multan in parallel to the annual Deobandi Tableeghi Jamaat gathering in Lahore. Needless to say, the state inclines to the latter as presidents and sons of chief ministers attend the international event. Maulana Ilyas Qadri also has his own TV channel where he addresses his extremely dedicated followers. Looking at the properties he owns in the big cities of Pakistan one marvels at the accumulative patience of the man. He is more careful than Tahir ul-Qadri when it comes to political expression, but his Mall Road mosque in Lahore clearly manifested signs of support when the other Qadri announced his Long March.

Tahir ul-Qadri's wealth emanates from Islamic charity which pours in not only from his indigenous outreach but also, according to him, from ninety countries where Minhaj-ul-Quran has its branches. He boasts 600 schools and colleges inside Pakistan and an international university. He can spend half a billion rupees on hiring buses when he wants to mobilize his disciples. When he spreads his money around it has the same effect as when Ilyas Qadri has the congregation of his Dawat-e-Islami in Multan, uplifting the city's economy through the 'demand-push' presence of his 'million' strong followers.

Charity versus the State

Pakistanis contributed Rs 140 billion (US $1.7 billion) in 2009 to charity. Most of the giving is religion-related. Even if you choose to build a liberal charity, like looking after the poor, you have to appear to your donors as a religious-looking person. The secular charity of Abdus Sattar Edhi benefits from the clerical look of the founder. He is addressed with the religious prefix of Maulana.

The remarkable phenomenon of Imran Khan—the cricketer who built Pakistan's first state-of-the-art cancer hospital—can be explained as a part of his religious transformation. His autobiography, explaining his born-again experiences, stands in for the beard he still doesn't boast but Edhi does. Edhi doesn't challenge the political order; but Khan does. It may be an accident but men who grow big on charity finally decide to reform the state too. The latest candidate in 2013 was Amir Liaquat Hussain who gathered big funds from the pious for his TV shows of pop evangelism; but his increasing reference to political and foreign policy issues pointed to his possible development as a challenger.

A challenger was already in the field on 14 January putting Islamabad under siege saying he wanted to save the state from venal politicians. Tahir ul-Qadri built his educational empire with charity. His wealth was fabulous, which he didn't hide through pious modesty of any sort. He may have spent over a billion rupees on his January 2013 campaign. Imran Khan was half-tempted to join Tahir ul-Qadri but was saved at the last moment by the 'politicians' he had recently taken in as 'electables'. Few know that Ilyas Qadri of the Green Turbans too was tempted but kept his peace and did not use the TV channel he personally owns to challenge the state. His followers too would do anything he wants them to do, including sit-ins in the heart of Islamabad. He may be chastened by what transpired with his predecessors,

Riaz Gohar Shahi of Anjuman Sarfaroshan Islam and Yusuf Ali alias Kazzab, both billionaires of Pakistan's charity underworld, who died by reason of 'power miscalculation'.

Some years ago, another big charity man was Maulana Akram Awan of Chakwal who grew rich on the money and property earned by *zikr* (chant) madrasas and by penetrating the rank and file of the army. A Naqshbandi strongman with a lot of dedicated following, he was the first charity saint to think of invading Islamabad when it was being ruled by General Musharraf. That was a mistake: you don't go against the army; you come out when it wants you to come out. Another 'mistaken' up-coming charity king was Maulana Murtaza Malik who became big because of the patronage of General Aziz Khan, once chairman of the Joint Chiefs of Staff Committee, who allowed Malik to become rich by publishing books for army libraries and by running two charity institutions maintained on zakat. Imran Khan, then thinking of branching out into education, was attracted to him the same way he was attracted to Tahir ul-Qadri, but some thought it could be an army nudging from the above-mentioned general. Malik was murdered in Lahore after he fell out with a local property-grabbing strongman.

There are other different kinds of charity operators in Pakistan, using a bit of extortion from the timid and dishing out 'empowerment' to those who pay up. By one count there are 116 charity groups wedded to a discourse of religion but doing mild or intense forms of terrorism on the side. Their modus operandi is: instil fear into the locality in focus and receive what is called bhatta (protection money). Those who offer this 'charity' benefit from a feeling of empowerment over fellow-citizens when the state is too weak to protect them. The state of Pakistan has lost its 'monopoly of violence' that normally underpins the internal sovereignty of a state. Its past forays into asymmetric and covert jihad outside its borders have produced a large number of armed non-state actors who now share its writ.

The charity pantheon of the country features men grown charismatic because of the funds they can deploy. They however need protection against the menacing presence of jihadi strongmen. They therefore use charisma to challenge the state and demonstrate peaceful muscle needed to defy their more powerful competitors. The unprotected will gravitate to them, as did the Hazara being ethnic-cleansed in Quetta, announcing support for Tahir ul-Qadri's Long March. He attracted more minority groups like Christians victimized by the Blasphemy Law, and Hindus haunted by forcible conversion and marriage because the state was in a phase of 'shrinkage' in the face of the Taliban and the al-Qaeda. The political parties, as remnants of the state that once operated the democratic order on the basis of 'internal sovereignty', will be forced to seek terms with these charismatic charity men to make up for the loss of their halo of non-violent legitimacy.

7

Penetrated by Al-Qaeda

On 8 September 2014, a Pakistan navy spokesman revealed that its dockyard was attacked by 'some miscreants' two days earlier, on Pakistan Defence Day, and that 'the group tried to penetrate the Pakistan navy Dockyard area at Karachi. Pakistan navy security personnel responded valiantly and in the ensuing encounter killed two intruders while apprehending four miscreants alive.'

He didn't say the attack was on PNS Zulfiqar, a missile-equipped warship built jointly by China and Pakistan in the shipyard factory four years ago. He didn't say that the latest attack had come from the sea. He didn't say either that the attackers were Pakistan navy defectors working for al-Qaeda although the 2011 attack on the navy's Mehran airbase was owned by the same terrorist organization. It had taken place ten days after the assassination of Osama bin Laden in Abbottabad and was triggered by the navy's alleged refusal to release scores of its employees arrested on charges of defection to al-Qaeda. Pakistani journalist

Saleem Shahzad who reported on the Mehran Base attack was mysteriously killed by someone after he revealed the extent of al-Qaeda's penetration of the navy.

What made the event more significant than hundreds of past such terrorist assaults was that the navy's response was robust: it killed two and captured four of the attackers 'alive'. The captured terrorists—clearly signalling a weakening of the ideological hold of al-Qaeda in the wake of Pakistan army's operation Zarb-e-Azb against it—had failed to kill themselves as per their SOPs and were made to 'sing' enough to enable the intelligence agencies to nab more al-Qaeda abettors from Punjab, the Tribal Areas, Balochistan, Khyber Pakhtunkhwa and Sindh, almost all of them—'no fewer than seventeen'—employees or ex-employees of the Pakistan navy.

For the first time Sindh was named as the new grazing ground of al-Qaeda: one Sindhi naval defector, Owais Jakhrani, said to be son of a senior police officer, was found drowned at sea as a member of al-Qaeda assault team—which immediately led, together with later discovery that the attackers had actually landed on PNS Zulfiqar—to the speculation that the attack had come from the sea. The infiltration of the navy looked massive given the total strength of the Pakistan navy: 35,700.

According to official statements released from time to time, 'in 2008, the Pakistan navy had approximately 25,000 active duty personnel, with additional 1200 Marines and more than 2500 Coast Guard, and 2000 active-duty navy personnel in the Maritime Security Agency. In addition, there were 5000 reserves, total combined forces exceeding 35,700 personnel'.

The Pakistan navy also tried to lessen the weightage of Punjab among its employees. According to official figures, 'In 2007, the navy gave commission to the first Baloch naval squadron, consisting of around fifty-three women officers and seventy-two Baloch sailors. In 2012, the navy pushed up its personnel strength from Balochistan after sending a large formation of Baloch university students to Navy Engineering Colleges and War College as well as staff schools to complete their officer training requirements. The navy established three additional facilities in Balochistan to supervise the training to its personnel.'

Enter AQIS

Al-Qaeda and the Taliban owned the dockyard attack through their spokesmen but one announcement had to wait till 11 September to coincide with the anniversary of al-Qaeda's 9/11 attack inside the United States. This came from 'Osama Mehmood', the spokesman of al-Qaeda in the Indian Subcontinent (AQIS) set up by the top boss, Ayman-al-Zawahiri. He added little to the details already revealed:

'The operation near Karachi shore was an attack by al-Qaeda in the Subcontinent. The attackers were former Pakistan navy officers-turned-jihadis . . . hijacking a missile ship to stage an attack on an American aircraft-carrier . . . They had taken over control of the ship and were proceeding to attack the American vessel when they were intercepted by the Pakistani armed forces.'

Mehmood's pledge that al-Qaeda would 'soon be releasing a video of the attack', opened another can of worms about the Pakistan navy and the extent to which it has been infiltrated.

In the first week of September, Ayman-al-Zawahiri, who is probably stationed somewhere in Pakistan, spoke to the world in an hour-long video vowing 'to return India to Islamic rule'. Does al-Qaeda have a base in India? An Indian terrorist, Zabihuddin Ansari alias Abu Jandal, arrested in Saudi Arabia and surrendered to India in 2012, actually revealed connections between the Mumbai attack of 2008, carried out from the Pakistani soil where he was present, and India's local Muslim radicals, for the first time.

American journal *Foreign Affairs*, wrote on 12 September 2014: 'Militants do have a presence in India—and a history of responding to Hindu nationalist provocations. A radical offshoot of the Jamaat-e-Islami-Hind known as the Students Islamic Movement of India (SIMI) broke away from its pacifist parent organization in response to the intensifying Hindu nationalist movement of the 1980s and was radicalized by the destruction of the Babri Mosque and other instances of violence against Muslims in 1992. Protesting the rise of Hindu nationalism—and the moderate response of India's Islamic institutions—SIMI openly called for jihad against the Indian government and the creation of a caliphate. Today, the group is believed to have about 400 full-time operatives and 20,000 members.'

Had al-Qaeda been successful in hijacking PNS Zulfiqar it would have been a 'suicide ship' as its fighting days would have been curtailed in short order by two strong naval presences in the Indian Ocean and Arabian Sea: India and the United States. Targeting an American ship would have proved difficult. An exchange of fire with missiles would have made short work of the adventure clearly meant to publicize al-Qaeda now that the region has other more savage competitors like ISIS. But could India too have been endangered?

According to the late Saleem Shahzad, al-Qaeda carried out the 2008 Mumbai attack with the help of Pakistani radicals, some of whom—like Ajmal Kasab and David Headley (formerly Daud Gilani)—made lengthy confessions after being arrested. It is almost certain that it would have worsened the already uncertain relations between India and Pakistan. Even as things stand after the failure to launch a warship from the Karachi naval dockyard, the outlook remains dicey.

A retired Indian diplomat, G. Parthasarathy, a former High Commissioner of India to Pakistan (1998–2000) known for his hard-line views, put a negative gloss on al-Zawahiri's video message, making it look as if inspired by Pakistan. He wrote in the *New Indian Express* soon after the Karachi attack:

'It is striking that the Zawahiri diatribe is couched in language used by the Pakistani military establishment over the past six decades. He describes the creation of Bangladesh as a "conspiracy" by "agents" of India. He reflects Pakistani animosity towards the secular Bangladesh government of Sheikh Hasina, as enjoying "the blessings of both India and America" and calls on scholars in Bangladesh to "fulfil the role Islam has given them to fight against secularists and atheists". India is predictably called an "enemy of Islam ".' He notes: 'The events in Bangladesh and Burma are not too distant from the oppression and killings of Muslims in Kashmir, or the racial cleansing in Assam, Gujarat and Ahmadabad earlier.' Coming after Operation Zarb-e-Azb in North Waziristan, which resulted in the wholesale exodus of foreign elements, particularly the Haqqani Network, from Pakistani territory, the above statement would appear patently emotive and divorced from the new reality. Unfortunately, most countries in the neighbourhood of Pakistan nurse such a negative view of Pakistan. In Afghanistan there is a consensus even among the Pakhtun that Pakistan is actually involved in the terrorist activity in the region. This view was prevalent in Washington too. In 2011, Admiral Michael Mullen, chairman of the Joint Chiefs of Staff, testified before the US Congress that the Haqqani Network—a branch of the Afghan Taliban based in Pakistan's tribal areas—operated as a 'veritable arm' of the Pakistani state.

What was more worrisome for the Pakistani military strategists was the internal contradiction of the charge: how is it that the Taliban—if it is the 'veritable arm' of Pakistan— is frequently seen as attacking and killing Pakistani troops and kidnapping prominent Pakistanis and keeping them in the same areas, described by the critics as a 'safe haven', provided by Pakistan? It was worrisome because it pointed to possible internal contradictions of the Pakistani state and conversion of state employees to the worldview of those whom it calls terrorists. It is not often that Pakistan officially recognizes this fact the way it did in the case of the naval dockyard incident.

Acts of Infiltration

There are countless cases where an interpenetration of the state with its enemies has come on record. The most symbolic personality was Khalid Sheikh Muhammad, half-Pakistani and half-Arab, who plotted the 9/11 attack on the US and got al-Qaeda to adopt it. In pre-9/11 days, al-Qaeda's external terrorism was staged from Pakistan, its perpetrators travelling to Pakistan freely before and after the acts of violence in Africa and the Middle East. It is claimed that even the Hamburg cell of terrorists who inflicted 9/11 on America travelled to Pakistan to reach Osama bin Laden in Afghanistan to receive his blessings before going to the US.

Saleem Shahzad gives us an estimate of al-Qaeda's mind-control in Pakistan: 'Since 1979, at least 100,000 Pakistanis were active members of different Jihadi cadres. Over 1 million students were enrolled in various Islamic seminaries, and there were several hundred thousand supporters of Pakistan's Islamic religious parties. The main handler of the Afghan Jihad against the Soviets had been Pakistan's army, which itself was not immune to the influence of radicalism.

'Several army officers had pledged their allegiance (*bayat*) to different Jihadi spiritual leaders, including Maulana Akram Awan of Chakwal. These groups were known in the Pakistan army as *pirbhai* groups. Although General Pervez Musharraf had purged some of these elements from the Pakistan army after 9/11, including his very close friend, the then deputy chief of army staff, Lt General Muzaffar Usmani, he was unable to completely eradicate the radical tendency, which had become deep-rooted in Pakistan's security services during the period from 1979 to 2001.'[1]

After he ordered the jihad in Kashmir closed in 2003, General Musharraf was attacked, not only by the jihadi organizations but also officers and employees from within the military. His successor General Ashfaq Pervaiz Kayani too got a taste of the same tough medicine after he was seen by al-Qaeda-affiliated groups as becoming soft on the Americans, a factor that may have nurtured in him a hesitation to grasp the nettle of North Waziristan's 'safe haven'.

In 2003, Musharraf nearly got killed after attacks from al-Qaeda through Abu Faraj al-Libi, Jaish-e-Mohammad and some Pakistan Air Force personnel. He wanted a counterattack in South Waziristan but was thwarted by his corps commander in Peshawar, General Ali Muhammad Jan Aurakzai, who preferred retirement to an operation. The succeeding corps commander Peshawar General Safdar Hussain, was from the ISI, its second most important member, DG Analysis. He made peace with the Taliban commander, Nek Muhammad, at Shakai in 2004, binding him to not attacking in Afghanistan and getting rid of the 'foreigners' in return for amnesty. Nek Muhammad did not abide by the peace accord.

Journalist Zahid Hussain in his book, *The Scorpion's Tail*, recounts that General Safdar Hussain told him he wanted the Americans trapped in Afghanistan. He was seen on TV dubbing Nek Muhammad a soldier of Islam.[2] After Nek Muhammad was killed by a drone in June 2004, General Hussain signed another peace accord with Taliban leader Baitullah Mehsud at Sararogha and gave him half a million dollars to pay back the payoff he and his commanders received from al-Qaeda before shifting loyalty for money. He too did not abide by the terms of the accord.

Journalist Carey Schofield, who was for a time attached to the combat formations of the Pakistan army as a military historian, in her book, *Inside the Pakistan Army: A Woman's Experience on the Frontline of the War on Terror*, narrates the story of Major General Feisal Alavi of the SSG commando brigade who was gunned down by renegade Major Haroon Ashiq on the orders of another arguably ex-commando Ilyas Kashmiri who had joined al-Qaeda and wanted Alvi punished for making things tough for al-Qaeda in the Tribal Areas. Haroon was arrested but finally acquitted by a court in Rawalpindi but may still be in custody. His brother was an al-Qaeda hero, too—Captain Khurram Ashiq, dead in Helmand in Afghanistan fighting the British army section of ISAF forces. Khurram was an assault commander of the elite anti-terrorist Zarrar Coy from Pakistan's Special Service Group (SSG) in 2001 when he 'flipped'.[3]

Retreat of Civilian Leaders

After schoolgirl Malala Yousafzai was brutally assaulted by terrorists in 2012 in Swat, the then president Asif Ali Zardari frankly admitted to a delegation of South Asia Free Media Association (SAFMA) that he could do nothing to avenge her near-assassination. He said Pakistan was not yet ready for the extremist blowback if North Waziristan was attacked by Pakistan. He gave the following three reasons: 1) Pakistani political parties were not united over what the attempt on Malala's life meant for Pakistan; 2) The extremists ready to side with al-Qaeda-Taliban were too strong and widespread in the country to risk challenging the terrorist blowback from North Waziristan; and 3) Pakistan was different from what it was in 2009 when he could put together a national consensus when a relatively unknown girl was flogged by the Taliban in Swat.

Clearly, this was coming out of the briefings he was receiving from the army chief, General Kayani. What he couldn't say, although he was aware of it, was that there were difficulties being faced purging the military of elements converted to al-Qaeda. In 2014, General Raheel Sharif proved his predecessor wrong with Operation Zarb-e-Azb. It effectively curtailed al-Qaeda's terrorist outreach and opened up the possibility of an internal clean-up of the armed forces.

It is easy to see that, compared to the 2011 attack on the navy's Mehran airbase, al-Zawahiri's latest attempt was a failure. This time around, the navy faced the challenge effectively and defeated the al-Qaeda plan to mount an adventure in the Indian Ocean putting Pakistan on the wrong side of India and America. Suddenly, with the appointment of a new army chief, the prospect of tackling terrorism appeared promising. The reason was not far to seek: the army calls all the shots in policymaking, given that Pakistan is self-confessedly a national security state. Was the Pakistan army, ensconced in the cockpit of power, discharging its duties as the country's top institution?

Under General Sharif's proactive stance, it was discovered that it was not, by deliberately or unknowingly misdiagnosing the process of the dismantlement of a jihadi state. After having created jihadi armies—boasting 25,000 to 100,000 men under arms—it was incorrect for the old top brass to assert that terrorism radiating from these desperados was for the police alone to tackle. It is no use facing outward to deter India when the trouble within is in various ways connected to military strategy. The Pakistan army must delink itself from the state's textbook nationalist narrative and come to terms with the new world order in which Pakistan lives and has to make progress. Much of what needs to be done has been discussed in *Crossed Swords: Pakistan, its Army and Wars Within* by Shuja Nawaz, a definitive work on the Pakistan army:

'The Pakistan army, a well-organized entity, has tried to fit into an underdeveloped political system. While responding to the unequal challenge of next door India, it has ended up cannibalising the state it is supposed to defend. Its acts of trespass and usurpation have sapped its professional function and habituated it to reinterpreting its defeats as victories. At birth, the ideology framed for the state by politicians facilitated its mutation into an Islamic army that sat back and let jihad undermine the state itself in the 1980s.'[4]

The Making of the Pakistani Mind

Is the Pakistani civilian mind militarized by the dominance of the army or by the history of the people who formed Pakistan? Does Pakistani nationalism postpone the civilianizing of the Pakistani mind or is it the army that pulls Pakistan towards the collective dream of a winnable 'just war' with India? Out of this theorem emerges the phenomenon of the Islamic soldier—anywhere from the COAS to the mid-ranking officers—who heroically questions the legitimacy of Pakistan's foreign policy clinch with the US, thus enlarging the challenge of the army's mission statement and making it potentially adventurist and dangerous. After so many misadventures in the new millennium, the mission statement must change from an India-centric charter that ignores, if not opposes, regional economic challenges, disarm the fears of neighbours and global expectations of ground zero possibilities of nuclear Pakistan by preventing the ship of the state from sinking. The challenge is internal and it comes from self-generated centres of violence by deliberately ignoring the prevalent theory of the modern state and its monopoly of violence.

Today, by turning inward and launching Operation Zarb-e-Azb, the army has earned the gratitude of all Pakistanis and the world at large. The Pakistan navy was able to stand up to al-Qaeda's attack in Karachi because of the change in the balance of terrorist power in the country. The state must assert its power against militancy to prevent the peaceful citizen from losing faith in its capacity to secure him against criminal behaviour. The purge of unwanted elements was not unknown in the past. The killer of an FIA officer getting close to the al-Qaeda spoor in the assassination of Benazir Bhutto in 2008, was an al-Qaeda agent but was the son of a brigadier fired from the army for his radical links. Now the purge must be deep-cutting and broad in the wake of the new environment created by Zarb-e-Azb.

Some facts, however, must be framed within the narrative of national security. The period of the jihad in Kashmir was the period of remarkable economic recovery in India and sharp economic decline in Pakistan. Pakistan's fixed 'national interest' had to be modified—but was not—in the light of the country's shifting security perspective characterized by a diminishing writ of the state. Although some voices were raised in favour of a review debate, Pakistan's national discourse remained overwhelmingly military-oriented.

Textbook Barriers

Textbook indoctrination and the vested interests formed around jihad coalesced to put up a joint front against new security perceptions. The Pakistan army saw its own corporate interest in standing behind the surrogate armies of the mujahideen 'keeping the Kashmir dispute alive'. As political leadership declined under the 8th Amendment and as civilian leaders ran up against the textbook indoctrination of confrontation, the army took to the task of building up the strength of the seminary-based religious leadership. As the mujahideen and the army emerged as the two dominant 'weaponized' forces in Pakistan, the institutions of the state gradually surrendered to their extra-constitutional power.

Religion, instead of being Pakistan's ideology, became the force that increasingly challenged and defeated the writ of the state. The army stood behind the exemption given to the jihadi militias and their aggressive leaders from the law of the land. As civilian governments found themselves helpless in the face of street power of the warrior priests, policy began to be formed outside the state institutions. Policies initiated by elected leaders to take account of the changed security perceptions were forcibly reversed by the bureaucracy who saw the army calling the shots. The ability of the jihadi leaders to create events on the ground actually became a part of the process of policy-formation. The state constantly adjusted to the 'advances' made on the ground by the surrogate armies. Finally, the outside world became mistrustful of the state of Pakistan itself. The civilian governments paid lip-service to the diplomacy of 'keeping the Kashmir dispute alive'. While the politicians thus exposed themselves to charges of insincerity, the army remained convinced that Pakistan had a case.

Today, all that has changed. And the change is nowhere more visible than in Khyber Pakhtunkhwa, the province most crippled by terrorism coming from the tribal areas adjacent to it. The daily *Dawn* (16 September 2014) observed: 'The current, comparatively calm and peaceful, Peshawar seems surreal. Since mid-June, the scenario has changed. Breaking news about suicide bombings and car bombs in Peshawar are almost none. Ambulance sirens have almost become silent . . . The comparative peace has been prevailing in the provincial capital despite the fact there were fears of a strong backlash from terrorists when operation Zarb-e-Azb was launched in North Waziristan Agency on 18 June this year . . . The monthly security report of the Conflict Monitoring Centre (CMC) released on 1 July 2014 also said that militant activities were drastically decreased after the launch of operation Zarb-e-Azb in Federally Administered Tribal Areas and Khyber Pakhtunkhwa.'

8

Modi and Pakistan

In 2014, the Bharatiya Janata Party swung back to power in New Delhi and a hard-line right-wing leader Narendra Modi was the new prime minister of India with a heavy mandate. The nation chose him through a free and fair election; and the liberals and pluralists in India who didn't vote for him would have to adjust and carry the moral burden of rebuking Modi whenever his government takes a misstep, coping with a powerful prime minister after decades of debilitating coalition politics.

Pakistan's immediate reaction came from Prime Minister Nawaz Sharif when he invited Modi for an official visit to Pakistan; Modi responded by inviting Sharif to his investiture. After a moment of quandary, according to reports, Sharif decided to attend, which was seen by many as the opening of a new door in India–Pakistan relations.

Modi had invited leaders from Afghanistan, Bangladesh, Bhutan, the Maldives, Nepal, Pakistan and Sri Lanka to his swearing-in on 26 May. It was said that he did so without advice from his party hierarchy and upset Ms Jayalalitha, the chief minister of Tamil Nadu, over his invitation to Sri Lankan President Mahinda Rajapaksa. The Muslim leaders of India-administered Kashmir however expressed appreciation of his gesture towards Sharif, which may have finally been the deciding factor for Islamabad. Modi took the risk of getting rejected, which is what the anti-Indian lobby in Pakistan would have liked to happen. Sharif was the first South Asian leader to invite Modi for a state visit.

But the announcement from Islamabad of the acceptance of Modi's invitation was late in coming. Despite advice to attend by the Foreign Office—which normally indicates the assent of the army too—Sharif hesitated, it was said, in the face of non-state actor jihadi reaction that could swell before he could take off for New Delhi. His office told the press that he would make the decision on 26 May, the very day the investiture was to be held, and spoke of three options before him: one, that he go himself; two, that he send his adviser on foreign affair Sartaj Aziz; or three, he let the Pakistan high commissioner in New Delhi attend the ceremony. But T.C.A. Raghavan, the Indian High Commissioner in Islamabad, let the cat out of the bag saying 'the prime minister has accepted the invitation to be present at the ceremony'.

On 23 May, Lahore's Chauburji Chowk was a venue of the religious parties' meeting in which chief of Jamaatud Dawa Hafiz Muhammad Saeed asked Sharif not to go: 'New Delhi has been fuelling separatist movements in Balochistan, Sindh and Khyber Pakhtunkhwa besides funding and training terrorists in Pakistan, killing and maiming Kashmiri Muslims, and blocking waters of rivers.' Then he added what could be interpreted as a threat: 'You will face public wrath if you visit India.'

This message of course could have gone to the prime minister much earlier through advice from his security agencies. The 'late decision' to go to India therefore could have been a security measure anticipating pre-emptive agitation by elements Pakistan no longer controls. Media analysis saw the visit as 'surrender' to Indian hegemony in the region, likening Modi's investiture ceremony to a 'darbar' under the British Raj where loyal princes used to symbolically bend the knee to the viceroy.

Modi Modifications

The world too has to adjust to Modi; but that means it will be a two-way process: Modi will tweak his sails now and then to get more of the world on board. But does the same apply to the region? Modi will approach the neighbours with messages of good cheer, but India's periphery will have to do most of the adjustment, some morally necessary but a lot realistically opportune. The yardstick of selfish gain will be constant, not 'principles' that prop up 'national honour'.

Modi will ignore border disputes and mend ties with China. When he was chief minister of Gujarat he spent thirteen years inviting Chinese, Japanese, and Middle Eastern investors and officials to his state, while America and Europe had largely turned their backs on him after 2002. He will also mend ties with America where his entry was banned as a killer of innocent Muslims. America will match his suppleness because it needs India on its side in the South East Asian 'pivot' against China.

This will put pressure on the Indian periphery. Bangladesh has learned to adjust, despite water disputes that clearly show Dhaka in the right. Sri Lanka will have to deliver on Tamils it is killing because Modi's approach will compound the international pressure on Colombo to respect human rights. In the past, Sri Lanka has behaved more realistically with India than other South Asian states have.

Pakistan's Indiacentrism as an unspoken state doctrine will complicate the Modi challenge. Some of the difficulty will belong in the category of Pakistan's bleeding-heart guardianship of the Muslims of India. The media is ringing with references to the 'Godhra massacre' by Modi but this drumbeat is hollow as it ignores what is happening to Muslims in Sri Lanka.

The 10 May 2014 issue of *Newsweek Pakistan* reported the following: 'The Sri Lanka Muslim Congress, the largest Muslim party, detailed 241 attacks on Muslims during 2013. These attacks included mosques being stoned, Muslim-owned shops being struck by Buddhist monks, calls for the hijab to be outlawed, and a successful campaign against halal meat. Four-letter obscenities against Allah have been scrawled on mosque walls and pig's heads drawn on their exteriors or even tossed inside.'

Islamabad first hesitated, then made some unwise noise about the hanging of clerics in Bangladesh this year because of Pakistan's rather murky transnational nexus with Jamaat-e-Islami in Bangladesh; but the generally more realistic reaction in Pakistan favoured leaving the issue well alone. Will Pakistan be likewise pragmatic with Modi?

Prime Minister Nawaz Sharif should have been just the right man waiting for a Modi visit; but last time he did it with BJP's infinitely more statesmanlike Vajpayee it didn't work, landing him first in prison, then exile. He has won the 2013 election on 'trade with India' slogan backed by all the economists and chambers of commerce and industry in the country. But this time around he could be running a greater risk.

Absent Governance

Pakistan sinks in amnesia when discussing foreign policy and behaves like a state with its internal sovereignty intact. It has actually handed over the conduct of its foreign policy to jihadi elements it no longer controls. It also forgets that any 'reformulation' of policy by the elected government may run up against the ingrained mindset of these non-state elements. Indeed what is amply proved on the streets is the capacity of these 'instruments' of policy to also be the formulators of policy. Many 'incidents' have to be 'owned' by the state through the paradox of denial, that is, instead of punishing the instrument, denying that the instrument has orchestrated an event.

Pakistan has suffered economic damage pursuing the unchanging 'principled' policy of revisionist challenge to India but this may not have hurt it enough to make it repent. In his latest comment, ex-World Bank Pakistani economist Shahid Javed Burki says: 'The past process was "India-centric" in the sense that Pakistan tried, sometimes with desperation, to balance India's growing military might. That approach proved costly. In a 2007 report, I wrote I estimated the cost to Pakistan of the running dispute with India over Kashmir and other issues. I estimated that the Kashmir dispute alone had cost Pakistan 2.25 per cent to 3.2 per cent a year of growth loss in GDP terms.

'Compounded over a period of six decades, this suggests the magnitude of the colossal damage Pakistan has done to its economy by following this particular quarrel with India. This study used purely economic factors; it did not take into account the undeniable fact that some of the cost of this approach towards India contributed to the rise of Islamic extremism in the country. That, too, has resulted in serious economic losses.'

Modi thinks India too has damaged its economy through the anti-business Nehruvian model, which his predecessor prime minister began to overturn but failed to complete the job. Prime Minister Sharif can hit it off with Prime Minister Modi but will be hampered by elements that force the world to call Pakistan a failed state by reason of lost 'internal sovereignty'. Modi will take the trade-first option offered by Sharif; but if he is squeezed on the 'Kashmir-first' option he will join the rest of the world on squeezing Sharif with 'do-more' pressure against Pakistan's 'instruments of foreign policy', the non-state actors.

Internal Demons

An impetuous interior minister in Islamabad stubbed his toe on the presence in Pakistan of a Mumbai don named Dawood Ibrahim. He assumed that Modi had made progress with Pakistan conditional to Pakistan coughing up Dawood Ibrahim, wanted for terrorism in India. It developed that Modi hadn't said anything about Dawood Ibrahim. But in the coming days, the Mumbai don and many others in the gallery of non-state rogues, let off with fig-leaf verdicts by Pakistani courts according to international opinion, will become a major agenda of bilateral discussion. Pakistan will balk; and Pakistan will suffer for being transfixed in a policy rut.

Most foreign policy experts in Pakistan study events keeping their eyes averted from how much Modi can gain from international reaction to Pakistan's gallery of internal rogues. In 2008, a UN Security Council committee, on India's request, designated Jamaatud Dawa the frontal organization of Lashkar-e-Taiba, as a global terrorist organization and its leader Hafiz Mohammad Saeed, Zaki-ur-Rehman Lakhvi, chief of operations of Laskhar-e-Taiba, and Haji Muhammad Ashraf, chief of finance of the group, as terrorists. America went ahead and placed $10 million on Saeed's head.

While in jail, Lakhvi has been allowed to wed again and, after regular cohabitation, become the father of a baby. Unfortunately for Pakistan, in 2012, a terrorist called Abu Jandal but actually Zabihuddin of India, repatriated to India by seemingly friendly-to-Pakistan Saudi Arabia, revealed all. While Zabihuddin was doing R&R in Saudi Arabia after training in Pakistan, Lakhvi phoned him triumphantly from his Rawalpindi prison to tell him that he was having the time of his life four years after his trial started with no end in sight in 2013.

In 2013, the Supreme Court of India pronounced that the 1993 serial bombings in Mumbai, which killed 257 people, were the result of 'the management and conspiracy of the blasts by Dawood Ibrahim and Tiger Memon, and that it was executed with the help of the ISI which played a vital role in imparting training to the accused'. Dawood Ibrahim is officially not in Pakistan but his movement is apparently not restricted by any niceties of security although some Karachi publications have come under pressure for reporting his whereabouts. Rumours hit Lahore in April when he visited the city to shop for another wedding in the family.

The Afghan Factor

Islamabad is making up his mind about what policy to adopt for the post-withdrawal Afghanistan with a pro-India Abdullah Abdullah as President armed with a bilateral security agreement with the US. So far the strategy was to oppose the Indian presence in Afghanistan and make it tough for India by getting the Taliban and foreign militants through cross-border terrorism. This policy, dividing the Taliban into 'good' (who attacked Afghanistan) and 'bad' Taliban (who attacked Pakistan) was flawed because of the linkages the two categories developed when Islamabad tried 'peace talks' with the 'bad' Tehreek-e-Taliban Pakistan.

Pakistan's 'trade-first' approach to India will sort out other complicated strategic issues. The 'foreign militants' being nursed by Pakistan on its soil are hurting its friend China. In the latest incident on 20 May, a Chinese tourist was kidnapped in Dera Ismail Khan in the Khyber Pakhtunkhwa province and taken to North Waziristan, followed by a Taliban spokesman announcing that the Chinese tourist would be released if China were to free a number of Uighur warriors from its prison in Xinjiang. Next day, 21 May, the Pakistan air force bombed North Waziristan, killing seventy-one men, including, according to Inter-Services Public Relations (ISPR), Taliban commanders and 'foreign militants'.

In the coming days, Modi will mount friendly pressure on Pakistan to 'do more' on its non-state actors and the 'foreign militants', a strategy he will pursue in tandem with the US and, more delicately, China. The global view of these elements has been vague. More reliably, Pakistan's doyen of commentators on the Taliban, RahimullahYusufzai, reported in the *News* of 28 May 2014:

'Around 12 groups of foreign militants are listed, the prominent ones being the al-Qaeda led by late Osama bin Laden's successor Dr Ayman-al-Zawahiri, the Islamic Movement of Uzbekistan (IMU), the Islamic Jihad Union which is a breakaway faction of the IMU, the East Turkestan Islamic Movement (ETIM) made up of the separatist Chinese Uighur Muslims and headed by

Abdullah Mansour, the mainstream Afghan Taliban movement and the powerful Haqqani Network affiliated with it.'

Modi's rise seems to coincide with Pakistan's change of Afghanistan strategy, namely, its reliance on the instrumentality of the 'good' Taliban to defeat India in Afghanistan. Under the new government in Kabul, the odds of the success of this strategy are stacked against Rawalpindi–Islamabad. The process of peace talks with the 'bad' Taliban was a part of this strategy with which the Pakistan army was not in agreement. Prime Minister Sharif thought that if the strategy was inflexible and obdurately fixed, then he should at least make his government minimally functional in the midst of the pro-Taliban terrorist affiliates and madrasa-linked clergy spread across the country. That policy has luckily come to grief.

Peace in South Asia

There is a speculative consensus in India that Modi will need peace around the region during his tenure to actualize his policy of bringing big money into India. He will therefore be attracted to any trade-first overture from Pakistan end-loaded with a comprehensive dialogue on bilateral issues that could go on forever. This consensus however carries a caveat: Modi will have zero tolerance for any future attempt at cross-border terrorism by Pakistan's non-state actors.

The caveat becomes nuanced when seen in the light of Prime Minister Sharif's trade-first overture to India. If the two countries are embarked upon normalization and fast-track some of the trade-route and economic integration agreements signed under South Asian Association of Regional Cooperation, a common strategy of avoidance of war can be fashioned against Pakistan's non-state actors and can be adopted with the assistance of a grateful international community. A Modi-Sharif partnership can resolve many South Asian crises, including the internal turmoil of both states stemming from decades of hostility.

9

The Dacoits of Lyari

On 2 October 2014, the police in Karachi killed two men guilty of kidnapping for ransom after a siege during which the kidnappers 'attacked the police and opened fire and threw hand-grenades'. It was later announced that 'two captured citizens were recovered from a house of Model Colony, picked after tracing the telephone location of one of the kidnapped persons'. More significantly, it was announced that the dead kidnappers, Abdullah alias Shera and Nasir alias Bangali, were brothers of Arshad Pappu, one of the ringleaders of the famous Lyari gang war, whose brutal murder and dismemberment in 2013 changed the map of Karachi's violence through a new balance of criminal power.

Slaying as Signature

In a recent book, *Karachi: Ordered Disorder and the Struggle for the City*, Laurent Gayer graphically described the ritual killing of

Pappu by a rival gang under Uzair Baloch in March 2013. Pappu's old rival Rehman Dakait had been killed in a 'police encounter' in 2012; now it was his turn at the hands of Dakait's successor:

'The Dakait Group organized a public execution which, even by Karachi standards, was unprecedented in its brutality. The exact circumstances of this event remain shrouded in mystery, but Lyariites claim that, following the abduction of Arshad Pappu (the arch-rival of the PPP-favoured People's Aman [Peace] Committee leadership), the residents of Afshan Gali were invited through the loudspeakers of local mosques to attend, and even, according to some accounts, to take part in his punishment.

'Pappu was tortured/beaten to death, tied to a car, dragged naked, before being beheaded with a knife. As graphic photographs published by the local Urdu press attested, his headless corpse, along with that of his brother, was later paraded on a donkey cart around the area of Gabol and Aman Park, until it was chopped into pieces and burnt, with the ashes being dispersed in a *nullah* (open sewage canal). This gruesome performance culminated in the armed cadres of the PAC—including the military commander of the group, Baba Ladla—playing football with his severed head.'[1]

A Den of Many Dons

Shaken by the details of the event, the Supreme Court of Pakistan took note and ordered an inquiry into the March 2013 outbreak of the gang war of Lyari. Insensitive to the refinements of law, the gang war quickly entered into its next phase. A strongman within the Rehman Dakait gang broke with the new don Uzair Baloch in April and declared his own satrapy in the city. Baba Ladla, perhaps egged on by the security forces, has caused the latest rift in the Lyari gangland to perpetuate a criminal war in which many innocent citizens get killed, while corrupt police officials make money blinking mayhem.

The latest reconfiguration of violence in 2014 caused the community once supported by Pappu to flee to areas outside

Karachi to avoid being slaughtered. Called Kutchis, these Gujarati Memons, represented in Lyari by the highly respected Memon family of Abdullah Haroon of Lyari's Khadda Market area, worked at the Karachi Port as dock labour before being targeted 'because we are resisting extortion by the Lyari gangs with political patronage'. The Baloch community—most Sindhi feudal landlords are Baloch in origin—complain the Kutchis support the Muttahida Qaumi Movement (MQM) in its efforts at a takeover, meaning a restart of the Pappu era.

Lyari was declared one of the eighteen towns of Karachi in 2001. A municipal administration has since been set up for it for a population of 607,922, divided into nine union councils.

The Lyari Lot

Who owns Lyari? The Kutchis and the Baloch lay claim to it but the dacoits have de facto ownership, riding atop an increasingly corrupt administration and political parties contending for control over Karachi. There is the story of Abdullah Haroon who arose from a hawker to being the 'sugar king' of Pakistan and his sons Yousaf and Mehmud becoming chief minister of Sindh and mayor of Karachi, respectively. According to a historian of Karachi, Gul Hassan Kalmati quoted by Gayer, the bulk of Kutchis had come to Karachi during the development process of Karachi Port between 1901 and 1905.

If the Kutchis arrived from Gujarat in the twentieth century or even earlier, the Baloch are equally early in their arrival in Lyari. The Sindhi elite today itself traces its origin to the warlike tribes of Balochistan. In the twentieth century, Lyari attracted India's mainland politics, and a Muslim leader from north India, Muhammad Ali Jauhar, came to Lyari and addressed the crowds here promoting his Khilafat Movement against the British Raj. From the Gujarati–Ismaili community arose the founder of Pakistan, Muhammad Ali Jinnah, enthusiastically supported by the Haroons of Lyari.

Lyari also gave rise to Baloch subnationalism predating similar movements in other parts of the country. It is here that one of the first Baloch nationalist organizations, the Baloch League, was founded in the 1920s by leaders including Allah Baksh Gabol, the grandfather of the former MNA from Lyari, NabeelGabol. Organizations such as the Baloch Students Organization (BSO) were also founded in Lyari, focusing more on education and political awareness than on agitation. It was after the alienation of the dominant Baloch dacoits from Nabeel Gabol after his election to the 2002 National Assembly that Lyari tilted into its latest crisis. Gabol's alleged backing of the MQM-aligned Pappu gang began a new phase of Lyari politics away from the PPP.

Gayer writes: 'Lyari's first residents were Sindhi fishermen and Baloch nomads from Makran, Lasbela and Kalat districts, fleeing drought and tribal feuds. A first influx occurred around 1725, a few years before Sindhi banias (Hindu trading class) settled in Karachi and committed to expand it. A second wave of Baloch settlers arrived around 1770, when Karachi came under the control of the Khan of Kalat, following an accord between the Khan and the Kalhoro rulers of Sindh. A third wave of Baloch migration took place after 1795, following the annexation of the city by the Talpur rulers of Sindh, which attracted Baloch tribesmen from interior Sindh and the Seraiki belt.

'Finally, in the second half of the nineteenth century, the British occupation of Sindh and the modernization of Karachi's port, as well as the construction of railway connections between Sindh and the Punjab, brought to Karachi a number of Baloch settlers from the Iranian part of Balochistan, most of whom settled on the banks of the Lyari river . . . Today, these Baloch of Iranian descent would constitute the largest share of Lyari's Baloch population.'[2]

Mushrooming of Meanness

The mushroom growth of Karachi after the 1947 transfer of populations between India and Pakistan disturbed the ethnic balance and catapulted some parts of the city into violence, followed by crime. From this disturbed soil grew the poisoned tree of Rehman Dakait, the Iranian Baloch don who was enriched from Lyari's thirty-three dens of drug-peddling and gambling, local beer traffic and other illegal activities, to be politically important. He was rich, a patron of people's causes, and in control of the megacity's security apparatus. When Benazir Bhutto landed in Karachi on 17 October 2007, and the procession was attacked with explosives, he was in charge of her security. Rehman helped Benazir shift from her armoured bus to a private vehicle which he was seen driving.

Gayer notes: 'In a picture published by the *Telegraph* the following day, Rehman can be seen holding Benazir's arm, helping in her transfer. It is therefore in the company and under the protection of Karachi's most wanted criminal that Benazir dealt with this life-threatening crisis, and that she reached the Bhutto residence.'[3]

Rehman Dakait was doubtlessly the don of Karachi, a man of means who could fund social activities like soccer among the Baloch youth and award scholarships to Lyari boys and girls who went to Lahore's prestigious Lahore University of Management Sciences (LUMS). How did he fall from grace after getting the upper hand in his infighting with Arshad Pappu and his gang? Did he die in a police encounter because he had gotten too big for his shoes in the eyes of the governing PPP? Gabol and PPP's acting chairman Asif Ali Zardari tried their best to get Rehman to come to heel but failed. A special relationship developed between Lyari and the PPP over the years as the residual stronghold of the Sindhi party in a city gradually falling to the MQM. In 1987 the wedding reception of Benazir Bhutto and Asif Ali Zardari took place here. The following year, Benazir Bhutto was elected to the National Assembly with a big Lyari vote. Two years later her husband followed suit from a Lyari seat.

Then in 2003, the big split took place within the criminal elite. Relations between Rehman Dakait and Haji Lalu, to whom he was also related by marriage, had started cooling in the late 1990s after Rehman's men kidnapped a Memon of Kharadar and Lalu asked Rehman to release him. They in fact split over the ransom that the hostage would bring; Rehman thought Lalu would take money from the Kutchis for the release. It got so bad Rehman split from the gang, which hurt Lalu's position as the top dog of the area. The war started when Lalu's son Arshad Pappu kidnapped and killed a transporter, Faiz Muhammad, a relative of Rehman and father of Uzair Baloch, the don who succeeded Rehman later. Pappu also desecrated the grave of Rehman's father, Dadal, with bulldozers. At this point the mixing of politics with crime came out in the open. Pappu represented the MQM and Rehman became proxy for the PPP. The war took 500 lives by 2008 and became a part of the general death toll of ten-a-day in the luckless city. Crime became politicized and politics became criminalized.

Dealing in Dead Dons

Nobody is quite clear why it happened but Rehman was killed by a police posse in Steel Town (Bin Qasim Town) in August 2009 led by SP Chaudhry Aslam—himself suicide-bombed by the Taliban in 2014. Significantly, PPP spokesperson, now-deceased Ms Fauzia Wahab, said shortly after Rehman's death: 'He was flying high to become a self-proclaimed leader of the area. His ambitions were threatening everyone and he spoiled institutions, culture, peace and everything in the area.'

In 2011, the resignation of Sindh home minister Zulfiqar Mirza made public the extent to which the PPP-MQM rivalry was feeding into the gang war of Lyari. Given to bluster which his party boss Asif Ali Zardari found distasteful he even confessed that he had provided scores of gun licences to Rehman Dakait's Peace Committee which was often seen in Karachi as the killing arm of the PPP against the MQM. But Mirza waved away his own confession about the licences by declaring that the PPP government in Sindh had actually got rid of the Dakait.

The gangland of Lyari was nothing if not deeply internecine. Rehman himself was the acolyte of the big-time narcotics don, Haji Lalu, who was an understudy of his father, the first Lyari super-don, Dadal. Rehman alienated Lalu as he grew in stature and was finally to deal with Arshad Pappu, the toughest of the many sons of Lalu. Rehman was succeeded as head of the Baloch gang by Uzair Baloch who, according to rumours, ultimately trapped Arshad Pappu and killed him with such brutality. Some observers suspect that intra-gangland wars are encouraged by the administration to break the stranglehold of the dons over Lyari where police raids fail with dull regularity because of non-cooperation from its inhabitants. Uzair Baloch now faces the challenge of an even more savage internal rival, Baba Ladla.

In 2008, Haji Lalu, the top don who sired the crime microcosm of Lyari, was in prison with his three sons while the fourth, Arshad Pappu, was out free. The latest news is that two out of them have been killed after they kidnapped some people for ransom and were discovered by the Karachi police. It is Karachi's routine that dangerous criminals are allowed to walk by courts because of lack of eyewitnesses. One can almost be certain that Lalu's sons had been let off, after which they immediately took to their earlier practices.

A Graveyard of Governance

If the death toll in Karachi to crime of all variety, including religious, is ten-a-day, the daily take of robbed money is over $100 million. This maintains criminal gangs in power and finances al-Qaeda's regional and global adventures. The big kidnappings end in the Tribal Areas while small-time grabs are managed by dumping the victims in stolen cars that keep going around on Karachi roads till the affected families cough up the money.

On the tenth of Muharram, the Day of Ritual Mourning of their community, the Shia of Karachi are routinely decimated in their processions. Sunni madrasas pay the price for these massacres when 'unknown' killers revenge themselves on their leaders. Insincere expressions of mystified grief cover up for the fact that most Shia-killing jihadi warriors are openly trained in these madrasas with funds that come from the Middle East. This mayhem is compounded by the three warring political parties—MQM, ANP and PPP—whose agreed mantra is not to name one another, while allowing the police only to pronounce the killers they nab as 'belonging to a political party'.

For the other deaths the city offers as burnt offerings to the terrorist organizations—named after at least half a dozen dead or alive Pakhtun strongmen in the Tribal Areas—the police chiefs routinely blame 'foreign conspiracy', easily interpreted by the nation as America's evil design on Pakistan. This stratagem has been invented as a cover for the incapacity of the police to enter Karachi's almost two dozen 'no-go' areas where normal governance died long ago.

The twenty-five key al-Qaeda- and Taliban-linked militant groups with strong signs of link-ups with the Lyari gangland have Karachi by the throat. They are led by factions of Lashkar-e-Jhangvi, Lashkar-e-Jhangvi Al Alami, Qari Zafar group, Qari Shakeel group, Akram Lahori group and Farooq Bangali group.

Then there are three factions of the Tehreek-e-Taliban Pakistan (TTP), Commander Waliur Rehman group (from South Waziristan), Badr Mansoor group (from North Waziristan) and Mullah Fazlullah group (from Swat). The remaining jihadi-cum-sectarian groups in Karachi include Sipah-e-Sahaba Pakistan (SSP), Sipah-e-Muhammad Pakistan (SMP), Sunni Tehreek (ST), Dawat-e-Islami (DeI), Harkat-ul-Mujahideen (HuM), Harkat-ul-Mujahideen al-Alami (HUMA), Jaish-e-Mohammad (JeM), Jamaatul Furqan (JuF), Harkatul Jihadul Islami (HuJI), Tehrik-e-Nifaz-e-Shariat-e-Mohammadi (TNSM), Jandullah, Tehrik-e-Islami Lashkar-e-Muhammadi (TILM), Lashkar-e-Islami (LeI), Mehdi Militia (MM), Hezbollah, Kharooj, Tawheed Brigade (TB), Al Mukhtar Group, Punjabi Mujahideen etc. According to reports, there are eleven areas of Karachi currently under the control of these groups.

One of the 'overlapping sovereignties' in Karachi mentioned by Gayer has been established by the criminal underworld. Crime has ballooned because at least one son of every lower-middle-class family breaks bad after seeing what a good time he could have snatching cell phones before graduating to target-killing for money. Sons of Sindhi feudal landlords, living in bachelor apartments along with their bodyguards, often run their own gangs of extortion and trafficked girls. They are more often than not joined by the sons of the big bureaucrats and police officers with clout fattening on 'reverse-bhatta', that is, money taken from the criminals in return for exemption from 'mischief of law'.

What has died actually in Karachi is governance. The city is the paradigm of what is happening gradually in other cities of the country, like Quetta, Peshawar and Islamabad. The death of Arshad Pappu's brothers at the hands of the police is a sign of decline of one don which unfurled during the gang wars. The police know that killing the underworld men would make their own officers vulnerable to attacks they simply can't stand up against.

10

The Lal Masjid Secret

On 16 December 2014, seven suicide bombers, sent by Tehrik-e-Taliban Pakistan, killed 140 in a middle-and-secondary Army Public School in Peshawar, 131 of them boys aged between ten and twenty; and this was Taliban chief Fazlullah's response to the military operation in the Taliban safe havens in North Waziristan. The school catered to 500 sons of the army personnel. The job was done with hand grenades and AK-47s at close range for over nine hours while under siege by the security forces. Pakistan changed that day, some calling it Pakistan's 9/11. The Parliament got together to pass a unanimous resolution of condemnation while even heretofore friendly-to-Taliban clerics joined the national consensus of outrage. But not the chief of Lal Masjid—or the 'red mosque'—of Islamabad: Maulana Abdul Aziz. His mosque-cum-madrasa complex is situated in the heart of Islamabad. It was discovered only after a commando operation that it had a vast underground residential and educational facility where 'guests'—militants—could be lodged.

There are some culpable religious leaders that Pakistan will not or cannot punish under the law. They have been allowed to become too powerful through proxy jihad and now partake of the 'monopoly of violence' of the state. Others are equally 'untouchable' because they are backed by other proxy warriors, and removal of their impunity by the state will likely create fissures within the ruling establishment. Grasping this fact, the judiciary equally 'empowers' itself by favouring them in its judgements. It blinked the acts of vigilante violence committed by the Lal Masjid seminarians against innocent citizens in Islamabad in 2007 and rewarded it with compensatory allocations after it was attacked and shut down by the government.

In 2015, after Maulana Aziz failed to condemn the massacre of schoolchildren in Peshawar, civil society protested. There was a modest gathering of citizens outside his mosque protesting his failure to answer a summons from the court of law asking him to explain his stance. They pointed out once again that his madrasa had been involved in terrorist activities. Preliminary investigation had revealed that the suicide bomber who blew himself up at a police picket in Wah the same month had been a student at his seminary. The terrorists took notice. Jibran Nasir, the lawyer-activist leading the protest, reported receiving a call from the spokesperson of a Taliban faction, Ehsanullah Ehsan, threatening him with consequence for criticizing Aziz. There was nothing anyone could do, and the deadlock was finally broken by the cleric saying he was sorry he had 'failed to unconditionally condemn the Peshawar massacre'. The court, having summoned him for 'supporting' the massacre, quickly forgot all about it. When Ehsanullah Ehsan speaks you'd better listen. And Aziz was no small-time preacher; his impunity was bought at the cost of Pakistan's relations with its 'all-weather' friend, China.

A Sectarian Oracle

Lal Masjid or Red Mosque was established in the 1980s knowingly as a sectarian seminary by General Zia who had fallen foul of the

Shia with his controversial zakat tax. It came to be favoured in the following decade by al-Qaeda as its client in central Islamabad. Like many religious leaders, doctors, nuclear scientists, and members of the armed forces, the founding family of the mosque admired Osama bin Laden and met him in the mountains of Afghanistan to pledge their allegiance to his jihad. In due course, the head of the family was killed in what was reported as a sectarian hit. But the family thought otherwise.

The Urdu daily *Jang* (3 January 2013) quoted Umme Hassan, wife of Aziz, as telling the Lal Masjid Judicial Commission that her father-in-law Maulana Abdullah Ghazi was killed in front of her own eyes. Abdullah had gone and met bin Laden in Afghanistan and was advised by the agencies to keep mum about the meeting but he decided to reveal the facts in a speech he made at a Lal Masjid Friday congregation. He was therefore killed on 18 October 1998 by a boy who walked in and shook hands with Abdullah Ghazi before emptying his revolver into him. She said she ran after the killer who jumped into a white car before fleeing the scene. Later no FIR was allowed to be lodged because Maulana Ghazi was considered dangerous for Pakistan. His son Rashid Ghazi was picked up by the ISI and kept in custody for putting too much pressure on the government for the investigation of his father's murder.

Abdullah Ghazi was a graduate of the anti-Shia incubator Jamia Banuria Madrasa, Karachi, like Maulana Masood Azhar of Jaish-e-Mohammad whose trained terrorists were often found living within the Lal Masjid compound. Rashid Ghazi echoed his father's sectarian worldview when he told a TV channel during the commando operation against the mosque that 'the government may have brought out Shia warriors against his besieged acolytes'. Lal Masjid was feeding ideologically into the anarchic order of Talibanization in the Khyber Pakhtunkhwa and the tribal territories (FATA). Eighty per cent of the acolytes in its residential seminaries were from FATA and from the provincially administered tribal region of Malakand, Swat and Dir. Aziz and his younger brother Abdur Rashid Ghazi regularly harangued the 'state within the state' of the 'FM radio mullah' Fazlullah of Malakand who was also connected with al-Qaeda. No one paid heed to this. No one registered the trend of increased al-Qaeda 'appearances' in Islamabad either.

The phenomenon was simply not understood. No intelligence agency took note that Aziz had started seeing 'sacred dreams'—numbering 300—in which the Holy Prophet in person ordered him to raise the standard of revolt, declare jihad and implement the sharia on his own. Timely information on this proclaimed project would have prepared the ground for some state action, but no one cared. General 'President' Musharraf who ruled the country with his commando panache had no clue he would have to quit because of crazy Aziz. He was taught a lesson about how not to take the right-wing conservative crutch of the Muslim League who would cave into the equally conservative Urdu media swinging in favour of Lal Masjid.

He was let down by his minister of state for religious affairs, then-MQM's Amir Liaquat Hussain. Hussain ignored his own party line on the mullahs to give a most ill-advised TV interview, indirectly defending Lal Masjid's revolt on the basis of 'sharia backslidings' of the government. His line was picked up by the clerical coalition of MMA in Khyber Pakhtunkhwa which taxed the government with failing to implement the sharia. Hussain actually pointed to 'lewd' signboards—staid by international standards—as a moral failure of the government, in unison with the MMA.

A Not-so-silent Operation

Finally the general took action in July 2007. It was a commando assault named Operation Silence, at first delayed by the intelligence that Aziz could call in help from Waziristan in the shape of suicide-bombers and could also count on the help of students from other seminaries in the vicinity. (There were eighty-eight unregistered madrasas in Islamabad in 2007.) Musharraf was also off the mark in his assessment of the coverage of it by the electronic media. However, the stratagem of turning off the electricity in Lal Masjid quickly forced its 6000 militant boys and girls to start surrendering. Once the operation was afoot, curfew declared and the army deployed, the dreaming mullah of Lal Masjid was disabused of his divinity in short order.

The lateness of the operation inclined a lot of people to speculate that the government had actually used the clerics to divert attention from the judicial crisis unfolding against Musharraf. Almost the entire opposition used this 'convenient' interpretation to rubbish the government. Even after the onset of the operation, opposition politicians were recommending 'negotiations' in a situation that no longer brooked negotiation. Only the PPP chairperson Benazir Bhutto appropriately asserted that on coming to power she would wipe out religious extremism in Pakistan. More than a hundred persons from the fastness of the seminary were killed in the operation, including Ghazi, as Aziz escaped concealed as 'a lady in burqa'. According to the inspector general of police, Islamabad, 102 people were killed during the operation: ninety-one militants, ten SSG commandos, and one paramilitary ranger. The blanket term 'militants' covered some seminarians who fell fighting the commandos.

The Chinese Factor

The operation against Lal Masjid was triggered by a vigilante attack launched by Aziz in June. A group of seminarians— including ten burqa-clad girls—raided a Chinese massage parlour and acupuncture clinic in one of Islamabad's wealthiest neighbourhoods. They grabbed the three guards, entered the house and ordered the seven Chinese staff and their Pakistani clients to accompany them. When they refused, they were beaten and taken to the Jamia Hafza madrasa, the girls' section of the Lal Masjid seminary where 'a spokesman announced to local press that clinic was used as a brothel house; and, despite our warnings, the administration failed to take any action; so we decided to take action on our own.' Months earlier, the Lal Masjid vigilantes, true to their sectarian indoctrination, had attacked another 'brothel run by a Shia lady', thrashing the inmates and kidnapping four policemen for good measure.

In 2009, Aziz's wife Umme Hassan was still obstinately committed to attacking entertainment and other obscenity. She was asked by a reporter:

'If the government provides free education to all, gives them health coverage and finds jobs for our youth, but also allows people to pursue arts and music and live their life as they want to live, would that be acceptable to the clerics?'

'No, it cannot be permitted in an Islamic republic', she replied,' 'Our Prophet destroyed 365 idols and broke musical instruments at the conquest of Makkah; and he fought against Abu Jahal, who believed in Jahiliat and profanity. But we in Pakistan are promoting a culture of dance and music.'[1]

But the kidnapping of the Chinese this time was like crossing a strategic threshold. As Andrew Small tells it, Beijing reacted with understandable fury, the assertive section of Chinese society taking it as 'a test of the Communist Party's backbone'. To give point to their reaction, 'mocking packages of calcium pills' were sent to the foreign ministry.

Wasn't Pakistan China's closest ally? How could it allow seven Chinese nationals to be picked up in its capital? Most Pakistanis were unaware that President Hu Jintao in Beijing was getting regular briefings from his diplomats in Pakistan as the kidnap drama in the name of religious piety unfolded in Islamabad. The irony was reinforced by the fact that China was about to compensate Pakistan for a 2005 US–India civil nuclear deal with the expansion of its Chashma nuclear power plants. As it turned out, no religious piety was involved. The madrasa was holding Uighur terrorists from Xinjiang and only the Chinese and the Lal Masjid clerics knew it.[2]

Before 2007, Lal Masjid was known as a watering-hole of all kinds of organizations the world recognized as terrorist, mostly al-Qaeda-linked Taliban not clearly defined as anti-state by Pakistan. After its opening in the 1980s, it 'welcomed fighters in transit to Afghanistan and Kashmir alike'. Its founder was overwhelmed by the warrior charisma of bin Laden during a trip to Kandahar in 1998 to 'pay homage' to the Taliban's leader, Mullah Omar. His younger son Abdur Rashid was with him. At the end of the meeting, Rashid picked up bin Laden's glass of water and drank from it. An amused bin Laden asked him the reason for his action, to which he replied, 'I drank from your glass so that Allah would make me a warrior like you.'[3]

After Abdullah Ghazi's assassination, sons Abdul Aziz and Abdur Rashid Ghazi ran the seminary, the former as its administrator and Ghazi as a firebrand behind-the-scenes inspiration who issued a reckless pro-Taliban fatwa, declaring that 'those killed in the battle against Pakistani forces are shaheed (martyrs)'. Ghazi was in time accused of a plot to blow up the President's house, the Parliament building, and the army GHQ, but was let off the hook by federal cabinet minister Ijaz ul-Haq, the son of General Zia-ul-Haq who had helped the Ghazis set up the mosque in Islamabad. That had emboldened the brothers who in time began a campaign of 'correction' in the capital city, deploying 'vice and virtue' groups that attacked music and DVD shops for their 'obscenity', abducted people of 'loose moral behaviour', and took them to special Lal Masjid sharia courts for punishment. Pakistan tolerated this and thus laid the foundation of the 'normalization of the abnormal' in Pakistani society.

Bad Vibes in Beijing

Even as President Hu Jintao of China kept anxious track of the abductees of the Chinese massage parlour, the Chinese ambassador in Islamabad, Luo Zhaohui, was pursuing the matter with great determination. Tall in height, he was no ordinary diplomat; his regional expertise was equally reflected in his diplomat-scholar wife who had translated Benazir Bhutto's memoir. Luo got around too, unlike the average Chinese diplomat, and approached the 'influentials' who could help out, working with the leader of the party in power, PMLQ, Chaudhry Shujaat Hussain—who patronized the Chinese parlour—and Maulana Fazlur Rehman of the powerful Taliban-connected Jamiat Ulema-e-Islam. The ambassador was soon talking on the phone to Ghazi in the mosque.

The ISI took out the other Taliban-friendly 'influentials' from the madrasas of Karachi and made them plead with the Ghazi family of Lal Masjid but to no avail. They also got their home-grown proxy warrior Maulana Fazlur Rehman Khalil to intercede but he too failed, not knowing what was driving the Ghazi brothers. Lal Masjid abided by the message from al-Qaeda's Ayman-al-Zawahiri who had said during the Operation: 'This crime can only be washed away by repentance or blood . . . If you do not retaliate . . . .Musharraf will not spare any of you. Your salvation is only through jihad.' At one point, Ghazi seemed to relent. He allowed Ambassador Luo to talk to the hostages and promised their release; but in the end he did nothing. Then the marathon five-hour telephone negotiation began, with President Musharraf himself interceding, while deputy commissioner and senior superintendent of police Islamabad begged and pledged all sorts of 'corrective action' against 'mixed-sex massage parlours' in Islamabad.

That pledge finally clinched the deal. The Chinese prisoners were released with Ghazi pompously announcing: 'We released them in view of Pakistan–China friendship. After receiving a number of complaints regarding "sex business", our students and people of the area took an action that should have been taken by the government. We greatly respect Pakistan–China friendship but it doesn't mean that foreign women can come here and indulge in such vulgar activities. Even housewives used to tell us by phone that the parlour charged Rs 1000 for massage while, by paying additional Rs 500, something else was also available.'[4] The Chinese women came out of the seminary wearing burqas!

Back in Beijing, Zhou Yongkang, China's public security minister, publicly declared on 27 June that 'we hope Pakistan will look into the terrorist attacks aiming at Chinese people and organizations as soon as possible and severely punish the criminals'. Author Small observes: 'Word leaked out that, in the course of bilateral talks, China was attributing the instigation of the kidnappings to the influence of militants from China's Uighur minority at Lal Masjid'.[5] What the Chinese knew was news to Pakistan, so out-of-bounds was the Lal Masjid set-up for Pakistani intelligence agencies. After Operation Silence, which almost destroyed the seminary, Afghan and local warriors were found among the dead. Out of the dead, twelve were Uighurs.

Officially China was tight-lipped. Wrote *Shanghai Daily*, 'Within days of the 27 June meeting between China's minister of public security Zhou Yongkang and Pakistan's minister of interior, Aftab Ahmed Khan Sherpao in Beijing, Musharraf ordered Operation Silence (renamed Operation Sunrise) to commence on the mosque. The operation lasted about a week, at the end of which the Pakistan military finally had control of the mosque.' Musharraf covered up by saying he had attacked Lal Masjid because 'I was personally embarrassed. I had to go apologize to the Chinese leaders, "I am ashamed that you are such great friends and this happened to you".' But that was no longer enough. His fall had begun and China, whose workers Pakistan had regularly killed in all the provinces including the tribal areas, didn't matter.[6]

Lal Masjid Gets Even

Lal Masjid retaliated soon enough. While the siege in Islamabad was still on, three Chinese engineers at an auto-rickshaw factory in Peshawar were murdered by gunmen 'shouting religious slogans'. That year al-Qaeda announced the foundation of the Tehreek-e-Taliban Pakistan (TTP), throwing aside all 'peace agreements' with the Pakistan army, extending the TTP's control over areas not 60 miles away from Islamabad. Symbolically, the Chinese-built Karakoram Highway came under threat.

Two months after the Lal Masjid siege, an eighteen-year-old boy blew himself up inside the high-security base of Zarrar Company, the elite commando unit responsible for Operation Silence; twenty-two commandos were killed. It was an insider job. Pakistani journalist Zahid Hussain wrote the following dreaded paragraph in his book, *The Scorpion's Tail: The Relentless Rise of Islamic Militants in Pakistan and how it Threatens America*: 'One of the officers identified was Captain Khurram Ashiq, who had served in Zarrar Company. Captain Khurram Ashiq died in Helmand fighting on the side of al-Qaeda. His brother Major Haroon Ashiq too worked for al-Qaeda, killing another SSG commander Major General Feisal Alavi in Islamabad. He was acquitted later by an anti-terrorism court in Adiala Jail.'[7]

What happened to Maulana Fazlur Rehman is also very sobering. The clerics who visited the mosque to intercede with the Ghazi brothers included Grand Mufti Rafi Usmani of Karachi, Harkat-ul-Mujahideen commander Fazlur Rehman Khalil and the infamous al-Qaeda lawyer Javed Ibrahim Paracha. Maulana Fazlur Rehman of JUI was at first opposed to the Ghazi brothers for not listening to advice, and rebuked them publicly, till he was tamed by fellow-clerics through a reprimand at a grand Deobandi congregation at Multan. What subsequently transpired is recorded by Andrew Small: 'In April 2007, a mysterious rocket attack was launched on Maulana Fazlur Rehman's home in Dera Ismail Khan. A few months later, Pakistani intelligence discovered his name on a Taliban hit list. In April 2011, he was the target of two attacks in two days. On the first occasion, a suicide bomber killed twelve and injured more than twenty members of a group waiting to welcome him in Swabi, barely minutes before he arrived.

'The next day, twelve more people were killed as another suicide bomber struck a police van providing security to his convoy in Charsadda. A few weeks later, Pakistani security officials confirmed that he was now top of the new hit list prepared by the Taliban leadership. By the time China had got round to cultivating him as a broker who could help navigate its own complex relationships with Islamic extremists, it was already too late.'[8]

In July 2008 a bearded suicide bomber walked into a group of policemen in Islamabad at the end of a conference commemorating the first anniversary of the storming of Lal Masjid by the army and blew himself up, killing all of them.

Beijing Will Be Bemused

The anniversary conference at Lal Masjid was, needless to say, welcomed by the entire political spectrum after General Musharraf's resignation as President under threat from impeachment by the new 2008 parliament. It was the most secure gathering because it was taking place under the 'pax' of al-Qaeda. (The police should have mounted a strict security for its own personnel, which it did not, and was caught in the posture of a sitting duck once again.)

The speakers at the Lal Masjid were the usual suspects: former 'double agent' MNA Shah Abdul Aziz, the rising star of the Tribal Areas, was seen as the prospective ruler of Pakistan in tandem with Baitullah Mehsud, after an al-Qaeda takeover. Outlawed Sipah-e-Sahaba was at the conference in strength, under the leadership of Maulana Alam Tariq, heir to the sectarian throne after his assassinated father, Azam Tariq. The great Lal Masjid conference was graced by such panjandrums of Pakistan's world of clerical extremism as Grand Mufti Rafi Usmani—brother of the internationally renowned Taqi Usmani advising the Arab states on Islamic banking—although the Constitution of Pakistan doesn't mention the post of a grand mufti. Resolutions were passed demanding the death sentence for President Musharraf and the banning of his ministers Aftab Sherpao and Ijaz ul-Haq from entering any seminary in Pakistan. They demanded that the army get out of the Khyber agency and not plan an operation in Waziristan.

Andrew Small must provide the tailpiece to the Lal Masjid saga: 'Fairly or not, Pakistan's approach to the Uighur issue has become the totemic example for those on the Chinese side who have started to raise broader concerns about the creeping "Islamization" of the Pakistani army . . . "We're not worried about the generals, we're worried about the brigadiers," argued one Chinese expert.'[9]

But, in 2012, the Supreme Court was still wedded to compensating the Lal Masjid terrorists for the 'folly' of China-inspired Operation Silence. Wrote Prof Pervez Hoodbhoy in May:

'The honourable Chief Justice of Pakistan says he is losing patience with the Capital Development Authority (CDA). In a court-initiated (suo motu) action, he wants a quick rebuilding of the Jamia Hafsa madrasa, flattened by bulldozers in 2007, after it became the centre of an insurgency. A three-judge bench of the Supreme Court, headed by the CJ, is now dragging procrastinators over the coals by issuing notices to the CDA chairman, Islamabad's chief commissioner and the interior secretary. The court has also expressed its "displeasure" over the status of police cases against the Lal Masjid clerics and ordered the deputy attorney general to appear before it next week.'[10] The court had ordered that Lal Masjid be gifted 20 kanals of the choicest land in sector H-11 of Islamabad in compensation.

Aziz did flee the mosque in 2007 in burqa but he became more radicalized in later years, thanks to popular support, judicial inclination and vilification of General Musharraf. By the 2013 election, Army Chief General Kayani had created a mood of reconciliation to terrorism with his reluctance to face up to the growing strength of the Taliban, inclining the political parties to 'peace talks' with them, which indirectly meant accepting al-Qaeda as an interlocutor. The Taliban promptly named Aziz as their representative at the talks. Today, General Musharraf (retd) is under trial for having wronged the seminary and may possibly face a death sentence for his Operation Silence. Beijing will be bemused.

Another Commission of Omissions

In December 2012, the Supreme Court of Pakistan set up a Lal Masjid Commission, led by a judge of the Federal sharia Court, to inquire into the 'causes of the circumstances' that led to Operation Silence and consequent death of 103 people. The Commission called in twelve witnesses from the Islamabad city administration who submitted their depositions in writing but none of them was from the intelligence agencies who clearly took part in diffusing the crisis. The Commission Report is characteristically inchoate in the construction of its narrative of events.

It mentions persons without apparently comprehending the significance of their background. It is not even clear whether the Commission grasped the identity of the persons being named. For instance, it mentions Khalid Khwaja as a member of the Lal Masjid management; it also says: 'According to another report, four Taliban, including Khalid Khwaja, a former ISI official, were arrested from Bhara Kahu and charged under Section 7 of the Anti-Terrorism Act.'

Had the intelligence agencies helped the Commission, the inquiry would have made the connections it could not make. Khalid Khwaja, an ex-ISI officer, killed in South Waziristan in the last week of April 2010, fitted the description of an adventurer: a man without principles and moral qualms who seeks the confidence of mutually hostile factions and makes his fortune amid suspicion and lack of trust. Playing all sides at once, Khwaja shone on TV and print media, but his lack of conscience finally caught up with him. The Taliban warlord Hakimullah Mehsud despatched him with his own hands 'for betraying the Lal Masjid martyrs by persuading Lal Masjid chief Maulana Abdul Aziz to escape as a woman wearing burqa.' Before his death, he confessed to working for the ISI even after retirement.

The Report mentions Mufti Rafi Usmani as one of the 'advisers' who tried to disarm the Lal Masjid clerics with good advice without avail, but did not give his background. Usmani is the son of Mufti Muhammad Shafi who founded the Deobandi Darul Ulum in Karachi in 1951. Given to extreme views, Rafi Usmani had become involved in jihad and had visited Afghanistan during the Taliban rule. Witnesses who deposed in front of the Commission named Uzbeks and Chechens among the inmates of the mosque, apparently ignorant about the correct nationalities of these non-Afghan, non-Pakistani terrorists.

The Commission Report names Member of Parliament (MNA) Shah Abdul Aziz brought in to intercede with Lal Masjid. He was earlier arrested in June 2009 for the killing of a Polish engineer in Attock and carrying a letter of Taliban chief Baitullah Mehsud in his briefcase. According to the *News* of 28 June 2009, 'The letter was addressed to a former high-profile ISI general known for his strong pro-Taliban views.' In October 2009, in a TV programme, Shah Abdul Aziz admitted that he had assisted 'in the kidnapping of two Chinese engineers'. Aziz is a descendant of Shah Abdul Aziz (1745–1823) of Delhi who wrote a famous tract against the Shia faith which today figures as the founding document of the Islamic State as led by Abubakr al-Baghdadi.

Two other 'intercessors' were brought to Lal Masjid during the siege, but only one, Maulana Fazlur Rehman Khalil—known as Osama bin Laden's 'post office'—is mentioned in the Report without any elaboration. The other person, known as 'al-Qaeda lawyer', was Javed Ibrahim Paracha, also a 'persuader'. Both these persons have an interesting background, Khalil additionally carrying a $5-million head-money as a terrorist.

Mariam Abou Zahab, in her paper, *The Regional Dimension of Sectarian Conflicts in Pakistan*, writes: 'The sectarian killers went to Afghanistan for training and sanctuary under the protection of Harkat ul-Ansar (HUA) led by Maulana Fazlur Rehman Khalil who was attached to al-Qaeda. Khalil later changed his militia's name to Harkat-ul-Mujahideen (HUM) and served the government of Pakistan closely through the ISI and is today living safely in Islamabad. His official line is that he does not indulge in the killing of the Shia, but he cooperates nonetheless with the

Deobandi killers from SSP and its offshoots.' He has figured in the 'million march' organized by Hafiz Saeed of Jamaatud Dawa against the PPP government's policy of free-trading with India.

Javed Ibrahim Paracha was to become the organizer of many sectarian clashes in Kohat and Hangu before he became an advocate of al-Qaeda welcoming its fleeing members into Kohat in 2003. In 2006, he was the leading lawyer in the NWFP defending al-Qaeda operatives caught and prosecuted by the government. According to Jason Burke in his book, *9/11 Wars*, he had helped in the release of 600 al-Qaeda terrorists. Paracha was arrested that year and taken to face the FBI where he said he did not know bin Laden but he thought him a soldier of God. He said he had named his own son Osama bin Laden. Jason Burke in *On the Road to Kandahar: Travels through Conflict in the Islamic World*,[11] writes about the suicide-bombing of a Shia shrine in Islamabad called Bari Imam in May 2005 which killed twenty devotees, saying Paracha was rumoured to be behind the attack. The Bari Imam incident was to be Lal Masjid's revenge for the killing of its founder, Maulana Abdullah Ghazi.

Responding to TOR (term of reference) Six requiring grounds for fixing the responsibility of the Lal Masjid crisis on the 'security agencies', the Commission rambles at length, collecting statements from dozens of establishment figures—but no one from the intelligence agencies—without coming to a conclusion.

11

Side-stepping the Yemen Trap

At the end of an Arab League summit convened in Sharm el-Sheikh in Egypt on 29 March 2015, representatives of the Arab states announced the setting up of a joint Arab army to deal with the crises besetting the region, including the war in Yemen. Saudi Arabia's King Salman bin Abdulaziz, harassed by uprisings on the two north-south borders, was able to mobilize the League against what he perceived was Iran's strategic encirclement of the Gulf. A thoroughly shaken Saudi Arabia wanted its friends to come and participate in its war in Yemen where a minority Houthi tribe, supported by Iran, threatened to take over the country as the Saudi-supported Sunni tribes remained divided by their disputes. A realistic assessment of the threat felt by the Saudis also took account of the two anti-monarchy Sunni terrorist groups operating in Yemen: al-Qaeda and Islamic State.

The friends of Saudi Arabia heeded the call: according to the official Saudi Press Agency, Egypt, Jordan, Morocco, Sudan,

Qatar, Kuwait, Bahrain and the United Arab Emirates (UAE) agreed to take part in Operation Al-Hazm (Decisive) Storm, a sea-and-land invasion of Yemen to tame the Houthis and Sunni tribes allied to them. The Saudi-owned Al-Arabiya news channel said on 26 March, the UAE had sent thirty jet fighters to Saudi Arabia to take part in the air strikes against Yemen, while 'Jordan will be participating with six aircraft', adding significantly that 'Egypt and Pakistan will dispatch jet fighters and warships to take part in the campaign'. America, next door in Bahrain in the shape of its 5th Fleet, assured Saudis of 'logistical and intelligence support'.

Will Pakistan send its 'warships and jet-fighters'? On the morning of 26 March, the kingdom said it had attacked the Houthis inside Yemen 'to reinstate the legitimate government of President Abd Rabbo Mansour Hadi', the Saudi-backed President of Yemen who had replaced another Saudi-backed President, Ali Abdullah Saleh, a Houthi-baiter Sunni who has now turned to Houthis, backed by a fragment of Yemen's Sunni army. The air-attack focused on enemy positions in Sana'a, the Yemeni capital, including the airport, and the group's political headquarters. Did Pakistan send its F16s whose first batch was bought from the US with Saudi money in the 1990s? On 10 April, the Parliament in Islamabad in a joint session unanimously declared that Pakistan would fight 'shoulder to shoulder' with the people of Saudi Arabia if its territorial integrity was violated.

SOS: Send Army

On 26 March, the media in Pakistan reported that Prime Minister Nawaz Sharif had consulted his top defence and national security aides on the situation in Yemen and his meeting with Saudi Crown Prince Muqrin bin Abdulaziz earlier in the month—his third visit to Saudi Arabia this year—'to know about Pakistan's decision on kingdom's call for deployment'. Judging from past conduct, this meant Pakistan was hesitant about getting into this new war; but then a meeting attended by Defence Minister

Khawaja Asif, Foreign Policy Adviser Sartaj Aziz, Chief of the Army Staff General Raheel Sharif and Chief of the Air Staff Air Marshal Sohail Aman, issued the following one-liner: 'Any threat to Saudi Arabia's territorial integrity would evoke a strong response from Pakistan.' On 7 April, as if 'defending' Saudi Arabia on Pakistan's Iranian border, Pakistan's terrorist group Jais al-Adl claimed responsibility for attacking and killing eight Iranian border guards—Iran is backing the Houthis—followed by another two the same week.

Although meant to 'delimit' Pakistan's entry into the fray after the Iranian-backed Houthis had entered Saudi territory, the statement in Islamabad aroused intense polarized local reaction. Leading the opposition in Parliament, the PPP warned against 'getting burnt' in yet another war and was seconded by most other parties not too friendly with the ruling PMLN. But the clerical underworld of Pakistan was confessionally co bifurcated: the erstwhile anti-Iran Sipah-e-Sahaba, now naming itself Ahle Sunnatwal Jamaat (ASWJ), whose leader had recently dubbed all Shias as infidels in a recent TV programme, called upon the army to go to the defence of the Two Sacred Houses of Islam (the Urdu media often refers to Saudi Arabia in this way). Amin Shaheedi, leader of the euphemistically renamed Shia party, Majlis Wahdatul Muslimeen, pointedly recommended dousing the fires of violence in Pakistan instead of participating in the war in Yemen. Some pro-war leaders even presumed that Pakistan had joined the grand battle of Yemen. Hafiz Saeed, the most powerful and militant pro-Saudi cleric heading the largest religious formation Jamaatud Dawa, appealed to the government to send troops to defend Saudi Arabia against 'the intrigues of Israel and America'.

On 27 March, a rather nervous Defence Minister Khwaja Asif arose in the National Assembly to say: 'We have neither decided to commit forces to the conflict nor have considered it', only to get the rejoinder of opposition leader Khursheed Ahmed Shah that the government 'either convene a joint session of the two houses of Parliament or at least convene a meeting of the leadership of all political parties before taking a decision'. Asif's much reduced parting shot was that if there was a danger to Saudi Arabia's integrity then 'Pakistan will definitely defend it'.

Does Democracy Deter?

Rather than a direct refusal, the PMLN chose to use signs and tokens to indicate its unwillingness to participate in a war in Yemen. It was reluctant to send a clear message because the Kingdom would not understand it as being one of the 'shortcomings of democracy'. Democracy was never a hurdle in the past when Pakistan took unannounced favours from the House of Saud. Yet the map of currently ignited wars in the region was so confusing, that most leaders of the states pledging action in Yemen were scratching their heads over the lack of a clear definition of the enemy. Saudi Arabia has always loomed menacingly over Yemen to diffuse its own sense of insecurity 'from the south', but couldn't stop the Yemenis from falling to the lure of terrorism offered, first by al-Qaeda, then the Islamic State, the two Sunni, mutually contending, groups threatening the 'kingdom' of Saudi Arabia 'because it is not a caliphate'.

In the north, neighbouring Iraq was fighting the Sunni-supported Islamic State countered by Iranian generals leading Shia fighters on the ground. Its foremost security guarantor, the United States, its 5th Fleet ready after a $580-million base expansion in 2014, was actually thinking of getting cosy with an Iran which was stabbing Saudi Arabia in the back through Houthis who—to compound the confusion—were not even 'proper' Shia as their Zaidi faith would reduce them to a 'victim' minority had they lived in the Iran of today.

Evil Springs from Arab Springs

The United States and its Western allies were victims of their own confusion. Ideological blindness afflicted them again after the Iraq war of 2003 when the Arab Spring came around in 2013. They ignored the post-2003 warning delivered by American journalist Fareed Zakaria in his book, *The Future of Freedom: Illiberal Democracy at Home and Abroad*. The gist of his message was:

'Democracy is no panacea if it curtails liberty, maltreats the minorities with the assent of the majority population and punishes free thinking on the yardstick of nationalism. Under Tito, Yugoslavia was a dictatorship but it was liberal; after 1999, elections have tilted its divided society into more intolerance. Under Suharto, Indonesia was doing well economically and was tolerant, but after democratization it is economically worse off and socially intolerant. The prince in Kuwait wants women to have the right to vote but the elected parliament bans women from representation. Generally speaking, the monarchies and principalities in the Arab world have more features associated with a democratic society than the so-called republics. If elections were the only requirement, Iran would top the list of democracies, but it has no opposition and its footballers can't keep long hair just like the Taliban couldn't shave.'

The West was again spastic about the 'springs' of Egypt, Syria, Libya and Yemen. (It may be proved wrong even about Tunis after the growing inability of the elected moderate Tunisian parliament to stand up to the Salafi terrorists infesting the country, sending the largest batch of jihadists to beef up the Islamic State in Iraq.) Saudi Arabia put its money behind the West-supported anti-Assad rebels in Syria and was proved wrong after al-Qaeda went in and confused the battleground. It feared the growing Iranian clout in Iraq, Syria and Lebanon and sought to curtail Iranian financial outreach in the region by refusing to cut its oil production after the global recession in 2013, thus sharpening the bite of American sanctions on Iran.

Iran responded by soft-pedalling on its nuclear programme and got on the right side of the permanent members of the UN Security Council plus Germany, called P5+one, negotiating a nuclear restraint deal with Tehran. The Spiritual Leader in

Tehran, Ayatollah Khamenei, deftly adopted 'heroic flexibility of Imam Hassan'- rather than Imam Hussain—with his bomb and brandished a fatwa disallowing nuclear weapons under Islam—thus delegitimizing Pakistan's bomb—which annoyed Riyadh. Its Supreme Leader effected a deft course-correction. 1) He announced 'heroic flexibility' on the nuclear programme; 2) Declared through fatwa that Islam disallowed making of nuclear weapons; and 3) banned Iranians criticizing and saying negative things about the Caliphs of Islam preceding Ali in power. The Saudis achieved more clarity with Egypt by welcoming the military takeover, giving—together with the UAE—approximately $12 billion to its new ruling general. Everyone who didn't go with Saudi Arabia hasn't escaped some measure of inner regret, but the moral confusion of the regional conflicts it is fighting is confronting its beneficiary states with a dilemma as they face 'payback time'.

Shell-out Time: How Much?

Prime Minister Nawaz Sharif must chafe under the obligation of 'payback time' a little more than others in the Muslim world. He was rescued from his prison cell in 2000 serving a life sentence under General Musharraf and sheltered in a comfortable eight-year-long exile in Riyadh. In 2014, when Pakistan was nearing bankruptcy with only $2 billion in the kitty, the current king and then crown prince, Salman bin Abdulaziz, gifted him $1.5 billion. That year, more money was also pledged through Saudi purchase of Pakistani conventional weapons. The world will understand that Pakistan's democracy stood in the way of Pakistan's direct participation in the Yemen war but it will closely watch Prime Minister Sharif who is personally deeply beholden to the House of Saud.

The prime minister looked troubled on TV on his three visits to Saudi Arabia this year, but no one could fathom the seriousness of the challenge put before him. Once again, it was ex-CIA man

Bruce Riedel who got it right. Writing on the Al-Monitor website on 16 March, he stated, 'Saudi Arabia's campaign to build a broad Sunni alliance to contain Iran has apparently suffered at least a setback from Pakistan. Islamabad has opted, at least for now, to avoid becoming entangled in the sectarian cold war between Riyadh and Tehran.' It must have been tough to rebuff the King who had met him at the airport 'to underscore the importance of the talks' focusing on 'Iranian aggression in the Arab world and the impending deadline for the P5+1 negotiations on Iran's nuclear project'.

Sending battleships and aircraft was different from introducing subtle changes in policy, as Pakistan quietly did in connection with Syrian President Bashar al-Assad who was finally asked to step down by Pakistan last year, disconnecting from the Chinese policy of neutrality over the Syrian crisis. This time, however, the Foreign Office in Islamabad was firm about what Pakistan couldn't do. Spokesperson Tasneem Aslam denied the Houthis were backed by Iran: 'I have not seen anything [to indicate] that Iran is backing the rebels,' she told journalists at the weekly media briefing on 26 March. The 3000 Pakistanis in Yemen were asked to head home, which could be interpreted also as an indication of Pakistan eventually joining the war.

The commitment as it stood on 27 March was that Pakistan will mobilize if Saudi Arabia was penetrated by the Iranian-supported militias. Stratfor thought: 'If the al-Houthi successfully consolidate their power in Yemen, the southern Saudi provinces of Jizan and Najran will become vulnerable to al-Houthi expansion in the long run because of the significant Shiite-Ismaili populations that live there. Certainly the Iranians would welcome this outcome, influencing their support for the Zaidis. 'Saudi Arabia's own Sunni Yemenis in these provinces have a record of rebelling against the Saudi royalty till Riyadh was forced to take action against them. After Yemeni Osama bin Laden became an 'outlaw' in Saudi Arabia his top warriors were drawn from the southern provinces. Finally, of the nineteen-member al-Qaeda suicide squad that carried out the 9/11 attacks, eighteen were Yemenis.[1] Reports, according to Riedel, were that, 'Talking to Nawaz Sharif, Salman specifically wanted a Pakistani military contingent to deploy to the kingdom to help defend the vulnerable southwest border with Zaidi Houthi-controlled north Yemen and serve as a trip-wire force to deter Iranian aggression'.

Reflex Not Yet Pavlovian

Will Pakistan stick to the precedent of 'military assistance' of the past? In 1980, the UAE was inducted into a Gulf Cooperation Council (GCC) together with Bahrain, Kuwait, Oman, Qatar and Saudi Arabia, specifically to fend off the threat posed by across-the-Gulf attacks from 'Revolutionary' Iran. Saudi Arabia experienced its first Shia revolt in a long time in 1979, just after the Iranian Revolution. There was serious consideration given to GCC having a military defensive aspect to it. Pakistan was the most natural ally from outside the region: it had a large expatriate population working in the GCC states and had a tradition of sending military advisers to the Middle East. General Zia-ul-Haq was close to the Arabs on many counts, having served as a military attaché in the region. There were rumours in Pakistan in 1982 that the GCC states had threatened to expel all Pakistani workers if Pakistan refused to 'lend military teeth' to the GCC.[2]

Riedel wrote: 'There is precedent for a Pakistani army expeditionary force in Saudi Arabia. After the Iranian Revolution, Pakistani dictator Mohammad Zia-ul-Haq deployed an elite Pakistani armoured brigade to the kingdom at King Fahd's request to deter any threats to the country. In all, some 40,000 Pakistanis served in the brigade over most of a decade. Today only some Pakistani advisers and experts serve in the kingdom.'

Quite naively, General Zia then tried to play neutral in the Iran–Iraq war which had begun in 1980, and tried his peace-making with Imam Khomeini which went badly wrong. According to Vali Nasr in his book, *The Shia Revival: How Conflicts within Islam will Shape the Future*, Imam Khomeini treated the general to a diatribe of choice words. Subsequently, much was to go wrong with Iran–Pakistan relations in Afghanistan under the Pakistan-propped Taliban government in 1998 when six Iranian 'diplomats' were killed in Mazar-e-Sharif.

In 1991, when the Kingdom was threatened by Saddam Hussein from its border with Iraq, Pakistan sent troops to defend the Two Sacred Houses, but no one noted that it could also be a reaction, under Pakistan's secret defence agreement with the GCC, to the invasion of Kuwait by Iraq. No favours were one-sided. When Pakistan set up the Taliban in Kabul in 1996, Saudi Arabia and the UAE were the only states to recognize the savage regime. In 1998, Pakistan exploded its nuclear device and the only states to welcome the test were the same two friendly states. Then, when Pakistan was under sanctions because of the bomb, Saudi Arabia supplied it oil for free for three years. In 2011, when during the pro-democracy riots in Bahrain, Saudi Arabia sent in troops, many Pakistani ex-servicemen were inducted into the law-enforcement agencies there.

Courting Coy Pakistan

Why were the Pakistanis increasingly reluctant to go for the defence of the Two Sacred Houses in 2015? Clearly there is a growing tendency to stay neutral in a conflict perceived as a Muslim-versus-Muslim confrontation. Tens of thousands of lives were lost in Pakistan's sectarian war in the last two decades of the twentieth century; and the mayhem continues. A very tolerable level of Sunni-Shia tension was inherited by the country from the British Raj, but the two sects squared off violently only after 1980. Like all internecine conflicts, the war of the sects has been characterized by extreme cruelty. It coincided with the onset of the Islamic Revolution of Imam Khomeini in Iran and the threat its 'export' posed to Saudi Arabia and other Arab states across the Gulf.

Pakistanis invariably blame Saudi Arabia and Iran for the violence since they funded if not trained the partisans of this war. They are aware that Pakistan was subjected to someone else's 'relocated' war. Much of the internal dynamic of this war remains hidden from public view, which bows to the formulation that the West is setting Muslims against Muslims. A kind of embarrassment over the phenomenon of Muslim-killing-Muslim has prevented Pakistanis from inquiring frankly into how the two hostile states were able to transplant their conflict in Pakistan.

Pakistani Shia politician Syeda Abida Hussain writes in her memoir, *Power Failure*, that in 1990 after her dreaded Shia-killing political rival in Jhang, Punjab, who was the chief of the religious militia Sipah-e-Sahaba, Haq Nawaz Jhangvi, was killed by unknown assailants, she thought of a 'white-flag' meeting of condolence with Jhangvi's widow. Her brusque answer to the request to meet was: 'No need for you to come. You can recite SuraFateha on the phone; I do not need your assistance. My brother Osama bin Laden looks after all my needs. You must have heard of him. He is a very famous and rich Saudi, much richer than all of you kafirs put together.' Nobody knew bin Laden then but the Sipah clearly had support from Saudi Arabia. Hence, the growing opinion in 2015 to shun the Yemen war. The Voice of America on 20 January 2015 quoted on its website Pakistan's Federal Minister for Inter-Provincial Coordination, Riaz Hussain Pirzada, as saying that 'the Saudi government was creating instability across the Muslim world, including Pakistan, through funding aimed at promoting its ideology' and that 'it is time to stop the influx of Saudi money'.

Real Islam with the Saudi Riyal

But Pakistan is not entirely blameless. General Zia coming to power after toppling and killing the elected prime minister, Zulfikar Ali Bhutto, used hard Islam to roll Bhutto's 'socialism' back. An Islamic Summit in Lahore in 1974 had highlighted the ongoing tussle for Arab leadership between Saudi Arabia and Libya which Bhutto exploited, but lionized Libya's more radical President Gaddafi—also financially committed to Bhutto's nuclear enterprise—and ignored the Saudis. Lahore's Gaddafi Stadium reminds one of that fateful 'pivot'. Bhutto had also sought funds from Saudi Arabia and had paid back his debt to them by apostatizing Pakistan's Ahmadis. General Zia was in luck too. He had Iran on the wrong side of both America and Saudi Arabia and needed money given the post-Bhutto state of the national treasury.

Saudi Arabia asked for the enforcement of zakat in Pakistan, the 2.5 per cent 'poor due' collected from all earning Muslims from their money and assets. King Feisal gave Zia the 'seed-money' to start the zakat system in Pakistan with the condition that a part of it go to the Wahhabi party called Ahle Hadith in Pakistan. Since most of the Ahle Hadith (Wahhabi) parties were headquartered in Lyallpur in Punjab, Zia renamed it Faisalabad. Zia lost no time in signing the Zakat and Ushr Ordinance (1980). Shockingly the framing of the law came from an Arab jurist, Dr Maruf Dualibi, 'specially detailed by the Government of Saudi Arabia' who sat in the Council of Islamic Ideology in Islamabad and imposed the tax on the Shia who have historically paid their parallel tax *khums* at 5 per cent to their own institutions and not to the state, thus touching off the first Shia public protest in Pakistan that year.[3]

Zia encouraged the clergy to open more seminaries to receive Rs 50,000 each immediately from the Zakat Fund he had started, courtesy the Saudis. In a matter of months hundreds of new seminaries cropped up—some of them just signboards— on the Lahore-Islamabad highway, to net the funds being doled out. The distribution of zakat was suitably reinterpreted as it did not allow payments to institutions. The Sunni madrasas increased from 401 in 1960, when Pakistan remained secular in governance, to 1745 in 1979, when ideology was emphasized and was finally enforced in the form of sharia in two years of General Zia's government!

During the Saudi-Iranian standoff in 1980, Pakistan was drawn to the Saudi side for a number of reasons. It had a large expatriate labour force stationed in the Arab Middle East, particularly in the region of the Gulf where the Gulf Cooperation Council (GCC) was formed in 1981 to ward off the Iranian threat. Almost 80 per cent of Pakistan's 'foreign remittances' were earned from this region. Saudi Arabia was also the most important ally—after the United States—in 'frontline' Pakistan's war against the Soviet Union in the 1980s. Saudi Arabia funded the jihad, it bought Pakistan its first instalment of the forty F-16 warplanes from the United States, it gave Pakistan the seed-money for its Zakat Fund which in 2008 stood at almost Rs 12 billion annually to be distributed among the poor but which went predominantly to the seminaries during the 1980s. Saudi Arabia allowed Pakistan to buy Saudi oil on 'deferred payment' which was deferred only in name as it meant free oil. The Islamization of Pakistan under the military ruler General Zia-ul-Haq proceeded under the tutelage of Saudi Arabia.

It is not possible to examine the Saudi-Iranian conflict exclusively in a non-sectarian perspective. The schism was reflected in the Afghan jihad, but after the jihad ended, it was reflected in the ouster, from the first government-in-exile, of mujahideen belonging to the Shia militias. The Afghan mujahideen government was set up in Peshawar in 1989, but, under Saudi pressure, the Shia militias were not given representation in it. The rise of the Taliban in 1996, quickly recognized by Saudi Arabia and Pakistan, was in a way a reversal of Iran at Saudi hands in the final count. The Taliban were recruited from the Deobandi and Wahhabi outfits, which were historically anti-Shia.

The Saudis also set up an International Islamic University for Islamabad with money decreed by the Saudi king to consolidate the growing involvement of Pakistan with hadith-based dogmatic Islam. This was the university where the intellectual founder of al-Qaeda, Abdullah Azzam, was to locate himself as a teacher. Azzam was killed in Peshawar where he had established al-Qaeda's first office because he disagreed with bin Laden's favourite al-Zawahiri over killing Muslims in the war against America and the West. Mullah Krekar, a Kurd from Turkey who 'exported' terror from Pakistan and is now in Norway as an asylum-seeker, also taught at the university. In 2009, the university was suicide-bombed, killing three students and injuring scores, after the PPP government tried to 'liberalize' it. Zia was rewarded with a multi-million-dollar mausoleum by Saudi Arabia, rivalling that of the founder of the nation, Quaid-e-Azam Mohammad Ali Jinnah, in Karachi.

Game-changing Gas from Iran

From the nadir of relations with Pakistan during the 1980s, Iran tried a radical eastward approach that would have changed Iran itself: the offer of a gas pipeline to Pakistan that would connect with India and China. In the following decade, Pakistan alternated between pro-Saudi and pro-Iran governments of the PMLN and PPP, and the project kept getting snagged till it collapsed under American sanctions, and the $7.5 billion, 1600-km-long pipeline became stalled. Mindful of eastward isolation but open to India and China because of the 'exceptions' granted to them under sanctions, Iran kept building its side of it and completed it in 2013 when President Zardari committed to President Ahmadinezhad that Pakistan would complete its side of it. Iran offered $500 million, or a third of the estimated $1.5 billion cost of the 750-km Pakistani section of the pipeline. When nothing moved under the government of Nawaz Sharif in December 2014, Pakistan was to start paying $200 million a month for not buying Iranian gas, but Iran waived the fine.

In 2015, the crunch-time was back and Pakistan had to choose once again between Saudi Arabia and Iran. Internally, the country was disinclined to fight on the side of Saudi Arabia if the Yemen war escalated, barring the hard-line clerical organizations enjoying power leverage over the state because of private Arab handouts. But since the war-front in the Middle East was confused, Pakistan's dilemma was further complicated. What if Iran clinched a deal with the West over its nuclear programme and was freed of sanctions? Pakistan's geopolitical interest would incline it to restart the 'game-changer' Iranian pipeline at the risk of alienating the Gulf powers in the GCC from where 3 million expat Pakistanis send over most of the $13 billion as remittances annually because they can't own businesses there. The regional strategic trap remained open and Pakistan was obviously not strong enough to sidestep it.

The Secret Treaty

Finally, on 19 April 2015, Finance Minister Ishaq Dar, who is related to Prime Minister Nawaz Sharif, went ahead and revealed something that was not generally known. He said in a briefing in Washington: 'Pakistan and Saudi Arabia had signed a military protocol in 1982, which entitles the kingdom to seek Pakistani troops.' He disarmed reporters who had pointed out that '$13.3 billion in the last nine months' as remittances from expat Pakistanis could be jeopardized if the GCC states decided to expel them. A UAE minister had warned Pakistan that if it didn't come to help in the Yemen war 'it will pay a heavy price'. On 21 April, the Arab bombing of Yemen Houthis had come to a halt.

People in Pakistan obviously didn't know about the 'defence protocol' because a question had been raised in the joint session of Parliament about it in March, members demanding to know the details of such an agreement 'if it existed'.

It is not possible to know from Mr Dar's comment if the 'protocol' was actually signed with Saudi Arabia as he claimed or with the Gulf Cooperation Council of which Saudi Arabia is a member. It was formed in 1981 in response to the 'Iranian threat'. It is quite possible that Pakistan had agreed, under pressure some say, to provide 'military teeth' to the GCC. This happened under the military ruler General Zia-ul-Haq who was close to the Arabs, having served as a military attaché in the region.

While clearly an ally of Saudi Arabia, Zia was inclined to be neutral in the developing Iran–Arab confrontation. There were rumours in Pakistan in 1982 that the GCC states had threatened to expel all Pakistani workers if Pakistan refused to 'lend military teeth' to the GCC. There is very little on record because of the extreme caution exercised by the rulers of the UAE. Most books on the Gulf States discuss the GCC as a harmless organization, but a clearer indication of what was at stake is indicated by Christopher M. Davidson in his book, *The United Arab Emirates: A Study in Survival*. According to him the plan for an anti-Iran axis existed up until 2001: 'Until 11 September 2001, many of the strongly anti-Iranian emirates had favoured a "Sunni axis" comprising the UAE, Saudi Arabia, Pakistan, and the Afghan Taliban, in an effort to curb potential Shia expansion.' The author footnoted that his information had come from 'personal interviews, undisclosed locations, 2003'.

12

Who Needs 'Big' Leaders?

Leader of the second largest political party by popular vote, Imran Khan said in Lahore on 10 April 2014 that Pakistan needed big leaders capable of taking big decisions. He referred to Mandela and Jinnah as leaders who brought about great changes in their polities. He was certainly referring to 'vision' too because that is considered the prescription for change in the Third World facing an international order where the rules are firmly set against radical change.

This discussion is not meant to denigrate Imran Khan whose hospitals and a university are solid achievements, but to reflect on what criterion the people have on which to judge leaders and what is meant by 'big decisions' that they presumably demand. Is the case for big leaders beyond dispute or do we simply need to revisit a twentieth-century view of governance? After stubbing their toes in a vast number of cases, do the developing states need 'big' leaders with hard-hitting defiant programs, or 'average' leaders obedient to laws laid down in the constitution and dictated by the global economic order which they can't defy?

Big leaders have done big things in the last century. They called for self-determination for enslaved nations and got the people out on the streets using violence and non-violent civil disobedience to bring down the colonial structures set up to exploit communities not yet evolved enough socially and politically. They led them on long marches and made them die in their millions to actualize the utopias they wished to replace colonialism with. The same century ended with a firmly established global order under the United Nations and more or less uniform economic principles, deviation from which was less plausible than in the beginning of the century.

Is the state in the twenty-first century ready for the 'big change' with revolutionary overtones? Does the state really want fundamental change or simply a higher degree of observance of the law it has laid down, remaining a little this side of utopia that requires punishment beyond the endurance of the people? Most 'great' leaders committed themselves to big change 'for the sake of the common man' and ended up being excessively 'confiscatory' towards the rich—whose wealth had a way of disappearing into the interconnected global economy—while imposing 'equality' on their nations.

'Big' Is Subjective

Certain subjective yardsticks tend to become dangerous when used unconsciously by people to assess the 'big leader'. Above all, it is the narrative of nationalism—always unrealistic and flecked with the intent of war—which confers on politicians the big-leader halo. More often, this concentrates the leader's mind on weapons and less on the economy. People hail the making of a nuclear bomb but treat shabbily the 'big' leader once the economy starts reacting badly to the bomb. People promise stoicism in the face of global hostility in a moment of nationalist spasm, but no one sticks to belt-tightening for long.

Imran Khan referred to Mandela and Jinnah as big leaders. He is right because neither wanted war. Mandela didn't want revenge for apartheid and Jinnah didn't want to fight India and wanted the kind of normalization we want today after fighting useless and self-damaging wars. Mandela was proved right while still alive; we had to 'reinterpret' Jinnah to justify going to war with India time and again.

But nationalism is the resort of the non-intellectual. One recent example is the 'popular' 2012 decision taken by the Pakistan Cricket Board to defy the 'big three' attempt to control international cricket. Then-chairman Zaka Ashraf leaning on the 'big leader' myth thought international isolation wouldn't hurt if he grabbed the emotional appeal of opposing India, a country that single-handedly supports cricket with big money. The media worked itself up in an anti-India frenzy and supported Ashraf's decision to virtually sideline 'honour-driven' Pakistan in international competitions with nothing in the PCB's kitty. Funnily, when the PCB ate its words and rejoined the big three (Australia, India, England) together with the entire cricketing world, the media reached down into the dark recesses of nationalism to make sarcastic comment on this 'nikah' (wedlock) of regret.

In our day, the weakened state gave birth to 'big' institutional leaders not conforming to the yardstick of popular election. A judge with the bob-nailed bludgeon of 'public interest litigation' in his hand can make the imperfect executive of a Third World state crawl. The suo motu judge can actually become a national leader without being elected by the people. He can appear to the public as the righteous man questioning high prices and dragging the bureaucracy into the court to answer questions only a professional economist should frame.

Poison of Economic Populism

One judge, enveloped in the murky wake of the retired judicial-aggressor chief justice, Iftikhar Muhammad Chaudhry, let loose a broadside on the economy: 'The dogs of rulers eat marmalade . . .

if you can't give inexpensive flour to the poor, give them rat-killing pills.' He made familiar reference to the 'Islamic welfare state' that is supposed to succour the poor. Instant populism, just heat a little and serve. He forgot that thousands of special shops, called Utility Stores, selling controlled-rate flour to citizens, have made shipwrecks. Price control mechanisms have failed all over the world. The last resort is state subsidy whose negative fallout redoubles the suffering of the masses supposed to benefit from the 'welfare' state. The judge was reminded that Pakistan already spends Rs 40 billion on 'flour subsidy' which sadly benefits not so much Pakistan as the regional food market extending to Afghanistan and Central Asia. The state frontier is not guarded enough—by reason of proxy war exigencies—to contain the effect of subsidy within Pakistan.

The vision of 'big change' must be pronounced as being for the benefit of the masses. In other words, it must be pledged that goods of daily use will become cheap, the wages will go up, and the exploitative classes will be squeezed and forced to disgorge their illegal riches through confiscatory reforms to enable the poor to become better-off. President Hollande of France did the bidding of the French voter unwilling to take the rough ride of a slipping economy, and is today hiding from his angry supporters, consoling himself with love affairs. The big leader falls with the fall of the big decisions taken by him. Pakistani leaders should take time off from the Bolivarian revolt of South America to focus on the 'chavizmo' of Venezuela's leader-of-the-poor, the late Hugo Chavez who presided over a state with the largest oil reserves in the world and left it bankrupt with the poor agitating in front of shops with empty shelves in 2015.

As Alan Greenspan stated, 'The practitioners of economic populism are clear about the specific grievances to be addressed; but their prescriptions are vague. Unlike capitalism or socialism, economic populism does not bring with it a formalized analysis of the conditions necessary for the creation of wealth and rising standards of living. It is far from cerebral. It is more a shout of pain. Populist leaders offer unequivocal promises to remedy perceived injustices.'[1]

If 'pleasing the people' is the only criterion, then going to war or pretending to go to war or simulating outrage and bad-mouthing states you can do nothing about, is the playbook for you. An unsmiling 'shouting' leader dying for a dose of isolationism teaches the masses to be morally outraged about causes of anguish lying outside the state. He attains size by taking on outsize enemies. If he does a good job of it, he can become a prophet. Chavez led into bankruptcy a country that earned $20 billion a year from its oil when he could have dealt with 'rascally' America profitably with the lesser charms of a small leader.

~

Imam Khomeini read the mind of his people—those who thought differently had fled Iran—and challenged the neighbourhood. He also challenged America and besieged the US embassy in Tehran for over a year for the emotional satisfaction of the Iranian masses. What he earned for his oil-rich state was global isolation, which is another name for defeat. After him, President Ahmadinejad thought he could retain the popular adulation showered on Imam Khomeini but ended up hurting the national economy: oil exports down by 60 per cent and currency down by 90 per cent in value. Even the authoritarian fiat of the Supreme Leader could not prevent the rise to power of a moderate president whose ticket is 'normal' rather than 'big' leadership.

The big dilemma of the modern third world state is the economy which functions only when unsullied by populism. You can get away with some populism if you are a global hegemon, but as a third-world growth-challenged state you have to live with incremental adjustments within the global template. If you grow rapidly, be prepared to face the rich–poor gap like India and not succumb to the economics of subsidy like India. Pakistan has had its big leaders. And we have had their big decisions too.

Looking back, it appears we are hurt more grievously by the big leaders and their big decisions. Small leaders—we can call them 'normal leaders'—have hurt us less because they lived within the system, tinkered with it realistically without upsetting it, and were appreciated in hindsight. This applies to most countries, especially in the West where the systems are settled and would be endangered by 'big leaders' if people elected them.

Global Order versus 'Big Leader'

The international order today preordains far more internal change in the state than in the past. If you impose too much religion leading to violation of human rights you can be isolated like Iran, which is another way of saying you are punished for doing something your people want. If you impose too many non-tariff barriers to 'protect' the masses, you are shunned globally and made to suffer economically for lack of foreign investment. Once you become economically wobbly, you are placed under IMF conditionality which you have already dubbed 'begging-bowl diplomacy' to capture the popular vote. You can become a big leader by defying the IMF but the masses will suffer the consequences of this defiance.

The hate-India Pakistani leader went down just as the hate-America leader will go down. Sabre-rattling was tried by civilian leaders and they were knocked over by military dictators who took seriously the popular textbook battle-cry but came to grief and, at times, faced treason trials for their pains. Living within the global template of status quo is the only way to live and flourish in our times.

This applies to India too. Ex-foreign minister Jaswant Singh in his book, *India at Risk,* laments that 'ersatz pacifist' Nehru didn't fight China properly in 1962 'and security got relegated to a much lower priority'. In consequence, independent India simply abandoned the 'centrality of strategic culture as the first ingredient of vigorous and bold national policies'. Nehru didn't fight properly, but has that hurt India? Pakistan fought India 'properly' and has got badly hurt.[2]

Pakistan had big leaders who fought India and gave the people 'strategic culture' that Singh wants for India. Thanks to these big leaders, Pakistanis are still not able to start trading with India to improve their lives. Jaswant Singh should recall his BJP colleague—and somewhat of a namesake, foreign minister Yashwant Sinha—who actually told Pakistan in 2003 that by not being 'revisionist' towards China, India had benefited economically through trade. He had said: 'I hope our western neighbour [Pakistan] will not keep its eyes forever shut to this truth.' Nehru was probably right not taking on China. And the smaller leaders that followed him were right not letting India become 'revisionist', forever locked in conflict like Pakistan while the economy went belly-up. But Nehru is not big anymore in the eyes of those who want India to come out of its 'Nehruvian model' of growth. They say when India kicked it in the early 1990s it began alleviating poverty, raising 300 million above the poverty-line.

The 'big leader' label doesn't stick either. President George W. Bush thought he could become the big leader like Reagan—who destroyed the Soviet Union!—by spreading democracy through regime-change, using overwhelming high-tech military force. He had at his back the Chicago philosophers of neo-conservatism, Leo Strauss and Albert Wohlstetter, and their pupils in Secretary of Defence Paul Wolfowitz, Vice President Richard Cheney, and Chairman of the Defence Policy Board Advisory Committee, Richard Perle. The intellectual ballast behind the neocons was substantial. Today Bush is not hailed by the world as a 'big' leader.

Endangered by 'Vision'

Small leaders don't need any 'visions' either. Everything is spelled out in the constitution and in international law. The global community secures the international order by punishing Pakistan for fighting proxy wars, no matter how popular they are with the people of Pakistan. Judging from past reversals, Pakistani leaders should be 'small' rather than 'big' and they should be prevented from having 'visions'. Above all, 'hate America' or 'hate any state' should be outlawed as slogans as they corrupt the mind of the expat Pakistani who runs the risk of become a deportable pariah.

When we moan about lack of great leadership we actually complain of lack of a death-wish vision. We want our leaders to be 'visionary'. There is something about the word 'vision' that is charismatic. Is it kosher to talk about vision without understanding what we mean by it? Especially, what do we demand of our political leader when we insist that he have a vision? Is it just another name for 'programme' or 'party manifesto'? We know what these two documents stand for in popular speech when they are likened to excrement.

One thing is certain. Vision relates to the future. It is embedded in human memory. It recalls the prophets and seers of ancient history. At some level in our subconscious, we attach the divine with the great leader. Do we want a Gilgamesh? But the desire for a greatly manipulative leader representing the power of good is there. Before the world became interdependent and free trade made it subservient to the same laws handed down by the World Bank, the IMF, WTO and other lending institutions, the vision was essentially a map of conquest and domination. Vision is also the undying longing for utopia. Most constitutions pledge all sorts of welfare-state conditions like 'roti, *kapra* and *makan*'; but when we go to the Supreme Court demanding that the government in power make them happen we get the answer: these pledges are things to aspire to, not a precondition of governance.

Europe got tired of big leaders after suffering a number of punitive wars in the twentieth century and thought up a clever device to cut them down to size by adopting proportional representation. PR today means 'less government' but what it really aims at is the near-impossibility of a majoritarian government almost always led by a great 'visionary' leader. India didn't think of it but has been visited by a variable device called 'coalition government' since 1989. No matter what the 'big leader' does, he can't impose his 'big vision' on the country. The downside of course is the possibility of the demise of the global economic template that could lift India from the subsidy-led cycle of low growth. If the BJP leader Narendra Modi decides to have his vision—in fact he is the scandalously visionless free trade man—India will be in trouble.

Vision and Its Punishment

A great leader has to promise utopia to persuade the masses to submit to his leadership. In India, Nehru's vision was a left-wing controlled economy making things easy for the poor masses. It didn't work. What worked was the non-utopian non-vision of Manmohan Singh who came from an international organization actually set up to kill visions. The truth is, all the laws are in place for the internal and external management of the state. The economist is now found everywhere trundling out his macro-economic prescriptions that no one can question: collect income tax, provide law and order, don't fall to the lure of high tariffs or non-tariff barriers, avoid international isolation no matter how 'heroic' it is, and don't go to war, no matter what.

Vision is dead. So if the PPP says it will give roti, kapra and makan, no one takes it seriously. But when Bhutto gave us this vision we swallowed it. His follow-up was nationalization which went badly wrong. Muslims have to be utopian because of the vision of the city-state which is a part of their sharia. The irreducible programme that emerges from it is the welfare (falahi) state that Imran Khan too is presenting as his vision. On the ground, it means a lot of subsidizing that the IMF will not allow or your trading partners will not accept. Vision is either followed by regimentation and tyranny or economic disaster. The big leader is more likely to unleash this tyranny—which could be actually consensual because of his charisma—while the ordinary forgettable leader will accept safe prescriptions and leave behind a viable state.

After the emergence of an interdependent world with an agreed body of laws about economic behaviour, the West is not supposed to have great 'visionary' leaders. The nation-state with its warrior leaders is no longer required. Populism based on vision is dead too. Paunchy central bankers growling over public spending are more acceptable. Let's not demand vision. Let's demand that prosaic recipes like law and order and writ of the state be applied, that taxation be taken seriously and impunity either on the basis of religion or sheer extra-legal power is removed. Follow Lee Kuan Yew, the non-visionary model ruler of today. For Pakistan, no vision is required. In fact some of the vision that we embraced at independence about what kind of state we would build should be modified. Let's not demand vision from our leaders. Let's not have 'big' leaders with 'big' decisions that take their toll on the lives of the people.

13

Seven Furies that Torment Pakistan

Pakistan's policy of covert wars—much strengthened by the 'deniable' international military effort against the Soviet Union in Afghanistan during the 1980s—resulted in the country following contradictory strategies. The post-Soviet era saw elected governments in Pakistan struggling to pull Pakistan back into normality but found the non-state actors of Afghan jihad too strong to tame. While handling the non-state actors caused institutional splits, more dangerously, there were cases of 'reverse indoctrination' that challenged the state from within.

Pakistan tried to become 'normal' by partially reverting to democracy in 1985. All the state institutions were not yet ready to allow a radical shift to representation, which resulted in 'restraints' on civilian rulers that sadly continued into 2014. The 1990s saw the politicians toppling each other from power till 1999 when even this process couldn't save normal governance. Thus began a period of ambivalence that caused the military leadership of

President General Musharraf to experience the double jeopardy of dissimulation at the global level and a dangerous tendency of subversion of Pakistan's internal sovereignty.

Strangely, Pakistan was reported upon by a bunch of foreign journalists treading dangerously through the late 1980s when the military still called the shots and the indigenous media was not entirely free. Interestingly, the most notable foreign journalists in these years were all women. Their reporting tended to reveal aspects of the state that male reporters somehow couldn't get access to. One 'lady reporter' actually got attached to the army as 'military historian' and ended up writing a most revealing 'insider' account of the army's dealings with the Taliban terrorists.

Emma Duncan of *The Economist* went through the perilous times of the late 1980s and was the first to produce insights in her book, *Breaking the Curfew,* that most upset Pakistanis. She was followed by the *Sunday Times*'s Christina Lamb who was actually expelled from Pakistan for displeasing the institution whose anger the ruling PPP could not resist. (The Liberal PPP is resilient in the face of non-state actors and the Taliban, which develops into walking in lockstep with the army more than the right-wing PML-Nawaz is prepared to do.) She was followed by the London *Times'* Carey Schofield, Kathy Gannon of the Associated Press, Kim Barker of the *Chicago Tribune* and, given her book that uncovered the same sort of characteristics of the protean state, Benazir Bhutto. The latest entry into this list of seven furies gnawing at the vitals of Pakistan for its ongoing hubris is Carlotta Gall of the *New York Times* whose book was given a curtain-raiser *What Pakistan Knew About Bin Laden* published in the *NYT* on 19 March 2013.

Carlotta Gall: She Has the Gall

Carlotta Gall made the mistake of scanning Quetta—for her pains she got slapped on the face by an officer—during the period General Musharraf was leaping through hoops to hide the Taliban government-in-exile known as Quetta Shura. (Declan Walsh, reporting for the *Independent* and the *Guardian* of London, was the latest man ousted for reporting too close to the well-known truth.) Gall, writing of the madrasas of Quetta, quotes a Pashtun leader: 'The madrasas were a cover, a camouflage. Behind the curtain, hidden in the shadows, lurked the ISI. The Pakistani government, under President Musharraf and his intelligence chief, Lt General Ashfaq Parvez Kayani, was maintaining and protecting the Taliban, both to control the many groups of militants now lodged in the country and to use them as a proxy force to gain leverage over and eventually dominate Afghanistan.'

But what has angered the establishment and the TV chat-show anchors most is her revelation that the Pakistan army actually knew that Osama bin Laden was living in a safe house in Abbottabad. Wisely, the government didn't react despite challenges from Urdu journalists who demanded that the US ambassador be called and rebuked officially. It was enough officially to recall that Washington had accepted the position taken by Islamabad that neither the army chief, General Kayani, nor the ISI chief, General Pasha, knew about the whereabouts of bin Laden. Also, Peter Bergen, author of many books on bin Laden, claims that all top officials from the US government with access to the best intelligence on OBL told him that Pakistani officialdom knew nothing about his presence in Abbottabad.

What hurt Pakistan eventually was Gall's claim: 'Only one man, a former ISI chief and retired general, Ziauddin Butt, told me that he thought Musharraf had arranged to hide bin Laden in Abbottabad.' Butt was no ordinary officer. He was the first head of the army's Strategic Plans Division which controls nuclear weapons and Prime Minister Nawaz Sharif made him Director General of the ISI in 1997 and promoted him to army chief in 1999 after dismissing Army Chief General Musharraf, which led to the overthrow of the Sharif government. As noted by the *News* on 22 March, he was quoted on the Jamestown Foundation website as saying: 'Osama bin Laden was kept in Abbottabad under the instructions of Intelligence Bureau Director Brigadier Ijaz Shah.'[1]

He added for good measure that Shah was also responsible for hiding Omar Saeed Sheikh 'who had killed journalist Daniel Pearl', adding that 'Prime Minister Nawaz Sharif had set up a ninety-man commando team to track and kill Osama bin Laden but it was disbanded after he was ousted in a military coup.'

Emma Duncan: The First Fury

Emma Duncan's *Breaking the Curfew: A Political Journey Through Pakistan* offended a Pakistan still unfamiliar with media freedom. She took readers on a journey into 'the murkier side of Pakistani society—its banditry, its lucrative drug trafficking and arms smuggling, and its efficient, corrupt civil service, which cuts red tape to keep the government viable'. She reported sympathetically on people suffering the wrath of a security state struggling with freedom of expression. Najam Sethi, in and out of jail, recalled her coverage of what happened to him after he published books the government didn't like: 'General Zia-ul-Haq didn't like me. I had published *From Jinnah to Zia* by Justice Mohammad Munir (retd) after every major publisher in the country had turned it down because it was overly critical of the dictator. After the author's death a couple of years later, a khaki emissary advised me to quietly withdraw the book from sale. "You can ban it," I had demurred.

'Then I published a book on US–Pak relations whose cover was taken from a painting by the famous artist Mian Ijazul Hasan. It showed the US Aid emblem in which there are two clasped hands in friendship, except that Mian Ijaz had rendered one of the hands as a skeleton and squeezed a drop of blood out of it.'

Duncan's coverage of Sethi's ordeals in jail didn't help much: later, in the 1990s he got into trouble again with Prime Minister Nawaz Sharif and was 'picked up' as a traitor and subjected to 'questioning' by Pakistan's notoriously sadist intelligence sleuths.

'One of the central figures in the country in the past couple of decades' told her: 'There are two sorts of nations, he said, those rooted in the soil, and those rooted in the ideas. India belongs to the first category; it has grown gradually out of things that have happened to a particular bit of earth. When Nehru died, he asked for his ashes to be scattered over his native soil. Pakistan, on the other hand, was created by descendants of people who thundered into the area from Tashkent, Afghanistan, Iran, Saudi Arabia, with a sword in one hand, the Koran in the other, and an idea in their heads—an idea of conquest, expansion, or conversion.'

She couldn't have realized that the championship of the ideas that Pakistan wished to uphold would shift from the state to the Taliban whom it had declared outlaw.

Christina Lamb: Who Wouldn't Go Away

While Christina Lamb reported for the *Financial Times*, she was asked to leave Pakistan for having discovered the nexus between the military and the mullah; and the notice of extradition was served by the government of Benazir Bhutto, whom she had interviewed in London in 1987, and whose wedding she had been invited to in Pakistan later that year. From here, she began her life as a foreign correspondent in Pakistan, journeying through Kashmir and along the frontiers of neighbouring Afghanistan, a place where the mujahideen were fighting the Soviet 'occupiers'. She interviewed and became good friends with many in the local community including future Afghan President Hamid Karzai. She was deported because she had offended the ISI. She then wrote *Waiting for Allah: Benazir Bhutto and Pakistan*.

In October 2007, Lamb was back in Pakistan, part of Benazir Bhutto's campaign bus in Karachi, only to see dozens of Bhutto's supporters killed by two suicide bombers. Bhutto survived but died two months later on the second attempt in Rawalpindi. Lamb received an OBE and was named 'Foreign Correspondent of the Year' by the British Press Awards and Foreign Press Association for

her reporting from Pakistan and Afghanistan in the *Sunday Telegraph*
following 9/11. As if that was not enough of a provocation, in
2013 she co-authored the autobiography of Malala Yousafzai, *I
Am Malala: The Girl who stood up for Education and was shot by
the Taliban.* Today the national consensus is against Malala, and
Lamb is a universal persona non grata, having flagged the extent to
which Pakistan is blindsided by the Islamic persuasion of terror.

Lamb focused on the ISI chief Hamid Gul quite a lot. Why
had the Taliban collapsed so easily after 9/11, she asked him? 'It's
not over,' he replied. 'The Russians lost in ten years, the Americans
will lose in five. They are chocolate cream soldiers.'

Her verdict on Gul: 'The more he is proved wrong the stronger
he becomes by reason of his Muslim strategy of *dattjanachahiyay*
(never give up). General Pervez Musharraf is the villain of the piece.
He doesn't adhere to the Tariq bin Ziad syndrome that forms the
centre-piece of Hamid Gul's frozen worldview.'

She also defines the mind of Pakistan: 'There is dishonour
in being as cunning as the Hindus next door. Being brave—and
achieving its adjunct, isolation—is the mark of the warrior that
Hamid Gul continues to portray. Defeat and repeated falsification
of strategic claims are the badges the nation wants him to wear.'

Kathy Gannon: Double-game Origins

Kathy Gannon was the Associated Press correspondent in Pakistan
and Afghanistan from 1986 to 2005 when Pakistan was managing
two Afghan wars and their two blowbacks and allowing the
Pakistani mind to be formed in the light of its policy meanders.
Her book, '*I' is for Infidel: from Holy War to Holy Terror, 18
Years inside Afghanistan,* tells a nuanced eyewitness story of what
happened in Afghanistan.

Gannon's main source on Pakistan's dealings with Mullah
Omar was Mullah Muhammad Khaksar when he had been
demoted from the job of intelligence chief—and Mullah Omar's
constant companion—in the Taliban government in 1999. He

saw Mullah Omar being flattered by Pakistani clerics as the True Caliph in 1994 and was put off to see that Mullah Omar was being seduced out of his normal humble character by it.

Mullah Omar was too witless to understand that he was making a dishonest use of the Holy Cloak just like King Amanullah before him. If Amanullah disclaimed something (modernism) through the cloak, Mullah Omar claimed it (tradition); but both did the insincere thing for which they were punished. Isolation came because of Mullah Omar's hubris and unfortunately the Holy Cloak caused it.

Gannon tells us that the clerics who were sent by the ISI to greet Mullah Omar are well known and their remarks about the man can still be collected from the Urdu press of those days. They compared him to the Prophet and Caliph Umar to his face and came home saying the Caliphate of the Companions had been revived. A retired chief justice went to see him after growing a flowing beard on his face. A very popular TV cleric predicted that under Mullah Omar the army of Imam Mehdi was taking shape, who will soon conquer the world with it and Islamize it.

Mullah Khaksar told Gannon that Mullah Omar didn't know Osama bin Laden before he arrived from Sudan in 1996 but was given, in Jalalabad, into the safe hands of warlord Maulvi Yunus Khalis by the ISI. Bin Laden himself courted Umar with a wheedling letter which worked; he loved being flattered. They met finally after the Taliban had captured Kabul. Gannon tells us how the Taliban began by securing the Bamiyan Buddhas against vandalism by issuing edicts from Mullah Omar describing them as Afghanistan's cultural heritage in 1999. In 2001 Osama bribed Umar's deputy prime minister and defence minister into convincing him to issue another edict for their destruction!

Pakistan's ISI chief General Mahmood Ahmad was in Washington when Osama struck his US targets on 11 September 2001. He is supposed to have accepted President Bush's 'terms' in consultation with General Musharraf back home. Washington told Musharraf to tell Mullah Omar to hand Osama over to the

US or be prepared to be invaded. General Mahmood Ahmad was asked to go to Kandahar together with a group of hard-core clerics from Pakistan and do the persuasion.

Gannon writes: 'The general was a religious zealot very much like Mullah Omar. He had been central to the military takeover of Pakistan in 1999 by General Pervez Musharraf. A hawk with pan-Islamic visions, he had been a staunch supporter of jihadis both from Pakistan and elsewhere. This was the man Musharraf sent to negotiate with Mullah Omar.

'People present at the meeting and within the ISI revealed that General Ahmad had a message for Mullah Omar quite different from the one that Washington had pressed his government to convey. He took the slow-talking leader aside and urged him to resist the United States. He told Mullah Omar not to give up bin Laden. General Ahmad travelled several times to Kandahar, and on each visit he gave Mullah Omar information about the likely next move by the United States.

'By then General Ahmad knew there weren't going to be a lot of US soldiers on the ground. He warned Mullah Omar that the United States would be relying heavily on aerial bombardment and on the Northern Alliance . . . Neither Osama bin Laden nor Pakistan's ISI chief explained to him the extent of the devastation that would be linked to his name and his movement.'

Carey Schofield: The Inside Track

Carey Schofield who was for a time attached to the combat formations of the Pakistan army as a military historian, in her book, *Inside the Pakistan Army: A woman's Experience on the Frontline of the War on Terror,* gives us the following account of the authority of corps commander Peshawar, General Hamid Khan:

'In May 2006 the retired General Muhammad Ali Jan Aurakzai was appointed Governor of the North West Frontier Province. In September he struck a deal, at a Grand Jirga in Miramshah, with the Utmanzai Wazirs. Maulana Gul Bahadur Khan and

Maulana Sadiq Noor, key Taliban commanders in North Waziristan, were party to this deal. Jalaluddin Haqqani of the Haqqani Network and Tahir Yuldashev of the Uzbek IMU were also present when it was signed. Under this agreement, known as the Waziristan Accord, the Taliban pledged to eject foreign fighters, prevent cross-border attacks into Afghanistan, stop running camps in FATA and return seized weapons and pay reparation.

'In fact the deal only helped the militants. After South Waziristan, the militants shifted to North Waziristan and then on to Bajaur and Swat. In July–August 2007 there were attacks virtually every day, especially around Miramshah and Mir Ali. The Pakistan army was losing control of territory, but Governor Aurakzai was determined to try to preserve the Waziristan Accord. In August in South Waziristan the army was faced with the worst episode yet in its struggle against the militants.'

General Masood Aslam, who succeeded General Hamid Khan as corps commander, described to Schofield the fiasco of the Pakistan army's infamous surrender to the Taliban on the road to Laddha Fort:

'General Aurakzai began negotiating with the tribes, and the tribes began moving the goalposts. Finally, they produced a list of prisoners held by the government, saying until they were released, our soldiers would be held prisoner. Aurakzai took the list, and would not share it with the rest of us.'

Aurakzai bent to the Taliban's demands but finally failed to give Baitullah what he wanted: 'In mid-December he resigned as governor. This was his way of telling Baitullah that he had played it straight, to persuade the tribes that he had behaved honourably. Otherwise, Baitullah would have gone after Aurakzai. He would have been a marked man. Aurakzai never wanted to discuss what he was doing with the army with the bureaucrats or with politicians. Nobody could control him.'

The bombshell that fell on Pakistan through Schofield was a letter published in the *Times of London* by Major General Feisal Alavi predicting that he would be killed by elements inside the Pakistan army, and naming two serving generals who had actually joined the Taliban secretly (names blacked out by the *Times*). Alavi was eventually killed in Islamabad by renegade Captain Haroon Ashiq on orders from a Taliban warlord Ilyas Kashmiri. In 2011, Captain Ashiq was found not guilty by a court in Rawalpindi.

Kim Barker: Some Ass-grabbing

The *Chicago Tribune*'s Kim Barker's book, *The Taliban Shuffle: Strange Days in Afghanistan and Pakistan,* contains an account of how she had her backside pinched repeatedly by the lawyers of Pakistan:

'Wearing a black headscarf and a long red Pakistani top over jeans, I waded through the crowd to the vehicle carrying the most popular man in Pakistan. Iftikhar Mohammad Chaudhry was an unlikely hero, with a tendency to mumble, a prickly ego, and a lazy eye.

'Standing near the Chaudhry-mobile, I took notes, the men shouting they would die for Chaudhry. And then someone grabbed my butt, squeezing a chunk of it. I spun around, but all the men, a good head shorter than me, stared ahead blankly. In Pakistan, even the tiny men seemed to have nuclear arms. Sometimes I hated it here.

"Who did that?" I demanded.

'Of course, no one answered.

'I turned back around and returned to taking notes. But again someone grabbed my butt. We performed the same ritual, of me turning around, of them pretending neither me nor my butt existed.

'"Fuck off," I announced, but everyone ignored me.

'This time when I turned back around, I held my left hand down by my side. I pretended that I was paying attention to all the cheering and tossing of rose petals. I waited.

'Soon someone pinched me. But this time I managed to grab the offending hand. I spun around. The man, who stood about five feet tall and appeared close to fifty, waved his one free hand in front of him, looked up, and pleaded, "No, no, no."

'I punched him in the face.

'In Afghanistan, this never happened. Men occasionally grazed a hip, or walked too close, or maybe tried a single pinch. But nothing in Afghanistan ever turned into an ass-grabbing free-for-all. In Pakistan, the quality of one's rear didn't matter, nor did a woman's attractiveness.'[2]

Benazir Bhutto: Posthumous Fury

The late prime minister Benazir Bhutto in her book, *Reconciliation: Islam, Democracy, and the West,* linked the deep state with terrorism and feared she would be eliminated through this dark nexus. According to her, Pakistan's establishment comprised the army, the intelligence agencies, religious leaders piously building political muscle through proxy warriors, and those brainwashed with textbook nationalism favouring a premodern Islamic state.

She named names in her book. The establishment remained impassive. She was attacked in Karachi by one of three assassination squads she had listed in her book. No special security was provided to her. Her reference to Saifullah Akhtar, a specially favoured jihadi leader in Pakistan who nearly toppled the Bhutto government in 1995 together with Major General Zaheerul Islam Abbasi, goes to the crux of the discussion that the furies have carried on.

Assistant Secretary General of the United Nations, Chilean diplomat Heraldo Munoz who headed a UN inquiry commission on Benazir Bhutto's assassination, writes: 'Akhtar had joined hands with Major General Abbasi, a former intelligence officer, not only in an attempted coup against Benazir Bhutto in 1995 but also in an attempt to remove the army leadership. After Akhtar spent five months in jail, he was released from detention. Years later, arrested in the United Arab Emirates for plotting to murder Musharraf, he was handed over to Pakistan; but after being held in jail for a couple of years, he was quietly released by the government after the Supreme Court inquired as to his whereabouts.'

Who did Benazir Bhutto name as her potential killers? In a letter sent to President Musharraf she named former ISI chief Hamid Gul, the Intelligence Bureau retired chief Brigadier Ijaz Shah; and then-chief minister of Punjab Pervaiz Elahi, plus former Sindh chief minister, Arbab Ghulam Rahim. The prosecutor investigating her assassination, Chaudhry Zulfiqar Ali, was killed in Islamabad.

Former Director General Federal Investigation Bureau and a senior police officer Tariq Khosa wrote in *Dawn* of 10 June 2013, under the caption *Deep State*: 'Chaudhry Zulfiqar Ali was gunned down on 2 May in Islamabad. A pamphlet with misleading contents was found at the scene of the attack carrying the name of the hitherto unknown Mujahideen-e-Islami. The risks of undertaking the investigation were known. The investigators were pitted against militants and their possible patrons in the deep state armed with a vast armory of devious methods and deadly weapons, including coercion, deceptive leads, blackmail, slander, kidnapping and even elimination.'

14

The Afghan National Army

The 2014 election in Afghanistan surprised the world. More than seven million Afghans turned out to vote on 6 April, defying Taliban militant threats that served as a message to them to boycott the poll. During the media coverage, the voters made it clear that they were voting against the Taliban who staged nearly 112 terrorist attacks to disrupt the process. One-third of the voters were women.

Out of the eight candidates for the job of President, three frontrunners—former foreign ministers Dr Abdullah Abdullah and Dr Zalmai Rassoul, and former Finance Minister Ashraf Ghani Ahmadzai—all announced their resolve to sign the Bilateral Security agreement (BSA) with the US, enabling the posting of approximately 20,000 post-withdrawal American troops plus the drone bases targeting the Taliban and al-Qaeda in Pakistan. Outgoing President Karzai had refused to sign the BSA in order to be better able to make a deal with the Taliban, somewhat on the same lines as Pakistan on its side of the border. All three have, off and on, held Pakistan responsible for terrorism inside Afghanistan. The second-round face-off between two winners will be held in May.

Prime Minister Nawaz Sharif has congratulated the Afghan people saying his government is not betting on any one candidate and has sworn non-interference. The Foreign Office, perceived closer to the army than Sharif, has repeated the assurance on non-interference; but the world knows Pakistan doesn't really control the Afghan Taliban and their Pakistani allies enough to back this assurance with credibility. One proof of this lack of credibility was Kabul's refusal to allow cross-border voting for the latest election among the Afghan refugees in Pakistan.

Not Ethnic at First

Most media analysts in Pakistan were proved wrong: voting this time was not ethnic-based. Dr Abdullah was upbeat despite his Tajik background, Ghani counted on support among the new urban youth, and Dr Rassoul was backed by the establishment of the outgoing President. Dr Abdullah, who pulled out of the 2009 vote before the second round spewing allegations of irregularities, has hailed Sunday's poll as a success. Significantly, Abdullah again wanted to make a deal with Ghani before the second round in May, and, since Ghani didn't want it, some analysts believed him to be the final winner.

The people of Afghanistan have reposed confidence in the Afghan National Army (ANA) while outside Afghanistan the neighbours have misgivings about the ability of the ANA to face up to the Taliban and their Pakistani allies. India has reason to be perturbed about the 'endgame' following the withdrawal of the Americans from Afghanistan in 2014. It has abstained at the UN vote against Russia after the Ukraine crisis, counting on Moscow to help out in the post-withdrawal phase. China has been more scared than India. It has pulled out from the copper mines near Kabul, expecting the breakout of civil war in the country. Western analysts think China should be persuaded to return to Afghanistan to keep Pakistan's 'strategic depth' doctrine at bay.

Elections in Afghanistan have always been ethnicity-driven. And since the country never got 'centralized' it also never got 'devolved'; hence the various ethnicities living without a common stake in the state. Afghanistan is supposed to be 'unconquerable', but invaders never had difficulty—because of this lack of common stake—in crossing this state 'without state attributes' to go and invade a juicier India. Many think Afghanistan was not allowed by its neighbours to become a normal state. Today, it is a 'scorched' state like Somalia and Yemen where invading armies get stuck.

Will the Afghan Army Defend Afghanistan?

Today, things are different. Afghanistan is supposed to be able to defend itself. It has now an army that will defend Afghanistan against invaders. The countries that invaded it in 2001 under a UN Security Council fiat will have left behind the largest army Afghanistan had in history, 350,000-strong, if you count the police also. The second largest Afghan army was fielded by President Najibullah, 40,000-strong, left behind by the Soviet Union. If America and its allies don't fund the ANA it won't be able to prevent the civil war imposed on it by its neighbours, in 2015. Najibullah's army collapsed after the Soviet Union stopped funding it, and he was shot and hanged by the Taliban who themselves never had more than 20,000 men under arms when they conquered a fragmented Afghanistan.

In 2010, Pakistan's Army Chief General Kayani had told the Americans the ANA will fracture and evaporate after the international forces leave Afghanistan, abandoning the country to familiar warlordism. He had flagged Pakistan's India-specific concerns, including unresolved issues, India's military capability and its Cold Start doctrine. He had said, 'We plan on adversaries' capabilities, not intentions.'[1] In Pakistan, everyone believes that the insurgency in Balochistan is fomented and funded by India with collusion from Kabul. In Kabul, all ethnicities including the Pashtun, believe that terrorism inside Afghanistan is organized by Pakistan.'

Some years ago, a number of ANA soldiers were attacked and killed by the Taliban in the Kunar province while they were asleep. Left to ANA by the Americans for some odd reason, Kunar is now home to the Pakistani chief of the Taliban, Mullah Fazlullah, a psychopath leading Pakistan through a *khattak* dance of peace talks he never really meant to lead anywhere. Pakistan has Afghanistan's terrorist organization, the Haqqani Network, on its side of the Durand Line, attacking a number of Afghan provinces across the border.

Ahmed Rashid in his book, *Pakistan on the Brink: The Future of Pakistan and the West,* discusses the Afghan army: 'US recruitment policy includes a strict ratio established in 2003 among all ethnic groups. Thus Tajiks could not be over 25 per cent in the army, but in 2010 they constituted some 41 per cent of soldiers and officers in the army, while Tajik officers commanded 70 per cent of the units.'[2]

But the latest report by Paul D. Miller in *Foreign Affairs* (2 April 2014) says things have improved: 'Fortunately, the international community has already set the Afghan army on the second course, ensuring that its ranks are ethnically mixed. Tajiks are overrepresented, constituting 39 per cent of the officer corps, well above the official target of 25 per cent. But their overrepresentation comes at the expense of the smallest groups, including Uzbeks and Hazara, not Pashtuns. Pashtuns made up 42 per cent of the officer corps and 43 per cent of the enlisted ranks, just below the official target of 44 per cent.'

Addiction and Desertion

Michael Kugelman, who watches the scene from Washington's Woodrow Wilson Center, shows a dark side to the $60 billion enterprise, 'far better trained and equipped than the Northern Alliance ever was'. In 2012, half of Afghanistan's army was addicted to drugs; sixty-five employees with the main spy agency in 2013 were fired because they were hooked on opium. Illiteracy too haunts the already punch-drunk ANA. A staggering 95 per cent of military and police recruits are robustly illiterate. In 2013, 30,000 soldiers deserted out of a total force of 185,000 under the ministry of defence. Because of their poor level of comprehension, ANA soldiers have killed American troops in a manner the American psychologists can't fathom. Next they might kill because of the ethnic divide, too, considering that ethnicity in Afghanistan is often defined through sect.

But one can't ignore the fact that the ANA is well-trained and may fight better once the Americans are gone after the signing of BSA. It has been observed that in the late 1990s the Northern Alliance never surrendered to the Taliban in five years of fierce conventional fighting, but the 1998 massacres of Mazar-e-Sharif by Pakistan-backed Taliban might still send shivers down the spine of most ANA fighters who have not already fled north with deserting Pashtun fellow-warriors. As for the numbers on both sides, the Taliban will likely be constantly supplied with fighting manpower from the non-state actors of the Punjab. Yet the changed map of war can't be ignored. The Taliban and their reinforcements from Pakistan cannot expect a walkover like the one in 1998. The big change in 2014 was the universal antipathy felt in Afghanistan for Pakistan; and that includes the types of Taliban sitting in the Quetta Shura, meaning those 'hosted' by Pakistan for achieving the objectives of its 'strategic depth'.

If the ANA Doesn't Fracture

What if the ANA doesn't fracture, keeps united under a charismatic general, and is faced by an invasion from Pakistan? If that happens, the ANA will become the most powerful entity in the country, more powerful than the state of Afghanistan. It will immediately enlist the sympathy of the luckless population haunted by the corruption and incompetence of decades of the Karzai government. This has happened before in the region. Pakistan's army, pitted against many-times-bigger India, incrementally became stronger than the state and took it over barely a decade after its birth in 1947. In Afghanistan, it may be sooner than that. The purist may not like it when it happens—and he has been proved right several times in hindsight. But after the Arab Spring and experience of Pakistan and Bangladesh with representative democracy, an ANA-ruled Afghanistan might actually settle down to better governance.

Many neighbours don't like living next to Iran which is 'democratic' and arguably incorrupt; and the Iranian army has not yet taken over the state. But Afghanistan is already ripe for the plucking after it ranked 175th on Transparency International's Corruption Perceptions Index, the third-worst in the world. Needless to say, the champions of freedom of speech and liberation of women in Kabul, who could mercifully breathe again during the US–ISAF order in Afghanistan, will all be swept aside in no time once this order gives way to the foreordained Islamic one. And there will be ample cause for this: only 47 per cent of Afghans say that they trust the Afghan parliament to do its job, 45 per cent trust government ministers, and 43 per cent trust the court system. A vast 77 per cent of them identified corruption as a major nationwide problem.

Pakistan's Best Bet?

The ANA is thought to be still 'work in progress'. Top Pentagon officials say: 'While Afghan troops are earning tactical victories on the battlefield, they struggle to hold cleared territory and still need much help in areas like transport and intelligence.' And if Pakistan proceeds according to its old proxy playbook, it will attract the attention of all sorts of scared governments from the regional neighbourhood, not because they have a 'strategic alliance' with Afghanistan like India, but because they fear the unintended expansionism embedded in Pakistan's 'strategic depth' doctrine that doesn't include controlling the non-state actors it will unleash.

Writes Kugelman: 'Yet for now, and in all likelihood for the foreseeable future, militants are continuing to pour into Afghanistan. Afghan officials and Taliban commanders claim that since announcing a ceasefire with Islamabad on 1 March, the Pakistani Taliban—already very active in Afghanistan—have been deploying fighters into the country. Meanwhile, Pakistani researchers estimate that hundreds of militants from Pakistan's Punjab province—ranging from sectarian extremists to anti-India jihadists—have relocated to the tribal areas in preparation for assaults on Afghanistan. And Indian security officials assert that their chief indigenous Islamist militant threat, the Indian Mujahideen, have branched out to Afghanistan to fight alongside the Afghan Taliban.'[3]

Last time its non-state actors went into Afghanistan, Pakistan suffered, and continued to suffer in 2014 at the hands of the 'returned warriors' waging armed rebellion in favour of an Islamic order pledged to transforming the state into a premodern utopia called the Caliphate. Pakistan has no clue what will finally jell in Afghanistan and how it will affect Pakistan's much-weakened state as it sleepwalks through a process of slow surrender it calls peace talks. The ANA is in fact Pakistan's best bet. It can prevent the Afghan Taliban and Pakistani Taliban from succeeding together and becoming a power that Pakistan cannot face up to without yielding territory that the latter are already demanding in peace talks. The civilian mind has the flexibility needed to get out of this losing situation, but the Pakistan army doesn't want the Pakistani mind to bend enough to dissolve the India-centric clot in its brain. The diktat doesn't come directly—indeed the consensus in Pakistan was that the army was hands-off in 2014— but when it comes to India, the non-state actors hit the road chanting textbook slogans against 'free' bilateral trade.

The Afghan national consensus behind the ANA may yet be hardly any use, just like Pakistani consensus behind democracy, because terror empties all such popular devices of their meaning. Over the years, it is not Afghanistan that has become more and more like Pakistan but vice versa: the destruction of ANA will complete the process despite Pakistan's large standing army. Unlike Afghanistan, the change will be internally induced.

15

Jaish Rides Again?

In the first week of February 2014, Pakistan seemed to have decided to break the unspoken embargo on the movement of Maulana Masood Azhar, chief of the outlawed terrorist outfit Jaish-e-Mohammad, and got him out of his ISI-protected madrasa fastness in Bahawalpur to speak to a public gathering of thousands in Muzaffarabad, the capital of Pakistan-administered Azad Kashmir. His job was to castigate India for unfairly killing Afzal Guru, a 'freedom-fighter' of the Indian-administered Kashmir hanged in India last year for allegedly helping Jaish mount an attack on the Indian parliament in 2001. He ended up delivering a recorded speech.

Masood Azhar had to be released in 1999 from an Indian jail by the BJP government in exchange for the release of the crew and passengers of an Indian Airlines plane hijacked from Kathmandu in Nepal and taken to Kandahar in 'friendly' Taliban-ruled Afghanistan. His speech in Muzaffarabad echoed the quietly gelling consensus about General Musharraf as a collaborator of the United States. 'Musharraf made Pakistan a stooge of the US and offered its resources for the massacre of innocent people of Afghanistan,' his recording roared, as quoted in the press.

A fire-breathing advocate of holy war, Azhar was also supposed to grace with his presence a debating contest in the University of the Punjab Lahore on the topic of jihad to decide the best speaker, but failed to turn up once again. A batch of radical students calling themselves Al Morabitoon—'the connectors'—told *Newsweek*, 'We were forced to call it off. The administration said we were violating campus rules; they even threatened us with violence.' The Morabitoon is headed by Mufti Muhammad Asghar Khan Kashmiri, a guerrilla fighter rumoured to be Azhar's most trusted lieutenant. When the Jaish elements, ensconced in an unknown place, were phoned about the whereabouts of Azhar, they said, 'He is in Srinagar. Until India leaves Kashmir, it will remain our enemy. We have been fighting this battle for the last fifteen years and will continue to do so.'

Pakistan has showcased a number of its non-state actors—known internationally as terrorists—to dampen the popular wish of easing relations with India. The bridegroom of the 'carnival' of the pious, which went to Islamabad last year to protest 'normalization' with India, was Hafiz Saeed, the most powerful man in all sorts of ways, including financially, flanked by none other than Maulana Fazlur Rehman Khalil of Harkat-ul-Mujahideen which fractured in 2000 into Harkat and Jaish because Azhar was too big for Khalil to order around.

A Pakistani economist at the Brookings Institution, Washington DC, speaking to an audience in Lahore in 2014 at the International Growth Centre said that, for reasons that couldn't be stated in public, Pakistan had started malfunctioning economically after 1992 in comparison with India, which actually took off that year. The entire audience knew what he was referring to: the blowback of the policy of fielding terrorist militias in proxy wars in Afghanistan and India in the 1980s by a military-ruled Pakistan. The 1990s was the decade of the rise of non-state actors when warriors like Azhar and Khalil were allowed to team up with Osama bin Laden, causing the proxy war to be fought on the cheap.

Azhar attacked the Indian parliament and was caught and imprisoned after he travelled to India on a fake passport, to be later sprung through a hijack that many foreign observers thought was 'arranged' by Pakistan. On the latest 'outing' of Azhar an Indian newspaper stated: 'Maulana Masood Azhar, one of the three terrorists released by India on the last day of 1999 to end the Kandahar hijack, is back in action. A flurry of intelligence reports has warned that Jaish-e-Mohammad, the terror group created by Azhar after his release, and which was responsible for the attack on Parliament in 2001, is planning a wave of suicide attacks at rallies across India.' Feigning innocence about Pakistan's major foreign policy instrument, the Jaish chief, the ministry of foreign affairs spokesperson, Ms Tasneem Aslam admitted, 'We have also seen media reports of Azhar's resurfacing. This is probably a one-time event. He escaped scrutiny, but his organization is banned in Pakistan and its activities are regularly monitored.' (sic!) Pakistani diplomats are not supposed to know that someone else, and not they, actually mould the country's foreign policy by 'creating events' meant to be of help to Pakistan.

Two Offshoots of Jaish

If Khalil's appearances on TV talk shows is any precedent, Pakistan could be about to thumb its much-thumbed nose to the world by parading Azhar too on TV to thunderous applause by a Talibanized population. There are more ominous signs: two new militias emanating from Jaish have already joined the Taliban in their 'war of correction' against Pakistan. The first is the outfit called Ansarul Aseer (Helper of the Imprisoned) led by an ex-air force mechanic, Adnan Rashid, trained in terrorism at the notorious Mansehra camp near Abbottabad run by Jaish on Osama bin Laden's money.

The second is Maulana Umar Qasimi's Ahrarul Hind which attacked a district court in Islamabad in March, killing a 'liberal' judge and over a dozen innocent people through suicide bombers. The luckless judge was labelled 'liberal' because in April 2014 he had dismissed a petition filed by the son of Lal Masjid cleric Abdur Rashid Ghazi asking that a case be registered against former President Pervez Musharraf for ordering the 2007 operation on the mosque.

As *Newsweek* noted in the issue of 12 July 2014, Adnan Rashid, a Pashtun from the Swabi district of Peshawar and a former air force officer-turned-terrorist, who was under a death sentence for having attempted to kill General Pervez Musharraf in 2003 was sprung from a jail in Bannu last year after a Taliban raid that was hardly resisted by the prison guards. The Taliban declared after the jailbreak that they had spent 'over Rs 2 crore on the operation'.

The money almost certainly went to those who transferred a dangerous terrorist from the military stronghold of Rawalpindi to Bannu, a semi-tribal area where the Taliban virtually rule in a doubtful diarchy with the local administration. After this clear case of 'complicity', Adnan Rashid talked to an English-language Taliban journal on the Internet (March 2013) and revealed how he had landed at Mansehra after joining the jihad:

'Brother X urged me to join the Taliban Air Force that needed skilled men. He kept on giving me Dawa (invitation to Islam) and kept on calling me to the path of Allah and His Prophet. Then I and Brother X left the [PAF] squadron. Brother X had some terms with Maulana Masood Azhar, so he took me to the Jaish-e-Mohammad office and then to the Mansehra Training Camp. He introduced me to them and then went back to his duty in Peshawar. I stayed in their camp for 23 days waiting to go along with some other brothers to Afghanistan; meanwhile, I was interviewed by many commanders; finally, they said that they had made my *Tashkeel* (delegation) back to my [PAF] Air Force Squadron. They told me that I should work there and give the Dawa of Jihad.'

The Ahrarul Hind raid on a district court in Islamabad in March 2014 brought to light another Jaish connection. The Tehreek-e-Taliban Pakistan (TTP), engaged in peace talks with the government of Nawaz Sharif, dissociated itself from the raid, led by a non-Pashtun this time, one Maulana Umar Qasimi from Jhang, a southern Punjab city that is home to Sipah-e-Sahaba, the mother of all sectarian militias unthinkingly used by the state in its proxy wars. This time a Punjabi was leading a gang of Pashtun suicide bombers. Qasimi moved from Jhang to Bahawalpur, close to the Indian border, and enrolled in a seminary run by Maulana Masood Azhar from his ISI-guarded grand madrasa Usman-o-Ali in Bahawalpur city.

Qasimi is said to have moved to the tribal agency of Mohmand, already home to the local TTP warlord Umar Khalid Khorasani, and developed an apparently rebellious attitude to the TTP shura (council) which increasingly feigned opposition to Khorasani's savagery towards Pakistani troops. Qasimi's attack on the district court was also not owned to by the TTP spokesman, which is hardly credible. Both Khorasani and Qasimi are supposed to be located in Kunar in Afghanistan and not in North Waziristan. The fact that the TTP chief too is not in North Waziristan, points to an impotent TTP shura issuing bogus disavowals to cover up for the indiscriminate savagery favoured by the Fazlullah–Khorasani–Qasimi trio. If not that, then the policy of denials is simply another ruse that Pakistan is dying to accept to award impunity to the killers it is talking peace with. Another incident not owned to by the TTP was the attack on a Christian church in Peshawar in September last year, killing seventy-eight innocent Christians during a service. The attack was owned by another al-Qaeda-linked outfit, Jandullah, which has Qasimi as one of its leaders.

Rise of Punjabi Taliban

A 2009 intelligence report presented to Punjab Governor Salmaan Taseer, who was to succumb to terrorism himself while still in office in 2012, says Masood Azhar was very much in control in

Bahawalpur, often visiting North Waziristan to discuss plans of action with then TTP chief Baitullah Mehsud, receiving Afghan warriors from North Waziristan, liaising with dangerous Lashkar-e-Jhangvi killers from neighbouring Rahimyar Khan, and sending warriors into Iran in coordination with Jandullah.

In Madrasa Usman-o-Ali angry discussions took place about Pakistan—read ISI—playing a double-game with Jaish and betraying the Islamic warriors to America. The report also noted a Jaish connection with TTP's Punjabi representative Asmatullah Muawiya who trained Punjabi suicide bombers for the TTP, and Sipah-e-Sahaba chief Ahmad Ludhianvi who admitted visiting the Shia-killer Malik Ishaq in a Lahore jail 'on the request of Mian Shahbaz Sharif'. Of course, all this, while Pakistan denied that Azhar was in Pakistan, like Indian underworld don Dawood Ibrahim who was in Lahore in the last week of February 2014 arranging the dowry for the wedding of his second daughter.

Was Pakistan putting the world on notice about its next move? If so, it was also a signal for all Pakistanis to get ready for more punishment. Every time Pakistan notches up proxy victories against India or the United States, the people of Pakistan have to pay a heavy price for it because this home-grown terrorism is structurally dependent on finances raised through bank robberies, kidnapping, *bhatta* (protection money) and an all-out assault on the national economy.

Masood Azhar was the most famous alumnus of the Banuri seminary in Karachi, son of Allah Baksh Shabbir, a teacher of the Quran from Bahawalpur. His family was connected to the pre-1947 fundamentalist movement of the Ahrar. Azhar was born in 1968 and graduated from Karachi's Arab-funded seminary where he then taught for two years till 1989, becoming a favourite of its head, Mufti Nizamuddin Shamzai, who inspired him to jihad.

Azhar's brother Ibrahim went to Afghanistan at the age of nineteen. Later he took along his father too. A sister, Rabiya Bibi, worked for the Taliban government in Afghanistan. His elder brother was a computer salesman in Bahawalpur but made many trips to Afghanistan for jihad. Ibrahim Azhar held the Bahawalpur office of the banned Harkat ul-Ansar and is said to have participated in the hijack of the Indian airplane to get his brother released from jail in India.

Azhar is the author of twenty-nine jihadi tracts and was the organizational genius behind Harkat-ul-Mujahideen, for which he toured abroad and collected funds. He was caught carrying fake dollars at Jeddah airport during one of these trips. He was instrumental in getting terrorist organizations Harkat-ul-Mujahideen and Harkat Jihad Islami to merge for some time. He was in Somalia in 1993 while Osama bin Laden was based in Sudan. Azhar was arrested in Anantnag in the Indian-administered Kashmir in 1994 while trying to coordinate the activities of another outfit named Harkat ul-Ansar.

He went to Saudi Arabia on a Pakistani passport, from where he went to Dhaka. When he flew to Delhi from Dhaka, he was carrying a Portuguese passport. Azhar is said to have met Osama bin Laden in Madina in 1994 when both were disguised. Azhar's mission was to bring his jihadi organization under the aegis of al-Qaeda. In 2000, following his release from jail and return from Afghanistan, he immediately announced the foundation of Jaish-e-Mohammad.

Masood Azhar was devoted to Maulana Haq Nawaz Jhangvi, the fanatically anti-Shia and anti-Iran founder of Sipah-e-Sahaba, who was murdered in 1990, which in turn led to the murder of an Iranian diplomat in Lahore, thus starting the great sectarian war of the decade of the 1990s and attracting Arab funds to Deobandi warriors. Azhar's Jaish first claimed the attack on Indian parliament in 2001, then went back on it; but it remained the most aggressive fighting arm of jihad in Pakistan together with Lashkar-e-Taiba.

It is said that his separation from Harkat-ul-Mujahideen forced his co-leader Fazlur Rehman Khalil to move close to Osama bin Laden, but the truth is that Azhar's trail in Somalia in

1993 links him and his Pakistani warriors with Osama-supported General Eidid's ambush of the UN troops in Mogadishu that killed twenty-four Pakistani troops doing UN duty. Later in 1999, the kidnapper of Daniel Pearl in Karachi, Omar Sheikh, joined him and confirmed the strong bond between al-Qaeda and Jamia Banuria, Azhar's alma mater.

A Pakistani working for al-Qaeda, Amjad Faruqi, with a bounty of Rs 20 million on his head, was killed in 2004 in Sindh after a five-hour gun-battle with the police. He was wanted for two abortive attempts on the life of General Pervez Musharraf in 2003, and the murder of the American journalist Daniel Pearl. His biggest link with al-Qaeda was his involvement in the 1999 hijack of the Indian airliner IC-814 which sought to free Masood Azhar from an Indian jail. Although Pervez Musharraf in his book, *In the Line of Fire,* clearly refers to Jaish as a terrorist organization, it was not seen as such by his entire establishment before it attempted to take his life at the behest of al-Qaeda. The government of Pervez Musharraf handled him as its favourite after his release from the Indian jail and let him roam freely in the country despite his avowed terrorist and sectarian links. In fact a lot of the sectarian slaughter that took place under Musharraf would have been avoided had he moved to stop Masud Azhar.

One reason Musharraf did not discuss Azhar in detail could be that Azhar's trail would have led him to parts of the establishment he himself did not want to upset. A *Terrorist Monitor* report by Jamestown Foundation, Washington DC, sketches the scene in Karachi in 2004: 'Karachi continues to be a safe haven for extremist religious groups like Lashkar Jhangvi and terrorist groups like Harkat-ul-Mujahideen and Harkat Jihad Islami. In fact Harkat runs forty-eight seminaries in Karachi. The biggest of these, Madrasa Khalid bin Walid, trains more than 500 students at any given point of time. A large number of his students fought the Northern Alliance during the Afghan wars of the 1990s. Some went to Kashmir to fight Indian Security Forces but none returned to their homes, choosing instead to make Karachi their home. Their collective objective is to turn Pakistan into another Taliban-style country.'[4]

The Favoured One

Why are Azhar and his Jaish being paraded now despite their links with al-Qaeda and the TTP? For the establishment obsessed with India, there is no plan B as far as the coming war in Afghanistan is concerned. If the past is any guide, see this report by Amjad Bashir Siddiqi in the *News* (5 August 2001):

'Jaish-e-Mohammad leader Maulana Masood Azhar, whose entry was banned in Sindh because of the wave of sectarian terrorism, was stopped at Karachi airport and was asked to go back. Azhar phoned someone and the ban was immediately lifted to allow him to enter Karachi, after which he had a meeting with home secretary, Sindh.' Azhar later went to Ghotki in violation of the ban and was ignored by the local administrative magistrate there. The officer was pulled up, but later still, when Azhar tried to enter Sukkur and was stopped by the district administration the local bureaucracy was pulled up, this time for not giving him unhampered passage to anywhere in the city.'

Most observers are worried about Afghanistan after the withdrawal of US–NATO forces from there end of 2014. It should be interesting to see what would happen to Pakistan once the Americans are gone. Islamabad's Jinnah Institute in its Briefing (25 July 2011) spelled out Pakistan's 'objectives' in relation to post-withdrawal Afghanistan. The most outstanding point made in the report pertained to India: 'Pakistani foreign policy elite accept that India has a role to play in Afghanistan's economic reconstruction . . . but Pakistani *security establishment* [thinks] a reluctance to address Pakistani misgivings increases the likelihood of a growing Indian footprint, and in turn, New Delhi's greater ability to manipulate the endgame negotiations and the post-settlement dispensation in Kabul.'

Withdrawal Symptoms

Will India get out of Afghanistan after the American withdrawal? From a statement of Indian prime minister Manmohan Singh ('we will support the Afghan people') it appeared that it planned to retain its presence in Afghanistan. The most likely post-withdrawal scenario is that there will be civil war in Afghanistan. A parallel war will take place between the Afghan National Army and the non-state actors from Pakistan. US commander in Afghanistan General John Allen told Congress in 2012 he thought a future 230,000-strong Afghan force was enough after 2017. That will be historically the largest army Afghanistan ever had. The Taliban will have 25,000 men, counting on the basis of the maximum muster managed so far. The uneven battlefield will be 'equalized' by inserting additional fighters from Pakistan. The TTP will raid across the Durand Line, but the manpower it mobilizes may not suffice. Pakistan expects Afghan Taliban, Haqqani Network, Hekmatyar's Hizb-e-Islami, ragtag warlords of FATA and Malakand to battle an Afghan army already inclined to defection.

But manpower will still be needed to even the scales and speed up defections. The Taliban will be helped by the Punjabi Taliban, of which Asian Tigers are already aligned to the Haqqanis. The Defence of Pakistan Council headed by powerful Jamaatud Dawa will oblige with more Punjabi manpower. Dawa leader Hafiz Saeed allegedly says he alone can muster 100,000. Pakistan is home to the armies that will enter Afghanistan but it hardly controls them. Therefore, the blowback from Afghanistan this time will be transformational for Pakistan. It may not survive the 'fund-raising' by its non-state actors through kidnappings and bank robberies in its major cities. This trend among the state-supported jihadi outfits has been in evidence. The Taliban in Pakistan have been criminalized. In affected areas, criminals are in the process of becoming Talibanized. Vendettas are carried out increasingly with suicide bombers because the Taliban are busy selling their surplus *fedayeen*. Karachi and Peshawar are already paralysed by kidnappings for ransom. From the 2014 trend in its Defence Housing Authority (DHA), Lahore too was expected to be targeted in a big away.

Under General Kayani, Pakistan ought to appease terrorism by becoming anti-American and pro-Taliban. After the withdrawal, a Talibanized Afghanistan will survive only if Pakistan too fulfils its promise of becoming a *khilafat*. The policy of appeasement will proceed to its logical end. The remaining attributes of the state will fall off, with religious parties plus madrasas with jihadi capacity increasingly exercising authority in its name.

16

A Council of Runaway Ideology

In Islamabad, the Council of Islamic Ideology (CII), an advisory body of clerics and scholars to assist the government to bring laws in line with the Holy Quran and the example of the Holy Prophet (PBUH), dropped one of its usual bombshells. On 10 March 2004, top cleric Maulana Muhammad Khan Sheerani announced after CII's deliberations that a man may not ask for permission from his first wife before marrying a second one. The latest 'decision' at the CII grated on many nerves because the law in force at present is that marrying the second time without asking the first wife will entail one year in jail and the paltry sum of Rs 5000 as fine. The law of 'permission' raised belly-laughs anyway because if the first wife refuses permission she can be divorced by the husband by pronouncing 'talaq' (divorce) three times, no questions asked. But the primitive anachronism of Sheerani's new 'advice' provoked the Human Rights Commission of Pakistan (HRCP) to condemn it as another sign of tightening up the faith in anticipation of the rule of the Taliban.

The CII released another bolt by allowing under-age marriage for girls, saying marriage 'of even minors can be solemnized but only with the consent of their guardians' but such girls can go with the bridegroom only after attaining puberty. No one can question the CII on the matter of the girl's own consent when she is a minor. The CII verdict will only validate the widespread practice of child marriage, occasionally interrupted by the police. It cannot have been ignorant of the fact that the founder of the state, Jinnah, had fought legal battles to ban child-marriage in India.

Sworn against Women

Somehow every newly 'discovered' law goes against women. For instance, in 2013 the CII decreed that the DNA test carried out to convict a rapist could not be regarded as conclusive evidence under the faith, thus indirectly confirming the widely held clerical view which conflates rape with fornication, requiring four eyewitnesses to what should normally be regarded as an act of violence. If the new law is enforced, a raped woman will have to bring four men or eight women—since the evidence of one man equals two women—as eyewitnesses to get the rapist punished. If she can't prove rape, she is to be whipped for 'qazf' or wrongful accusation.

Reacting angrily to the latest women-related 'correction' of law, Pakistan People's Party's Dr Nafisa Shah, coordinator of the PPP Human Rights Cell, stated: 'Why is the council concerned with men's four marriages and why have they done nothing to ensure that women get their property as enshrined in the Islamic Law?'[1] There was a time before 1947 when Islamic Family Law was more progressive than the Hindu Family Law because it gave a Muslim girl half of what a Muslim boy got in inheritance while the Hindu girl got nothing; however, in 1954, India's Prime Minister Jawaharlal Nehru changed the Hindu law and allowed full portion to Hindu girls, thus making Hindu Law more progressive in India.

The CII was set up by Pakistan's first Constitution in 1962 as the 'Advisory Council of Islamic Ideology'. It was 're-designated' as Council of Islamic Ideology in the 1973 Constitution by the more progressive PPP, thinking it would be able to ignore its 'advice' and carry on as usual; but incidents, as for instance by an institution like the Air Force which approached the CII for advice on the keeping of beards, which had previously been banned, strengthened the hands of religious elements. Malpractice has developed around the advisory and non-binding status of the CII. The council can frame new laws and pass them on to the ministry of religious affairs, knowing that no move (because advice is not binding under law) would be made by the ruling party to legislate the rendered advice into law. This has been followed by another evil practice of allowing radical clerics to populate the CII as a kind of bribe in return for the support of their parties in Parliament. This means that a certain kind of angry and revengeful perfectionist-literalist cleric can run the CII as an instrument of fear for such vulnerable sections of society as women and non-Muslims.

Redundant Yet Troubling

The CII has behaved accordingly. It duplicates the Federal sharia Court—the supra-parliamentary and therefore anti-democratic institution-with-teeth, which nonetheless remains impotent. Pakistani rulers began by appointing moderate scholar-clerics to the CII, mostly retired judges of the higher judiciary who did not want to rock the boat of the state by delving into the literalist foundations of Islam. Gradually, however, the trend changed and the CII became radicalized under Justice Tanzilur Rehman (retd) whom the Islamizing dictator General Zia appointed in 1980 before imposing zakat (poor due) tax on the nation.

Justice Rehman (1980–84) had written his book on apostatization and was ready to implement the vision of the dictator when an even more powerful personality of the Islamic world intervened and stole the show. Saudi Arabia, having helped

General Zia financially with the gift of Zakat Fund, sent an Arab scholar Dr Maruf Dualibi, to supervise Pakistan's transition to hudood (Quranic legal edicts). He was also instrumental in relocating the Sunni-Shia war raging in the Gulf to Pakistan.

A CII member, Syed Afzal Haider, in his book titled *Council of Islamic Ideology: Evolution and Activity*, tells us how the council came to its final draft of the Hudood Ordinance as it was later promulgated by General Zia. It records that Dr Maruf Dualibi visited the offices of the council. However, the council's own report to the government in December 1981 observed that Hudood laws were discussed by the council and the law ministry 'under the guidance of Dr Maruf Dualibi who was specially detailed by the Government of Saudi Arabia for this purpose'.

Sad Saudi Intervention

The Zakat and Ushr Ordinance (1980) was framed by Dr Dualibi in Arabic sitting in the CII office, which was then translated into Urdu by the government and applied equally to both the Muslim sects despite the fact that Shia traditionally did not pay zakat to the state. The first clash with the Shia community took place when it staged its 'long march' to Islamabad against the imposition on zakat on them not permitted by their jurisprudence. The consequence of going against good sense led to comic results. The Supreme Court first exempted all the Shia from paying zakat, which caused most Sunnis to submit certificates under oath that they were Shia, thus preventing deduction of the tax from their bank accounts. Later, the court, acting on equity, extended this exemption to Sunnis as well, thus making zakat voluntary, in violation of the traditional interpretation of Islamic law. Ushr, meaning ten (per cent), fared even worse.

Land Revenue expert, A.K. Khalid, member Board of Revenue Punjab for eight years, in his book, *Agrarian History of Pakistan*, has made a study of Ushr, coming to the conclusion that it was not correct on the part of General Zia to accept the clerical demand that Ushr be treated as zakat. The act of haste that produced the Zakat and Ushr Ordinance (1980) ignored the disparity of rates between the rain-fed land (10 per cent tax) and canal-fed land (5 per cent tax). The canal-fed land deserved the 10 per cent deduction, but the fear of a backlash from the ulema suspended reason. Now the subterfuge part of the policy on Ushr collection is that while Ushr on canal-fed lands is compulsory (on the basis of self-assessment), it is 'voluntary' in the case of rain-fed lands. And it is only 5 per cent! The word *ushr* which means 'ten' is therefore misapplied.

The next chief of the CII, given to somewhat fiery advocacy of laws on TV, often rebuking the Supreme Court for letting modern banking run in Pakistan, was S.M. Zaman who led it for two terms of three years each. He was said to be a graduate from Harvard but was nonetheless hard-line and was later in the academic council of Jamaat-e-Islami's Institute of Policy Research headed by Dr Khursheed Ahmed, featuring two distinguished retired ambassadors, Akram Zaki and Shamshad Ahmad Khan. After the rise of the Taliban and the consequent empowerment of the clergy, the PPP in its wisdom appointed Maulana Muhammad Khan Sheerani as chairman in 2010 and the Muslim League–Nawaz compounded this wisdom by giving him a second term in 2013. Only President General Pervez Musharraf acted in favour of moderation by not appointing the house of twenty 'hard-shell' members to the CII and kept it at the minimum strength of eight to allow it to be functional under the constitution. And he got Dr Muhammad Khalid Masud, a PhD in Islamic studies from McGill University, Canada, to head it.

Long Shadow of Sheerani

Why did the PPP leader Asif Ali Zardari give the CII to Sheerani? Pakistan's assassinated leader Benazir Bhutto—her killing was owned by al-Qaeda—wrote in her book, *Reconciliation: Islam, Democracy and the West*: 'And the living reformers like Muhammad

Arkoun, Abdur Rahman Wahid, Wahiduddin Khan and Khalid Masud would be able to preach and teach their modernizing theology without facing repression or marginalization by the state.' Muhammad Arkoun is an Algerian genius who is recognized in the West as the most gifted exponent of Islam who may not be able to live in Algeria because of his reformism. Abdur Rahman Wahid, an Indonesian religious and political leader, served as the President of Indonesia from 1999 to 2001. Maulana Wahiduddin Khan is the Indian moderate scholar whose message is appreciated all over the world but is rejected by the Muslims of India because of the dominance of extremism in their thinking.[2]

Benazir Bhutto mentioned Dr Masud because of his scholarly contribution to a rational understanding of Islam, including the 'Sixth Lecture' of the national poet-philosopher Allama Iqbal where the latter had bravely 'reinterpreted' the concept of hudood in Islam, recommending that punishments such as cutting of hands not be imposed in our times. Although it hardly matters today, Iqbal had seen nothing wrong with modern banking and, following the example of Sir Syed Ahmed Khan the great Muslim reformer of South Asia, had allowed bank interest in his writings.

A Brief Light

One can easily claim that the CII under Musharraf was run by enlightened scholars with international standing. The other well-known member of the CII was the popular Muslim evangelist Allama Javed Ghamidi who adheres to the Quran and Sunnah (way of the Prophet), and scrutinizes critically the dicey jurisprudence used by Pakistani clerics while formulating 'funny' laws. As long as the CII was led by Khalid Masud (2004–10) it sent down rational and non-controversial advice to the government, occasionally disturbing the clerical dovecotes by recommending pro-women changes in law—such as, that a wife's appeal to the court for divorce be considered unchallengeable.

Dr Masud was naturally not well-liked by the conservative circles. The late Qazi Hussain Ahmad, ex-chief of Jamaat-e-Islami, was greatly put off by his appointment in 2004, saying, according to the Urdu daily *Jang*: 'In the eyes of the government, moderation means saying the namaz while drinking wine. Pakistan is suffering because of riba (usury) which has instilled laziness (*kahili*) among people. CII has been filled with the wrong people, its chairman Khalid Masud is a man of no repute, and one member of the council had been editing a Qadiani magazine for ten years.'

In 2010, Ghamidi's seminary in Lahore was attacked and a teacher, mistaken for him, was murdered, forcing him to go into exile in Malaysia. His mistake was his criticism of Pakistan's infamous Blasphemy Law that had caused the assassination of the governor of Punjab, Salmaan Taseer. The *Guardian* had quoted him as saying: 'The blasphemy laws have no justification in Islam. These ulema are just telling lies to the people. But they have become stronger, because they have street power behind them, and the liberal forces are weak and divided. If it continues like this it could result in the destruction of Pakistan.'

In 2014, the Taliban were knocking at the door pledging to enforce all the 'advice' the CII has sent to the incumbent governments now gathering dust in old files. This 'ignoring' of the CII advice led to another practice: the extremist clerics in the council whose recommendations were set aside were leaked to the Urdu press where they started appearing regularly as 'chastisement' to the 'pagan' government in power. The following leaks to the press are noted with the comment that they have been once formally denied by the CII secretariat:

- The practice of printing photographs on banknotes be stopped, meaning that the portrait of the founder of the nation, Quaid-e-Azam Muhammad Ali Jinnah, be removed from the Rs 500 and 1000 banknotes.

- Special women's seats in Parliament be abolished because 'they are by and large terribly impressed by modernism and Westernism, and instead of believing in the Islamic principle of equity and justice, believe in the western slogan of gender equality.' (Quoted from a letter from the CII.)
- The council intended to recommend that anyone blaspheming against Allah too should be punished. It will also recommend that no woman be allowed to marry without the permission of her male guardian. It is expected to ban organ transplant and smoking.
- It became seized with the question of Christian hangmen executing Muslim convicts in Pakistan and recommended that they be replaced with Muslim hangmen. Among issues taken to the council by the religion ministry was the issue of girls marrying of their own accord.
- It endorsed the destruction of Afghanistan's archaeological heritage by the Taliban.
- It ruled that insurance of all kinds was against Islam and should be abolished forthwith.
- It came to the conclusion that soft drinks sold as non-alcoholic beer were not allowed in Islam. It said any drink which is not *sharab* (alcohol) could not be called sharab or that the name beer should not be put on it. It said preparation and trade of non-alcoholic beer inside or outside Pakistan was haram (prohibited).
- It advised change of the national flag twenty-three years ago. The recommendation was that *kalima* (avowal of faith) be inscribed on the national flag along with the battle-cry of Allahu Akbar.
- It said that women should be disallowed from appearing in advertisements and that only men should be used to promote products through photographs. It said that women were allowed to work as air hostesses but they should wear burqa or hijab on board. Also, no tailor should be allowed to sew the clothes for women and that only women tailors should be used for women.

- It recommended that ACRs of all state employees should contain sections indicating religious observance, and those not saying namaz should not be promoted.
- It declared that it was wrong to label jihad as a defensive war alone. The truth according to CII was that jihad could be offensive as well. It stated that Western propaganda against jihad had pushed it into the background, but everyone should be grateful to Afghanistan for having revived it. It said that the greatest act of piety was participation in jihad and one cause of the decline of the Muslims was their abandonment of it.
- It recommended to the government that it should fire civil servants who did not say their namaz, and that areas where people said their namaz should be selected for concessional development funds.
- It resolved in Islamabad that Pakistan should revert to Friday as the weekly holiday for Islamic blessings.
- It declared that sending anyone to prison was against sharia and recommended that prison sentences be abolished. Early Islam had no jails, no police, and no banks. Thieves used to have their hands cut off.

When Maulana Sheerani was appointed chairman of the CII by the PPP government in 2009, it was hardly welcomed by the non-clerical citizens of Pakistan. The Aurat Foundation defending women's rights in Lahore cringed at what might happen next. Led by Justice Nasira Javid Iqbal (retd), it demanded that the order appointing JUI's Maulana Sheerani as chairman of the Council of Islamic Ideology be revoked. The Barelvi sect felt the tremor too. The Qaumi Yakjehti Council of the Barelvi ulema protested the appointment of Sheerani as chairman saying it was like replacing a scholar with a cleric. The Barelvi ulema accused Sheerani of being 'disputable', saying Sheerani will violate Sunni rights and will 'blow to bits' the Islamic ideology. But the PPP had to make a compromise in 2009 with the JUI to retain its majority in Parliament; and one pledge in the compromise was to give the CII to Maulana Sheerani. The same dilemma was faced by the PMLN in 2013 and Sheerani got his second three-year term.

Divine but Murky

The provenance of the CII is murky. General Zia, who ruled Pakistan after hanging Prime Minister Zulfikar Ali Bhutto, rejected Allama Iqbal's view of ijtihad (reinterpretation) and not only imposed the cutting of hands for theft but also fired the then chairman of the CII in order to impose stoning to death which is not specifically mentioned in the Quran. It is not surprising that Bhutto's daughter too was killed in Pakistan because she possessed a level of intellect that Pakistanis usually reject as being heretical. Those who killed her will not allow innovative thinking—and dissenting intellect least of all.

The founder of the infamous Banuri Mosque complex in Karachi, Maulana Yusuf Banuri, was made a member of the CII by General Zia on coming to power in 1977. The Banuri mosque, funded by the Arabs, later became heavily sectarian under Mufti Shamzai, who was killed by the opposing sect. The CII has not been the most helpful place in guiding Pakistan on the path of wisdom. The great leader of jihad and a persistent thorn in the side of India since his bloody assault on Mumbai on 26 November 2008, Hafiz Muhammad Saeed, includes the CII in his trajectory of fame and power. After graduation in 1974 Hafiz Saeed was appointed lecturer at the University of Engineering and Technology Lahore in the Islamiat Department. He was sent from UET to Saudi Arabia 'for higher studies'. There he got together with the famous 'blind' Saudi high priest, Sheikh Abdul Aziz bin Baz—who insisted that the earth was flat—to pronounce the fatwa of jihad in Afghanistan in 1979. He returned to Pakistan and was selected as a research scholar at the CII, a several-years-long selection made by a panel of High Court judges.

On 17 December 2009, two years after al-Qaeda's establishment of the Tehreek-e-Taliban Pakistan, jihadist websites posted a new book by Ayman-al-Zawahiri titled, *The Morning and the Lamp: A Treatise Regarding the Claim that the Pakistani Constitution is Islamic.* Al-Zawahiri had probably written this book earlier but made it public after it had been translated and circulated to all the Deobandi-Wahhabi seminaries in Pakistan. The book does not merely call for radical reform of the Islamic Republic of Pakistan along the principles traditionally espoused by al-Qaeda and its local allies; it calls for the destruction of the state itself. Al-Zawahiri sought to prove that the Pakistani Constitution was in contradiction with Islam and the sharia. Needless to say, most Pakistani Islamists and religious leaders hold that while the constitution itself is Islamic, the Pakistani regimes have failed to implement it. CII chairmen too have in the past raised objections, while the custodian of Islamabad's infamous Lal Masjid (Red Mosque), whom the Taliban selected as their representative for parleys with the government this year, Maulana Abdul Aziz, has openly declared the constitution heretical. What are the points raised by al-Zawahiri in his polemic against the constitution?

Prefacing his case in the form of questions, he states: 'How is it possible that the Pakistani system is based on Islamic foundations:

- Yet the system results in corruption, sabotage, and subordination to the West and the Americans?
- The system teaches confusion which results in the creation of generations with a sentimental attachment to Islam, while in fact, practice, tradition, and general fascination are sympathetic to Western culture.
- The army—the uncrowned king in Pakistan—is subordinate to the Americans?
- And Pakistan has become the greatest ally of America in its crusading war against Islam?'

Zawahiri: The Guide

Emboldened and empowered by al-Zawahiri's case-building and the violence of the Tehreek-e-Taliban Pakistan, the religious scholars inducted into the CII would agree with all the points raised above. The book is critical of Pakistan because 'the constitution is based on the people's power to legislate; because the power to amend the constitution is also vested in the people which is a trespass on the authority of Allah; because riba (usury) continues to be practised under the constitution and women are allowed to go unveiled and be together at the workplace with men; Pakistan is not an Islamic state, it contradicts the Islamic sharia in a number of fundamental and significant ways like immunity granted to some office-holders from judicial prosecution, the non-restriction of important offices to male Muslims, and the fact that the word democracy is mentioned in the Constitution's preamble.'

Wrote Lahore's veteran journalist Aziz-ud-Din Ahmad: 'The CII comprises fossilized clerics trying to dictate to people living in the twenty-first century. They continue the futile attempt to push the wheel of history backwards. While the performance of the council since its inception has been uniformly dismal, under Sheerani it has surpassed past records. The government spends millions on this outdated fixture. There is a need to seriously consider if the candle is worth the oil.'

17

Judiciary Acts Up in South Asia

The Supreme Courts of India, Pakistan and Bangladesh went 'activist' in recent years and clashed with parliaments and executives in their respective states, not because they wanted the upper hand in a system where the separation of powers is embedded in the Constitution, but because of the poor-quality of governance characterizing most third world states. Claiming 'judicial review', they blocked the executive's unpopular actions. Becoming increasingly populist, they curtailed due process by removing the trial court stage of normal prosecution. More aggressively, they also at times challenged legislations and set them aside. They encouraged 'public interest litigation' (PIL) through their suo motu powers and were at times seen as trespassing in the domain of the executive.[1]

In India and Pakistan, the Supreme Courts suffered periods of coercive curtailment of their judicial powers by the executive and became reactively aggressive after the intrusion of the executive subsided. The Indian court launched into a twenty-year-long activism after the exit from power of Indira Gandhi whose attitude towards the court was dismissive. The 'activist' court was mostly appreciated by the man in the street but did not fail to evoke some professional criticism. Heads of government at times complained of 'judicial over-reach', but there was no for-and-against political divide over the court's actions.

The Pakistani Supreme Court, browbeaten by military rulers for decades, on the other hand, began to be influenced in the late 1990s by the post-Indira Gandhi 'liberation' of the Indian Supreme Court. It took on the last military ruler General Pervez Musharraf to whom it had earlier given powers to amend the constitution under the doctrine of 'necessity', was dismissed by him, only to bounce back in 2007, after he was ousted from power. After 2008, the court leaned even more on PIL and liberally used the suo motu jurisdiction to hound a clearly incompetent executive, and was seen as 'excessive' by its critics. The empowerment of the court was in measure with the disempowerment of the other two institutions through political discord.

In Bangladesh, the Supreme Court functioned in conditions of extreme political polarization between the two parties alternating in power. Also, the judiciary was undermined by the still backward Bangladeshi trend of 'political appointments' by the government in power. It went 'activist' in 2010 during the reign of the government of Awami League's Hasina Wajed after the 2008 general election. Encouraged by references made to it about the 'basic structure' of the Bangladeshi Constitution, it struck down the 'Islamizing' 5th amendment (1979) to the constitution inserted by military dictator General Ershad and banned the religious parties disallowed by the original now-reinstated secular constitution. On the other hand, in Pakistan the Islamization of the constitution by the generals has been adjudged as 'basic structure'.

This 'activism' is however threatened by the great political schism over what kind of state Bangladesh should be. Whereas in Pakistan, the Muslim League–Pakistan People's Party split has to some extent empowered the Supreme Court, the Supreme Court in Bangladesh may actually be rendered uncertain in its 'activism' by the political vendetta between Bangladesh National Party (BNP) and the Awami League. By setting up an 'international' War Crimes Tribunal, which is doling out death sentences to religious leaders, the Hasina Wajed government may have blunted the legitimacy of the court's activism.

The Indian Precedent

In India an 'activist' judiciary gave rise to mixed reactions. The clash with the executive in India came early and was in response to an aggressive and powerful executive. Speaking in the Constituent Assembly, Prime Minister Jawaharlal Nehru said: 'No Supreme Court and no judiciary can stand in judgement over the sovereign will of Parliament representing the will of the entire community. If we go wrong here and there, it can point that out but, in the ultimate analysis, where the future of the community is concerned, no judiciary can come in the way . . . '[2]

In 1952, the Chief Justice of India shot back: 'Our constitution contains express provision for judicial review of legislation as to its conformity with the constitution'.[3] After Nehru's daughter Indira Gandhi insulted the judges of the apex court during her Emergency—somewhat like Musharraf in Pakistan in 2007—the Indian Court became 'activist' and 'interventionist'. And that led to a proliferation of PIL litigation while three crore 'normal' cases continued to be pending.

The High Courts in India began to arrange admissions in colleges and organize routines in hospitals till the chief justice of the Delhi High Court issued an order that 'no judge shall take suo motu notice of any news item without his prior permission'. When 'activist' Chief Justice P.N. Bhagwati, serving from 1985 till retirement in 1986, invited the members of the public to bring to his notice violations of human rights, he was candid enough to call this a 'judge-led' and 'judge-induced' litigation.[4]

Later, it got so bad that President A.P.J. Abdul Kalam, speaking at the National Legal Literacy Day in 2005, had to say: 'What is required is a conscious realization of unseen boundaries that cannot be traversed without causing embarrassment and even injustice to the democratic system and the rights of its citizens.' Prime Minister Manmohan Singh had to repeat that warning to the judiciary in 2007: 'All organs, including the judiciary, must ensure that the dividing lines between them are not breached.'

Lawyers have generally endorsed the 'activism' of the courts in India, but there were some who saw this activism as an excess on the part of the judiciary vis-à-vis the jurisdiction of the executive. Indian lawyer A.G. Noorani wrote in 2009: 'A conference of chief ministers and chief justices of the high courts was held in New Delhi on 16 August which Prime Minister Manmohan Singh and the chief justice of India, Justice K.G. Balakrishnan, attended. Everyone was surprised when some chief ministers raised the issue of judicial overreach. At least two of them expressed concern over the manner in which courts summoned senior government officers to appear in court in minor issues.'

Pakistan's eminent Supreme Court lawyer Abid Hasan Minto complained that Pakistan's Supreme Court was leaning on the jurisprudence of the Indian Supreme Court in interpreting the constitutional phraseology 'in consultation with' in regard to induction of judges in the higher judiciary and other precedents, without regard to the political environment specific to the Indian decisions. The truth is that the Pakistani Supreme Court had started following the Indian Supreme Court's precedent of defying the executive since 1996. What was not duly noted by the court is the public reaction to the Indian Court's total removal of the Indian Parliament's oversight in the induction of the judges.

The complications that have arisen in Pakistan in the aftermath of the 18th Amendment were compounded by the vast public support the court was able to rely on. Civil society activists, determined to roll back the autocratic era of Musharraf, joined the aggressive phalanx of the lawyers' community to give the court the backbone it needed to further expand the intrusive questioning of the executive action under Musharraf. Perhaps the court expressed itself less as an 'independent' institution—which is allowed by the constitution—but more as a 'powerful' body owing its clout to the politicization of the judicial process.

India Rationalized Activism; Pakistan Didn't

In India, judicial 'activism' did not unfold in a landscape of violence, but in Pakistan it did, given the latter's different circumstances. Even then, strong voices were raised from within the Indian superior judiciary against the 'activist' tendency to fly off the handle. As A.G. Noorani noted: 'On 10 August 2010, Justice Markandeya Katju of the Supreme Court of India delivered a strong rebuke to judges of the court under whom judicial activism had run riot for over two decades to the dismay of informed opinion. His remarks followed close on the heels of those made by Justice S.H. Kapadia who had assumed the office of chief justice of India the same year. He said that the Supreme Court would not entertain "matters of policy". Justice Katju had added: "Can the Supreme Court convert itself into an interim parliament and make laws in vacuum? Supreme Court judges should do their job and not become a parliament and make laws."'[5]

In Pakistan, violence characterized the movement launched by the lawyers and civil society to get the government to reinstate the judges fired by Musharraf. This condition, specific to Pakistan in the reassertion of the judiciary, has affected the post-restoration Supreme Court and has set Pakistan apart from India. The lawyers in 2007 had threatened the Supreme Court with arson to get it to ignore government pressure and issue a verdict of their liking reinstating the Chief Justice. In a society where power is seen as the legitimizing principle, a judiciary grown 'powerful' may be conflated with the constitutional norm of an 'independent' judiciary. This came about in a violent swing of the pendulum of public reaction against a notoriously subjugated Supreme Court in the past. Predictably, the parliament felt the heat this change brought about: it faced subjugation to a judiciary that was now likely to set aside an amendment to the constitution.

The 'Basic Structure' Argument

It is to be noted that the Pakistani judiciary also followed the lead of its Indian counterpart in discovering a 'basic structure' in the constitution which even the parliament cannot tamper with while passing amendments. In India, most jurists accept the theory of 'basic structure' in the context of the Supreme Court's confrontation with Prime Minister Indira Gandhi who tried to undo the judicial findings about her invalid elections through lawmaking in Parliament. The Court referred to the *grundnorm* of the constitution's 'basic structure' to foil her attempts at validating her election through the legislature.

In the case of Pakistan, the obiter dicta (off-record remarks) of the Supreme Court judges while hearing an appeal against the 18th Amendment—aimed at inserting the role of the legislature into the mechanism of induction of judges—signalled that the court would rely on the text of the Objectives Resolution as the 'grundnorm' and 'basic structure' of the constitution to strike down the 18th Amendment. Supreme Court lawyer Salman Akram Raja took issue with this trend of relying on the Objectives Resolution to set up a principle of 'intervention' in the function of the legislature beyond the accepted norm of 'judicial review' on the ground that in the past the court had declared that 'no part of the constitution or any other statute could be struck down by the high courts or the Supreme Court on the basis of inconsonance with the injunctions of Islam'. The Objectives Resolution was thus held not to be the 'grundnorm' of Pakistani constitutionalism.[6]

The other trend the Pakistani judiciary 'borrowed' from its Indian counterpart was the suo motu expansion of PIL. The Indian Supreme Court as well as the high courts hauled up the bureaucracy before the court on the basis of newspaper reports and distress calls addressed by citizens. India experienced an expected backlash to this kind of activism with the result that the judges themselves became split on the issue and the trend was finally disapproved by the sitting chief justices. In Pakistan, Chief Justice of the Supreme Court Iftikhar Muhammad Chaudhry established a record in taking suo motu notices by starting up 6000 cases before Musharraf ousted him from his post. But after his restoration, the high courts too began to shake up a dormant bureaucracy in the provinces with suo motu notices.

Disturbed by the negative effect PIL had on the backlog of normal cases before the courts, Supreme Court lawyer Ashtar Ausaf Ali, like many other lawyers devoted to the 'independence' of the judiciary, had this to say: 'As far back as 1958, the Supreme Court of Pakistan declared that the high courts do not have suo motu powers under the then 1956 Constitution. In 1971 the Supreme Court made a similar declaration in respect of the 1962 Constitution. The provisions vis-à-vis powers of high courts in the present constitution of Pakistan more or less resemble those in the 1962 Constitution'.[7] It appears that the terminal effect of the suo motu resort of the judiciary has been the same in India and Pakistan.

In the post-Musharraf 2008 elections, two mainstream parties, ousted from the political process by Musharraf, achieved success and were committed to act together in the matter of the restoration of the judiciary whom the President had fired. However, the PPP coalition led by President Asif Ali Zardari took its time restoring the chief justice, which had two important consequences: the rift between the two mainstream parties; and a perceived rivalry between the restored Supreme Court headed by Chief Justice Iftikhar Muhammad Chaudhry and the PPP government. What followed the restoration—achieved at the behest of Pakistan's army chief in 2009—is an unfolding of judiciary-versus-the-executive war that dimmed some of the hope that civil society had of establishing an order free of old biases.

The Court displayed its lack of knowledge of, or opposition to, the free market economic order prevailing in Pakistan when it quashed the privatization of the Pakistan Steel Mills undertaken by the Musharraf government. The court seemed not to have registered the harm it did to the process of privatization of loss-making industries by rolling back the process in the Steel Mills case. In 2013, the mills are making a loss of Rs 1.6 billion a month and no foreign buyers are interested in taking them off the hands of the government. The post-restoration Court has further compounded its economic activism by indulging in price-fixing in an economy governed by supply and demand after decades of pitiful examples of market 'intervention' through special 'utility' stores. The tendency of the court to resort to aggressive obiter dicta has also attracted the comment that the 'judges should speak only through their judgements'. The Chief Justices while asserting the primacy of national law over international law actually referred, inappropriately, to Pakistan's 'nuclear power'. The damage done by this 'activism' in the crucial energy sector may turn out to be more lasting than most observers calculate.

The most irreversible damage done to any court process is the politicization of the judicial process. The best judgement is rendered useless if delivered in an environment polarized by politics. This is what is happening in the case of Pakistan and Bangladesh. The ruling PPP thinks it is being hounded by the court while the opposition PMLN is let off the hook, if not brazenly favoured. Some of the cases brought against the PPP have recoiled badly on the court to bring the judicial process in disrepute.

The case of the alleged corruption of the Chief Justice's son Arsalan Iftikhar Chaudhry, although disposed of lightly by the court, has given rise to speculation about the integrity of the Chief Justice's family. On the other hand families of politicians have been firmly pursued, including that of an incumbent prime minister who was finally dismissed from office by the court through conviction in a contempt case. Senior lawyers pointed to the fact that the Chaudhry Court functioned mostly without any dissenting note from the bench. The violent conduct of some of the lawyers' community that supported the court, did not cover the judiciary with glory.

Barrister Aitzaz Ahsan, once the champion of the movement for the restoration of the Supreme Court, wrote in *Newsweek* Pakistan (13–20 September 2010): 'The court has consistently limited the power of Parliament and kept it subject to judicial review. If the Supreme Court of Pakistan follows the same line of reasoning, there may be a clash between the two institutions. Lawyers, whose movement sapped a military regime of undiluted power, ushered in the democracy and an independent judiciary, have a stake in both institutions, the parliament and the court.'

Former judge of the Supreme Court of India Justice Markandey Katju wrote in *The Hindu* (21 June 2012): 'How can the court remove a prime minister? This is unheard of in a democracy. The prime minister holds office as long he has the confidence of Parliament, not the confidence of the Supreme Court. I regret to say that the Pakistani Supreme Court, particularly its Chief Justice, has been showing utter lack of restraint. This is not expected of superior courts. In fact the court and its Chief Justice have been playing to the galleries for long. It has clearly gone overboard and flouted all canons of constitutional jurisprudence.'

In the past, the executive had been so powerful under autocratic or dictatorial rule that it ignored the verdicts of the court, so much so that the court took to postponing the decisions it thought would offend the executive authority. But the PPP in power was a weak executive, out of favour with the army, at loggerheads with the other big party, the PMLN, fearing the jihadi militias that looked at it as an American stooge. The powerful factor of agitating lawyers who could rough up anyone at will, including the police and media-persons, could not be ignored.

This situation however may not last. The lawyers' movement or the opposition politicians may not be willing to lend a helping hand to the judges. The army may not despise the next government in power and thus cease being the assumed 'jubilant' third party (tertium ludens) that scares the PPP today. What is to be feared is 'correction' through a swing of the pendulum against the judiciary. Stefan Troches and Graham Leung of the International Commission of Jurists (ICJ) travelled to Pakistan in 2011 to meet serving and retired judges, lawyers, politicians and officials to compile a comprehensive state of the judiciary account. The Chief Justice Iftikhar Chaudhry declined to meet this team despite their requests. The ICJ report highlighted three critical areas: 1) relating to the appointment of judges; 2) suo motu cases including their interplay with the media; and 3) separation of powers.

It observed that in case of the 19th Amendment the Supreme Court seemed to have done away with the principle *nulls index in cause sue* [i.e. no-one should be a judge in their own cause] and not only adjudicated a matter in which it was an interested party but also 'concluded that in a conflict between Parliament and the Judiciary, the latter ought to have a stronger position'. It suggested that the assumption (on the part of the Pakistani judiciary) that any involvement of political institutions in judges' appointments is incompatible with the rule of law and the respect for human rights, was 'rather disingenuous'.

The report concluded: 'We heard insinuations that the Chief Justice picked colleagues who would determine cases or reach decisions in the way he would have himself decided the case. There were also suggestions that judges who were considered partial to his views in a given case would be given preference for selection in hearing a matter.'

Judicial Activism in Bangladesh

In February, Dhaka witnessed a scene reminiscent of the Arab Spring demonstrations of Egypt's Tahrir Square. The city's Shahbagh Square had thousands of youths demanding—not democracy and civic rights—but death for a convict who had been sentenced to life imprisonment. Abdul Qader Mollah, one of the thirteen leaders under suspicion of various crimes, had come out of the court making a victory sign. At Shahbagh Square they wanted the Jamaat-e-Islami leader dead like Abdul Kalam Azad, another Jamaat leader who had been awarded capital punishment a month earlier.

The big development had come in Bangladesh in January 2010 when the Supreme Court of Bangladesh ruled that the constitutional 'Islamic amendments' inserted into the 1972 constitution by military dictators were null and void and that the four 'basic' principles of the original constitution stood revived: democracy, nationalism, socialism and secularism. The military rulers who had headed the conservative elements of Bangladesh, were not reconciled to the secularism of the founder of the new state, Sheikh Mujibur Rahman. Rahman, who took his country out of Pakistan, had in turn reacted to the constitutional evolution of an Islamic state determined to prevent East Pakistan's perceived relapse into India.

In January 2010, the Bangladesh Supreme Court threw out the 5th Amendment of General Ziaur Rahman, founder of the opposition Bangladesh National Party (BNP). Introduced in 1975, after the assassination of Rahman, the 5th Amendment added the Islamic phrase of inception: Bismillahhir Rahman nir Rahim (In the name of Allah, the most Beneficent and Merciful) and replaced pro-India Bengali nationalism with anti-India Bangladeshi nationalism, and removed the constitutional provision banning the formation of religious parties. Coming to power in 1982, General Ershad further sought support from the conservative and religious parties through the 7th Amendment making Islam the religion of the state.

The constitutional reversion by the Supreme Court was backed by an overwhelming three-fourths majority in Bangladesh's unicameral parliament by founder Rahman's daughter, Hasina Wajed's Awami League (AL) after the 2008 elections. The stubborn practice of inducting judges to the higher judiciary on political considerations compounded the revengeful trend further. Despite legitimate grounds for strict separation of the judiciary from the executive, the AL government has leaned on politicization of the courts in the country.

But even a big majority in Parliament did not embolden Prime Minister Wajed to go the whole hog as intended by the Supreme Court. Sporting a more conservative dress and a Muslim rosary when she returned from her exile in 1981, she had signalled her recognition of the Islamization of Bangladesh in the interim. So in October 2010, sitting down to consider the consequences of the court's overturning of the 5th and 7th Amendments, she agreed with her advisers not to remove the Arabic blessing of General Ziaur Rehman. She also agreed not to remove General Ershad's insertion of 'Islam as state religion' in recognition of the new 'reality' in Bangladesh. (Pakistan's leader Benazir Bhutto had also returned to Pakistan from exile in 1986 fingering prayer beads in recognition of the same reality.)

This decision had serious repercussions for the 'reform' in laws suggested by the Supreme Court decision and has angered the liberal-secular centres of opinion in the country. It has also pushed back the widespread demand for the banning of religious parties clearly suggested by the verdict. How can a state with Islam as its official religion ban Islamic parties? The Dhaka high court reacted by forbidding a women's college to impose a Muslim dress code on its students, saying the Supreme Court verdict had automatically reverted the country to secularism. Most Islamic scholars insist that separation of religion and politics in public life under secularism was abhorrent to Islam.

But the AL government moved to target the religious parties in another way: by reviving the International Crimes Tribunal Act of 1973 to punish Crimes against Humanity and Genocide and setting up two National Tribunals in 2010 and 2012. Foreign Minister Ms Dipu Moni was at pains to clarify the status of these courts in January 2013, saying: 'The International Crimes Tribunals in Bangladesh is not "international" in nature, but for all meaning and purposes they are "domestic". The only international element in the whole scheme of things is the nature of the offences, that is, the international crimes.'

The opposition in Bangladesh was never as crushed. General Zia's widow Khaleda Zia who leads the right-wing BNP has ruled in the past with the help of the religious parties led by Jamaat-e-Islami. (Two BNP members faced charges at the war crimes tribunals.) Most observers thought it would take a long time to revive BNP and its partner parties unless a natural calamity or a steep deterioration of the economy compels people to join the most prominent trait of the nation: violent street protest. There was enough ammunition for agitation in 2014 by AL opponents: stuffing of the courts and tribunals with political appointee judges.

Bangladesh has been called politically dysfunctional. Will its next 'dysfunctionality' come from what its courts hand down in the coming days? Wrote William Milam, US ambassador to Bangladesh (1990–93) and to Pakistan (1998–2001) in the *Friday Times*: 'The Awami League has come to power in the worst of all possible ways, with an overwhelming majority in Parliament. This led immediately to a majoritarian approach to governance, which seems inherent in the politics of South Asia. As in many developing countries, when one of the political parties wins an election by a large margin the victory appears to give the leader of the winning party the impression that he or she embodies the nation, and is, according to one scholar, the main custodian and definer of its interests and is entitled to govern as he or she sees fit, constrained only by the hard facts of existing power relations and by a constitutionally limited term of office.'[8]

Lawyers in Dhaka who didn't like what was building up in the country discreetly pointed to flaws in the justice system under the AL in the face of an unusually strict contempt-of-court routine practised by the judges (another development not in line with precedents in India and Pakistan). In Bangladesh, the law, or absence of it, allowed the government to make the Supreme Court appointments without 'meaningful consultation' with the chief justice. Justice Ruhul Quddus Babu was among the seventeen new judges appointed in April 2010. He was an accused in the 1988 murder of a leader of the student wing of the Jamaat-e-Islami but the case against him was dropped shortly before his appointment, drawing sharp criticism from the Supreme Court Bar Association.

As a further public relations fiasco, the then Chief Justice refused to administer the oath to Mr Babu together with two more appointees who had been accused of kicking the door of the chief justice's room in 2006 as 'an act of vandalism'. The said chief justice, who offended the government by not administering oaths, was replaced in September 2010 with a more pliable judge by superseding two senior appellate division judges. The Dhaka Supreme Court Bar Association declared that the appointment had laid bare the 'government's intention to control the next caretaker government, which will conduct the national elections in 2013, which are normally overseen by the last retired judge of the Supreme Court'.

Judicial secularization in Bangladesh may not succeed because of political polarization. Pakistan's polarization in favour of an activated Supreme Court has been more one-sided than Bangladesh's because of the right-wing and the growing Islamist extremism dictated from abroad by Arab friends in a state in Pakistan 'softened' by al-Qaeda and the Taliban. The Supreme Court in Bangladesh is stymied by the procedural excesses of the government, such as the induction of judges, which will be pursued by AL's opponents whenever they come to power. But Bangladesh is less internationally isolated than Pakistan therefore its internal bipolar fracture is not exacerbated by unfriendly neighbours and international terrorism.

Justice is marred by politicization even when immaculately delivered, that is, when one side of the political landscape thinks the courts are discriminatory. This has not happened in India as much as in Bangladesh and Pakistan. There are bound to be corrections in the long run but not before much damage is done through exaggeration of illiberal forces in Pakistan and secularist dreams—which can't be fulfilled—in Bangladesh. Judicial strictures in Bangladesh will however be less damaging than in Pakistan where the bankrupt state is in retreat and governance minimized by its eroding outreach. India's economic performance—and to some extent Bangladesh's—will cushion the consequences of judicial overdrive in those two countries, but in Pakistan people may have to suffer more strife because of the sense of irremediable grievance and victimization created by it.

The Indian higher judiciary has already responded to criticism through self-correction in the realm of public interest litigation—the infamous suo motu. In Pakistan, where vendetta-prone politicians use litigation to get even with one another, the Supreme Court has emerged as the strongest of the three pillars of the state, at times challenging Parliament itself, and it may take a while to moderate its reactive overdrive. In Bangladesh, it is clearly the overgrown muscle of Parliament after 2008 that is trespassing on the judicial turf through political inductions. Sadly, vendetta politics, borrowed from Pakistan, has steered the state repeatedly to dysfunction.

18

Saint Qazi (1938–2013)

In November 2007, the leader of Tehreek-e-Insaf Imran Khan, paid a visit to his fans at the Punjab University Lahore but was roughed up by the Islami Jamiat Tulaba, the student wing of Jamaat-e-Islami, before being handed over to the police. The chief of the Jamaat Qazi, Hussain Ahmad immediately condemned the attack, thus setting the trend—since grown strong—of distancing the Jamaat from the wilder forays of its Lahore student wing. He went further. He took his inner circle at the Mansura headquarters of the party and called on Imran Khan at Zaman Park, making his dissociation from the act of violence real by apologizing to him. The Khan was visibly touched because Qazi Sahib had a way of being persuasive with sincere understatement. The consequence was that when Imran Khan's father died, it was Qazi Sahib who led the funeral prayer at Zaman Park in March 2008. He laid the foundation of Tehreek-e-Insaf–Jamaat relations that continued after his retirement as emir ameer.

Taliban Revenge

Qazi died of cardiac arrest on 6 January 2013. He had already had two by-passes, the fruit of being at the helm of a religious party for four stormy tenures, during which he removed the hard edges of the party ideology, personally growing into the high status of a wise man wedded to the Islamic principles of *adl* (middle path) and *ihsan* (concession) which he kept articulating in his last days. He had to take the party away from the anathema of being host to early al-Qaeda terrorists and being counted among the 'non-state actors' of Pakistan that the world abominated.

He may have succumbed finally to the stress he endured a few days earlier during an attempt on his life in the Mohmand Tribal Agency by a woman suicide bomber sent by the Taliban chief Hakimullah Mehsud through the Mohmand warlord Omar Afridi. Qazi was to be punished for his remark on TV in April 2012 that 'the Afghan Taliban's resistance against the US-led coalition forces in Afghanistan is true jihad but that of the Pakistani Taliban in Pakistan is un-Islamic.' A video CD released by Hakimullah had him saying that ex-ameer Jamaat-e-Islami Qazi Hussain Ahmad 'is a traitor to the cause of jihad (jihad-*farosh*) and a secret member of the Jewish Lobby because he favours democracy'. What he said next gave a measure of how much Qazi had grown out of the mould of a traditional religious leader: 'There was a time when educated people, students, ulema and others used to respect you a lot. But I can no longer trust you, Qazi Sahib. Why are you calling our battle *fasaad* (disorder) instead of jihad?'

Smoothed by Circumstance

Qazi's moderation came from the process of adjustment to the political kaleidoscope, taking his party from a jihad-oriented religious organization in the 1980s to a more democratic identity in the 1990s—in other words, from a covert war led by Jamaat to a covert war led by the Deobandi consensus in the tutelage of Al

Qaeda. His personality helped the Jamaat to make the transition from jihad to politics-as-usual under democracy. His rare mix of tough posture and tolerance for variants of view was a hard act to follow for his successor, Syed Munawwar Hasan, whom some observers see as a bit of an ineffectual stormy petrel trying to radicalize the party in step with the Taliban.

Born in 1938 in a village near Nowshehra in Khyber Pakhtunkhwa province, Qazi never really took seriously his father's naming him after the All India Deobandi Jamiat Ulema-e-Hind leader Hussain Ahmad Madni. (Madni had had an argument with Allama Iqbal, Pakistan's national poet, over the nature of the modern state; Qazi never tired of quoting lines from Allama Iqbal.) Given his family's religious background, he could not have become secular-liberal as some of the Pashtun youths had chosen to under the influence of the All India Congress Party, but he never aspired to the status of a maulvi and was not scared of admitting it as ameer of the Jamaat. He became active in the Jamiat, the student wing of Abul Ala Maududi's party—till he had reached the top of its ladder.

In 1979, after the Soviet Union invaded Afghanistan, the Pakistan army was in the saddle in Pakistan. Its chief, General Zia-ul-Haq, took the decision of fighting the Soviets on the side of the United States and his patron state Saudi Arabia. As if in preparation for the role set for him, Qazi had stayed away from the madrasa, completing his MSc in geography from the prestigious Islamia College in Peshawar, getting busy with his family business, and joining the Jamaat only in 1970, to soon climb to the top of the party hierarchy in his province. In 1978 he had become the secretary general of the central Jamaat—just in time for the mounting of the first Afghan jihad in our times.

A Pashtun for Jihad

A deniable war was unfolding in Afghanistan, spearheaded by the Pashtun youths of Afghanistan and Pakistan most of whom were inspired by the urban-based Jamaat. The strategists of Pakistan perhaps had a hand in getting Pashtun Qazi to head the Lahore-based party whose Punjabi chief was not known to be politically too bright. Qazi became chief of the Jamaat in 1987 even as the covert jihad in Afghanistan was winding down and resurfacing in India-administered Kashmir. Qazi was charismatic albeit deceptively stern of visage. He had become acquainted with the leaders of the Afghan militias while they bided their time in Peshawar under the auspices of the Pakistan army. One relationship that he cemented with the leader of Hizbe Islami, Gulbuddin Hekmatyar, proved to be empowering because Pakistan's Inter-Services Intelligence (ISI) leaned in favour of the Afghan warlord in terms of funds and weapons.

Most people thought the Qazi–Hekmatyar friendship was based on an identity of views. More correctly, it was based on Hekmatyar's deep reverence for Qazi, unfortunately offset by the former's pathologically suspicious and stubborn nature. Qazi never encouraged his friend to fight with other mujahideen commanders as he disliked the Pashtun–Northern Alliance split on the eve of victory against the Soviets. A Pakistani journalist visiting Iran in 2001 together with Qazi observed:

'Qazi Sahib met Hekmatyar, who had sought sanctuary in Teheran, and criticized him for not making an effort to reach out to the Northern Alliance leader Ahmad Shah Massoud, commander of the Jamiat Islami militia. He saw no merit in the infighting of the mujahideen. Hekmatyar defended himself while showing utmost deference to Qazi Sahib.'

Days before he passed away, Qazi's advice to the Pakistan army was: 'Stay out of Afghanistan and let the Afghans sort it out among themselves. Don't fear India's presence in Afghanistan because the Afghans will never allow Indians to dictate to them. Afghanistan must be a state in which the Pashtuns of the south live as brothers to the non-Pashtun of the north.'

With Qazi Hussain Ahmad as ameer the Jamaat became Pakistan's major pawn in the 'deniable' US–Saudi-supported jihad in Afghanistan. Its branch-line, the Hizbul Mujahideen militia, had indigenously developed in India-Administered Kashmir as a pro-Pakistan resistance group. Being a Pashtun was important in those days of radical activism. He was the ideal ameer, a favourite of the student wing, the Jamiat. He was to leave his imprint on the Jamaat and on religious politics of the country, remaining unchallenged within the party during four re-elections, 1992, 1994, 1999 and 2003.

A Radical Qazi

The mellowing of Qazi Hussain Ahmad was a gradual process and it was good for the Jamaat as it suffered the spectacle of other schools of thought—the Deobandi and Ahle Hadith—monopolizing the arena of jihad in Afghanistan and India. But the early days were Qazi's radical phase. In 1990, he turned his attention inward and sought to revolutionize Pakistani society through 'social justice' and 'equality' enforced by his newly founded youth outfit named Pasban. The slogan was: 'If we don't succeed in bringing about equitable redistribution of wealth, we'll equitably redistribute hunger and poverty.' Qazi himself came out at the head of aggressive processions with the slogan: *'Zalimo!* Qazi *aa raha hai!'* (Oppressors, Qazi is coming!) Qazi was the inventor of dharna (sit-down protest) with which he demonstrated party muscle to subdue the government and attracted the middle class to his 'alternative power'.

Perhaps Qazi learned his most useful lesson handling Pasban which, he soon discovered, had been penetrated by the intelligence agencies. It may also be the only blot on his career. In 1994, he decided to say goodbye to the threat of violence Pasban was using and dismantled it. He formed Shabab-e-Milli which he controlled more effectively but the response of the activated youths to Shabab was lukewarm. The spark ignited by Pasban was gone. The Shabab got busy as a youthful ancillary helping organize Jamaat's campaigns. The 'trouble-shooting' activities were taken up by the other rising stars of jihad, Deobandi Jaish-e-Mohammad and Wahhabi Lashkar-e-Taiba, who charged a fee for helping citizens 'obtain justice informally'. Unfortunately the terrorists of Somalia stole the name Shabab and gave it to the world's most blood-thirsty militia.

Loyal to Maududi Legacy

Qazi was a personable man of piety who forswore the status of a preaching mullah. He was loyal to the inspiration and lesson of the founder of the Jamaat, Abul Ala Maududi, and maintained his contacts with the Ikhwanul Muslimeen (Muslim Brotherhood) of Egypt whose founder Hasan al Banna the Jamaat celebrated in its publications. Ikhwan intellectual Syed Qutb had accepted Maududi as his inspiration for the establishment of an Islamic state. Qazi must have later grasped the irony of choice on the part of al-Qaeda when it adopted the Taliban and Lashkar-e-Taiba in lieu of the Jamaat when the Pakistani state controlling the jihad took the baton away from him. Al-Qaeda today boasts Syed Qutb as its preceptor.

There were other ways in which Qazi paid homage to Maududi. He kept away from the Sunni-Shia rift among the religious parties and tried his best to keep Pakistan out of the sectarian war developing in the Gulf between Saudi Arabia and Iran. After General Zia was attracted to the side of the Sunni states in the Gulf for confessional as well as economic reasons, Qazi carefully kept the Jamaat out of the sectarian war that killed Iranian diplomats in Punjab. On one occasion when the fanatics were ransacking an Iranian cultural centre on the Mall in Lahore, he surprised everyone by appearing on the scene to talk sense to the mob.

Disenchantment too taught some lessons. Eyewitness Riaz Muhammad Khan, ex-foreign secretary of Pakistan, in his book, *Afghanistan, and Pakistan: Conflict, Extremism, and Resistance to Modernity*, tells the story of the so-called Peshawar Accord among the mujahideen in 1992 on the future governance in Afghanistan:

'It was arranged for Qazi Hussain Ahmad to meet the two leaders on the afternoon of 20 April in Peshawar, where he was to join Prime Minister Nawaz Sharif to meet the Tanzeemat leadership. After meeting for several hours with rival leaders Rabbani and Qutbuddin Hilal, Qazi Hussain Ahmad came to the governor's house for the prime minister's meeting frothing at the mouth, exceedingly upset with the Jamiat (Tajik Massoud) and Hizb (Pashtun Hekmatyar) leaders. When asked about his discussions, he remarked: 'There was a time when these people had turned up at my doorstep in tatters. Today they refuse to listen to me.' Throughout the evening's meeting, which lasted for nearly five hours until well past midnight, Qazi Hussain Ahmad sat stone-faced without making a single intervention.'[1]

Not His Finest Hour

There was an episode in the life of the Jamaat that Qazi wanted desperately to live down: his party's taking part in the 2002 general election in which General Musharraf, allowed by the Supreme Court to be army chief cum president with powers to selectively amend the constitution, let the religious parties win in the NWFP and Balochistan with some help from the ISI. Qazi was president of Mutahida Majlis-e-Amal (MMA), an unlikely alliance of religious parties of all stripes, which the Shia had also joined in hopes of sitting among their killers for security.

In 2003, another trauma was endured by Qazi, this time in Balochistan where his alliance MMA was in government. Scores of Shia had been massacred during a procession. GEO TV interviewed the imam of the Hazara Imambargah at Quetta after the event. The imam said the attack was carried out by Sipah-e-Sahaba, Jaish-e-Mohammad and Lashkar-e-Jhangvi. Qazi Hussain Ahmad who was present on the occasion was asked by the Shia imam to intercede with others in the MMA to stop the bloodbath.

Qazi replied in his familiar honest style: 'The government is responsible for the killings and since MMA is in the government it is equally to blame.'

The wages of ignoring Qazi's moderate voice is that today the state watches as the Hazara Shia of Quetta silently fall to the firing squads of the jihadi outfits backed by Pakistan's madrasa network. Out of 600,000 Hazaras in Quetta 800 have been killed in what the Hazaras call Shia genocide. Qazi was saint-like to people who met him. The secret of this disarmament of fear was his non-threatening personality, unlike your regular maulvi who warns you of the punishment in the hereafter and challenges the neighbouring states with pious terror. As a Pashtun he was a violation of the Pashtun type: he was flexible in the treatment of enemies. He had the gift of compassion and called on his enemies as well as friends in times of their duress. His slogan was embedded in the politics of 'confluence of the politically unlike'. After the fracturing of the MMA—which had imposed the draconian Hasba Bill on the NWFP and allowed Swat to fall under the guns of Taliban—he put together a milder Milli Yakjehti Council, this time based on a peaceful articulation of principles.

The MMA phase was not his finest hour. It saw the Jamaat decline in influence in the face of the rising power of the Taliban and their Deobandi backers. A nadir was reached when the rising star of jihadi radicalism, Sufi Muhammad of Swat, denounced democracy and the Constitution of Pakistan as un-Islamic, denigrating religious leaders like Qazi as ideological deviants. It would be wrong on the part of a liberal to claim Qazi as his own by ignoring his quintessentially religious character. It was expected of him even as a moderate to challenge TV programming in Pakistan as vulgarity under law. But he was devoid of the schadenfreude that allows some to feel joy over the misfortune of rivals. Amazingly, the nation felt a unanimous warmth for someone with whom it did not agree all the time. Right-wing columnists in Urdu indulged in an apotheosis no one actually disagreed with, and that is saying a lot for Qazi the man.

Najam Sethi, TV anchor and publisher of the liberal weekly the *Friday Times,* remembered him fondly after his death: 'When I was being hounded by Saif ur Rehman [the 'accountability bureau' attack-dog of Prime Minister Nawaz Sharif] and the *Friday Times* was banished from its printing press, it was Qazi Sahib who came to the rescue. The liberal magazine was actually printed at the Jamaat-e-Islami press! I will never forget that!'

19

Grasping Many Thistles

Akbar Ahmed had a good homecoming to Pakistan in 2013, and his message was embraced by the state of Pakistan, Army Chief General Raheel Sharif presenting him with a shield after his lecture in December at the Pakistan army's premier institution, the National Defence University in Islamabad. The navy chief was so impressed he sought his permission to reprint his latest book, *The Thistle and the Drone: How America's War on Terror became a Global War on Tribal Islam,* for the Pakistan Navy Book Club.

Once Akbar Salahuddin Ahmed, which he for a time compressed to Akbar S. Ahmed, this is probably his best book, if not for its substance then for the kind of impact it made in the world, including the United States, where he holds the Ibn Khaldun Chair for Islamic Studies at American University and is a non-resident senior fellow at the Brookings Institution in Washington DC. The European Union, perhaps also moved by his 'centre versus periphery' thesis announced its opposition to America's use of drones in Pakistan and Yemen because of the human rights they violated.

Ahmed holds a PhD in anthropology. His mind is shaped by the discipline's non-partisan, non-judgemental approach to the study of all human communities. He abhors labelling and stands apart when rivals go at each other's throat with Manichean reductionism. He hates the 'metanarrative' of Clash of Civilizations and tries against all odds to make religions communicate with one another with mutual acceptance. When he met its nonagenarian inventor of the term, Bernard Lewis, at a forum he was reported as 'helping the ninety-five-year-old Professor Bernard Lewis climb the stage; during the pleasant discussion that followed, Professor Ahmed even opened a water bottle when Professor Lewis seemed to choke; and the warmth continued in the cool November evening.' The upshot was the realization that Lewis's 'Clash of Civilizations' had been de-contextualized and misunderstood.

Bite Like the Thistle

His thesis, in his own words, is cast like this:

'These suffering people [targeted by the war on terror] had one thing in common—they were all part of communities living on the periphery and margins of the state. Those who represented the centre of the state usually called them "primitive" and "savage". Some said their time in history was up. Love of freedom, egalitarianism, a tribal lineage system defined by common ancestors and clans, a martial tradition, and a highly developed code of honour and revenge—these are the thistle-like characteristics of the tribal societies. Moreover, as with the thistle, there is a clear correlation between their prickliness, or toughness, and the level of force used by those who wish to subdue these societies, as the Americans discovered after 9/11.'[1]

In *The Thistle and the Drone*, the tribal 'thistle' that 'bites back' has been framed in such a way that it cannot be ignored—like the way Pakistan ignored his earlier studies of the tribal communities of Pakistan. His campaign to make Islam understood through an interfaith TV dialogue did not succeed in the United Kingdom when he was Pakistan's high commissioner there, but his broad acceptance of all faiths in his book has been well absorbed after disenchantment with the solutions sought through 'unmanned aerial vehicles' called drones that kill with precisely-targeted 'Hellfire missiles'.

An anthropologist knows his subject community more deeply than other researchers because he lives within it and identifies with it to a fault, as an extreme act of exorcism divesting oneself of the indoctrinated judgements imposed by society or state. Ahmed speaks for the 'peripheral' people who live sandwiched between the central state and the rebellious 'thistle' reacting against its intrusion. He warns against taking his views as judgements: 'While explanations of the violence are provided in this book, they cannot justify or rationalize it in any way.' As he speaks for them, he reveals details so far hidden from view. The terrorist attack by nineteen Arabs on 11 September 2001 in the United States was not merely an 'Arab action' as often claimed by Pakistani analysts but was carried out by a group of individuals belonging to the alienated 'peripheral' community of southern Saudi Arabia. The province of Asir is populated by Yemeni tribes living on the basis of a tribal code shared by all 'segmentary-lineage'-based communities in the world.

Yemenis in the Works

According to Osama bin Laden's bodyguard Nasir al-Bahri, a Yemeni born in Saudi Arabia, '95 per cent of al-Qaeda activists were Yemenis, meaning they were either from Yemen, were ethnic Yemenis whose families had moved to Saudi Arabia, or were from ethnic Yemeni areas in Saudi Arabia, most prominently from the Asir region, or indeed elsewhere.'[2]

Although the leader of the nineteen, Mohammed Atta of Egypt, has become the best known of the 9/11 hijackers, he was not the driving force behind the plot. He was your typical malcontent reacting to the perceived condition of the ordinary man in his native Cairo and 'blamed the corrupt national leadership with its Western support for their miserable situation'. Contrary to claims made in Pakistan that the nineteen had nothing to do with Pakistan, he arrived in Karachi, 'still searching for a cause and met members of bin Laden's group and was brought to Afghanistan.'[3]

But eighteen out of the nineteen hijackers were Yemeni. Ten were from the tribes of Asir, whose role in the 9/11 operation was acknowledged by bin Laden himself who declared: 'Asir's tribes formed the lion's share [of the 9/11 perpetrators, including those from Ghamed, Zahran, etc., all Asir tribes.' Author Ahmed explains: 'The largest single tribe represented in the group was the Ghamdi tribe of Asir, with four members: Ahmed and Hamza al-Ghamdi who were brothers, Saeed al-Ghamdi, and Ahmad al-Haznawi. Others from Asir were Abdul Aziz al-Omari al-Zahrani of the Zahran tribe, the brothers Wail and Waleed al-Shehri, and Mohand al-Shehri of the Shahran tribe, and Hani Hanjur, who can be identified with the village of Hanjur in the area of the Abidah tribe in Asir.

'Fayez Banihammad, who was born in the United Arab Emirates (UAE), may have had family ties to Asir as he attended university there and was also commonly identified as Fayez Ahmed al-Shehri, which would indicate an affiliation with the Shahran tribe of Asir. By providing their full names, they were giving a clue to their tribal identity and lineage. The other ethnic Yemenis included Khalid Muhammad Abdallah al-Mihdhar, whose family was from Yemen, although he grew up in Mecca. Marwan al-Shehhi claimed descent from the Qahtani tribes. Ziad Jarrah of Lebanon may be connected to the Jarrah tribe, part of the larger QahtaniShammar tribe.

'Majid Muqid Mushan bin Ghanim can be identified with the traditionally nomadic Ghanim tribe of the Taif area, which is a branch of the Qahtani Thaqif tribe. The three remaining hijackers, Satar al-Suqami and the brothers Nawaf and Salem al-Hazmi, are probably Yemeni as their family names are place names in Yemen, although they were born in Saudi Arabia. In all probability, keeping in mind Mohammed Atta's Egyptian nontribal background, eighteen of the nineteen hijackers on 9/11 were Yemeni tribesmen or descendants of Qahtan.'[4]

The 'warrior' characteristic of the peripheral communities has come in handy, for the UK in relation to the Yemenis, and Pakistan in relation to the Pakhtun of its Tribal areas, both states using them in national wars. Well known British scholar of the Middle East, Fred Halliday, in a letter to the BBC in 1996, reacted angrily to the growing prejudice in the UK against its Arab community. He recalled that most of what the British accused the Arabs of first was tried out by Europe. He was particularly put off by a *Sunday Express* article titled 'We Owe Arabs Nothing'. Halliday found opportunity to praise the Yemenis who first came to the UK in large numbers and helped build it. The Yemenis today form the majority of the Arabs in the UK. They served in the Royal Navy in the Second World War and laid down their lives for their adopted country and are remembered on a memorial at Liverpool.

The book goes on to describe and interpret at length the other 'peripheral' communities at war with their central governments: Pakistan, Iran, Yemen, Mali, Somalia, Nigeria, Algeria, etc., and makes remarkable revelations about the uniformity of conduct among the tribal people fighting the centralized state across the Asian and African continents. To trap him with an exception, a TV chat-show host asked Ahmed whether Iran too was fighting its peripheral communities like Pakistan, Iraq and Syria. His answer was a bit of a surprise for the host: 'Iran treats its Arabs, Kurds and Baloch the way Pakistan does its tribal people.'

The book records: 'If Iran treats the Kurds, Baloch, Ahwazi Arabs, Turkmen, and Azeris harshly, it does the same to the Jews and Bahai. Take Pakistan as another example. Its recent treatment of its periphery in the Tribal Areas and Balochistan is far from satisfactory and compromises the vision of the founder of the nation, Mohammad Ali Jinnah, but its handling of Hindus and Christians and even sects like the Shia and Ahmadis is not much different.'[5]

Non-state Actors and Ungoverned Spaces

Ahmed catalogues all the incidents of terrorism including those caused by the 'non-state actors' from the plains of Punjab affiliated with al-Qaeda that the state had been using in its proxy wars with the 'peripheral' Taliban at war with the state after it joined the global 'war on terrorism' following the UN Security Council Resolution 1373. This complicates the role played by the deep state in the undoing of its internal sovereignty. Pakistan's ex-foreign minister Ms Hina-Rabbani Khar, speaking at the Lahore Literary Festival in February bluntly stated: 'The biggest threat to Pakistan's existence are the non-state actors created by the state itself to fight its proxy wars.'

Daniel S. Markey, who held the South Asia portfolio on the Secretary's Policy Planning Staff at the US Department of State from 2003 to 2007, writes in his book, *No Exit from Pakistan: America's Tortured Relationship with Pakistan,* 'Fighters trained by Lashkar-e-Taiba (LeT) routinely work with other radical groups focused on the Afghan front and beyond. Many of these groups are completely untethered, even opposed, to the Pakistani state. For instance, the al-Qaeda-linked perpetrators of the July 2005 London bombings trained in LeT camps before carrying out their attacks.

'David Headley's LeT handlers also shared him with al-Qaeda, who sent him to conduct surveillance in Denmark against the newspaper that had published what al-Qaeda considered blasphemous cartoons in preparation for a planned attack in 2009. These facts belie the notion too often voiced by Pakistanis that Washington's concerns about LeT are overblown or driven merely by an eagerness to cultivate better relations with India.'[6]

In Pakistan LeT is now known by the name of Jamaatud Dawa, but in the Kunar province of Afghanistan, the perch from where the Taliban terrorists target Pakistan, it still interfaces with al-Qaeda and works in tandem with it. Pakistani journalist SaleemShahzad who, in his book, *Inside Al-Qaeda and the Taliban: Beyond bin Laden and 9/11,* revealed this nexus, was mysteriously abducted and killed by no one knows who. However, the focus remains on the 'wrong' of America's war on tribal Islam as it was based on a lack of understanding of the affected people. When the TV host asked him whether America's policy toward Pakistan was that of hatred aimed at destroying the country, Ahmed replied: 'America's policies are not based on emotion but rational analysis.' It is on the rational basis that the book challenges the 'drone' of the war on terrorism aimed at the 'thistle' of Tribal Islam.

In Liberal–Radical Crossfire

It is easy therefore to misunderstand Akbar Ahmed on both sides of the divide among his readers, those who have welcomed his latest thesis and those who have a history of denigrating him. The 'liberals' have doubted his enterprise of championing Islam by 'sucking up to the fanatics'; the fundamentalists on the other hand have rejected his advocacy as fake Islam in the garb of 'Jinnah's Islam'. Writing in Lahore's the *Friday Times* he took on the liberals:

'There is also the failure of the elite to come to grips with the problems of Pakistan. Many of its members, like Pakistani 'liberal' commentators, reflect ideas picked up from Washington or London think tanks such as the War on Terror. They simplify what is happening in Pakistan as an Islamic movement. Their analysis is replete with words and concepts like jihadis, Islamists, and salafis, which explain little and add to the confusion. Not fully understanding the problem, like their western colleagues, they are incapable of offering solutions.'[7]

And the so-called 'liberals' continue to fail to see where Ahmed effectively supports their worldview, especially when he takes on the extremism of the faith while analysing the worldview of the founder of Pakistan, Mohammad Ali Jinnah. In 2003, Ahmed wrote his book, *Islam under Siege: Living Dangerously in Post-Honour World*, and put his hand in the hornet's nest of radical Islam gelling in Britain. When Akbar was making his Jinnah film and trying to talk to the 'other side' in an interfaith dialogue that he led on TV, a whole lot of Muslims were put off. Islam giving itself over to dialogue with any other faith was unfamiliar to them. Ahmed was disliked by the secular intellectuals in Pakistan who browbeat him despite the fact that his books,which came out regularly, persistently challenged the current extremist views of Islam. Somehow his personality kept getting between the people and his books.

In the UK where he began his project of talking to Christianity on behalf of Islam, the aggressive local Islamists didn't like it one bit. One was Sheikh Umar Bakri, the unpleasantly frothy founder of Hizbut Tahrir, the near-violent organization that damns everything if it is not khilafat. Bakri was quoted as calling him 'chocolate Muslim' and 'an Uncle Tom' [sic] because of his 'admiration of Western civilization more than Islamic civilization'. 'He is a sincere Muslim but sincere is not enough', he said. In October 2001 Bakri sent his followers to Afghanistan for jihad. That was what was missing in Akbar Ahmed who was merely dialoguing!

When he was making his movie on Jinnah, Bakri once again fired from both barrels. Ahmed noted: 'In Britain, Sheikh Umar Bakri's *Khilafah*, the journal of Hizbut Tahrir, attacked Jinnah as a kafir, an insult for a Muslim. Moreover it accused Jinnah of being an enemy of God and the holy Prophet (PBUH) because Jinnah supported women, Christians and Hindus, and advocated democracy. Why, I asked myself, did they pick on Jinnah? Because, I concluded, Bakri saw him as a major ideological opponent. Significantly, after the American strikes in Sudan and Afghanistan in 1998, Bakri emerged in the media to claim that he represented bin Laden in Europe.'

Later, when Ahmed started visiting Christian and Jewish gatherings to present the Islamic view he was attacked by HizbutTahrir in the press. 'I was walking perilously close to the fatwa territory,' he wrote. He has not stopped doing that: his book recounts how he spoke at the Holocaust Museum in the US and condemned what had been done the Jews whereas many Muslims believe that Holocaust never happened! He reveals that many of his relatives were killed by Taliban leader Fazlullah in Swat and that their descendants were residing in Islamabad today vowing tribal revenge on the man.

Minefield of Hyper-asabiyya

Muslim readers ignored his earlier work, *Postmodernism and Islam: Predicament and Promise,* and failed to look at him as someone who understood the intellectual legacies of both the West and Islam enough to enter into a reasonable dialogue between what are being increasingly viewed as two opposed 'logospheres' in our day. Paying tribute to the first great 'anthropologist' in human history Ibn Khaldun, who wrote in the fourteenth century, he explained the new radical identity crisis of Islam by extending his concept of *asabiyya* (identity). He felt that some among the Muslims had become extreme and wanted fellow-Muslims to revert to the old *asabiyya* through violence. This violent principle of organization he calls hyper-asabiyya and rejects it out of hand as being against the spirit of Islam. To him, post-modernity bothers the West— 'a period of gentle apocalypse'—but it completely confuses the Muslims who failed earlier to climb out of the colonial period into the twentieth century.'

Writing in Pakistan, he put his finger on the crux of the problem: 'Every citizen must accept the challenge to take back and re-establish the writ of the state. But time is running out. The situation warrants a long-term and radical strategy to re-establish the writ of the state. It needs to be holistic and long-term. The path ahead will be difficult and will require courage, wisdom and compassion from the leaders of Pakistan.' As a part of this holistic approach he wants the army to withdraw from the Tribal Areas at some stage; he wants the re-establishment of the old system of self-governance based on tribal elders, religious leaders as supported by the political agent with an anthropological 'non-judgemental' approach to the peripheral society, tempered with 'reconstruction' of its educational and health infrastructure.

But how much reconstruction will Pakistan itself need is anyone's guess. The state has been evolving from a 'soft' to 'hard' Muslim identity and has come to the final stage of hyper-asabiyya because of the state's policy of allowing a premodern interpretation of jihad. Most 'non-state actor' formations in settled territories proclaim that jihad is no longer the exclusive function of the state. The consequence is the 're-tribalization' of a rapidly urbanizing country, often called Talibanization. Pakistan's national consensus, as articulated by an all parties' conference in 2013, comprises the following pro-Taliban components:

A Furtive Re-tribalization

One, the drone attacks must be stopped because they infringe the sovereignty of Pakistan and cause impermissible collateral damage, swelling the ranks of tribesmen whose revenge is then visited on Pakistan; two, the war on terror (against the Taliban) is not, and never was, Pakistan's war and was joined by then-ruler General Musharraf with treasonable intent; three, consequently Musharraf has become the symbol of the policy Pakistan has abandoned and should suitably face a case of high treason in Pakistan for imposing martial law in 2008; four, Pakistan demands, in unison with al-Qaeda, the release of Afiya Siddiqi, an agent of al-Qaeda according to the US, from an American prison; five, that the attack in 2007 by the state on an al-Qaeda watering-hole in the heart of Islamabad, Red Mosque, was a criminal act; and six, as and when the Taliban deny responsibility for an act of terrorism, the real culprit must be the 'external enemies' of Pakistan, read America, India and, for good measure, Israel.

The Huntingtonian thesis of 'Clash of Civilizations' or 'West against the Rest' that Akbar Ahmed opposes, together with a myriad European scholars of good standing, has been espoused by both sides. The Muslim world is bristling with anti-West prejudices starting with a 'crusades' complex rising from the reversion of the Muslim mind to the past. The 'clash' may have poisoned the minds of some policymakers of the West but it suffuses the worldview of entire Muslim nations with consequences they have not yet analysed as they fight their internecine national and sectarian wars and their refugee populations throng the borders of the West. Akbar Ahmed may get hurt by this polarization because what he says is still right.

For the first time however Ahmed has not run into opposition from the people of the faith he supports. Those who still doubt his credentials should go back to his book, *Islam Today: A Short Introduction to the Muslim World,* and judge for themselves. That he is an apologist there is no doubt when he praises the conceptual excellence of Islam while rejecting the Muslim praxis. On the question of Islamic punishments, he tried to disabuse the Western opinion about the supposed cruelty of the Quranic 'hudood' by pointing out that the concept of *ihsan* (mercy) had so far prevented the Muslims from cutting hands off, barring of course Sudan and Saudi Arabia. Today, in Pakistan, sentences of hand-cutting and stoning-to-death are routinely passed but, he would be dismayed to learn, the victims are let off after an average of eight to ten years of imprisonment by the higher judiciary through what is known in Pakistan's still 'westernized' judicial system as 'due process'.

The Thistle and the Drone is focused on the clash between the state and the peripheral communities. It maintains a dispassionate approach towards the dramatis personae of this game now enveloping the world—Ahmed is strictly 'non-thistle'—except for the American policy of 'renditions' where Washington has sought to conceal its policy of torture without trial by using locations outside America. What the book was not supposed to discuss was the fate of Pakistan as an ideological state irresistibly journeying to the hyper-asabiyya of the Taliban. Had it not been happening in other Muslim states, Pakistan would have been treated like an aberration, but it seems the world will have to cope with the current Muslim cycle one way or other. It would be of immense help if it read Akbar Ahmed's very erudite book.

On the last page, the message is that of compassion: 'In asking God "Am I my brother's keeper?" Cain is raising a question that is at the centre of this study. Cain has just killed his brother Abel—committing the world's first murder. God's answer is explicit and repeatedly stated throughout the Bible. It is an emphatic yes.'

20

Lambs to the Slaughter

In Pashtun-dominated Quetta, capital of Balochistan province, they look different. Fair-skinned but with mongoloid features, they arouse curiosity and primal hatred. They belong to the Shia sect in a hard-line Sunni city where the presence of Afghan and Pakistani Taliban has produced a terrorist mix seldom seen elsewhere in Pakistan. The Hazara of Quetta are in the crosshairs of the sectarian manifestation of the Taliban–al-Qaeda dominion in Pakistan. On 21 January 2014, a bus carrying Hazara youths returning from a pilgrimage to Shia shrines in Iran—many mixing business with faith—were blown up by a suicide bomber's car in the Mastung district approaching Quetta. Over twenty-four mangled bodies were extracted from the wreck of the pulverized bus. The Hazara of Quetta went through their routine of laying the dead bodies out on Alamdar Road and refused to bury them till the state of Pakistan pledged to take action against the killers. They pointedly rejected any assurances from the provincial government which they had long perceived as impotent.

Two days of vigil by men, women and children alongside the limbs collected from Mastung produced results: Federal Interior Minister Chaudhry Nisar Ali Khan accompanied by Information Minister Pervaiz Rasheed flew to Quetta and vowed to take action. Accordingly, on 24 January, paramilitary Frontier Corps and the police swept through Mastung with a 350-strong force and arrested dozens of suspected 'militants'. Special military flights were arranged for the rest of the Hazara pilgrims stranded on the Pakistan–Iran border-post to avoid another bloodbath. This was not the first target-killing on the Mastung Road. In the past months, the Hazara were repeatedly offloaded from buses by gun-toting men, stood before a firing squad and executed as the non-Hazara passengers looked on and cowered. The Mastung Road approach to Quetta is a deathtrap despite the fact that the district contains a cadet college supplying Baloch manpower to the army. (In the other stricken province, Khyber Pakhtunkhwa, the district of Bannu too has a cadet college but is entirely at the mercy of the Taliban.)

But the 2014 massacre recalled the biggest act of mass murder in the city of Quetta. Earlier, on 10 January 2013, over a hundred Hazara, including women and children, died after a vehicle full of a quantity of explosives not seen in the country before destroyed a market town where the Shia have become ghettoized. The mourners refused to leave the street where they had assembled the dismembered bodies of their families till the government ensured action against the killers. The Hazaras didn't believe a word of what the politicians said because their extermination had become routine, often referred to as genocide. This routine began years ago with the rise of the Punjab-based Lashkar-e-Jhangvi, a sectarian outfit whose name appears on the al-Qaeda flag along with Taliban Tehreek-e-Pakistan and Jandullah, the last-named specifically targeting Iran.

In 2011 too, at least twenty-six Hazaras were shot dead execution-style on Mastung Road. Terrorists had intercepted a bus going to Taftan, the border-town near the Iran border, had singled out all Hazara men, and shot them dead. Terrorists stayed at the scene for ten minutes, firing with AK-47s to ensure no one survived. Then they ambushed and killed several Hazaras rushing to the scene to take their dead relatives to the hospital. From 2008 to 2012, Balochistan witnessed 758 Shia killed in 478 incidents. Of these, 338 victims belonged to the Hazara community, indicating that Hazaras remain the prime target of this violent schism.

Hazara and the War in Afghanistan

Lashkar-e-Jhangvi issued the following proclamation in 2011: 'All Shiites are worthy of killing. We will rid Pakistan of unclean people. Pakistan means land of the pure and the Shiites have no right to live in this country. We have the edict and signatures of revered scholars, declaring Shiites infidels. Just as our fighters have waged a successful jihad against the Shiite Hazaras in Afghanistan, our mission in Pakistan is the abolition of this impure sect and its followers from every city, every village and every nook and corner of Pakistan.

'As in the past, our successful jihad against the Hazaras in Pakistan and, in particular, in Quetta, is ongoing and will continue in the future. We will make Pakistan the graveyard of the Shiite Hazaras and their houses will be destroyed by bombs and suicide bombers. We will only rest when we will be able to fly the flag of true Islam on this land of the pure. Jihad against the Shiite Hazaras has now become our duty.'

In 2012, instead of any action against the Shia-killers, Pakistan released the leader of the dreaded Punjabi group Lashkar-e-Jhangvi, Malik Ishaq, from jail where he had faced seventy charges of sectarian murder. Reason: death/refusal of witnesses to appear against him in the court of law. Ishaq was led from his Lahore prison to his home in Rahimyar Khan in south Punjab in a large procession of admirers which mushroomed as it progressed. Soon thereafter, Ishaq broke the judicial embargo on his movement and left the country to visit Saudi Arabia, becoming a symbol of the state's surrender to terrorists. To strengthen his group's sectarian sinews further he deepened his ties to the mother of all sectarian organizations in the country, Sipah-e-Sahaba Pakistan. It was rumoured that he did so after talking on the phone with some provincial ministers.

That year, provincial governments were vying with one another to reach a modus vivendi with the power centres linked to al-Qaeda, to save their politicians from being assassinated. In Punjab, where such a new relationship was set up to 'sanitize' the elections in south Punjab in favour of the government, police chiefs were in the habit of blaming terrorism on Israel and India. Malik Ishaq, killing the Hazara in Balochistan, was a challenge to Pakistan's sovereignty that Pakistan was reluctant to face. And there were reasons for that.

In 2012, the Shia of Pakistan quaked as they saw Malik Ishaq on the stage of a Defence of Pakistan Council rally in Multan protesting against Islamabad's policy of normalizing relations with India. The ex-ISI boss Hamid Gul, who attended the rally, denied that Malik Ishaq was present on the occasion and charged that a photograph revealing the truth was actually a doctored one. The Defence of Pakistan Council went into partial eclipse after the retirement of the then ISI chief General Ahmad Shuja Pasha, but there is no guarantee that it may not raise its head again, this time in defiance of the state. Matthew Green of *Reuters* wrote that year: 'The grip Lashkar-e-Jhangvi exerts on Quetta is difficult to appreciate from the drawing rooms of Islamabad, where brief reports of bombings or assassinations carried on the inside pages of newspapers fail to capture the scale of the persecution now faced by the city's 500,000 Hazaras.'

During the Ashura (ten days observing the martyrdom of Imam Hussain) of 2003 and 2004, the Shia Hazara community of Quetta was struck twice, yielding fifty-three dead. Pakistan blamed India but the Shias were pointing clearly to the three well known sectarian jihadi militias and some quite respectable clerical leaders of Pakistan. When nothing was done and more Shias were killed at the Pakistan space agency Suparco in Karachi, someone hit back in a desperate gesture and shot dead the 'elected by mistake' member of the National Assembly, Maulana Azam Tariq, leader of the anti-Shia religious party Sipah-e-Sahaba, in Islamabad.

Matthew Green thought the Quetta killings could be stopped: 'The onslaught against the Hazaras could easily be blunted — if the will existed to do so. This is not an isolated village in the Hindu Kush, nor is it an intimidating metropolis on the scale of Karachi, the mega-city of 18 million people where Lashkar has also been hard at work. With a population of about two million, Quetta, the capital of the vast province of Balochistan, has a small-town feel. It is easy to predict where the attacks will take place. Many occur on Spini Road, which links Mehrabad to Hazara Town, the other main Hazara enclave which lies on the other side of Quetta. The assassins roar up on motorbikes, open fire, and are gone. They are never caught. It is a measure of their confidence that they do not bother to wear masks.'[1]

There is an unforgettable TV discussion of a 2003 massacre that deserves revisiting: GEO TV (12 September 2003) had host Hamid Mir interviewing the imam of the Hazara Imam Bargah at Quetta where the Shiite community was blown up by suicide bombers. The imam said the attack was carried out by Sipah-e-Sahaba, Jaish-e-Mohammad and Lashkar-e-Jhangvi, and this information had been given to the administration in Quetta. Qazi Hussain Ahmad was present at his side when he stated this. He added that Qazi Hussain Ahmad was a member of the clerical electoral alliance MMA and should take measures to persuade people in the MMA to stop doing what was being done. Qazi Hussain Ahmad instead said that it was the responsibility of the government to end terrorism. The Hazara killings followed the distribution of anti-Shia fatwas in Quetta, a fact mentioned by the Hazaras on TV.

Why are the state-generated, Taliban-appended militias killing the Hazara? Is it religion or are there other reasons which may become more apparent after the Americans leave and the Taliban re-establish themselves in Afghanistan? Roy Gutman in his revealing book, *How We Missed the Story: Osama bin Laden, the Taliban, and the Hijacking of Afghanistan,* points to the real reason and it goes back to the 1997 unsuccessful invasion of the Taliban of the northern city of Mazar-e-Sharif with a large Hazara presence. The invasion was orchestrated by the ISI which managed the defection of the Uzbek warlord Rashid Dostam in favour of the Taliban. Seeing Pakistan involved, Iran weighed in on the other side, arming and training the Shia warriors. Uzbekistan and Tajikistan also sided with forces arrayed against the Taliban onslaught.

The Taliban warriors easily occupied Mazar and began doing things not agreed prior to the invasion. Pakistan recognized the Taliban government at this point, ignoring the violated undertakings by its client. Soon, the trouble started and victory began to derail. The Taliban went to the Hazara quarters in the city and asked them to disarm. Scared of the sharia-based revenge against their faith, they refused and began roaming the city looking for the Taliban. They killed 350 of them including their commander Mullah Razzaq. They ended up bagging 3000 of them as prisoners whom also they executed.

The book says Pakistan was the dominant power behind the scenes. But uncannily it also sent in Pakistani jihadis of Kashmir vintage as military assistance. Hamid Gul told Gutman, 'ISI brokered a deal but it was the wrong one'. Col Imam, the ISI officer called Ruler of Herat, later denied that the Mazar defeat was a big fiasco and funnily also claimed that the Taliban who invaded Mazar were unarmed and were mostly traders! He put the blame on Iran for asking the Hazara Shias to resist and start the massacre.

The Taliban finally got hold of Mazar in 1998 and inflicted a massacre on it to shame all massacres. They killed the Iranian diplomats in the Mazar consulate and the killers were the Sipah-e-Sahaba boys sent in from Pakistan, as Iran complained. The book also gives another version: the Sipah boys arrested the officers but, after taking their cash, handed them over to the Taliban for the killing.

Who Are the Hazaras?

Balochistan's inspector general of police, Shoaib Suddle also put his finger on another cause of the Shia extermination: The Hazara were an upwardly mobile community; their children were more motivated to acquire a good education and did well at school and college levels and ended up winning the best government jobs specially in the education sector. The community was comparatively prosperous and inward-looking, thus arousing envy and hatred. In *The Hazaras of Afghanistan: An Historical, Cultural, Economic and Political Study,* author S.A. Mousavi gives the ethnic background:

'Hazara sociology points to their Mongol or Moghol background as most Hazaras designate ideal behaviour as being moghol. Most classical historians agree with this theory, as do anthropologists who see the Hazara features as distinctly Mongol. Greek historian Curtius wrote about Alexander invading Central Afghanistan to tame the stubborn Hazaras. Firdousi also mentions the fiercely resistant warriors of Barbaristan which can be identified as Hazarajat or the central province of Bamyan. Famous Chinese traveller Hiuen Tsang passed through Central Afghanistan in 644 AD and mentioned two capitals, Ho-See-Na (Ghazni) and Ho-Sa-La (Hazara) in Arachosia (Afghanistan). Ptolemy too notes Ozala in Arachosia. This is supposed to prove that the Hazaras were ancient natives of the region.'[2]

Afghan historian Habibi thinks that the Moghol troops settled in Central Afghanistan, then adopted Persian as their language. The commanders who owned a thousand horsemen-warriors were called Ming (thousand) in Chinese, which translated as hazar in Persian. Hence, the name Hazara, although the Hazaras pronounce their name as Azra. Another expert on the Hazaras, Alessandro Monsutti, classifies the Hazara migration from Bamyan in Afghanistan to Balochistan in the following phases:

'From 1878–1891: Following the second Anglo-Afghan war, the first Hazaras came to Quetta to seek employment in British-run companies under the Raj. They are thought to have worked on the building of roads and the Bolan Pass railway as well as enlisting in the British army of India. At that time, there could have been no more than a few hundred Hazaras in Balochistan.

'From 1891–1901: The subjugation of Hazarajat by Emir Abdur Rahman, between 1891 and 1893, triggered a mass exodus of Hazaras to Turkestan, Khorasan and Balochistan. From 1901 to 1933: The situation in Afghanistan returned to normal under Habibullah (1901–1919), the son of Abdul Rahman. He offered amnesty to the Hazaras but this proved to be of little help in improving the lot of the Hazara community in Afghanistan. In 1904, the 106th Pioneers, a separate regiment for the Hazaras formed by the British, offered greater career prospects, social recognition and economic success. In the sixties, one Hazara rose to the job of commander-in-chief of the armed forces of Pakistan, General Musa Khan, who probably foresaw the fate of the Hazara in Pakistan and left a will to get himself buried in Mazar-e-Sharif in Iran.

'From 1933–1971: The regiment of Hazara Pioneers was disbanded in 1933. Deprived of this social and professional outlet, Hazaras went to settle in Quetta between the 1930s and 1960s, although the process of migration never completely dried up. From 1971–1978: Following the 1971 drought, Hazaras then settled in Quetta or went to Iran in search of work. Between 1973 and 1978, tensions over the Pashtunistan issue between the Daud government and Pakistan were an additional factor in the Hazara migration. After 1978: Following the Communist coup in April

1978 and the Soviet intervention in December 1979, the migratory movement assumed hitherto unprecedented dimensions.'

The State of Pakistan and the Hazaras

Pakistan in 1996 backed the Taliban government in Kabul and, together with Saudi Arabia and the UAE, was the only state that extended recognition to an intolerant sharia-based government; but out of three states only Pakistan allowed a Taliban embassy to be opened in Islamabad. Today Islamabad's Afghan policy continues to be heavily pro-Pashtun and it has deliberately eschewed traction with the Afghan communities enlisted with the non-Pashtun Northern Alliance because of its ideological intelligence bias. In the coming days as the Americans and their allies leave Afghanistan, Pakistan must anticipate a free-for-all civil war in Afghanistan, perhaps erroneously preening itself for having backed the 'friendly' Taliban instead of the 'India-friendly' non-Pashtuns.

The Taliban in Afghanistan are killing the Hazara the same way as Pakistani groups are killing them in Quetta. AFP stated on 23 January 2014 in its report, 'Death Road Blocks Afghan Hazara Minority from Homeland,' that the Kabul-Bamyan Road, like the Mastung Road, had become the killing-fields of the Hazara: 'A 30-kilometer stretch of two paved lanes heading west from the town of Maidan Shahr in central Afghanistan has seen many beheadings, kidnappings and other Taliban attacks in recent years against members of the minority ethnic Hazara community. Nowadays, nearly all drivers avoid it. The highway is the main route between the Afghan capital and Hazarajat, the informal name of the 45,000-square mile region of highlands and rich pastures where Hazaras have traditionally settled.'

This is the underside of Pakistan's military vision. It sees Afghanistan through the Pashtun goggles, and that means letting the Shia be put to the sword. This is how Pakistan has survived in the past and this is how it hopes to survive with the doctrine of strategic depth. The Hazaras are the dividend Pakistan's military thinkers are offering to the holy investors in jihad. Will the Hazara go as lambs to the slaughter organized by failing states no longer able to allow them to live?

The Hazaras have finally rejected the Shia propaganda line— emanating from Iran and embraced by the Shia leaders of Pakistan in general—that the Shia are being killed by the Americans through their paid killers, the Taliban. They now name the killers. Their leaders in Quetta have challenged Declan Walsh, the *Guardian* correspondent expelled by Pakistan for reporting too close to truth, on the label of 'Sunni killers' used by him: they are clear about the Deobandi section of Sunni Muslims carrying out the carnage; they go so far as to exclude such 'moderate' Deobandi organizations as Tablighi Jamaat, reminding him that a Tablighi Jamaat gathering was massacred in Swat when the current Taliban chief Fazlullah was ruling the valley. (An attack in 2013 on a Tablighi Jamaat mosque in Peshawar was not owned by the Taliban.)

After the Mastung carnage, the Shia of Pakistan staged countrywide protests, including the one in front of the Governor's House in Lahore which actually told Imran Khan's Tehreek-e-Insaf workers not to offer sympathy to them because they considered the Khan too pro-Taliban. The Hazara ask the following stark questions on the Internet.

One: in February 2013, two killers of Lashkar-e-Jhangvi, Usman Kurd and Daud Badini, were condemned to death by an anti-terrorism court in Quetta. They were picked up from the Quetta Cantonment prison and sent to Afghanistan in a military truck. Who was behind this? Two, in May 2013, Pakistan army took Shia-killers of Lashkar-e-Jhangvi Muhammad Umar Lehri and Mir Ahmad Lehri from the Quetta Cantonment police station and made them disappear. Three, these two were arrested by the paramilitary Frontier Constabulary after repeated complaints from the Hazara community; why were they released? Four, why are the Lashkar-e-Jhangvi terrorists able to buy thousands of kilos of explosives in Quetta but the Baloch insurgent BLA is not able to do so?

Death of the Jihadist State

If there ever was a sign of the demise of the Pakistani state it is the killing of the Hazara community of Quetta. The Hazara, after getting killed like flies, are a stigma for Islamabad's Foreign Office earning its daily bread rebuking the world for finding fault with Pakistan.

Reuter's Matthew Green reported ('The Killers of Quetta') in October 2012: 'According to Khaliq Hazara, chairman of the Hazara Democratic Party, many attacks take place within sight of checkpoints manned by security forces. Hazaras say they have not heard of a single case of a Lashkar suspect being prosecuted . . . In private, some members of the security forces are less than sympathetic to the Hazaras' plight. One officer argued—in apparent seriousness—that wealthy members of the Hazara community were orchestrating the attacks on their poorer brethren to win sympathy from Western governments to make it easier to obtain visas.'

Of course, the chief minister of Balochistan that year, Nawab Aslam Raisani, told reporters he would send a 'truckload of tissue paper' to mourning Hazaras so they could wipe away their tears. After that Hazaras turned to human-smugglers to somehow get them out of Pakistan, like their fellow-Shia of Kurram Agency, the Turis, many of whom died trying to get to Australia as 'boat people'. Ali Dayan Hassan of Human Rights Watch says: 'In April 2013, some sixty Hazaras died when their boat capsized in Indonesian waters en route to Australia.'

The lives of 50,000 Hazara are under threat in Quetta. There are over 13,000 members of the community living in Karachi too. In Hussain Hazara Goth, where their mosque called imambargah is located, they fear for their lives, often pointing out that 'our community, especially in Balochistan, is among the most literate and educated; they envy us, our people are in the police, government and everywhere; and out of the four female pilots in Pakistan, one is from our community.' The pride in being Pakistani is irrepressible in this dying community.

I.A. Rehman of the Human Rights Commission of Pakistan wrote: 'The Hazaras question the failure of the all-powerful Frontier Corps to go for the trigger-happy members of the Punjab-based militia [Lashkar-e-Jhangvi] that enjoys the freedom of not only Mastung and Khuzdar but also of Quetta. They make no attempt to conceal themselves or hide their weapons in the street or the mosque. They have already destroyed Balochistan's reputation as a peaceful multicultural society.'

21

The Rapids of Subnationalism

The situation is apparent to most. Water-stressed Pakistan's irrigation is faltering because it cannot store water. Its cities are awash with ill-managed sewage while groundwater levels sink. Its barrages are old and in need of improvements it can't afford. Its canals are tapering off at the tails because of low supply from the rivers. And it keeps losing water disputes with India because of its warlike approach to the water crisis.

Pakistan's lower-riparian concerns about India stealing its waters are similar to Sindh's fears about the Punjab. This latter discord is back in the news as the Sukkur Barrage, the oldest and most historically significant of Pakistan's ten barrages, silts up. Commissioned in 1932, the Sukkur Barrage gave birth to Sindhi nationalism, which split the province's Muslim and Hindu populations, and, ultimately, made the creation of Pakistan possible.

Two new books—Saiyid Ali Naqvi's *Indus Waters and Social Changes: The Evolution and Transition of Agrarian Society in Pakistan*, and Daniel Haines's *Building the Empire, Building the Nation: Development, Legitimacy, and Hydro-politics in Sind, 1919–1969*—present a compelling case about the barrage's impact on Pakistan's present-day water tensions within and without.

Originally named the Lloyd Barrage, the Sukkur Barrage, Naqvi writes, 'delivers water to the world's largest irrigation system, serving a cultivable command area of 6.54 million acres'. It feeds seven canals: Rohri, Nara, and two Khairpur canals on the left; and the Northwest, Rice, and Dadu canals on the right. The barrage became world famous because some of these canals fanning out from it are larger than the Suez.

In arid Sindh, where rainfall averages between 100 to 200 millimetres per year and the evaporation rate is between 1000 to 2000 millimetres, people live off the Indus River. Sukkur Barrage, the first constructed across the Indus, has reportedly developed a large delta which allows silt deposits to build up in the middle of its storage area. This has reduced its capacity from 1.5 million cusecs to less than 1 million. This in turn has squeezed the three canals on its right side, threatening agriculture in Sindh. Farmers fear that the depletion of the barrage may render 62 per cent of its command area barren, inflicting a loss of 3.39 per cent to the country's GDP or more than Rs 413 billion. They want a new barrage built.

London sanctioned the Sukkur Barrage project in 1923 to improve the reliability of irrigation water to more than 1.5 million acres of existing agricultural land, and irrigate for the first time more than 2.6 million acres. This was not entirely propelled by altruism; it was also to increase land revenue receipts. To Sindhi Muslims, Sindh's separation from Bombay province was conceived as an ideal after imagining the barrage as a source of wealth that Bombay was unable to provide.

Sukkur Barrage Awakens Sindh

Syed Mohammad Shah, a member of the 1928 Royal Statutory Commission on Reforms, had argued that the separation of Sindh from Bombay would help it develop its own infrastructure. This Sindhi nationalism, linked to the Sukkur Barrage, included all its Muslim communities as well as some Gujaratis. Jamshed R. Mehta, president of the Karachi Municipality and a prominent Parsi politician and financier, asserted in 1928 that separation would result in better health, sanitation, education in Sindh—and prosperity for the whole country.

'All that has to be done,' Mehta said, 'is that in the Ledger of the Government of India, on the page of the Sukkur Barrage account, the debtor should be entered as the Sindh Provincial Government rather than the Bombay Provincial Government.' The Hindu majority opposed to separation held that the Sukkur Barrage was too big a project for Sindh's financial and administrative capacity. Since Bombay had to foot the bill, they said, it tied Sindh irrevocably to Bombay.

The barrage's political significance was attested by former Pakistani leader Benazir Bhutto in her posthumously-published book, *Reconciliation: Islam, Democracy and the West:* 'The British ended Muslim Sindh's separate identity by integrating it into Hindu-majority Bombay. My grandfather . . . had long struggled for the separation of Sindh from Bombay. The British said that the waterlogged, saline Sindh lacked sufficient revenues to be independently governed as a separate administration. My grandfather then initiated the Sukkur Barrage project to turn the arid lands of upper Sindh fertile. With the completion of the Sukkur Barrage, Sindh gained sufficient revenues for my grandfather to argue that Muslim Sindh be separated from Hindu India. He was successful, and Sindh once again emerged as a separate entity under British rule.'

Before or around the same time as Sir Shahnawaz Bhutto's advocacy for the barrage, prominent Sindhi landowner–politician

Mohammed Ayub Khuhro asserted in a 1930 pamphlet that the Sukkur Barrage was 'the greatest irrigation scheme in the world' and that Sindh was 'honour-bound to accept responsibility for its success or failure'. Khuhro articulated the 'national' marker the barrage had become: It 'had become inextricably entangled with Sindh's existence as a self-conscious entity,' writes Haines.

The rift was becoming visible: the 'separatists' were arguing for greater control over their own affairs while those opposed called for government-by-bureaucracy. Soon afterwards, the Round Table Conferences, convened in London in 1930 and 1931, included a subcommittee whose task was to determine the desirability or otherwise of separating Sindh from Bombay.

Sir Frederick Sykes, the then governor of Bombay province, feared that allowing Sindhis to dominate the hypothetical new province entirely would run the 'risk that a policy of Sindh-for-Sindhis will lead to the exclusion of immigrant cultivators from the Punjab to take up lands [in the Sukkur Barrage zone], which would still further increase the burden and possibly render the scheme unproductive. Expressing an earlier assessment of Sindhis as farmers, he thought Sindhis would not farm the land effectively, thereby not earning money that could be taxed' and 'leaving the government without increased revenues to compensate for the debt [from] building the barrage and renovating the canals.'

Goodbye, Bombay!

Separation eventually occurred in 1936. Sindh became an autonomous province under the terms of the 1935 Government of India Act. This triggered the overarching tendency among Sindhi Muslim nationalists to support the Muslim League's demand for a separate homeland. This move, from small separation to a big one, was the result of the Sukkur Barrage, which stands as a monument in the annals of the Pakistan Movement. Sindh became the only province to support Jinnah in the early phase of the Pakistan Movement while Punjab and the Frontier were ruled by anti-separatism parties.

But the Sukkur Barrage also triggered an early competition with upper-riparian Punjab. Water in the new canal network in the Punjab was, to Sindhi nationalists, water stolen from Sindh. The new Punjab colonies were established after the canals got going. From 1945 to 1946, the canals made a net profit of Rs 4,099,000—more than three times their cost of construction. The officials in charge of the Sukkur Barrage put forward big revenue estimates to get London interested. And Sindhi cultivators were preferred over non-Sindhis: 350,000 acres (nearly a quarter of the land brought under cultivation by the barrage) were set aside to be granted to existing landholders in the barrage command area at a 'nominal' rate of Rs 15 an acre.

A British officer actually recommended 'that a Land Alienation Act should be introduced to offer landholders greater legal protection against potentially destabilizing outsiders.' Had it been done, as happened in the Punjab, the rancour against Hindu financiers taking over farmland would not have occurred. Haines writes: 'Muslim [landowners were] at risk of obliteration by Hindu [moneylenders]. This tightened the colonial administration because their system of control was dependent on the cooperation of [the] Muslim [landlord], and not on the Hindu moneylenders, who could often take over the land of borrowers who had failed to repay their debts.'

The Sukkur Barrage gave birth to Sindhi nationalism vis-à-vis Bombay. It became the root of the Hindu-Muslim divide in Sindh because Hindus didn't want separation from Bombay. This was followed by a Sindhi-Punjabi split after British officers 'imported' Punjabi farmers to ensure proper revenue from the barrage waters. In time Sindhi nationalism became a willingness to support Pakistan's separatism from India. As the barrage dries up today, it excites Sindhi lower-riparian alarmism against the Punjab, as Pakistan expresses the same kind of alarmism against upper-riparian India.

Today, Sindhi nationalism is directed at the Punjab province and has been supported sporadically by the other two small provinces, Balochistan and Khyber Pakhtunkhwa. This nationalism draws its strength from its opposition to the 'dream' dam that will end Pakistan's water shortage during droughts: the Kalabagh Dam. In its water disputes with India Pakistan is often rebuked by international experts for not storing its river waters when the flows are normal or excessive. The World Bank leads the international financial institutions in encouraging Islamabad to undertake the construction of new dams, particularly the Kalabagh Dam.

Kalabagh: The Negative Inspiration

Kalabagh Dam was conceived in 1953 as a multi-purpose project to store water in order to keep the water supply going in the lean months. In 2000, as the existing dams silted up by one-third of their capacity, the shortfall in water availability in the country went up to 40 MAF in 2004 and to 108 MAF by 2013. Kalabagh Dam was proposed to be built with a height of 260 feet and a length of 11,000 feet with a storage capacity of 6.1 MAF. It was also to generate 11,750 KW hours of cheap electricity and irrigate 2.4 million additional acres. The cost of the Kalabagh Dam in 2004 was estimated at 10 billion dollars when President Musharraf tried to persuade Sindh to support the dam and got nowhere.

Nationalism becomes critical with consensus: in Sindh political parties otherwise mutually hostile to the point of violence, support the Sindhi stance on waters. The PPP, which is the only party with an all-Pakistan national status, was supposed to rationalize the sharp edges of this subnationalism but is less and less able to do so as its hold outside the province shrinks and it is made to rely on its electoral dominance of Sindh to survive. At the best of times, however, it was seen as 'moderate' on the question of the Kalabagh Dam while its leaders in Sindh remained hard-line. The four-way political divide in the province among the PPP, MQM, ANP and the nationalists, has not undermined the consensus against Punjab which remains the only unambiguous supporter of new mega-dams in the north of Pakistan.

Sindhi subnationalism however is owned and championed seriously by the Sindhi 'nationalist' parties: Jeay Sindh Mahaz and its better known offshoot Jeay Sindh Qaumi Mahaz (JSQM) which was once led by its founder-secessionist Ghulam Murtaza Shah or G.M. Syed; Jeay Sindh Mahaz (JSM) and Jeay Sindh Mutahida Mahaz (JSMM). The other two influential parties with a growing following in the country of Sindh are: Qaumi Awami Tehrik (QAT) led by Ayaz Latif Palijo; Sindh Taraqi Pasand Party (STP) led by Dr Qadir Magsi; Sindh United Party (SUP) led by Jalal Mehmood Shah; and Sindh National Movement (SNM) led by Ali Hassan Chandio. The second group is non-secessionist but wants a new social contract by the state. Emphasizing the smaller-province resentment against Punjab, the nationalist parties are united at the all-Pakistan level in Pakistan Oppressed Nations Movement (PONAM), bringing together a Sindh-Balochistan consensus of grievances.

Sindhi experts diligently collect evidence to underpin the province's case against Punjab, solidifying what may appear at times to be mere distrust, in some cases, arising from proven excesses committed by upper-riparian Punjab. Interestingly, the grievances highlighted by the experts go back to the British Raj and the construction of the Sukkur Barrage. A distrust of Punjab and its rapidly growing 'canal colonies' grew in 1901 when Sindh was a part of Bombay Presidency and had put the government on notice about Punjab 'taking water from rivers Indus, Chenab, Jhelum, Ravi, Sutlej and Beas without the prior permission of Sindh'. In 1919, a committee set up by the Government of India had recommended that 'Punjab government should undertake no new project, till the construction of the Sukkur Barrage had been completed and Sindh's water requirements had been met'.

The Sukkur Barrage touched off a nationalism that has many strands now. Sindhi resentment of Punjabi farmers relocated to areas watered by the barrage aroused a mild and natural xenophobia against 'outsiders' which grew as the barrage brought prosperity and caused old cities to flourish. Migration, external and internal, exacerbated the situation as urbanized populations gravitated to Karachi and stymied the Sindhi farming communities' own transition from the village to the city. Sindhi subnationalism draws strength from its 'hydraulic' grievances against Punjab and the usurpation of indigenous space by external settlers.

Something similar happened to Maharashtra in India without the hydraulic aspect of the strife. In Maharashtra's case, the animus was directed mainly at the Gujarati population dominating Bombay's economy by reason of its superior consciousness based on centuries of trade in Gujarat when its city Surat was the only port of India. Bombay and Karachi were built to benefit from this 'superior consciousness'. But unlike Bombay, the indigenous population failed to assert its rights through organization and violence. Bal Thackeray the strongman of the 'wronged' indigenous population and leader of Hindu-extremist Shiv Sena dominated Bombay; but the Sindhi assertion remained rural-based surrendering urban space to Altaf Hussain, the leader of the immigrant MQM.

Bal Thackeray died on 16 November 2012 and the *Hindustan Times* headlined the news 'Bal Thackeray the mascot of Marathi pride'. It went on to describe his real power: 'Bal Thackeray protested the right of the Marathi on Mumbai, a city dominated by "outsiders". His pro-Marathi plank propounded Maharashtra for Maharashtrians, and chose even to offend his ally the BJP by backing Congress's presidential nominee, Pratibha Patil, who was a Maharashtrian.'

Migrations lead to violence. Those who migrate, clash with the local population on the basis of different identities. The immigrant is insecure because he wants a place under the sun; the local person is insecure because he fears losing his place under the sun. Fear gives way to hatred and hatred to violence. Both in Bombay and Karachi the local populations were either marginalized or their relocation from countryside to the cities delayed through 'interloper' communities.

Ethnicity produces more durable violence than any other identity. More internal émigré communities in Karachi took to using strong-arm methods. Altaf Hussain opposed violent reaction with violent response. Communities hounded by religious extremism seek shelter under Altaf Hussain's wings, who, like Bal Thackeray, remains aloof from the politics he presides over. If Karachi is the stronghold of the Urdu-speaking muhajir community, it is also the biggest Pashtun city of the world. Bal Thackeray challenged a functional Indian state and was therefore demonized by India; Altaf Hussain challenged a dysfunctional Pakistani state and achieved acceptance from political parties beleaguered by terrorism.

Heroic Isolation of Sindhi Nationalism

The Sukkur Barrage revived agrarian Sindh and postponed the forced relocation of population from the village to the city. It aroused fear too because the Sindhi thought this lifeline could be disrupted; it compelled him to ask for more guarantees against betrayals of the upper riparian. As other grievances accumulated, this fear coalesced with real dangers of marginalization and neglect. Nationalism usually relies for its survival on exaggeration and in this case too, a realistic fear grew into what may be called 'lower riparian alarmism', thwarting all solutions and promoting only secessionist extremism—somewhat like Pakistan's own 'hydraulic alarmism' vis-à-vis upper riparian India.

Sindhi nationalism is isolationist as it militates, against international opinion recommending more upriver storage dams. It also repels international support by denouncing the Indus Waters Treaty of 1960 with India, which safeguarded the rights of lower riparian Pakistan and is held up as a model to be followed by other states. Pakistan compounds the problem by mixing nationalism with its water problems with India. Its crisis of confidence with Sindh could be defused if it cooperated with India instead of threatening war with it on the basis of a case-building that convinces no one outside Pakistan.

In December 2012, after rumours that the Kalabagh Dam project was to be revived, the Sindh Assembly, ruled by the PPP, simply blew its fuse. The judiciary had overreached itself in a mood of excess at the Lahore High Court, 'ordering' the construction of the dam favoured only by Punjab. The house unanimously cried 'shame-shame', indulged in inflammatory speech-making, before adopting the following resolution: 'The issue or even the idea of constructing this dam is tantamount to eroding the foundations of national cohesion, destroying the provincial fraternity in general, and creating socio-economic disaster for the province of Sindh in particular and this house vehemently condemns those who have been supporting it.' Amazingly, some of the speeches made by the members still referred to the Sukkur Barrage!

As the PPP consolidates in Sindh after being ousted from the Centre in the 2013 elections, it is challenged by the province's subnationalism, forcing its young patron Bilawal Zardari-Bhutto to refocus on Sindh and put his party on top in the province. His reference to 'mother Sindh' in a tweet after hearing MQM leader Altaf Hussain demand bifurcation of Sindh promises an intensification of provincialism: 'No 50/50, no number one or number two; only Mother Sindh. All men are created equal. All Pakistanis should be treated equally in the eyes of the Law.' The message was two-pronged: to rivals in the province and to the federal institutions including the judiciary seen by the PPP as biased against it.

The PPP government of Sindh is opposed to the federation because it suspects it of favouring a Punjabi 'plot' to build dams. It challenges the other Sindhi party, the MQM, on the urban–rural divide, posturing to represent the Sindhi of the Sukkur Barrage against the urban trespassers voting for MQM. Behind the slogans of 'wronged Sindh' looms the shadowy presence of secession, a reminder that if the PPP doesn't succeed in retaining the minds and hearts of the Sindhi masses, the separatists of Jeay Sindh will make inroads into the PPP vote-bank and marginalize it. As the dysfunctional state of Pakistan swings helplessly in favour of the terrorists, carrying a flag of extreme isolationism because of its ideological opposition to India and the United States, rising subnationalism represents a defensive reaction of the aggrieved masses.

22

Traitor or Trophy to Taliban?

Pakistan's ex-army chief General Pervez Musharraf (retd) was taken ill with stress while trying to present himself at a special court in Islamabad on 2 January 2014. He was removed to a military hospital where the doctors found he had high blood pressure. The Nawaz Sharif government has gone to the Supreme Court against General Pervez Musharraf under Article 6 of the Constitution which awards the maximum penalty of death for treason against the state. There is a kind of national consensus against the retired general who ruled Pakistan from 1999 to 2008, as army chief and President, 'wearing two hats'. Is he going to be a traitor or a burnt offering to the rising dominion of al-Qaeda in Pakistan?

The instinct of revenge is high in the 'national consensus' which in the simplest terms represents the anger of those who wish generals offending against democracy punished as traitors. But there are countless others who speak from rage of a personal nature: people affected directly or indirectly by his decisions. The sceptics were convinced that, as in past cases, he would be let off the hook and spirited abroad to live the high life in the Gulf on the basis of some deeply laid international plot which includes America at worst and the Gulf sheikhs at best. His defenders were few, the most cogent of them surmising that an army facing the terrorists in the Tribal Areas would not take the death of its ex-chief as a morale-booster—it could even persuade the troops subconsciously to think poorly of their seniors, who can be hanged by the civilians they pretend to defend.

The political party in power hates him because he deposed its prime minister, Nawaz Sharif, in October 1999 and put him in jail, charged with treason, no less. In the opposition, the Pakistan People's Party hates him because it believes that the 'deep state' under him killed its leader, ex-prime minister Benazir Bhutto, in December 2007. Less pragmatic than his father Zardari, party chairman Bilawal Bhutto-Zardari has said some harsh words about the ex-president of the country. Those in Parliament who should have no complaints against him have taken to joining the angry chorus because populism is the order of the day in Pakistan, thanks to a passionately anti-Musharraf media.

Justice or Vendetta?

Musharraf says what he faces is not a fair trial but a process of vendetta through which a number of parties seek revenge. He names the revenge-seekers: Mullah Fazlullah, the current boss of Tehreek-e-Taliban Pakistan, the Balochistan Liberation Army, elements of Lal Masjid (Red Mosque), and al-Qaeda, all of them banned as terrorist organizations in Pakistan. He avoided naming the party whose sense of grievance against him actually renders the process of justice suspect.

The judges of a special court hearing the treason case against him are a party in the 'vendetta', his lawyers say. Justice, a process of 'closure' of the cycle of violence, is said by experts to replace revenge, which is 'circular' in nature and therefore perpetual. A TV anchor actually wondered whether the government in power and the judges in Pakistan will act like Nelson Mandela of South Africa who favoured reconciliation or like Hasina Wajed of Bangladesh who favours revenge.

Musharraf doesn't name as his avengers the two big parties and the judges of the special court appointed by a Supreme Court whose members he had kept in confinement after deposing them and who have scores to settle with him. He doesn't equally name the religious parties and madrasas aligned with the Taliban baying for his blood, but may wish to include them in the 'blanket' reference to Lal Masjid, a stronghold of al-Qaeda in Islamabad, which challenged him in 2007 through its vigilante action in the capital. The entire Pakistani nation, drunk with anti-American passions, wants his head to roll, which means Imran Khan's Tehreek-e-Insaf too should want him punished, although Khan was once close to him as an 'alternative' to the bipartisan leaders he had ousted after coming to power.

Officers Abandon Musharraf

He didn't refer to the Pakistan Ex-Servicemen Society which had taken a stand against him in 2008 in the wake of his dismissal of the Supreme Court. Crowded with anti-American and anti-Indian ex-generals, the Society had resented his shutting down of proxy jihad against India in 2003 and his hasty tilt to the United States for economic assistance—to bolster a state made economically wobbly after the nuclear test of 1998—and subsequent American hounding of Pakistani scientists for their involvement in proliferation. He is supposed to be guilty of entering an American war in Afghanistan, which was 'not our war', surrendering scores of al-Qaeda terrorists to Guantanamo Bay prisons.

Musharraf thinks the army should stand by him and tell the Supreme Court not to prosecute him as he is subject to army rules that oust civilian jurisdiction. He returned from his exile thinking that his old deputy and then army chief General Ashfaq Kayani would shelter him from the slings and arrows of the judges he had kicked out in November 2007. But Kayani too succumbed to populism, which ironically prompted him to pursue another treason case in the 'Memogate' trial against the PPP chief Asif Ali Zardari; he struck a neutral posture and remained aloof.

Populism-driven hatred of Musharraf was owed to the media, which had caved into intimidation by the Taliban and found comfort in forgetting that it was Musharraf who had allowed freedom to newspapers and the TV channels. This freedom, held back for decades by elected governments, unleashed itself on his governance but tended to lose its legitimacy however when it prostrated itself helplessly—and perhaps blamelessly—to the power-to-kill of the Taliban and their terrorist affiliates. Freedom of expression can only be guaranteed by the state itself but when it becomes too weak to protect this freedom, then intimidation is the only governance any media will acknowledge.

Sensing that the judges will go for the kill in the treason case, he has once again appealed for intercession to the army chief, this time General Raheel Sharif, who was recently appointed by Prime Minister Sharif over the head of two other more senior generals, and is not expected to bail him out, although, were he to do so, the court may 'heed his advice' in the name of 'national security'. General Sharif may be daunted by the negative image of Musharraf within the army where many defections to al-Qaeda and the Taliban have highlighted a rising Islamist wave.

To his statement that the army was upset for him, a rebuttal came from four retired generals: General Aslam Beg (retd), Lt General Hamid Gul (retd), Lt General Ali Kuli Khan (retd), and Lt General Shahid Aziz (retd), calling it a 'bluff'. Barring Khan, the others are known for an almost pathological hatred of the US and an equally diseased reaction to the pro-US policy followed by a pragmatic Musharraf after the 9/11 attacks planned and prosecuted from the soil of Pakistan. The group of Arab terrorists who destroyed the World Trade Center all came to Pakistan and were facilitated in their onward journey to Afghanistan to meet Osama bin Laden in Jalalabad before infiltrating the United States.

Jihadi Officer as New Normal

How sane some of the anti-Musharraf generals are can be gauged from the opinion expressed by General Shahid Aziz in his book, *Yeh Khamoshi Kahan Tak: Ek Sipahi ki Dastan-e-Ishq-o-Junoon.* His diagnosis of terrorism in Pakistan is pro-Taliban: 'The bombs that kill innocent Pakistanis in bazaars and mosques are planted by friends of America, and this terrorism is done to persuade Pakistan to embrace America more closely, allow the government to pursue pro-America policies and to alienate Pakistan from the mujahideen. But this trend of support to the killers of Muslims is open rebellion against Allah.'

The general himself wonders if he is actually a sane man: 'Why am I full of contradiction? Why can't I be balanced? Then I console myself with the thought that a pendulum has a balance too; what use is balance that is static and frozen? Real balance is in movement. One should be flying back and forth on a swing.' Pakistan's anti-Musharraf media reports that Aziz's book is 'selling like hot cakes' in the army.

The 'unbalanced' officers are in sync with the general political trend symbolized by the 2013 all-parties conference approving 'peace talks' with the Taliban and a challenge to the US against its drone attacks. Ex-ISI chief Hamid Gul openly confessed his own and his sons' relations with the Haqqani Network in North Waziristan; and ex-chief Aslam Beg awaited trial for having rifled a bank to get at the money that he later distributed as bribes to obtain results of his choice in the 1990 election. Both Gul and Beg headed the anti-American lobby within the army that would overwhelm any military leader seeking a pragmatic solution to the challenge of extremism in Pakistan.

High-altitude Blunder

But Musharraf was not blameless. If the intent was to hang him, then the real case against him as army chief was the Kargil Operation. In his book, *Between Dreams and Realities: Some Milestones in Pakistan's History*, the current adviser on foreign affairs and security, Sartaj Aziz, wrote about the affair in some detail. In May 1999, General Musharraf briefed the prime minister on Kargil. This may not have been the first briefing but for Sartaj it was. The PM was accompanied by him, Abdul Majid Malik (minister for Kashmir affairs), Raja Zafarul Haq (minister for religious affairs), Shamshad Ahmad (foreign secretary), and Tariq Fatemi (additional secretary in the PM secretariat). Sartaj Aziz was among the dissenters, and what he said must be flagged as the intellectual thesis of the book: the Pakistan army is 'tactical' rather than 'strategic' in its thinking.

He told the meeting: 'I see that the tactics are brilliant but the strategy does not seem viable. And the objectives of the operation are even less clear.' Other Foreign Office diplomats were perhaps in the loop, unlike Sartaj. In the RAW telephone intercept of General Musharraf—and there have been many since—General Aziz Khan in Islamabad is heard telling the chief in Beijing in Appendix III of the book that while Mian Sahib was okay, 'Shamshad as usual was supportive' on the plan to invade Kargil.

Musharraf and his fellow trigger-happy generals, however, could be indicted for attacking Kargil—with regular troops backing non-state actors—because they were serving under an elected prime minister who may have given him the go-ahead, as the Sartaj Aziz book implies. Nevertheless, Kargil was arguably the most humiliating of the defeats Pakistan has suffered at the hands of India; and Musharraf, appointed by Prime Minister Sharif over the heads of several senior officers, was heading the defeated army. Crushingly, even China voted against Pakistan in the UN Security Council session on Kargil.

Musharraf could also be punished for the takeover of 1999, after which he humiliated the prime minister who had appointed him by putting him through a treason trial and keeping him and his inner circle of ministers locked up in the Attock Fort, a medieval practice favoured by the generals in Pakistan in the twentieth century. But speaking on TV on the first day of 2014, one of his ministers, Khwaja Asif, could not suppress his desire for revenge when he said he would like to see Musharraf consigned to the dungeons of the Attock Fort where he had spent time along with Prime Minister Sharif. However, the big hurdle in the way of clearing the decks in this case is the verdict of the Supreme Court that, in 2001, 'indemnified' his coup, exonerating him of the removal of an elected government. The court even gave him the right to amend the constitution.

A typically non-intellectual 'tactical' officer, Musharraf converted to 'useful' pragmatism after the Chapter Seven resolution of the UN Security Council allowing an international force headed by the United States to invade Afghanistan after Jalalabad-based head of al-Qaeda, Osama bin Laden, successfully caused the World Trade Center to collapse in 2001, and the Kabul-based government of the Afghan Taliban refused to cooperate. Considered objectively, his decision not to defy a UN resolution, not vetoed by Pakistan's friend China, may have been a wise one.

Pakistan's depleted economy benefited from American aid and raised the standard of living of a segment of the population. The chosen president, through a dubious referendum and further legitimized by the government that came to power after the 2002 election, was unable to forestall the country's looming energy crisis through hydropower projects that the world was willing to endorse. Scared by backlash from the army after he called off the proxy jihad—fought through non-state actors who would bleed the state of its internal writ—against India in 2003, he started playing a 'double game' with his external supporters. Sadly, the state today will not punish him for this 'terminal' damage to Pakistan, threatened today from the inside.

Bhutto Assassination

At some point Musharraf will have to face the truth behind the assassination of ex-prime minister Benazir Bhutto in December 2007 after he, under American pressure, let her return, most reluctantly, from exile just before the elections. The account of her target-killing in Rawalpindi has gradually revealed facts that the Musharraf establishment will find hard to answer. A member of the UN panel of investigators who inquired into the assassination, Heraldo Munoz has written a book pointedly titled *Getting Away With Murder: Benazir Bhutto's Assassination and the Politics of Pakistan*, which confirms Benazir Bhutto's own suspicion expressed in her book, *Reconciliation: Islam, Democracy, and the West*. Munoz is of the opinion that the ISI planned her murder through its non-state actors and army officers with terrorist contacts.

There seemed to be a pattern of practice in the military-dominated intelligence to get the 'enemy' Taliban and their affiliated non-state actors to commit crimes for the state. Benazir Bhutto could very well have been eliminated by Musharraf's establishment with or without his knowledge through a 'contract' with the Taliban boss Baitullah Mehsud, whose incriminating taped conversation was then produced in a public briefing by Brigadier Javed Iqbal Cheema, after being briefed from the ISI, says Munoz. After six years, in 2013, chief prosecutor of the Federal Investigative Agency (FIA) Chaudhry Zulfiqar Ali was target-killed in Islamabad by two al-Qaeda agents, one of whom was the son of a retired brigadier. Zulfiqar had just announced on TV that he had traced some leads to Bhutto's murder to the ISI and Military Intelligence officers.

Musharraf called off the Kashmir jihad in 2003. This caused outrage within the armed forces and the non-state actors being used in this asymmetrical war with India. Attempts were made on his life by elements from the military and non-state actors, including the one in Rawalpindi in which Jaish-e-Mohammad was found to be involved—the same banned organization that ran the jihadi training camps in Mansehra near Abbottabad. Then Musharraf had to incarcerate Hafiz Saeed of Lashkar-e-Taiba, temporarily, after informing him that it was merely a formality under pressure from America.

In 2005, when a big earthquake hit Azad Kashmir close to the strategic Line of Control with India, he allowed Lashkar to carry out rescue operations in the affected areas after ousting the various non-governmental organizations (NGOs) that had reached there earlier. The son of his security adviser, Tariq Aziz, headed the mission as a member of Lashkar. As his successor General Ashfaq Kayani was to discover later, he knew that the non-state actors had become too powerful to challenge because of their nexus with the army. The son of his chief minister in Punjab Pervaiz Elahi was an important member of the Taliban-favoured Tablighi Jamaat in Lahore, run unobtrusively by a retired ISI chief.

Endgame: Red Mosque

The Supreme Court, which will finally decide whether or not Musharraf will hang, has come under a lot of criticism during and after the tenure of Chief Justice Iftikhar Muhammad Chaudhry. It is well known that most apex courts of the world tend to be conservative rather than liberal, but in the case of Pakistan this conservatism is overlaid with a 'realistic' tendency to avoid confrontation with the al-Qaeda–Taliban combine that the weakened state can no longer confront.

One case that may never be laid at the door of the otherwise tainted court pertains to Lal Masjid (Red Mosque), which was attacked in June 2007 by Pakistan army commandos after proof of insurgent vigilante acts by its clerics. The reason for this populist 'forgiveness' is a reinterpretation of what really happened; but the fact is the clerics of the Islamabad mosque were favoured by the suo motu court through forced compensatory allotments of land where the whole complex destroyed by the army could be recreated.

Pervez Hoodbhoy wrote in *Dawn*: 'In early January 2007, Lal Masjid had demanded the immediate rebuilding of eight illegally-constructed mosques that had been knocked down by the CDA. Days later, an immediate enforcement of the sharia system in Islamabad was demanded. Thereafter, armed vigilante groups from this madrasa roamed the streets and bazaars. They kidnapped ordinary citizens and policemen, threatened shopkeepers, and repeated the demands of the Taliban and other tribal militants fighting the Pakistan army . . . Lal Masjid and the adjoining Jamia Hafsa had engaged in a full-scale bloody insurrection against the Pakistani government, state, and public.'

The clerics running the mosque had set up a parallel government in Islamabad, operating an unlicensed FM radio station, occupied a government building, set up a parallel system of justice, made bonfires out of seized cassettes and CDs, received the Saudi ambassador on the mosque premises, and negotiated with the Chinese ambassador for the release of his country's kidnapped nationals. The commando attack came finally in July 2007.

Lal Masjid was built in 1965 and took its name from its red walls and interiors. During the Soviet war in Afghanistan (1979–89), it played its role in recruiting and training local warriors to fight along with the Afghan 'mujahideen'. Its clerics enjoyed patronage from influential members of the government and establishment. Founder Maulana Abdullah Ghazi—dead in 1998 as a result of his running sectarian battle with the Shia community—was a veteran jihadi who had fought against the Soviets in Afghanistan and had close contacts with such radicals as Mullah Omar, Ayman-al-Zawahiri, Tahir Yuldashev and Osama bin Laden. Its direct patron from within al-Qaeda was Sheikh Essa, an Egyptian member of al-Qaeda, who according to Saleem Shahzad, died mysteriously in 2012 amid rumours that the deep state had silenced him, and who had wanted to make it a base for an apostatizing (*takfeer*) assault on the Pakistan army.

In more ways than one, the unfolding drama of Lal Masjid signalled the end of Musharraf's period in power. He was broken on the wheel of the army's incapacity to survive its nexus with the jihadi brood it had incubated.

Zahid Hussain in his book, *The Scorpion's Tail: The Relentless Rise of Islamic Militants in Pakistan and how it Threatens America*, noted: 'Lal Masjid clerics Abdul Aziz and Abdur Rashid had learned their militancy from their father, Abdullah Ghazi, who received funding and guidance from the Pakistani military and intelligence agencies for jihad. After the Taliban's victory in Afghanistan, Abdullah Ghazi became closely associated with al-Qaeda.'

In 1998 he travelled to Kandahar to pay homage to Mullah Omar, and took his younger son along. During this visit that enabled him to spend an hour alone with Osama bin Laden, Abdur Rashid Ghazi became radicalized. At the end of the meeting, he picked up bin Laden's glass of water and drank from it and said: 'I drank from your glass so that Allah would make me a warrior like you.'

Shifting Allegiance

In a June 2013 address to the National Assembly Prime Minister Nawaz Sharif said Musharraf had twice abrogated the constitution and would be tried under Article 6 of the Constitution: 'The federal government's decision is in line with the Supreme Court's decision and the Sindh High Court verdict which firmly held the view that holding the constitution in abeyance on 3 November 2007 by Musharraf constituted an act of high treason under Article 6 of the Constitution 1973.'

Would this suffice to convict Musharraf? Veteran lawyer S.M. Zafar says: 'Suspension or keeping the constitution in abeyance was not an offence in 3 November 2007, as it was added to the Article 6 in the 18th Amendment'. So where does the national consensus stand in light of the law? Or will the law simply do what the 'people want'?

The operative part of the Supreme Court judgement in the Sindh High Court Bar Association case says: 'From the above, the conclusions drawn are that General Pervez Musharraf (retd) in the garb of Emergency Plus and the Provisional Constitution Order made amendments to the constitution by self-acquired powers which are all unconstitutional, unauthorized, without any legal basis; hence, without any legal consequences.' Against this, the argument advanced is: It doesn't say that this is grounds for a case of treason under Article 6. Many discussants on TV chat-shows don't believe Musharraf will hang or even be prosecuted; others think Musharraf is being tried to distract attention from the spreading sectarian war in Pakistan. A few, considered close to the prime minister, seem to be advising him to back off before the army reacts in favour of Musharraf.

Under the last chief, General Kayani, the army seemed to appear weak-kneed while facing two centres of possible challenge to its supremacy—the non-state actors and the political consensus—and one word that would describe this change of attitude is: populism. It has undermined several institutions required to render verdicts on the basis of supreme national interest, regardless of how the people at large feel. For once, some in the army, in unison with the retired relative of his, General Shahid Aziz, may like to see Musharraf hang under this new unspoken doctrine. In 2013, tragically, the national consensus was veering to a shift of loyalty from the state to the Taliban which may require Musharraf to become the trophy the nation will present to the state's enemies as an earnest of its allegiance.

23

Dealing in Delusions

End of 2013, Pakistan experienced the consequences of its misdiagnosis of terrorism, as if it was a part of its delusions about the coming civil war in Afghanistan, end of 2014. The government of Khyber Pakhtunkhwa province led by Imran Khan's Pakistan Tehreek-e-Insaf (PTI) blocked the NATO supply route through its territory to force Washington into calling off its drone attacks on the Taliban–al-Qaeda terrorists, which they alleged result in the 'collateral damage' of innocent lives.

Few could protest against PTI because the rationale of its disruption of the supply route was based on an all-parties consensus in Pakistan against drone attacks. This consensus was based on yet another all-parties consensus tasking the government of Pakistan with holding 'peace talks' with the Taliban. Given the fact that 80 per cent of the Pakistanis hate the United States in Gallup surveys, it appeared as if Pakistan was set to pursue a Taliban-dictated change in its foreign policy. Another unavoidable perception is that, given Pakistan's international isolation, the state was in the process of shifting its allegiance to the Taliban as legitimate rulers. The state wished to survive on its robust delusion-dependency.

In Khyber Pakhtunkhwa, defeated by terrorism and broken in spirit, people were gradually shifting their loyalty from the 'dysfunctional' state to a new 'social contract' with the Taliban who would stop killing them under a superior Islamic order, a delusion encouraged by populist isolation. According to reports, the business community of the province paid 'protection' money to the terrorists while ignoring the federal bureau of revenue. The people have become submissive to terror under the leadership of Imran Khan: they had earlier rejected the government of clerics close to the Taliban and elected the 'secular' Awami National Party only to see its leaders killed by suicide bombers and the population decimated by IEDs.

Clearly, the Taliban became engaged in this process and were issuing orders they believed would be carried out. They warned the media against projecting the Khyber Pakhtunkhwa government negatively, particularly the leader of Jamaat-e-Islami, Dr Munawwar Hasan, who broke new ground in jurisprudence last month by declaring the Taliban leader Hakimullah Mehsud a martyr (shaheed) after he was killed by a drone. Shockingly, people in rural Sindh, fallen inconspicuously to the persuasive power of the banned but renamed terrorist–religious organizations, started rejecting polio vaccination of their children in tacit obeisance to the coming dominion of the Taliban. Many parts of Khyber Pakhtunkhwa had already done so.

Some Pakistanis thought it was wrong on the part of their leaders to succumb to populism aroused by terrorism and to embrace isolationism through an anti-American campaign. The Pakistan army itself changed tack in August 2013 when its chief, General Kayani, declared from Abbottabad that Pakistan was threatened from within, meaning the Taliban, and not from without, and additionally meaning India and the US. And yet the powerful clerical–jihadi Defence of Pakistan Council was allowed by its patrons within the army to demonstrate its massive non-state actor strength in the big cities, supporting jihad against the two states, thus indirectly rejecting the new Kayani 'doctrine'. Why was Pakistan behaving the way it was on the eve of another war that would start in the region by the end of 2014?

If you want to delve into the mystery of Pakistan as a state, the book to read is *Magnificent Delusions: Pakistan, the United States, and an Epic History of Misunderstanding* by ex-ambassador to Washington, Husain Haqqani, whose earlier thoughts in *Pakistan: Between Mosque and Military* on state conduct had deeply offended the Pakistan army. Today's delusion-based politics is traced by him to Pakistan's national security paradigm. A similar thematic shot-across-the-bow was fired earlier by ex-foreign secretary Riaz Muhammad Khan in his book, *Afghanistan and Pakistan: Conflict and Resistance to Modernity*. Haqqani's diagnosis is rare but he is not alone.

Birth of a Frozen Paradigm

Before we examine Haqqani's diagnosis of the Pakistani state in *Magnificent Delusions,* let us examine the offence his earlier book gave to the army who finally got him to resign from his post as ambassador in Washington (2008–11), leaning on the still-ongoing case against him of treason against the state at the Supreme Court of Pakistan. His thesis was as follows:

Pakistani nationalism was shaped in an anti-India mould to favour the military during the early years and during interregnums when the political parties ruled Pakistan under the tutelage of the military. By the time the politicians realized that nationalism was actually helping the military to remain on top they had also become alive to the already formed public mind that would not accept any alteration in nationalism without a trauma.

Back to his latest book, Haqqani investigated the doctrine of 'strategic depth' that continues to fashion the military worldview. Haqqani traces it, not to the timeline of the Pakistan army's decision to support the Taliban, but to Aslam Siddiqi's 1960 book *Pakistan Seeks Security*. Siddiqi leans on Fraser-Tytler's suggestion that the two states—Afghanistan and Pakistan—be fused into one. Siddiqi's typically military addendum to the theory was that since it can't be done by force—'fusion will lead to confusion'—Islamic ideology may be put to use. Today this very formulation is recoiling on Pakistan in the shape of the Taliban who owe allegiance to Mullah Omar whom they call emir and not to Pakistan.

The India-centrism of this thinking is backed by an almost universal resistance in Pakistan to any changes in the anti-India curriculum of textbooks which the provinces will not change despite orders from the central government. The resistance is not only from the bent mind of the state machinery but also to the mind within the army which will not remove its nexus with the non-state actors it used in the past and might use again after 2014. There is reference in the book to Fazlur Rehman Khalil of Harkat-ul-Mujahideen who was the logistics man of Osama bin Laden and had co-signed the 1998 fatwa of death against the Americans with him. He is still one of the central figures of the Defence of Pakistan Council in addition to Hafiz Saeed, the man for whose head the Americans will pay $10 million. He was in the camp [together with five ISI officers] when the US unsuccessfully targeted Osama bin Laden in Afghanistan after an al-Qaeda bombing of the American ship USS Cole in 2000.

The Defence of Pakistan Council was a well-known policy tool of the ISI used to deter Islamabad from getting too friendly to India. Khalil was once head of the Harkat-ul-Mujahideen fighting the state's covert wars, its command shared with him by another terrorist wanted in India, Masood Azhar. Both were close to bin Laden who was upset when they fell out and separated, the latter creating his own militia named Jaish-e-Mohammad. Bin Laden helped financially in this split, compensating both. When Azhar was arrested in India while pursuing Pakistan's proxy jihad, a secret plan was made to spring him from prison. An Indian airliner was hijacked and made to land in Taliban-ruled Afghanistan and its passengers swapped to free Azhar. The still-functional Mansehra camp near Abbottabad, training non-state actors in terrorism, was set up by Azhar, as disclosed by Adnan Rasheed an air force officer-turned-terrorist sprung by the Taliban from a Bannu jail. Needless to say, bin Laden was living in Abbottabad for five years to be close to the camp he was allegedly funding.

What came first, the army-sponsored India policy or army-sponsored Islamic extremism? Haqqani ends the book proving that it was the India-centrism of Pakistan that finally brought it to Islamic extremism. The myth of India not accepting Pakistan and India attacking Pakistan was concocted and survives the acquisition of nuclear deterrence by Pakistan. The army used jihad in the 'asymmetric war' the world calls cross-border terrorism; it used the 'mosque' to muster the warriors it needed to sharpen its revisionist irredentism. Prophetically, Haqqani thought normalization of relations with India was the only available solvent to what the military and cleric had done to Pakistan. He desired the survival of Pakistan through a change of policy in the light of the theory of gradual adjustment to circumstances. But the Pakistan army desired longevity through consensual stasis based on refusal to adjust.

Haqqani moved to the US in 2002 after serving as media adviser to the government of Nawaz Sharif (1990) and Benazir Bhutto (1993) both falling from power before their term. He produced his 2005 book while in exile, which he shared with Asif Zardari and Benazir Bhutto, while Nawaz Sharif licked his wounds of dismissal by General Musharraf in Saudi Arabia. Haqqani's latest book draws much from his advisorship with the two governments.

Military-driven Delusions

In his second book, Haqqani lays down his stance: 'I have always been convinced that the United States remains a force for good in the world. Pakistan has benefited from its relations with the United States and would benefit even more if it could overcome erroneous assumptions about its own national security and role in the world. Instead of seeking close security ties based on false promises, Pakistan must face its history and diversity honestly, and it should be neither dependent on nor resentful of the world's most powerful nation.'[1]

He studied the relations between the United States and its other partners to 'figure out why almost all post-World War II US allies have found prosperity and stability through this partnership, whereas Pakistan has not.' But when he tried to re-establish Pak–US relations on mutual trust, the 'major power centres in my own country resisted my vision'.[2] The ISI was let loose on him, the anti-US media was likewise unleashed with accusations against him of safeguarding US interests and helping the CIA expand its network of spies in Pakistan.

Islam and nationalism were the password with which even the erudite Pakistani approached the Pak-India equation: there was grave moral doubt not unmixed with self-flagellation about the conduct of Pakistan in getting involved with the global hegemon. The pragmatism of foreign policy was booby-trapped with piety. On the other hand, the US found fault with Pakistan as an ally on the following counts: 1) Pakistan developed nuclear weapons while promising the United States that it would not; 2) the US helped arm and train mujahideen against the Soviets during the 1980s, but Pakistan chose to keep these militants well-armed and sufficiently funded even after the Soviet withdrawal in 1989; and 3) from the American perspective, Pakistan's crackdown on terrorist groups, particularly after 9/11, was half-hearted at best.

IQ Ambushed by Ideology

While serving in the government of Nawaz Sharif in 1992, Haqqani saw the prime minister receive a letter of protest from the US Secretary of State James Baker through Ambassador Nicholas Platt 'which he left unread on his table'. He saw that during the meeting of the bigwigs of the state convened to discuss the letter—including the army chief and head of the ISI—the letter was still lying unopened in front of him. He asked Haqqani to summarize its contents while the prime minister himself 'gave instructions to his staff regarding snacks he wanted served to all of us—Sharif often asked for specific food items during meetings, as if it helped him concentrate his mind.'

Haqqani noted that the letter contained the following plaints: 'Your intelligence service, the Inter-Services Intelligence Directorate, and elements of the army, are supporting Kashmiri and Sikh militants who carry out acts of terrorism, providing weapons, training, and assistance in infiltration. We're talking about direct covert Government of Pakistan support.'[3] There was no reaction from the various pillars of the deep state except the ISI chief General Javed Nasir—notorious for an IQ effectively ambushed by 'high-church' Islam, complete with a flowing beard—who spoke first and wrongly accused Platt of being a Jew working for the Indo-Zionist lobby.

In the case of Nasir, the prime minister had erred in his selection as ISI chief, as he was to err again while choosing General Pervez Musharraf as his army chief in 1998. Take a sampling of the level of intellect of the Pakistani state as Nasir spoke: 'The Jihad in Kashmir is at a critical stage and cannot be disrupted. We have been covering our tracks so far and will cover them even better in the future. These are empty threats. The United States could not declare Pakistan a terrorist state because of our strategic importance. The Saudis and Pakistan are America's only allies in the greater Middle East, so the United States needs Pakistan to deal with the changing situation in Muslim Central Asia after the Soviet collapse. All we need to do is to buy more time and improve our diplomatic effort. The focus should be on Indian atrocities in Kashmir, not on our support for the Kashmiri resistance.'[4]

What was the effect of this patently idiotic strategic positioning? Prime Minister Sharif 'agreed with Nasir's assessment, which reflected the consensus of the meeting.' Only Haqqani and foreign secretary Shehryar argued that Pakistan needed to reconsider Pakistani support for Kashmiri militants as 'it would undermine Pakistani diplomacy, get Pakistan labelled a terrorism sponsor, and was unlikely to result in a settlement of the Kashmir dispute.' Shehryar actually said that Pakistan would probably be more successful by focusing on diplomacy and political action in favour of the Kashmiris instead of 'setting off bombs.' Nasir's response—a cliché echoing from cable TV even today when retired military officers fulminate against India— was that 'the Hindus do not understand any language other than force'.[5]

The meeting finally dismissed the concerns raised in Baker's letter. Sharif said, 'As long as Pakistan could be useful to the United States, the United States would remain favourably disposed toward Pakistan.' The ISI chief was sure he knew how to take care of the CIA: 'We know what they need and we give it to them in bits and pieces to keep them happy.' On this, Sharif said, 'It is important to talk to Americans nicely while doing whatever you have to and that there are always enough disagreements among American policymakers that anyone can find someone who supports them.'

According to Prime Minister Sharif, Pakistan could deal with allegations of sponsoring terrorism by reaching out to the American media and Congress. He would allocate $2 million 'as the first step' for that purpose and announced at the meeting that Haqqani 'would be in charge of this expanded lobbying effort.' Haqqani adds: 'He did not allow me to speak, and I had to wait until the next day to turn down the assignment.'

The army chief, General Jahangir Karamat, whom the prime minister was to get rid of later, made some sane remarks: that it was not in Pakistan's interest to get into a confrontation with the United States, but 'we cannot shut down military operations against India either.' He suggested that Pakistan get off the hook with the United States by making some changes in its pattern of support for Kashmiri militancy without shutting down the entire clandestine operation—and that is precisely the policy Pakistan adopted over the next few years till General Pervez Musharraf switched off the jihad in 2003 after committing the blunder of the Kargil Operation and overthrowing an intellectually unfocused prime minister.

This meeting decided Haqqani's future in a way. Disagreeing with what was said in the meeting, he wished to resign, but was instead let off the hook and sent to Sri Lanka as ambassador.

Fear of a Liberated Intellect

Of course, Haqqani will not own up to sharing the worldview of the people he once served after rising from the ranks of the youth wing of Jamaat-e-Islami—which most affected the worldview of the army—and which was to be the first host of al-Qaeda in Pakistan. The book is not introspective enough to take us through the process of intellectual transformation— from the salad days of dragging the steel ball of state ideology around his ankle to the realization of long kept-on-hold self-realization as he grew up to face the realities of state power— but it nevertheless points the way to how Pakistan can get out of the choppy waters of military-led ideology of war-making on borrowed money.

The military leaned on jihad to frontload its narrative. It had the scope of delusional innovation too, as General Aslam Beg, army chief for a brief period after General Zia's death, told Haqqani: 'Pakistan needs to show its spine to the United States; a nuclear Pakistan would tie up with Iran and China in order to create a third pole in a multi-polar world.'[6] The general had no clue about the Chinese mind and was obviously not reading the carefully worded signals from Beijing, busy at that very moment to 'normalize' its relations with India.

But Beg was stupidly 'defiant' while a more wily ISI chief, General Hamid Gul, went on duping the Americans into thinking he was their man while advancing a more lethal and Islamic version of Beg's view of how 'the ISI could wage covert wars throughout the region and change Pakistan's fortunes'. Today, in the aftermath of Osama bin Laden's discovery in Abbottabad, close to the Mansehra training camp for the militants, Gul is busy trundling out the story that bin Laden had actually died a natural death in 2005 and that the 2011 US attack which killed him was a 'put-up' job. One Supreme Court judge was actually heard in private repeating the story—an obvious plant from a divided 'deep state'.

The ISI briefed Benazir Bhutto about the Taliban's rise as a local phenomenon. She worried about their reported misogyny and their propensity for violence and asked Haqqani for his views on the ISI position that 'they could bring peace to Afghanistan and secure Pakistan's interests': 'I said that the ISI had previously said the same thing about Pashtun warlord Gulbuddin Hekmatyar. Bhutto agreed but laughed saying that we civilians could not stop the ISI even if we wanted to.'[7]

Ijlal Zaidi, senior bureaucrat serving Bhutto, was worried about the 'Taliban's core beliefs', wondering whether madrasa students with a narrow worldview and no modern education were equipped to run a country: 'They will ruin whatever is left of Afghanistan. They will kill Shias and then they will come after Pakistan.' Haqqani observes: 'The ISI's major general, Aziz Khan, said he could not understand why so many people in the Bhutto government were so averse to the spread of Islam.' This was a clear pointer to the crux of the crisis that now engulfed Pakistan: the ideology of the Taliban was the same as that of the state of Pakistan, and whose purity stood as a living rebuke to politicians grappling with the pragmatism of living in the present world. Saudi Arabia and the UAE recognized the Taliban government in 1996 but Pakistan was the only country to allow them an embassy on its soil.

General Aziz Khan probably knew where he was taking Pakistan. He was the architect under General Musharraf of the infamous Kargil Operation, against which even China voted in the UN Security Council, and which came to grief, forcing Prime Minister Sharif to intercede with President Clinton to get the Indians to allow a retreat. General Aziz's religious passions brought about the rise of the TV evangelist of Islam, Murtaza Malik—of dubious moral reputation—whose sex scandals shook Lahore before he was finally killed in a property row.[8]

The jihadis became a part of ISI's covert ambition to conquer countries other than Afghanistan. Benazir Bhutto had been warned about it but could do nothing. She was told by the Philippines government during a visit that Pakistanis were fighting alongside Muslim extremists battling for autonomy in Mindanao. Russia said they were among the Islamists fighting in Chechnya. Arab governments in Egypt, Algeria and Jordan also complained that their terrorists were among those living in Pakistan since the anti-Soviet Afghan jihad: 'But when the issue was raised in government meetings, ISI and interior ministry officials dismissed the reports as western propaganda.'

A Double-dealing Mind

Could Pakistan help all this? The pattern was that the prime minister told the US he was helpless in the face of military dominance combined with the coercive power of the fundamentalists. Sharif told deputy secretary of the US State Department, Strobe Talbott: 'If he wanted what the Americans wanted—not test the bomb—Talbott would find himself dealing not with a clean-shaven moderate like himself but instead with an Islamic fundamentalist.' But he had the son of old dictator General Ayub Khan, Gauhar Ayub, heading the Foreign Office, who recited the army's line to all comers, accompanied by foreign secretary Shamshad Ahmad who symbolized the Foreign Office bureaucracy as a satrapy of the army where diplomats advanced the thinking of the GHQ. Talking to Talbott, Ayub would call India a 'habitual aggressor and hegemon' and describe the United States as 'a fair-weather friend'. When Talbott spoke, 'Ayub and Foreign Secretary Ahmad rolled their eyes, mumbled imprecations under their breath, and constantly interrupted.'[9]

Strobe Talbott, in his *Engaging India: Diplomacy, Democracy, and the Bomb*, writes: 'While [Foreign Minister] Jaswant's team [in India] was highly disciplined some of Shamshad Ahmad's colleagues [in Pakistan] tended to be querulous, surly, and sometimes abusive. On one occasion, early in our dealings, a member of the Pakistani delegation exploded at our observation that his country seemed always to react in knee-jerk fashion to Indian moves. He rose out of his chair and lunged at Bruce Riedel or me, depending on whose neck he could get his fingers around first. He had to be physically restrained.'[10] The said Pakistani diplomat was later sent as ambassador to the US by the Sharif government!

Haqqani discloses that the 2008 Mumbai attacks, which Pakistan refuses to own as linked to its covert war strategy against India were carried out by Pakistanis and quotes the ISI chief Ahmad Shuja Pasha as admitting to CIA Director Michael Hayden that 'the planners of the Mumbai attacks included some retired Pakistani army officers' and that 'the attackers had ISI links, but this had not been an authorized ISI operation'.[11] This remark is significant because it signals splits of strategic ideology within the army. When in 1996, the warlord controlling Kabul, Ahmad Shah Masoud, paraded on TV ISI officers arrested while fighting on the side of the Taliban, Islamabad's response was the same: these were retired officers.

Is the army split on ideology between the normal India-centric officer and the ideological jihadi officer who also wants Pakistan changed on the lines advocated by the Taliban? Is the army actually reconciled with General Kayani's Abbottabad 'doctrine' that Pakistan is threatened from within or was he under threat from the same elements who tried to kill General Musharraf for his pro-America and anti-jihad policy tweaks in the past? Are the generals acting as guardians of national security with an ear cocked to what the ideological elements within are saying about them? Or, like Pasha, are all of them using extremism to extract more concessions from the US, which has actually been defeated in Afghanistan by an Afghan policy pursued by the GHQ in Rawalpindi?

The book offers evidence that the ISI dangerously stoked the fires of honour-based, intense nationalism to scare the US into offering more assistance to a 'beleaguered' Pakistani leadership: 'Pasha and the ISI continued to propel hypernationalist sentiment. Pasha once told me that this was one of the few tools Pakistan had for leveraging itself in an asymmetric relationship.'[12]

Split from Within

The author believes that Pakistan and the US are embarked on mutually opposed policies in Afghanistan; plus Pakistan is also under an ideological siege that views the US as a hegemon in decline hobnobbing with India to the detriment of Pakistan's own India strategy. (The Roman Empire lasted a thousand years but was in decline half of this time.) He recommends to both sides to come clean on their strategic targets and re-establish the current edifice of mutual distrust and fear on a more pragmatic footing. He is more critical of Pakistan in light of the 'scandals' it endlessly spawns because of its internal lack of cohesion.

Read this chastening passage: 'Soon after the Abbottabad raid, Grossman and CIA Deputy Director Michael Morrell travelled to Islamabad to propose actions that Pakistan could take to build confidence in its commitment to fight terrorism. They shared intelligence about a bomb-making factory run by the Haqqani Network in North Waziristan. According to the CIA, al-Qaeda as well as the Taliban and Pakistani Jihadi groups used improvised explosive devices (IEDs) made at this factory. Kayani and Pasha promised that the Pakistan army would send in troops to shut down the illicit factory that was manufacturing the IEDs. A few days later the CIA sent time-stamped photographs showing the facility being dismantled hours before the army's arrival. The dismantling began after a man on a motorcycle went into the factory, thus leading to speculation that he had come to tip off the terrorists about the impending army operation.'

General Kayani who handled the Afghan policy finally retired. Will his successors take Pakistan out of its delusional worldview based on deceit? In September 2011, Kayani's American counterpart and friend Admiral Mike Mullen testified to the US Congress that the Haqqani Network in North Waziristan was 'a veritable arm of Pakistan's Inter-Services Intelligence agency' and that anti-Indian terror organization Lashkar-e-Taiba was part of the Pakistani government's policy and served Islamabad's interests. After that, the ISI broke with the CIA and the army broke with the US army. And now Pakistan is afloat on the basis of the unconvincing policy that the Americans should stop their drone attacks without demanding that Pakistan expel Afghan terrorists from North Waziristan.

In 2013, Prime Minister Nawaz Sharif was presiding over a Pakistan on the verge of bankruptcy and in need of international help; in 1998, he was in a similar situation after stealing the thunder of the army by testing the nuclear bomb. Caught in a spiral of inflation and terrorism-induced capital flight, he was endangered by public anger and the rising tide of pro-Taliban defiance of the United States. Would his partial acquiescence in the country's shift of allegiance to the Taliban save him and the country? Elements in the army were still backing warlike organizations such as the Defence of Pakistan Council to restrict his options of survival. But the new army chief General Raheel Sharif, it developed, would deviate from the strategy followed by the Kayani–Pasha duo.

Last word: 'Pakistan cannot pursue its dreams of being India's military equal by seeking American aid. If 40 billion in US aid has not won Pakistani hearts and minds, billions more will not do the trick. Unless Pakistanis define their national interest differently from how their leaders have for over six decades, the US–Pakistan alliance is only a mirage. The relationship needs redefinition, based on recognition of divergent interests and an acknowledgement of mutual mistrust. Only then will Pakistan and the United States share the same reality.'[13]

24

NS in DC

Prime Minister Nawaz Sharif's Washington visit became Pakistanward-looking by the time he got to see President Obama on 23 October 2013. Earlier, he spoke about the drones in detail at the US Institute of Peace (USIP), a subject which resonated more in Pakistan than in the US It seemed as if Pakistan had sent NS to America with a single stark message: stop the drones. Added to it was the next demand: release Aafiya Siddiqi from an American prison where she was doing her eighty-six-year-long sentence for terrorism. To complete the catechism of honour, NS was supposed to ask a protectionist America to stop aid and allow reduced-tariff export of Pakistani products into its market.

NS had campaigned in the 2013 election with two opposed slogans, opening up to India and peace with Taliban. He dropped the India part earlier by raising the issue of Kashmir at the UN but embraced the Taliban part by talking about America's drone attacks in unison with Amnesty International and Human Rights Watch.

Disown the Drones!

The *Washington Post* revealed on the day he was to meet the US President that the drones were agreed between the US and the Pakistan army and gave details about the latter actually directing their targeting in some cases. Unmoved by Pakistani assurances, Taliban chief Hakimullah said the Pakistan army was in on the drone attacks and that's why he was attacking and killing its soldiers. The bitter truth for Pakistan was that, if the drones disappeared, the Taliban would win the Tribal Areas. The question was: if the Pakistan army didn't like him, why did it want the drones stopped?

Clearly, it wanted Hakimullah targeted—just as it did the earlier leader Baitullah—but not all the al-Qaeda-affiliated terrorists in the safe haven of North Waziristan. The all-Pakistan media brainwash on drones is nothing but populism embraced by General Kayani flecked with fear of internal dissent in the army. Chief Minister Pervaiz Khattak of Khyber Pakhtunkhwa, the province virtually in control of the Taliban, says he would have shot the drones down had he been ruling in Islamabad. The post-visit media opinion was frank: we want the drones stopped because the Taliban demand it.

The Pakistani consensus had aspects that could only be fathomed through psychoanalysis. Politicians and generals often accuse nameless 'foreign enemies' of Pakistan of carrying out the bombings that kill innocent Pakistanis because 'they don't want us to reach a peace deal with the Taliban'. The obvious reference is to the two arch-enemies, India and the US. This view was encapsulated accurately by a retired general, Shahid Aziz, in his memoirs published earlier this year:

'The bombs that kill innocent Pakistanis in bazaars and mosques are planted by friends of America, and this terrorism is done to persuade Pakistan to embrace America more closely, allow the government to pursue pro-America policies and to alienate Pakistan from the mujahideen. But this trend of support to the killers of Muslims is open rebellion against Allah.'[1]

India Trouble

In the Institute for Defence Studies and Analyses, New Delhi, an analyst wondered why Pakistan should hot up the eastern border when it needed to tackle the unravelling of the American presence on the western border. The answer may be: because, if NS normalizes with India, the India-centric strategy leveraged with terrorists in North Waziristan would be undermined on the western border. However, more sanely, Manmohan Singh was in China the same week, cooling down India's northeastern border to face up to the mounting heat on the Line of Control (LoC) with Pakistan. Of course Pakistan army denied it had anything to do with terrorists attacking Indian troops across the LoC and was backed by an increasingly jingoist national consensus.

The US was soft on Nawaz Sharif, with Secretary of State John Kerry anointing the policy of 'realignment'—after two years of bilateral trouble under General Kayani—with $1.6 billion of aid blocked in 2012. Back home, Pakistan was mildly shocked to learn that, starting 2001, it had pocketed nearly $26 billion from America out of which $17 billion had gone to the army. Some Pakistanis, habituated to hearing the army say it received nothing, thought the money was a loan, not a grant, and that most of it was raked back by Washington anyway.

Nawaz Sharif went out to the US saying we don't want aid, we want trade, despite the fact that his two advisers on foreign policy knew America was financially broke and Pakistan was no leafy haven for foreign investment in 2013. How much Hakimullah was devaluing Pakistani assets by the day through bomb blasts and kidnappings NS would discover only when he got down to privatizing the country's bankrupt state enterprises.

Ending 'Slavery' to America

It is clear that the media had sent Nawaz Sharif to the US to tell the Americans to generally get off Pakistan's back. Most discussants had recommended defiance. The entire gamut of political parties registered their opposition to American 'slavery' on a pulse-taking TV talk show. On 23 October, Sharif's USIP speech was reported in the Urdu press as a kind of medieval dare to America: 'Honour us and we will honour you; we want a relationship of equals; we want trade not aid.' The English-language press—in some cases owned by the same Urdu papers—eschewed reference to honour.

The 'non-equals can't be friends' dictum has caught on in Pakistan, which was mind-boggling, given the global canvas of balance-of-power relationships in which 'unequal' states like Taiwan, Japan and South Korea reaped untold advantages, and Pakistan itself had benefited in many ways from its relationship with China. If one read the post-visit joint statement, one became conscious of how an 'unequal' Pakistan was milking funds both from the US and China. One popular foreign policy guru insisted Pakistan should stick to its guns on terrorism—no give on North Waziristan and on non-state actors fighting proxy wars—because 'America will buckle as it has buckled on Iran and Syria'. Whence this suicidal strut? Clearly, there was an assumption that America would crawl because it needed to get out of Afghanistan in 2014 using Pakistani territory. Was this thesis realistic?

Withdrawal Leverage

It was estimated America would be faced with shipping 100,000 containers and about 50,000 vehicles out of Afghanistan by the end of 2014. Today the shipping cost is $6 billion but it might rise. If America was good to Pakistan the containers would pass 'safely'—whatever that means in the Pakistani lexicon. If America was mean to Pakistan and decided not to take its equipment out of Afghanistan, the cost would be $37 billion. However, if it went wrong, the one-time loss of $37 billion was nothing compared to the annual $112 billion America would save after 2014 by not being in Afghanistan. And, in extremis, it could either scrap the equipment or ship it more expensively through the northern route or by air. Pakistan could hurt itself by overblowing its leverage as a transit state.

If NS was not able to normalize with India and got embroiled once again in Afghanistan with India-centric hawks pointing the way, and the non-state actors' massive tail wagging the bankrupt state's dog, it would be endgame for a dangerously nuclear Pakistan. Rawalpindi's post-withdrawal Afghan policy suffered from one big flaw: it couldn't calibrate a proxy war whose actors wanted 'change', not in Afghanistan but in Pakistan. Tragically, NS's party might be forced to trace the footsteps of its predecessor-in-power, the Pakistan People's Party, which first defied the textbook 'security policy' centred on India and later swung back to it. This was indicated by Pakistan Muslim League's current water and power minister Khwaja Asif who accused India once again of stealing Pakistan's water and unleashing 'water war' on Pakistan; he also termed the Indus Waters Treaty (1960) as being unfair to Pakistan.

Frankensteins, All

Ominously, Karachi's monthly *Newsline* published an article 'Jamaatud Dawa Pakistan army's new Frankenstein',[2] in its October issue, noting how 6 September, once Pakistan's Defence Day celebrating 'victory' over India in the 1965 war, was now being showcased with the muscle of Jamaatud Dawa. Hafiz Saeed with $10 million American head-money riding on him swaggered in front of the Parliament in Islamabad with a scary procession of 10,000 vehicles, threatening India with war. Former Pakistani ambassador to the US, Husain Haqqani, whose new book on Pakistan, *Magnificent Delusions,* would endear him less with a Supreme Court waiting for him to come and receive an obvious verdict in a case of treason against him, said on the eve of NS's arrival in Washington: 'My countrymen will some day have to come to terms with global realities. Pakistan cannot become a regional leader in South Asia while it supports terrorism.'[3]

If the media is any indicator, Pakistan back home was angry that 'perfidious' America did not agree to stop drone attacks or free Aafiya Siddiqi. No anchor mentioned the North Waziristan 'problem' described by the ex-US chairman of joint chiefs of staff Admiral Mike Mullen as ISI's locus of illicit relations with the Haqqani Network attacking across the Durand Line. The US Government Portal on the Internet stated: 'Condemning terrorism in all its forms and manifestations, US President Barack Obama and Pakistan Prime Minister Nawaz Sharif on Thursday said that no country's territory should be used to destabilize its neighbours.'

Wanted: Hafiz Saeed

America gave no assurance on the drones, apart from a hint of cooperation on Pakistan's 'peace talks' with the Taliban that Sharif's spin-doctors insisted should be read as Washington's pledge to scale down the attacks. But Hakimullah Mehsud in his fastness in North Waziristan was more sure-footed: 'Nawaz Sharif went to America to get the aid restored not to get the drones stopped. We never believed otherwise before, nor do we believe otherwise now.'

The Americans gave Sharif a dossier of proofs of Jamaatud Dawa chief Hafiz Saeed's complicity in terrorism in the Mumbai attacks and involvement with Lashkar-e-Taiba fighting on the side of al-Qaeda in Afghanistan. Back home Saeed walked from courts declaring him innocent of all charges of terrorism while, like the rest of Pakistan, thinking nothing of the threats of war routinely flung by him at India. The jihadi strongman, thought to have a private army of over 200,000 warriors on call, is too strong to be even asked to tone down his brazenly uncivilized jihadi rhetoric.

Adviser on Foreign Affairs and Security Sartaj Aziz responded to the American case-making against Hafiz Saeed by saying Pakistan would not move against Hafiz Saeed because the proof against him was insufficient. However, Pakistan accepted that Lashkar-e-Taiba was involved in the Mumbai attacks and was trying some accused persons and their leader Zakiur Rehman Lakhwi. He didn't say Lakhwi was being treated very well in a Rawalpindi prison, using his cell phone to tell his friends he was enjoying frequent unions with his new 'facilitated' wife there. (The same month as NS was visiting Washington, India and the US signed an agreement on targeting the financial network of Lashkar-e-Taiba abroad.)

Yet, NS, judged by the yardstick of low expectations, scored diplomatically: he restored a relationship derailed by an army strongman acting on the basis of pique. Washington, despite its own persistent economic trough, promised to continue its assistance: by 2013, it had added over 1000 megawatts of power to Pakistan's national grid, helping over 16 million Pakistanis, constructed and rehabilitated Gomal Zam, Satpara, Mangla, and Tarbela dams, modernized Guddu, Jamshoro, and Muzaffargarh power plants, and provided loans for private sector 'wind development' in Sindh. But could NS deliver his side of the bargain? Could he guarantee the safe passage to US–NATO container trucks on the Ground Lines of Communication (GLOCs) through Balochistan and Khyber Pakhtunkhwa if his talks with the Taliban didn't take off?

A Visit of Non-gratification

His visit reopened the channels of communication blocked by two years of anti-Americanism at home exacerbated by paranoia historically associated with isolated states. The ministerial-level Pak–US Strategic Dialogue, which Secretary Kerry was to host in Washington by March 2014, might pull Pakistan out of its daze of unrealistic passions. As NS puts it, there are more important things than Kashmir to sort out to take the country out of its current financial nosedive. But the visit obviously didn't meet the expectations of emotional gratification back home. Taliban chief Hakimullah Mehsud said he had seen through the visit as a ruse;

Jamaat-e-Islami said NS had returned empty-handed; Hafiz Saeed said he shouldn't have gone to America in the first place; Pakistan Tehreek-e-Insaf said the visit was a flop because NS had failed to implement the all-parties-conference mandate of stopping the drones.

25

Breaking through in Balochistan?

Once again, Pakistan was hoping to tackle the troubled province of Balochistan after the May 2013 election, strengthened by a new government that seemed better equipped to normalize the insurgency-haunted region. A scandal-ridden Pakistan People's Party-led coalition had been ousted, allowing Nawaz Sharif's Pakistan Muslim League to choose the provincial executive more wisely. Instead of simply delegating government-forming to his local party boss Sanaullah Zehri, he gave the province over to a coalition of parties that in the past had looked like siding with the 'enemy'.

The sixty-five-member assembly in Quetta elected in 2008 had carried the stigma of naming all its members as ministers who might, in the just-completed tenure, have walked away with Rs 300 million each of the province's development budget. Keeping that in mind, Prime Minister Nawaz Sharif decided to plump for the 'secular-nationalists' from two parties: The National Party and the Pakhtunkhwa Milli Awami Party (PkMAP). Both had separatist reputations in the eyes of the conservative elements in the country, the first as secessionist from the state, the second as a secessionist from province. This could be a moment of breakthrough for a terrorized Balochistan.

Radical Baloch to the Rescue

The new chief minister was a Baloch with a radical background. Dr Abdul Malik was born in the southern-coastal region of Turbat, next to Gwadar, and did his school and college in Turbat before completing his medical studies at Bolan Medical College in Quetta and running his own medical clinic in Turbat. His middle class background took him into radical politics with the much-demonized Balochistan Students Organization (BSO); but soon he formed his own party, Balochistan National Youth Movement (BNM) in 1987. Instead of taking the path of rebellion, he took his party into elections the following year and won his seat in the assembly for the Balochistan National Alliance headed by Nawab Akbar Khan Bugti and Sardar Ataullah Mengal and was health minister in the provincial government in 1988; later, he was education minister in the cabinet of Nawab Magsi in 1993. In 2004, his Balochistan National Youth Movement was merged with the National Democratic Party of Mir Hasil Bizenjo to become the National Party. He was a senator from 2006 to 2012.

The ruling PMLN opted for Dr Malik because he was seen to enjoy the support of all the feudal lords called sardars, including those whose families were directly or indirectly involved in the Baloch insurgency against the state of Pakistan. Chief Minister Malik was expected to rule the province in tandem with Governor Dr Muhammad Khan Achakzai, a retired economist from the Planning Commission of Pakistan and brother of 'secular-nationalist' Mehmood Khan Achakzai of the PkMAP. Both the gentlemen don't agree with the 'security narrative' that makes the Baloch 'disappear' and kills the Shia community of Quetta.

Dr Malik stands up for the rights of the people of Balochistan who, in the prevalent Pakistani view, have been unfairly treated over decades. He had reservations about the action taken by the army against the perceived rebels.

As for The National Party's rejectionist background, here is a quote about its other well-known leader, Dr Abdul Hai Baloch. Talking to GEO (12 January 2006) Senator Sanaullah Baloch of the Balochistan National Party (Mengal Group), said: 'According to the Lahore Resolution of 1940 Balochistan was to be an independent state but after 1947 it was taken over by Pakistan. Five Baloch leaders, including Senator Abdul Hai Baloch, did not sign the 1973 Constitution and, for this reason, today the constitution needs to be amended so that only defence and currency should stay with the federation.'

A Political Masterstroke

Mehmood Khan Achakzai has disagreed openly with Pakistan's Afghan policy and proclaimed it in the new parliament in Islamabad challenging its foundational agitprop. His contention was that Balochistan had been deliberately radicalized through the transfer of Afghan refugees and the relocation of the Afghan Taliban to Quetta. He upset the establishment by saying in Parliament: 'We are harbouring foreign terrorists on our territory; we intervene in Afghanistan's politics and should stop that for the sake of peace. The establishment should stop its monopoly on policy and not decide things on its own. We should drop our grandiose ambitions about fighting the US and be aware of our limitations.'

Given the above worldview of the new government in Quetta, it was a masterstroke of mature politics that Prime Minister Nawaz Sharif brought the heretofore marginalized radicals into mainstream politics, thereby isolating the insurgents in a province where an overwhelming majority of the Baloch don't want to secede from Pakistan. Just before the election, in February 2013,

113 Hazara Shia were killed and 180 injured in a powerful bomb blast in Quetta. After the election and the installation of the new 'secular-nationalist' government, the Baloch insurgents destroyed the 'protected' rest house in Ziarat where the founder of the nation, Quaid-e-Azam Muhammad Ali Jinnah, had retired for a time to recover from ill-health. Within the week, Quetta saw the massacre of a dozen female medical students at the Bolan Medical College. The sectarian terrorist outfit linked to al-Qaeda, Lashkar-e-Jhangvi, announced that it had killed the girls by booby-trapping the bus used by the students. By the end of the month, another suicide attack in the Hazara Town area of the city accounted for twenty-eight dead.

The May 2013 election ended the situation created by non-participation of the 'nationalists' in the 2008 election. The political order that emerged seemed to reject both the extreme views in evidence in Balochistan: the 'separatist' slogans of the Baloch rebels busy staging insurgency; and the state agencies' charge that a 'foreign' conspiracy was behind the trouble being faced by the administration.

The Baloch are no doubt the aggrieved party owing to the low economic development of the province over the decades. Their leaders had disagreed with the accession of Balochistan to Pakistan after 1947 because they claimed they had a legal case because of the special status of the region under the British Raj. Balochistan was annexed to Pakistan but the resentment remained and increased after some Pakhtun-populated areas were included in the province, leading to complications for the Baloch nationalists claiming to be one nation demanding a separate state. Over the years, Baloch nationalism seemed also to become 'resource-based'—like Assam in India and Biafra in Nigeria—as gas and minerals were discovered in the province and any further exploration for natural resources in the region was targeted.

However, according to a survey conducted in July 2012, nearly 67 per cent of the Baloch population wanted greater autonomy for the province but did not demand independence.

Only 37 per cent of the Baloch favoured independence. Those who supported greater provincial autonomy may have grasped that a separate Balochistan state surrounded by hostile neighbours and two conflicting nationalisms within was hardly viable. The post-2008 federal parliament had amended the constitution to grant the provincial autonomy demanded in the past.

The 'Disappeared' and the Massacred

In 2005, an incident in the Bugti area triggered unrest which was put down by the army, resulting in the first big migration of the Baloch. In June 2013, Nawabzada Guhram Bugti led a fifty-five-day-long protest in Islamabad at the head of 400 tribesmen, demanding that 200,000 Bugtis displaced by the army be repatriated. He said: 'These people are living under the open sky for the last eight years in Jamshoro, Sanghar, Ghotki, Rohri and Karachi districts of Sindh.'

There were Baloch claims that thousands of Baloch had been made to 'disappear' by the army in its paramilitary Frontier Corps manifestation. The phenomenon of the 'disappeared' Baloch has moved the rest of the country, the media taking the lead in highlighting the tendency of the army to function without accountability when dealing with Baloch 'rebels'. An assertive Supreme Court headed by a former lawyer from Balochistan took note of the plight of the families looking for their sons. The Court held more than seventy hearings on the situation in Balochistan but to no notable effect. Apart from further persuading the public in the country that Balochistan was suffering under arbitrary rule, it has been unable to correct the status quo of oppression in the province.

British journalist Declan Walsh was expelled from Pakistan last year after his report, 'Pakistan's Secret Dirty War' appeared in *Guardian,* graphically describing the atrocities earlier also reported in the Pakistani media: 'The bodies surface quietly, like corks bobbing up in the dark. They come in twos and threes, a few times a week, dumped on desolate mountains or empty city roads, bearing the scars of great cruelty. Arms and legs are snapped; faces are bruised and swollen. Flesh is sliced with knives or punctured with drills; genitals are singed with electric prods. In some cases the bodies are unrecognizable, sprinkled with lime or chewed by wild animals. All have a gunshot wound in the head.'[1]

But there are other human rights violations too in Balochistan that cannot be ignored. In May 2012, the Human Rights Commission of Pakistan (HRCP) sent a large delegation of observers to Balochistan to inquire into the allegations of strong-arm methods by the security agencies and terrorism by the Baloch separatists. The report of this fact-finding mission was pessimistic. The province was undergoing rapid transformation, succumbing to Islamic radicalism encouraged by the state to counter the challenge it thought was coming from the 'secular-nationalists'.

Frederic Grare in his Carnegie Endowment paper of April 2013 writes: 'The most worrisome factor is the changing sociology of the Islamic radicalization in Balochistan. Unlike the Pashtun-populated areas of the province, the Baloch territory was until very recently largely secular. Today, the Tablighi Jamaat conducts its activities outside the Pashtun areas. Lashkar-e-Jhangvi is now recruiting in the Baloch population, and five of the most prominent leaders of the organization in Balochistan are said to be Baloch.'[2]

The *News* (25 May 2013) reported: 'Disturbing reports have emerged of members of the Quetta police having close links with Lashkar-e-Jhangvi. In a press conference on Monday, DIG Operations, Quetta Police, disclosed that Assistant Sub-Inspector Yahya and constable Karim were in contact with the banned terrorist organization, helping it in targeting the Hazara community.'

Before their ghettoization in Quetta, the Hazara Shia community was more spread out but now it is being uprooted from Loralai, Machh and Zhob and forced to move to Quetta hoping to be provided security. Well-funded religious parties were increasingly seen active in the province's far-flung areas. Their concentration in Quetta yielded a bloody crop of 550 Hazara killed between February 2008 and May 2012. The Hindu minority is scattered all over the Baloch-populated districts except those adjoining the sea. They were 22 per cent of the province's population in 1947 but had to leave at partition till their percentage dwindled to 1.6 per cent. The Pakhtun areas were always hostile but in 2012 it was discovered that the rest of the province too was under heavy religious indoctrination from powerful seminaries. In consequence, Hindus were coming under pressure in the traditionally tolerant communities and were subject to kidnappings by insurgents in need of money for weapons. The HRCP delegation discovered that 'over a hundred Hindus have been abducted in Balochistan, a majority of whom was released after a ransom was paid; those who did not pay up were killed and their bodies dumped.'

In its 2012 report, the HRCP said: 'No one from the government had come to the victims. Hindus could not get out of their houses. Their education had been suspended. They were forced to pay extortion money. About a fifth of the Hindu population has migrated from Balochistan. The rest could not leave because they were poor. They looked at the Hazaras and thought that the pain and suffering of Muslims was far greater than their own.'

Pakistan has been through the trauma of separatist movements before. In East Pakistan, a province that broke away and became independent as Bangladesh in 1971, local grievances were focused on the Punjab province in West Pakistan and the 'Punjabi army'. In Balochistan too, the nationalist rancour is directed against 'settlers', most of whom are local-born Punjabis. Professionally more competitive, like the Hazaras, the settlers have suffered deadly attacks by the Baloch Liberation Army (BLA), and the province has lost a number of greatly prized teachers and doctors manning its depleted institutions.

Secular and Religious Terrorism

In 2012, out of 1931 incidents of terrorism in Balochistan, 800 had been owned either by the Baloch separatists or sectarian killers of Lashkar-e-Jhangvi, an offshoot of the Punjabi Taliban declaring itself as aligned with al-Qaeda. No terrorist was caught and punished but there were cases of killers being allowed to escape from prison. There are over seventy gangs involved in kidnapping for ransom, some backed by Baloch feudal leaders, many whom keep private armies, and members of the Balochistan assembly.

Baloch and Taliban killers have their distinct patterns of behaviour—Baloch kidnapping and killing settlers and destroying gas pipelines; and Taliban killing the Shia—but they leave one another alone. This pattern goes back into history and is probably grounded in an unspoken 'peace' between armed tribal societies capable of doing great mutual harm. But now and then there is hostile reference to each other which could inflame into open war in some future time. And that time could be sooner rather than later if the Afghan Taliban take over once again in Kabul and cause the Pakistani Taliban to declare their own affiliated emirate in the tribal areas adjacent to Khyber Pakhtunkhwa and the northern part of Balochistan abutting on Afghanistan, including Quetta.

Although headed by two men of Baloch nationality, Sipah-e-Sahaba and Lashkar-e-Jhangvi in Balochistan are imports from Punjab ordered by the Taliban leadership ensconced in North Waziristan. Because of their strong base in southern Punjab and their long association with the Pakistan security establishment as 'non-state actors' for cross-border jihad, most critics of the Pakistan government accuse the army of fomenting sectarian pogroms to dampen the secular 'separatism' of the Baloch. The way the leader of the Lashkar, Malik Ishaq, was let off in Lahore in 2012 from hundreds of cases of Shia-killing 'because of lack of evidence through death of witnesses', convinces the Shia community in Pakistan that the state wants them exterminated.

Malik Ishaq was taken to his headquarters in Rahimyar Khan in south Punjab in a dancing procession, which was seen as a bad omen by the Hazara of Balochistan.

The Baloch uprising is said to be on the boil in the southern districts of the province: Kalat, Gwadar, Panjgur, Turbat and Khuzdar, the last-named Brahui-dominated but a part of the Baloch 'struggle'. More journalists have been killed in Khuzdar than in the rest of Pakistan. The most talked-about 'clandestine' force is the Balochistan Liberation Army or BLA, originally led by Balach Marri until he was killed in 2007. His son, Hyrbyair Marri, currently leads the organization seeking independence of a 'greater' Balochistan, including Iranian and Afghan areas. It is said to have approximately 3000 fighters, mostly tribal. Brahamdagh Bugti, in exile in Switzerland since the killing of his grandfather, Nawab Akbar Bugti, by the Pakistani army in 2006, leads another clandestine Baloch Republican Army advocating independence of a 'greater' Balochistan and opposes any sort of political dialogue, calling upon the international community to intervene to halt Baloch 'genocide'.

The Baloch Student Organization (BSO), created in the late 1960s, has been the incubator of many nationalist leaders and has constantly prevented them from becoming moderate. Middle-class in social origin it supports the BLA, the Baloch National Movement, the National Party, and the Balochistan National Party, while also providing a platform to such extremist leaders as Turbat's Allah Nazar who looks forward to the removal of sardars from the Baloch nationalist pantheon.

If the National Party, led by Abdul Malik Baloch, is a middle-class party that will take part in elections and therefore conditionally accept a status quo 'in need of correction', the Balochistan National Party, led by Akhtar Mengal, is a 'midway house' between those who 'accept' the state of Pakistan and those who don't. While Akhtar Mengal aggressively presents his case at the Supreme Court of Pakistan, his brother Javed Mengal is fighting the Pakistani troops in *parari* (hillside) camps. Dr Malik's first big achievement after coming to power was to successfully persuade Mengal to end his boycott of the Balochistan assembly.

The Six Points of Baloch Separatism

In September 2012, Sardar Akhtar Mengal, returned from abroad where he had fled after being freed from prison, appeared in the Supreme Court to present his six recommendations—'the bare minimum preconditions for the beginning of talks between disgruntled Baloch militants and leaders and the government'. Mengal's six points were: 1) all covert and overt military operations against the Baloch should immediately be suspended; 2) all missing persons should be procured before a court of law: 3) all proxy death squads operating under the supervision of Inter-Services Intelligence (ISI) and Military Intelligence (MI) should be disbanded; 4) Baloch political parties should be allowed to function and resume their political activities without any interference from intelligence agencies; 5) persons responsible for inhuman torture, killing and dumping of dead bodies of the Baloch political leaders and activists should be brought to justice; and 6) measures should be taken for the rehabilitation of thousands of displaced Baloch living in appalling conditions.

After his appearance in court, Mengal appeared on TV and likened his Six Points to the Six Points presented to West Pakistan by East Pakistan before it separated and became Bangladesh in 1971.

The Great Game Revived?

Because of the many interventions by the Supreme Court, people in Pakistan are generally aware of the hidden military rule in the province through the Frontier Corps and the ISI. The 'security narrative' generally accepted by the media and most right-wing parties links the Baloch insurrection to the presence of India—the largest contributor to Afghanistan's infrastructure development—

from where it helps the rebels with funds, weapons and possibly training.

The other factor may be the involvement of China in projects in Balochistan that the nationalists are opposed to. The BLA has killed or kidnapped Chinese engineers in the province, a practice they share with the Taliban who train rebels from the Chinese province of Xinjiang and want to create an Islamic state there. A Chinese company prospected for copper at Saindak in the Chaghai district—where Pakistan tested its first nuclear device—starting in 1995. The Balochistan assembly has joined the nationalists in demanding a bigger share than a mere 3 per cent. The Chinese company has had its contract renewed for another five years in 2012 while Balochistan's share has been increased to 5 per cent.

China has also developed the Gwadar port and has recently been awarded the management of the port facility, which the international analysts of global strategy see as one of the 'string of pearls' bases China has developed in the Indian Ocean—ports built for Pakistan, Sri Lanka and Burma. New Delhi sees Gwadar as a link in the chain of 'encirclement' of India, seen together with the Karakoram Highway in the north of Pakistan. The US too sees Gwadar in the light of China's general move to 'enter' the Middle East even as Washington makes it a strategic 'pivot' to South East Asia which the Chinese may see as a strategy of encirclement. India could be present in Afghanistan—which is a member of the South Asian Association of Regional Cooperation (SAARC) together with India and Pakistan—in response to Pakistan's own flanking movement through Bangladesh to foment trouble in India's northeastern provinces, as often reported in the Indian press.

Are the Baloch rebels clearly opposed to the Chinese in Balochistan? Sardar Ataullah Mengal, the doyen of the rebel sardars of Balochistan, told ARY TV (9 January 2006): 'Why shouldn't the Baloch bullets kill the Chinese? The Baloch opposed the Gwadar port. Everybody has weapons in Pakistan like the MQM in Karachi; why shouldn't the Baloch have their weapons and why should these weapons not be capable of killing the Chinese engineers?'

Civil servants and ministers in Pakistan who often refer to 'foreign enemies' as trouble-makers in Balochistan using Baloch rebels were inadvertently encouraged by Republican Representative Dan Rohrabacher who brought a resolution to the US Congress in February 2012, protesting human rights violations in Balochistan. The PPP government, perhaps unmindful of the reaction it would arouse within the security establishment, tried to get things cleared up by inviting the United Nations to send a team of observers. The UN team arrived in Balochistan in September 2012 and met almost a hundred citizens, but the mission was aborted as one-sided when the ISI and officers of the Frontier Corps refused to be interviewed by it. Both the US and United Kingdom thereafter made Pakistan more paranoid by expressing 'concerns' over the human rights situation in Balochistan during the 19th session of the United Nations Human Rights Council.

India Interfering in Balochistan?

There is hyperbole in Pakistan's claim that India has opened twenty-five consulates in Afghanistan. The truth is that India still has only four, which it always had, and Pakistan has produced no hard evidence to the contrary that could be accepted by the international community. But the latest essay, *A Deadly Triangle: Afghanistan, Pakistan, India,* written by William Dalrymple, tends partly to address the anxiety of the Pakistani establishment: 'A former Indian consul general in Kandahar privately admitted to me that he had met with Baloch leaders at his consulate there, but he claims his ambassador gave him strict instructions not to aid them in any way against Pakistan. Still, he hinted to me that RAW personnel were present among the staff at the Kandahar and Jalalabad consulates.'

Perhaps aware that most non-state actors sent into Kashmir by Pakistan were trained in Afghanistan, India made its own 'flanking movement' in Afghanistan with some help from Afghanistan's Northern Alliance and the Central Asian states. Dalrymple continues:

'As the Taliban, supported by regular Pakistan troops, pushed the Northern Alliance into ever smaller corners of Afghanistan towards the end of the 1990s, India as well as Iran continued to send supplies to the increasingly beleaguered Massoud forces. In 2001 India built a hospital at their airbase in Tajikistan so that there would be a place to which they could ferry wounded Tajik soldiers for treatment. Lt General R.K. Sawhney, the Indian commander who oversaw this programme of assistance to the Northern Alliance, recalled to me vividly and with sadness the day the hospital received its first casualty. It was Ahmad Shah Massoud himself, assassinated by two suicide bombers posing as cameramen.'

In 2013, Pakistan looked to be on the brink of a solution to the crisis of Balochistan. What needs addressing is what in Pakistan is referred to as 'civil–military' relations. That will bluntly mean reclaiming the formulation of Pakistan's foreign policy—now often called 'security strategy'—from the GHQ and taking initiatives in the region that Sharif promised in his election manifesto. Confronted with a possible civil war in Afghanistan and its bifurcation into the Tajik–Hazara-dominated north and the Pakhtun-dominated south after 2014, Pakistan must wake up to the dangers of blindly supporting the latter against the former. It must move quickly to normalize its relations with India through the 'free trade' regime in South Asia it has pledged in SAARC resolutions, giving itself the advantage of a median state between India and the Central Asian states. A frozen foreign policy based on immovable geopolitics has yielded only terrorism and insurgency. Any departure from it will make Pakistan more acceptable to a world now scared of Pakistan's ability to trigger global instability.

26

A Typical General?

In December 2012, Lieutenant General Shahid Aziz (retd) went public with the 'secrets' of the 1999 Kargil Operation conducted by the Pakistan army against India, the first act of war under civilian rule, which brought yet more discomfiture for the Pakistanis to bear. He had also just written a confessional book which contained chapters on the 'fiasco' brought on by Army Chief General Pervez Musharraf who was his relative by marriage. Musharraf in rejoinder has called him an officer 'without character'. Before the book came out, Aziz was paraded by keen anchors on TV programs luxuriating in the new scandals attached to the discredited ex-army chief, who had hastily slipped abroad and couldn't enter Pakistan for fear of being arrested for murder by the state or killed by the Taliban. Aziz said of Kargil in an interview, 'It was an unsound military plan based on invalid assumptions, launched with little preparations and in total disregard of the regional and international environment.'

According to Aziz, Musharraf did not even share plans of the war he was going to unleash on India with his corps commanders. Only four officers, according to him, knew about it: General Pervez Musharraf, chief of general staff Lt General Mohammad Aziz, Commander Force Command Northern Areas Lt General Javed Hassan and 10-Corps Rawalpindi commander Lt General Mahmud Ahmad. He revealed: 'Even the then director general military operations (DGMO) Lt General Tauqir Zia came to know about it later.' Aziz, himself director general of the Analysis Wing of Inter-Services Intelligence (ISI), had no clue. The Operation was not studied professionally because secrecy was paramount.

Confession as Sermon

Then the book came out. Titled *Yeh Khamoshi Kahan Tak*: *Ek Sipahi ki Dastan-e-Ishq-o-Junoon* it follows no recognizable format. Its chapters were simply phrases taken from poems giving no clue of the subject discussed under them; there is no index, so you have to plough through the unexamined gushings of an average man living on the basis of clichés to get at facts—or what Aziz thinks is analysis. An Urdu columnist, after reading the book, praised him for his Urdu style! The book in fact needed a going-over from a language-editor who could win readers' gratitude by excising several sprawling sermons palmed off as chapters. The great Pakistani poet Faiz Ahmad Faiz, whose lines are copiously strewn all over the book, would not have liked this extravagance in aid of bad prose.

Shahid Aziz was what one might call a typical success story in the army. Commissioned in 1971, he saw action in Kashmir and was smart enough to rise to the level where he was trained at The National Defence University before being appointed Director Military Operations. As major general, he was placed at the head of the Analysis Wing of the ISI from where he studied the Kargil Operation and came to the conclusion, as the war wound down to the discredit of Pakistan, that it shouldn't have taken place. He however shocked a deflated Musharraf by suggesting during a top-level meeting that certain defeat be avoided by expanding the war into other theatres. Aziz is a warrior typically not given to any holistic analyses that Clausewitz recommends to military leaders living under civilian governments. He is liberal with religious sermons while what he actually needs is examination of the functioning of national economy and global environment. Where he should have inducted regional and global factor-analysis he makes do with conspiracy theories that Muslims all over the world prefer over logical connections. On a study tour in the US he bowled over his American lecturer by calling Kissinger's book *Diplomacy* 'a Machiavellian' piece of writing.

A rare intellectual general, Major General Hakeem Arshad Qureshi (retd) says in his book, *The 1971 Indo-Pak War: A Soldier's Narrative*: 'We have displayed a tendency to enter a contest mostly on the rebound, with overly ambitious aims and without due thought and preparation and have usually given up the effort at the half-way mark for want of resources . . . We have also failed to understand the international interests and reactions in the event of an armed conflict on the subcontinent or to appreciate correctly the enemy's reaction to a major ingress.' Aziz gives no evidence of having read Qureshi's 'corrective' volume.

Musharraf brought in Aziz as his Director General Military Operations (DGMO) and in 1999 planned the overthrow of Nawaz Sharif's elected government. Aziz later commanded a division in Azad Kashmir. In 2001, after 9/11, Musharraf still thought he could trust his relative as Chief of General Staff, a post from where most officers ascend to the top job of army chief. If the book is to be trusted, it is here that Aziz woke up to the wickedness of America and its 'games' in the region. His last two years in service he spent as corps commander Lahore, falling prey to religious quacks and building his beautiful farmhouse near Murree—'no budget, expense doesn't matter . . . we have an amount of money we never thought of before'. He rues the fact that while in Lahore he was relentlessly pursued by 'dirty rumours'. He retired in 2005, decorated with the prestigious Hilal-e-Imtiaz medal. Musharraf quickly appointed him head of National Accountability Bureau (NAB)—but put him off the very first day by asking for immunity for one of his corrupt ministers, Faisal Saleh Hayat. He resigned from NAB one and a half years later. His NAB 'confessions' prove once again that Pakistan should stay away from accountability, which its leaders and institutions use more for revenge against enemies than for cleaning up corruption.

It is often said that Pakistani troops are of high quality but are poorly led by their generals. The book proves it once again. The pity of it is that Aziz thinks he is a maverick because of his religious passion rather than type-cast as a Pakistani general. His opinion actually adheres to the general ideological view entrenched in Pakistan, perhaps furtively anticipating reprisal from the terrorists if the truth is revealed. He repeats the platitudes daily unloaded on the already heavily indoctrinated public by our retired generals, led by ex-army chief Aslam Beg and ex-ISI chief Hamid Gul. He defers to the last-named by approving of his Council of Elders ruling Pakistan in lieu of the currently soiled 'Western system of democracy'.

Democracy comes in for condemnation on page 214, an 'ill-smelling' order where politicians make money hand over fist while the common man starves. The 'greedy intellectuals' who relentlessly speak for democracy also come in for scathing diatribes. Despite his stint in the analysis wing of the ISI there is scant reference to terrorism and the Taliban who with equal vehemence criticize democracy as being abhorrent to Islam. He abstains from taking a look at the al-Zawahiri treatise on Pakistan's Constitution, treated by many as the blueprint for Pakistan's next constitution when the Taliban finally rule from Islamabad.

America Is Killing Us

He mentions the current army chief General Kayani with deference but clearly doesn't accept Kayani's stated position that Pakistan faces internal danger and is not being threatened externally. In this he is with many retired officers, like one Shahzad Chaudhry who recently accepted that Pakistan faced internal rather than external threat but could not refrain in 2013 from connecting the Taliban attacks on Pakistan's expensive surveillance aircraft at Kamra and Mehran base as possibly 'India's deed' because these planes were targeted only at India. But Aziz is not even forgivably reductionist like Chaudhry; he has firm conviction and can't accept that the Taliban are the real threat: 'The bombs that kill innocent Pakistanis in bazaars and mosques are planted by friends of America, and this terrorism is done to persuade Pakistan to embrace America more closely, allow the government to pursue pro-America policies and to alienate Pakistan from the mujahideen. But this trend of support to the killers of Muslims is open rebellion against Allah'.

Of course he doesn't believe that the 9/11 attacks were carried out by Muslims. He buys into the theory that America destroyed the World Trade Center to give itself the grounds for attacking the Islamic world. The adoption by Musharraf of the slogan of 'enlightened moderation' is condemned by him as a double-faced slavery of America busy planning the roll-back of the true faith of Islam by making it lean on the false religion of the Mughal emperor Akbar and the latter-day 'rationalist' exegete of the Quran, Ghulam Ahmad Parwez. He condemns Musharraf for using this slogan to label orthodoxy as fundamentalist and militant and inviting society to become deviant from the path of piety, while dancing to the materialist drumbeat.

Aziz was a major at the Quetta Staff College. One day he made a presentation to his class responding to the challenge of a possible Soviet incursion into Pakistan after occupation of Afghanistan. He proposed that if and when the country was seen to be falling to the Soviet army, the Pakistan army and government leaders should be made to leave Islamabad–Rawalpindi and hide in the mountains in the region of Chitral and Kashmir from where to organize popular uprisings against the Soviet occupiers. He typically doesn't dwell on the scenario in full as that would involve discussion of the notorious 'resource base' of proxy warriors that our officers are not supposed to look at.

No St Augustine

He confesses that while on his course in the US he once got so drunk at night that he could not get his homework right and was reprimanded by his American teacher. But he is no Saint Augustine; his confessions are harmless and not detailed enough. Here too he fails the yardstick of analysis and is more focused on non-analytical opinion. Why do officers as gifted as Aziz shun intellect and fall prey to irrational connections which they confuse with intellectual activity? Chapter Five is titled 'Wave of Inspirations' describing his namaz and Quran routines in Kashmir instead of the realities of confrontation with a state who would deliver defeat after defeat to a revisionist Pakistan dismantled by costs of conflict. The Faiz poem at the end of the chapter, complaining of ideological oppression, has no relevance here.

The book is full of sermonizing on faith; and the author apparently doesn't tire of it. Yet he talks disparagingly of Lt General Ghulam Muhammad, commander of 10 Corps, known for his blatantly fanatic injection of faith into the army, which he titled Construction of Character, mainly based on how many incantations (Quranic recitations) the subject officer should know by heart, reinforced by his routine of blocking upward movement of officers who did not say namaz. Aziz ends the chapter by inappropriately inserting a long rambling poem, not by Faiz this time, but by himself, in English! His habit of rational disconnection perhaps became vaguely known to him on 'Why am I full of contradiction? Why can't I be balanced? Then I console myself with the thought that a pendulum has a balance too; what use is balance that is static and frozen. Real balance is in movement. One should be flying back and forth on a swing.'

Conspiracy Theory as Intellectual Activity

As a soldier, he is forgivably worshipful of Pakistan's nuclear weapons, but is rough in his condemnation of anti-nuclear peaceniks—who 'take money'—for attacking the bomb. His explanation for having violated the basic rules of nuclearization with the Kargil Operation is unconvincing, probably because of a weak control of the Urdu idiom, rather than reasoning. He goes on to claim Pakistan's bomb as a bomb of the Muslim world and accepts the West's reference to it as Islamic Bomb. (He ignores Iran where the Islamic Bomb of Pakistan caused alarm; and might ignore now the alarm the Iranian bomb has raised among the Arab states across the Gulf. He is obviously incapable of seeing the Iranian bomb as a Shia bomb, which makes Pakistan, an ally of Saudi Arabia, the possessor of a Sunni bomb.)

In the ISI his meditations on the media fly in the face of all theory about the connection of the freedom of expression with a strong private sector in the national economy under a democratic constitution. He relates media freedom to another conspiracy of the West to undermine Pakistan's civilizational foundations and replace them with a 'satanic system' through injections of money into a media marketplace where 'journalism is business'. He opposed the Kargil Operation which posited that after Pakistan cut India off from Siachen and internationalized the dispute, New Delhi would be forced to cough up Kashmir; but he is predictably tough on trade with India—which 'Americans keep pressuring Pakistan to allow'—because it would be a first step towards saying goodbye to Kashmir. He thinks politicians who promote trade with India are crippled in their thinking by their narrow political interests. He doesn't bother to analyse how India has handled its own 'Kashmir dispute' with China and how it has allowed trade without damaging itself while growing at the rate of 8 per cent of the GDP.

Far from being trained as a disciplined military thinker, he insists that Pakistan should focus on the grand conspiracy behind

America's imperialist dominance of the world. He knows that the theory is airy-fairy but proclaims that a large number of people around the globe believe it: 'The world order is not running by itself, it is being run according to a secret plan by a powerful secret organization that has first conquered global banking, followed by the media and entertainment. This plan is being worked out with the help of the United Kingdom, the IMF and the World Bank, the funded think tanks and their intellectuals, big corporations and reputable universities'.

Added Attraction: The Protocols

Perhaps the most interesting nugget in the book is Aziz's reference to the 'eye of Dajjal' (Antichrist) on the dollar bill, symbolizing the grand conspiracy set in motion by the Freemasons and many powerful families in league with the American Neocons. He thinks that whatever is happening in the world is in line with the Jewish conspiracy outlined in *The Protocols of the Elders of Zion*, a document that surfaced in Europe in the early twentieth century to rouse people into a fit of anti-Semitism and resultant holocaust. By a strange leap of logic, he thinks that the American imperium was following the programme of world domination through a shameless pursuit of sensual pleasure. 'Only the Quran stands in the way of this satanic way of life,' he writes.

Aziz is falling back on an elaborate campaign unleashed in Pakistan in 1995 against the New World Order proclaimed by an American President after the first Gulf War. Pamphlets circulating in Pakistan referred to the 'one-eyed pyramid on the left side of the one-dollar bill' calling the seal a deeply laid Jewish-American conspiracy to dominate the world. The eye on the note was called The Eye of Lucifer, also designated as the eye of the Antichrist Dajjal in the Muslim belief system. The pamphlet was titled 'The Pyramid, the Global System and Control Mechanisms'.

General Shahid Aziz's book badly needs good editing with special emphasis on style and removal of irrelevant matter passed off as inspiring verse. The great Pakistani poet Faiz who stood for a secular and pluralist Pakistan may be spinning like a lathe in his grave seeing the use Aziz has made of him to promote his own patently irrational and unrealistic worldview. (Aziz asserts that Pakistan is still secular even after the establishment of the Federal Sharia Court under a constitution declaring Pakistan as an Islamic state.) The book has been welcomed in Pakistan by an anti-American, anti-Musharraf and Taliban-frightened media. The author has been lionized for his 'bravery' in speaking the truth.

The truth however is that the book is yet more devastating proof of the defective military leadership in Pakistan where most Muslim officers, brought up on non-rational beliefs, decline into end-of-career religiosity and find fault with the world they think they are about to say goodbye to. The book has photographs of the adolescent Shahid Aziz 'in tight pants and pointed shoes', growing up normally.

27

American 'Retreat' and AfPak Secrets

When I walked up to him to get his book signed by him, Vali Raza Nasr surprised me by remembering my name. We had last met in 2007, when his book, *The Shia Revival: How Conflicts within Islam Will Shape the Future,* revealed to me that the Shia mayhem in Pakistan was started in Lucknow at Nadwatul Ulema by Rabita Alam Islami funding its chief cleric Manzur Numani to start the sectarian war with an incendiary book, finally, as I revealed in my own book, *The Sectarian War,* culminating in his demanding—and getting—'apostatization' fatwas against the Shia sect from all the major seminaries in Pakistan.

And now in Chicago—the native city of Richard Holbrooke—it was April 2013 and he had just spoken to an appreciative audience about his latest book, *The Dispensable Nation: American Foreign Policy in Retreat.* He had been senior adviser to the Special Representative for Afghanistan and Pakistan (SRAP) Richard

Holbrooke at the State Department and had criticized the White House in the American press for ignoring Holbrooke's advice on how to deal with Pakistan.

Nasr is Professor of Middle Eastern and South Asian Affairs at the Fletcher School of Law and Diplomacy and knows Pakistan well—his books on Maulana Mawdudi and Jamaat-e-Islami remain authoritative in the academic world—and he knows Iran, his native country, where his father Seyyed Hussein Nasr was once the top intellectual in the Shah regime. (I, as junior lecturer in Government College in Lahore in the 1960s, had met Hussein Nasr at the house of my friend Suhail Iftikhar. A handsome Iranian with a good command over English, he had just returned from a game of tennis, after paying his respects as a practising mystic at Data Darbar, the mausoleum of Lahore's founder saint. He was being hailed in Lahore for his latest book on the four great mystics of Islam.)

Vali Nasr agreed with Holbrooke that the Afghanistan crisis could be resolved by engaging with Pakistan and roping Iran in as an important interlocutor: Holbrooke thought that a political settlement was possible if Afghanistan's key neighbours (Iran and Pakistan) and other important regional actors (India, Russia and Saudi Arabia) could be induced to support it. Anyone living next to Afghanistan knows that the country's sovereignty is shared by its neighbours: Pakistan has unusual influence in Jalalabad, Iran virtually controls the economy of Herat in the west and Uzbekistan has influence in Mazar-e-Sharif in the north. Holbrooke thought the US should pay more (positive) attention to Pakistan because of its clearly expressed commitment to internal developments in Afghanistan, otherwise known as 'strategic depth'. He recalls:

'In October 2010, during a visit to the White House, Pakistan's army chief, General Ashfaq Parvez Kayani, gave President Obama a thirteen-page white paper he had written to explain his views on the outstanding strategic issues between Pakistan and the United States. 'Kayani 3.0', as the paper was dubbed (since it was the third paper the Pakistanis gave the White House on the subject), could be summarized as follows: You are not going to win the war, and you are not going to transform Afghanistan. This place has devoured empires before you; it will defy you as well. Stop your grandiose plans and let's get practical, sit down, and discuss how you will leave and what is an end state we can both live with.'

Hard-nosed Vali concludes: 'The Afghanistan fight is starting to eerily resemble Vietnam, with Pakistan acting roughly like Laos, Cambodia, and Maoist China all rolled into one.' He knows Pakistan is fielding 35,000 'non-state actors' to safeguard its interests in Afghanistan, among whom the largest number, 20,000 or more, were mercenaries. Holbrooke fell afoul of ex-CIA man Bruce Riedel whom Obama had asked to review Afghanistan: 'Holbrooke did not favour committing America to fully resourced counter insurgency and thought America would get more out of Pakistan through engagement.'

Holbrooke died in 2010, but what has followed since proves him right: there is no military solution to Afghanistan where a war against terrorism has gone wrong, thanks to Pakistan. He was not allowed to exhaust the diplomatic channels and was overruled by the White House through the simple stratagem of not listening to him. What he proposed was nothing outlandish: talk and fight, and fight in order to 'make your foe find talking more appealing'. He had enough knowledge of what was going on inside the Taliban Inc. to sense that the Taliban were ready to break with al-Qaeda and talk to America. But the CIA nixed the idea saying 'reconciliation was a Pakistani ploy to slow down the American offensive in Afghanistan and reduce American pressure on Pakistan'. The White House followed by undermining his diplomacy with Kabul.

Vali saw Holbrooke becoming obsessed with the idea of trans-Pakistan Indian trade, not so much for the unravelling of the war knot in Afghanistan as for its transformative role in the region. His persuasion was effective in Rawalpindi: 'That he got the Pakistan military to give its okay (given that the deal would connect Afghanistan and India economically and would require Pakistan to open its border to India) was a mighty achievement.'

But US–Pakistan relations plummeted thereafter and Pakistan backtracked in light of its own myopic strategic thinking pitting it against India and the US on the side of China. It backtracked ominously again, swallowing its word on giving New Delhi the Most-Favoured Nation status in 2012. The State Department, within which Holbrooke operated, warmed to the idea and proposed revival of the historic Silk Road trade with Central Asia, quickly dubbed as an American plot in Pakistan's hostile Urdu press.

If there was any meaningful American initiative in the region it was scuttled by the tiresome regurgitation of India–Pakistan rivalry cauterized into Pakistan's military memory by the fact that the two countries backed opposite sides during the Taliban's war on the Northern Alliance in the 1990s and 'continued to see Afghanistan's future as a zero-sum game that could change the balance of power between them'. India was convincing when it pointed to Pakistan's terrorist interference in India through its non state actors; Pakistan was less so about Indian interference in Balochistan given the embarrassing fact that the Baloch despised Pakistan as the army made them disappear on the charge that they not so much pressed their legitimate demands as a neglected nationality, as acted as instruments of Indian policy.

Vali Nasr's thoughts in the post-2010 period are encapsulated thus: 'America was trying to fix Afghanistan while actually escalating tensions with both Iran and Pakistan, as if peace could somehow be made to take hold in Afghanistan when the country's immediate neighbourhood was roiled by acute instability. A chaotic Afghanistan in a stable region was hard enough to handle; a chaotic Afghanistan in an unstable region, and with its two most important neighbours in conflict with America, seems nearly impossible.'

He is not sure that a 'wobbly' 300,000-strong Afghan Security Force will be able to fight the Taliban fielded by the Pakistan army. The book carries a blunt rejoinder by Pakistan's General Kayani to President Obama: It will not stand up for long. It will splinter and become cannon-fodder for the warlords who will rule Afghanistan once again. Hidden behind this prognostication was the likely fear that the Afghan Security Force will have trained a large number of Pakistan's enemies left out of the compass of Pakistani diplomacy in Afghanistan.

Then in September 2011 the outgoing Joint Chiefs chairman Admiral Mike Mullen told the US Senate Armed Services Committee that the Haqqani Network was 'in many ways, a strategic arm of Pakistan's Inter-Services Intelligence Agency. Wali Nasr traces the ISI policy backwards to Musharraf: 'In reality, Musharraf had been the architect of the Taliban revival. The Taliban surge of 2008 and 2009 would never have been possible without preparations, recruiting, training, and capability-building activities that the Taliban undertook in Pakistan or with Pakistani help and that went back several years—to the time when Musharraf was in charge. The fact was that Pakistan had strategic objectives in Afghanistan, and it was pursuing them with us there and despite its own budding partnership with us.'

But was it wise to hit back at Pakistan? 'Several levers came to my mind: we relied on Pakistan to supply our troops in Afghanistan with everything from fuel to drinking water; we needed Pakistan's cooperation to gather the intelligence necessary to make drone strikes effective; and above all we needed Pakistan to make our Afghanistan strategy work. Given these dependencies, we had done ourselves a disservice by taking an axe to the relationship. Bullying wasn't going to pay.'

The Mumbai attack had taken place in 2008 but the US decided to put a bounty on the head of Hafiz Saeed in 2012, which was seen by Rawalpindi as the extension of the American war on terror to Pakistan. Of course, the military mind unrealistically projected Pakistan as a pawn in China's imagined ingress into the region to ward off a similar America strategy with the help of India, in other words, setting up India as the unchallenged hegemon of South Asia. The frequent unsettling realization in the GHQ that China is unwilling to pit itself against either the US or

India—both important trading partners—goes without normal retribution for lack of brains.

The book sums up the American mistake: 'We could have managed Pakistan better. We did not have to break the relationship and put Pakistan's stability at risk. That course of action has not gotten us any further than the more prudent course of greater engagement—in fact, it's gotten us a lot less. We have not realized our immediate security goals there and have put our long-run strategic interests in jeopardy. Pakistan is a failure of American policy, a failure of the sort that comes from the President handing foreign policy over to the Pentagon and the intelligence agencies.'

Vali Raza resents the 'disengagement' with Pakistan as a part of a much larger 'demission' from the region of the Middle East, and confronting/containing China through Obama's 'pivot to Asia' policy— 'a forward-deployed diplomacy to face China in its backyard'. An otherwise pliant boss of Holbrooke at the State Department, Hillary Clinton, had concocted the strategic vision that Vali's book resents the most: She wrote in *Foreign Policy* magazine to argue that 'the administration's case that America ought to pay less attention to the Middle East and more attention to Asia; that China (and not the Middle East) is the real strategic challenge facing America.' Her verdict was: 'The future of the United States is intimately intertwined with the future of the Asia-Pacific; and global politics will be decided in Asia, not Afghanistan or Iraq, and the United States will be right at the centre of the action.'

The book insists that the Middle East should matter more to America because China sees the region growing in importance, even more than Africa or Latin America. He agrees that China doesn't favour confrontation with the US but it might cause it to happen through economic expansion; and that the American retreat from the Middle East, instead of strengthening the hands of Washington in its Asian pivot strategy, will simply lessen America's capacity to manage that competition.

We get an idea of the American 'retreat' and Chinese 'expansion' in the following statistics:

'Today the Middle East accounts for 5 per cent of US trade and only 1 per cent of its direct foreign investment ($54 billion out of $3.4 trillion), a paltry amount compared with the Asia-Pacific, which accounted for 16 per cent of American investment abroad. We are now doing less trade with the region than China is. The big story of the past decade that we missed amid our preoccupation with wars in the Middle East is the explosion of Chinese trade with the region.

'China's trade with Iran has grown from $1.3 billion in 1999 to $45 billion in 2011; with Saudi Arabia from $4 billion in 2001 to $50 billion in 2011; and with Egypt from less than a billion in 2001 to $9 billion in 2011. Since 2006 China has been exporting more to the Middle East than the United States does, and the same is true for imports since 2009. In 2010, Chinese exports to the region were close to double that of the United States (China is now the largest exporter to the region), and Chinese direct foreign investment took off, leaving America far behind: 30 per cent of China's global contracts in that year were with Arab enterprises. We have essentially ceded the Middle East to China and others to profit from just as we geared up to prevent the same happening in the Asia-Pacific and Africa.'

Why should Pakistan not be abandoned? Because China is going to use it to get close to the Indian Ocean: 'China has earmarked $12 billion to develop the port of Gwadar on Pakistan's Arabian Sea coast. The idea is to create a place where petrochemicals piped down from Central Asia (Kazakhstan and Turkmenistan) and minerals shipped from Afghanistan can be loaded onto tankers and cargo ships bound for China.'

He grasps the Chinese mind more accurately than most in Pakistan do. India too understands China as it increases its cooperation—instead of confrontation—in Bangladesh and Burma, apart from bilateral trade which is certain to go from $70 billion to $100 billion in the near future. He writes: 'China does not like it when Pakistan pushes too hard with India, or provokes American anger. China wants Pakistan as a strategic base, not a source of fresh headaches. Waves of extremists trained in Pakistan may stoke fires of separatism in Xinjiang, and, as happened before, countless Chinese engineers can be abducted by Pakistani tribesmen for ransom; yet China's true anger at Pakistan is directed at its threat of a regional power play. China wants to use Pakistan to serve Chinese interests, and it will not be made a pawn in Islamabad's regional games. So it was that even as China was stepping up its investment in Pakistan's military capability, it was winding down its support for Pakistan on the Kashmir issue.'

Unfortunately, Vali Nasr is confronting a rival that no one can win against—the shrinking American economy and the thoughts of global 'retreat' it inspires. Richard N. Haass, president, Council on Foreign Relations, writing in *Foreign Affairs* (May/June 2013) triumphantly expresses the prevalent point of view: 'Six and a half years ago, I wrote an essay for this magazine titled *The New Middle East*. The piece argued that the era of American domination of the region was coming to an end and that the Middle East's future would be characterized by considerable but reduced US influence . . . The Greater Middle East had come to dominate and distort American foreign and defence policy, and a course correction was called for. The Obama administration's vehicle for this correction was the announcement of a "pivot", or "rebalancing", towards Asia, a region home to many of the world's largest and fastest-growing economies and one likely to be more central than the Middle East in shaping the world's future.'

28

Eating Grass and Some Snakes

Brigadier (Retired) Feroz Hassan Khan is no ordinary author. He is an acknowledged 'insider' who was once a director at the apex nukes establishment of Pakistan, The Directorate of Arms Control and Disarmament, Strategic Planning Division (SPD), and has told the story of Pakistan's bomb as a legitimate undertaking which the world should now recognize as such.

Khan favours the theory that states nuclearize not so much on the basis of realism—which can actually deter acquisition of nuclear weapons—but 'strategic culture which stands as an important intervening variable between changes in the material cases of power and state behaviour'. Given Pakistan's 'martial persona', its ideological misrepresentation of jihad, and the dominance of the state by a coup-making military, security is defined in Pakistan in military terms. And today, if you think security should emanate from a buoyant economy flourishing on trade openings with states dubbed 'enemy' by nationalism, there are numberless non-state actors willing to use terror to cow you down and make you love the bomb that bankrupts the state.

Who in Pakistan erects the emotional structure of 'national humiliation' propelling these suicidal national security ideas even as 'failed states' like North Korea brandish their bombs to scare the world? How many lessons were learned from nuclear China that finally derived its real global clout not from the bomb but its economy? Had China aped revisionist Pakistan, nuclear war would have engulfed the world and destroyed the Chinese nation. Only ideology and nationalism make Pakistan ignore the low-IQ military leader who flourishes only by isolating the country internationally and unleashing non-state actors on civilian leaders. No one can ever tell a Pakistani jingoist that the nuclear example of India is less relevant to him than North Korea's: you can collapse as a state while your bombs rot in the attic.

The author remains steadfastly wedded to references that don't always present Pakistan as a sane nation: 'Such global prominence [through nuclearization] in Pakistani thought, harkened back to past civilizational glory, to the time when the Mughal Empire shared the global stage with the Safavids and the Ottomans. Additionally, for Pakistan, a country conflicted over whether it is a secular or theological Muslim state, nuclear weapons were a symbol of cohesion—they became one of the few issues about which there was national consensus.' In 2013, the fib about 'cohesion through the bomb' no longer stands up. The truth is that a revisionist state has gone haywire and said goodbye to realism too after going nuclear.

It all started in 1954 with Dr Rafi Mohammad Chaudhry in the high tension laboratory in the Physics Department of Government College, Lahore. When General Zia met him 'he raised his hand and saluted Chaudhry for his contributions to Pakistan's nuclear development'. After that, Cambridge-educated Pakistani physicist, Abdus Salam, recipient of the Nobel Prize in physics in 1979, helped the weapons programme by directing more British-trained nuclear manpower to the project. Bureaucrat I.H.

Usmani helped in attracting 'peaceful' nuclear technology from Canada. The Pakistan Institute of Nuclear Science and Technology (PINSTECH) emerged as an architectural masterpiece; and the Pakistan Atomic Energy Commission (PAEC) was given $350 million in 1975 for 'initiatives' including the uranium enrichment plant.

Nuclear Physics and Heavenly Horses

The Muslim mind conquered science and equated the bomb with the 'horses that had to be kept ready' according to an edict of the Holy Quran. Sultan Bashiruddin Mahmood, a PhD in science and nuclear engineering at the University of Manchester in the United Kingdom, had worked in the UK's Atomic Energy Authority on nuclear reactors, then at Risley Design Centre, a small facility 30 miles outside of Manchester. His job at this facility exposed him to design work for nuclear power plants, reprocessing plants, and enrichment facilities.

Back home from the UK, where religious humbug was not tolerated, Mahmood read a paper before General Zia saying he could produce electricity for the entire country from a single jinn, a supernatural fire-born entity mentioned in the Holy Quran. When the author asked him to explain his innovative approach to enriching uranium he said, 'I got the idea from Allah.' He was so wedded to the idea of 'horses' that he wanted war rather than peace, and Osama bin Laden next door in Afghanistan seemed to promise the Armageddon he aspired to. He retired in 1999, after protesting against Pakistan's perceived softening on the signing of a test ban treaty (CTBT). In 2001, he clearly signalled in favour of war 'without the state' by going—together with fellow scientist Chaudhry Abdul Majid, formerly of PINSTECH—to Afghanistan and meeting Osama bin Laden.

The Pakistani interface with terrorism had begun in the 1990s and Mahmood was one of the pioneers of it from the deep establishment. Writing about that period, Husain Haqqani in his book, *Magnificent Delusions: Pakistan, the United States, and an Epic History of Misunderstanding*, notes: 'Pakistan was the only country with a Taliban embassy, although Saudi Arabia and the United Arab Emirates had also recognized their regime. At one point the US embassy in Islamabad estimated that 20 to 10 per cent of Taliban soldiers were Pakistani. US diplomats acknowledged that the presence of Pakistani volunteers in Afghanistan solidifies Pakistan–Taliban relations . . . Pakistanis were fighting alongside Muslim extremists battling for autonomy in Mindanao, the Philippines, and Pakistanis had been among Islamists fighting in Chechnya. Arab governments in Egypt, Algeria and Jordan also identified their foes among those living in Pakistan since the anti-Soviet Afghan Jihad.'

Mahmood was divinely inspired like the rest in this great covert battlefield organized by nuclearized Pakistan now that it felt secure. Like generals Hamid Gul and Aslam Beg—and in 2013 General Shahid Aziz—Mahmood was temperamentally unstable. Author Khan calls it 'a rebellious streak' that made him present his 'viewpoints with force and passion', hiding behind ideology when challenged by his superiors. The bomb had become a part of the national catechism, mixing patriotism with faith, and everyone had to bow before it as if to a phallic god. If you can smell fascism in the maunderings of retired generals on TV chat-shows today, you can see it in the career of Mahmood too. The book also notes incompetence growing out of this sense of ideological authority:

'Sultan Bashiruddin Mahmood was one of the causes of the poor working environment in Project 706 [enrichment]. Though personally skilled and knowledgeable, his poor managerial skills caused precious hours to be wasted on conferences and petty administrative tasks, leaving little time for substantial work. In addition, Sultan Bashiruddin's hiring practices came under scrutiny. For example, he insisted on interviewing and selecting new employees on his own and did not include any of his subordinates in the hiring process. Many employees viewed this as nepotism, making the working environment even less pleasant.'

Enter 'Father of the Bomb'

But the nuclear establishment had another absolutist personality in the shape of Dr A.Q. Khan trying to transform the bomb project into his personal fiefdom. After his BSc from Karachi University, Khan travelled to Europe and earned an MS from the Technological University of Delft, Holland, and a PhD in copper metallurgy from the Catholic University of Leuven, Belgium. Thereafter, as an employee at the URENCO nuclear plant in Almelo, Netherlands, he had gained crucial knowledge of centrifuge-based enrichment operations before returning to Pakistan and joining the enrichment project in 1976.

Then nationalism cloaking a deep personal urge to dominate overcame all sense of ethic: overarching 'destiny' was knocking on his door. The biggest nuclear theft was going to take place through him, making him the 'father of the bomb' in Pakistan while he accumulated personal wealth hand over fist in Islamabad. However, the state could not carry the burden of his greatness much longer and succumbed to global pressures in 2004, forcing him to 'confess' to his evil enterprise and arm-twisting a jinn-taming 'jihadi' Sultan Bashiruddin Mahmood to take lie-detector tests from an FBI team—which he rendered ineffective by cleverly feigning fits of unconsciousness. The ruling general who made Pakistan's nuclear heroes suffer this humiliation, Pervez Musharraf, was facing charges of treason in 2013 and may succumb to 'divine justice' for having violated the sanctity of the bomb by maltreating its bearded uncle and clean-shaven father.

Then Abdul Qadeer Khan clashed with the other Khan who ran the entire nuclear establishment, chairman of the PAEC, Munir Ahmad Khan, who had done a stint at the International Atomic Energy Agency (IAEA) and was inclined to be less 'mission-driven' and more discreet, in total negation of the 'jihadi' commando action that Mahmood favoured, and the venality of Dr Khan. The 'secular' bomb-nationalism of Munir Ahmad Khan soon led to rumours about him being an Ahmadi, a community bestowed the with label of apostasy by a death-wish-driven nation. General Zia who had just placed further stringent disabilities on the Ahmadi community succumbed and made Dr Khan independent of Munir Ahmad Khan by giving him autonomous charge of what later became KRL (Khan Research Laboratory). Munir Ahmad Khan, whom the intelligence agencies reported to Zia as being a normal Muslim and not an apostate, was taken off the bomb project, which shows how a Muslim state, more attuned to medieval witch-hunting than rationality, wobbles when handling science.

What did Sultan Bashiruddin think of Dr Khan? The book offers us this nugget. 'Even after thirty years, Sultan Bashiruddin Mahmood held exceptionally strong feelings about those times, demonstrated by his lasting opinion of A.Q. Khan: 'A.Q. Khan was mentally sick. His mental sickness was such that he wanted everything in his possession, in his control, and he wanted that "it should be known that I am the super-genius, I am everybody".' The Pakistani bomb was doomed to be sired by a gang of scientists suffering from severe personality disorders. And one can extend that diagnosis to the state itself in 2013 as it prepares to bend to the will of the Taliban–al-Qaeda combine while carrying the payload of more than a hundred nuclear bombs in its bowels.

In a comprehensive analysis of Dr Khan as a person, *Deception: Pakistan, the United States, and the Secret Trade in Nuclear Weapons* by Adrian Levy and Catherine Scott-Clark states: 'Khan continued to collect awards and honours, many of them invented at his request. He became addicted to it. Between 1984 and 1992, the KRL chief scored eleven gold medals from organizations as diverse as the Lions Club of Gujarat, the Institute of Metallurgy and the Citizens of Rawalpindi. He awarded himself the "Man of the Nation" medal given by the Pakistan Institute of National Affairs in Lahore, and even wangled a recommendation out of the Abbasi Shaheed Public Hospital in Karachi, which, after receiving an envelope stuffed with cash, had a gold medal cast glorifying Dr Khan.'

General Zia versus General Beg

General Zia, presiding over Pakistan, was aligned with Saudi Arabia and Gulf Arabs against Iran, which threatened them with exportable revolution. His deputy in the GHQ, General Aslam Beg, was ideologically aligned with Iran and saw Arabs as allies of hegemonic America and favoured Dr Khan's proliferating contacts with Tehran. A dossier released by the London-based International Institute for Strategic Studies (IISS) in 2007, as a 'chronology of Dr A.Q. Khan's proliferation' indicates that he had visited Iran's reactor at Bushehr in 1986. Iran approached Dr Khan's 'network' to close a $3 million deal for centrifuge technology. The IISS dossier distinguishes between the 'Pakistan government' (meaning General Zia) and the 'Khan network' (excluding General Zia). Iran later disclosed the details of the dispatch of centrifuges to Iran by Dr Khan to the International Atomic Energy Agency (IAEA). According to the IAEA, he made the sale to Iran of all the required elements in 1987 in Dubai.

As Aslam Beg embraced anti-imperialism, General Zia was nursing his own bruises from the Arab–Iran rivalry in the region. Under Saudi tutelage he had made the mistake of clamping zakat (Islamic poor-due) on the Shia of Pakistan whose jurisprudence forbade them from paying it to the state. Then the Gulf Arabs set up the Gulf Cooperative Council (GCC) with Saudi Arabia as its patron and asked General Zia to provide it with covert military teeth. When he protested neutrality between Iran and the Arabs he was actually threatened with the repatriation of hundreds of thousands of Pakistani workers employed by the GCC states.

Kuldip Nayar's Fatal Interview

1987 was the fatal year. Dr Khan decided in an interview given to Indian journalist Kuldip Nayar—who was escorted by Pakistani journalist Mushahid Husain—to 'showcase' his bomb by admitting that Pakistan had gone beyond nuclear 'capability' and could actually nuke India. In his latest book, *Beyond the Lines: An Autobiography,* Nayar tells the story thus: 'I thought I would provoke him. Egoist that he was, he might fall for the bait. And he did. I concocted a story and told him that when I was coming to Pakistan, I ran into Dr Homi Sethna, father of India's nuclear bomb, who asked me why I was wasting my time because Pakistan had neither the men nor the material to make such a weapon.' Khan exploded and boasted that Pakistan had made the bomb, adding the threat, "If you ever drive us to the wall, as you did in East Pakistan, we will use the bomb."

After the Nayar article appeared, General Zia went ballistic and took action that may have had the effect of sabotaging General Aslam Beg's Iran project. Feroz Hassan Khan reveals: 'Islamabad's reaction to the publication of the interview was swift and severe. A.Q. Khan was first called to explain himself to Senate Chairman Ghulam Ishaq Khan; next he was directed to report to General K.M. Arif, the vice chief of Army Staff, who supposedly grilled Khan in his office. A.Q. Khan claimed that he was tricked (by Pakistani journalist Mushahid Husain) into meeting the Indian journalist. Finally, he was summoned to the President's house. Lieutenant-General Syed Rifaqat Ali, who was chief of staff to President Zia-ul-Haq, narrated to the author how the wrath of Zia fell on Khan. After a normally polite Zia had finished with Khan the latter was seen leaving 'trembling and perspiring'. The author adds: 'Soon afterwards, Zia directed the bomb-designing project to be taken away from Khan and returned to the dedicated team in the Pakistan Atomic Energy Commission (PAEC). Mushahid Hussain soon lost his job at the *Muslim.* The Zia government deprived the newspaper of all government advertisements, isolated it, and economically crippled it, putting it out of business. [But] damage to the nuclear policy could not be reversed.'

This tough double-take from President General Zia stemmed from three worries. First, the ramifications of the interview on US–Pakistan relations and the new $4.2 billion economic and military aid package were being stringently scrutinized by a cheese-paring

US Congress as the Cold War subsided. Second, at the regional level, he worried about India's reactions and the implications of this kind of 'signaling by a top scientist'. He had toned down the nuclear rhetoric and was assiduously damage-controlling a recent downturn in relations with the big neighbour. And third was the knock received by his nuclear security system as it lay ravaged by a nosy Indian journalist.

Touching Base with Prabhakaran

This was very close in time to what happened next. General Zia was killed in an air crash in October 1987 amid rumours that his deputy in the GHQ, General Aslam Beg, had masterminded it, probably for fear of being 'discovered' selling nuclear secrets to Iran. After becoming army chief, Aslam Beg tried selling the 'Iran project' to Prime Minister Nawaz Sharif who was equally averse to the idea because of his own closeness to the Arabs.

The book makes the following assessment about the activities of Dr Khan: 'The Pakistani government overlooked Khan's activities because it believed the benefit he provided outweighed the cost of corruption. A.Q. Khan was a go-getter, a people-pleaser, and a hero. He was a master at kickbacks and bribes which kept scrutiny away from his activities—at least temporarily. Also, many of those who observed his bureaucratic malpractices were themselves beneficiaries of the system.' It goes on to tell us about the 'proliferation' triggered by Dr Khan for personal gains, selling blueprints and centrifuges to North Korea, Iran and Libya, till he was finally caught in the act and had to be gagged and confined by the Pakistan army after a TV confession in 2004.

The most damning passage in the book relates to Dr Khan writing to the army chief of Sri Lanka asking for help in retrieving money owed him by a Sri Lankan. He actually threatened him if he did not do the needful and offered him a bribe of $300,000! The letter he wrote, on Government of Pakistan letter head stationery, introduced him as a 'federal minister' and stated that in case the army chief of Sri Lanka did not oblige, Khan would get in touch with Prabhakaran, leader of the terrorist Liberation Tigers of Tamil Elam (LTTE) to get the job done. This is also proof that Dr Khan had his contacts within the terrorist underworld of the region and could have been facilitated in this by the Pakistani establishment.

In the post-2004 period Dr Khan hid behind the skirts of powerful organizations despite his unshakeable status as the 'father of the bomb'—which was wrong; he had to actually gate-crash the group of PAEC scientists that tested the device in Ras Koh range in the Chaghai Division of Balochistan in 1998, according to the book. The state now had to worry about the security of the great scientist: he could be killed by rascally America or he could be kidnapped by al-Qaeda who would naturally like him to resume where Sultan Bashiruddin Mahmood had left off. That security came from an obvious quarter.

In *Osama's Revenge: The Next 9/11,* Paul L. Williams, an American journalist with a PhD who teaches and advises the FBI, informs us that Dr A.Q. Khan started appearing in the rallies of Lashkar-e-Taiba of Hafiz Saeed, a graduate from Saudi Arabia's King Abdul Aziz University. He goes on: 'Dr A.Q. Khan attended Lashkar-e-Taiba gatherings accompanied by other nuclear scientists of his establishment, including Sultan Bashiruddin Mahmood who enriched uranium at Khushab.' In 2013, Pakistanis knew who in Pakistan was fielding Jamaatud Dawa and who could have advised Dr Khan to attend its rallies. It is not only he alone who bends the knee to Hafiz Saeed for self-empowerment; many retired military officers and politicians do this to make an impression on whoever is ruling Pakistan and to deter the leader from normalizing relations with India.

29

Terrorists as Martyrs

After the drone-killing on 1 November 2013 of the chief of the officially declared terrorist organization Tehreek-e-Taliban Pakistan (TTP), Hakimullah Mehsud, national fury in Pakistan was intense. Officially handling the so-called 'talks' with the TTP, Interior Minister Chaudhry Nisar Ali Khan issued an acerbic anti-US diatribe in Parliament. It resonated with the all-parties consensus which politicians think is safe populism in a moment of weakness yielding new popular support. Soon there was a rush to outdo Khan's gimmicky speech: two powerful clerical leaders normally busy bad-mouthing each other jumped into the fray of competing statements.

Jamaat-e-Islami chief Dr Syed Munawwar Hasan, a bit of a loose-cannon orator, gilded the lily saying Hakimullah Mehsud was a martyr (shaheed) before Allah because he had died fighting an enemy of Islam. When some remnants of the liberal opinion protested, Hasan's rival, Maulana Fazlur Rehman, went a notch above him in demonizing America and said had the Americans killed a dog instead of the Taliban chief he would have dubbed the dog a shaheed. Residual moderates protested, but these days any hyped-up insult targeting America is kosher. Pakistan calmly pocketed the insult of awarding martyrdom to a semi-literate man who had killed thousands of innocent Pakistanis across the country. But then something unexpected happened, an act of personal ambition and spleen not found in ordinary politicians.

Army Excluded from Martyrs

Trapped into saying indiscreet things on TV by an anchor, Dr Hasan then delivered a fatwa-like judgement on the soldiers of the Pakistan army dying fighting the Taliban and routinely dubbed shaheed in the media. He declared that since the Pakistan army was fighting against those fighting the enemy of Allah, they could not be called martyrs. He said he had 'doubts about their being shaheed' and by saying so stepped on to the thin ice of the doctrine of martyrdom used by the nation and embraced by the army to console the families of those whose children give their lives in the battlefield. The media snapped at Hasan for being so blatantly a partisan of the Taliban destroying property and human life in Pakistan.

Sensing that the Jamaat chief was isolated in public, the army issued a statement through its inter-services public relations (ISPR) department condemning his denial of martyrdom to its soldiers, asking him to explain why he had chosen to hurt the feelings of soldiers under oath to lay down their lives for the country. The ISPR statement said: 'The JI chief's remarks are irresponsible and were made for political point-scoring. His statement is an insult to the thousands of Pakistani civilians and soldiers killed and needs to be recanted.'

A Stormy Petrel Silenced

The media chat-shows followed, with discussants calling Dr Hasan names that a religious leader has seldom suffered, asking him to apologize or face punishment from a court of law for treason. The political parties lost no time in bifurcating on the Martyrdom Affair: the PPP, ANP and MQM hauled him over the coals and took the opportunity to denigrate the Jamaat as well for having allied itself with dictators in the past against democracy. The PPP Chairman Bilawal Bhutto Zardari, appealed to the Supreme Court to take suo motu notice of Hasan's statement and try him under Article 6 of the Constitution punishing treason with death. The Sindh Assembly passed a fiery resolution demanding unconditional apology from Hasan amid speeches of extreme harshness made from the floor of the house.

Caught off-guard, the provincial JI boss in Lahore Dr Fareed Piracha, stated that Syed Munawwar Hasan's statement on 'the status of soldiers killed in the war against terrorism was his personal opinion and not of the party'. This internal jolt, which must have upset Hasan, was soon corrected by the Jamaatshura (council) giving their own punning response to the statement from the army: it turned around the army's reference to 'politics' to accuse the army of violating its oath of non-interference in 'politics' through the ISPR statement. Secretary-general of the Jamaat, Liaquat Baloch, a moderate party man who should have taken over after the death of the longest-serving emir, Qazi Hussain Ahmad, was made to deliver the defiant message to the army. Of course, assertions were made of favouring the past martyrdoms in the army without correcting the denial of it to those fighting the Taliban.

Dr Hasan had to overcome two handicaps that the party had suffered vis-à-vis the Taliban and al-Qaeda in the recent past, one of them deeply personal too. The Jamaat under former emir Qazi Hussain Ahmad had sought to distance itself from the two—at times twinned—entities to make the party more acceptable to the electorate: he had pulled the party in from open collaboration with al-Qaeda and had also sought to 'correct' the war of the Taliban by denying them the blessings of jihad by calling it *fasad* (chaos) when it killed innocent Pakistanis. He was also upset over the validation of suicide through suicide bombing ('fedayeen'

strikes) on non-combatants but found the going tough because
of the threat to his own life. He was charismatic unlike Dr Hasan
who gives the impression of a petulant schoolmaster at best.

The death of Hakimullah offered an opportunity to regain
lost ground. A significant development had been signalled in the
following news in November 2012: 'Taliban leader Hakimullah
Mehsud had followed the lead of al-Zawahiri to say in a video CD
that Qazi Hussain Ahmad was a traitor to the cause of jihad—
calling him 'jihad-farosh' or betrayer of jihad—and a secret
member of the Jewish Lobby because he favoured democracy.
On the other hand, Qazi Sahib had admitted in an article that
those who were most affected by the terrorism of the Taliban
were members of the Jamaat-e-Islami.' Significantly, after having
written this, Qazi Sahib had put the blame of the suicide attack on
him as 'the work of the Americans'.

Taliban as Martyrs?

Qazi Hussain Ahmad was attacked in Mohmand by a suicide-
bomber in November 2012 but he escaped unhurt; he died in
January 2013. He had stepped down as emir in 2009 after a record
twenty-two years at the helm, cultivating a moderation of stance
that made him politically acceptable in Pakistan and abroad but
not among the affiliates of al-Qaeda and Taliban. The new emir,
Dr Munawwar Hasan, his party still in the electoral doldrums after
an unimpressive round in power from 2002 to 2008 in Khyber
Pakhtunkhwa, needed to perk up the party ideologically and get
back in the good books of the Taliban poised to make a 'peace'
deal to their advantage with the parties in Parliament in Pakistan.
He could match neither Qazi's charisma nor his statesmanship
but he could re-empower the party by repairing the cracks that
had developed in its relations with Hakimullah.

The TTP spokesman Shahidullah Shahid was prompt in
praising what Dr Hasan had achieved: 'a return to the teachings
of the founder of the Jamaat, Abul Ala Maududi'. This was a

reference to the real course-correction with al-Qaeda warriors who acknowledge the founder of the Jamaat as an inspiration of Syed Qutb, the Egyptian prime mover of al-Qaeda.

The Jamaat is not the only party getting ready to greet what is thought to be the dominance of al-Qaeda and Taliban in Pakistan. The Deobandi madrasas and the parties affiliated to them have declared their allegiance to the Taliban—if they are not already part of their terrorist edifice—but the non-Deobandi clergy sees its doom writ large if the Taliban ever come to power even marginally. The Barelvi and the Shia have both condemned Dr Hasan's canonization of a murderer but the two schools of religious thought hardly matter to him as potential targets of inter-clerical assassinations after the announced debate on martyrdom between them and the Taliban. The sun has arisen on Jamiat Ulema-e-Islam (JUI) of Fazlur Rehman as well, who has used the hyperbole of equating a dog with a martyr 'if killed by America'. Had it not been for the army, the nation would have tamely accepted what amounts to the death of Pakistan's already complicated martyrology.

A Proliferation of Martyrs

In Christianity martyrdom is reserved for canonized saints who die, not in the battlefield, but in cities, tortured by infidel tyrants. But in Islam martyrdom (*shahadat*) is reserved for those who die 'in the way of Allah'. Before the advent of the proxy militias, there was no doubt that the nation-state alone could engage in jihad and whoever died in the battlefield defending the state was a martyr. Today of course this application of non-death—'the shaheed doesn't die and indeed lives among us'—has spread to non-state actors and complicated the concept. Already, shaheed is loosely applied to big leaders who die unnaturally. Further, almost limitless latitude is allowed by the tradition recorded in Al Bukhari and Muslim hadith collections saying: 'Shaheed is one who dies in a plague, the one who dies of a stomach ailment, the one who drowns, the one who is crushed to death, and the martyr in the path of Allah'.

Pakistan's long list of 'political' martyrs is contested impolitely according to who you are talking to. The current discussion is marred by the bitterness of this shifting definition. Prime Minister Zulfikar Ali Bhutto, hanged by an Islamizing military dictator General Zia-ul-Haq, is referred to as shaheed by his party, the PPP. His daughter Benazir, killed by the al-Qaeda–Taliban combine, is also canonized as shaheed on renamed airport terminals and cities; while General Zia, killed mysteriously in an air-crash is shaheed in the eyes of those—now dwindling in their numbers—who think he was a soldier of Islam killed by rascally Americans.

Presiding over this proliferation of martyrdom is the Pakistan army which has muddied the waters further by inducting jihad into its repertoire of cross-border aggression. In May 2012, a seminar on jihad in Islamabad had Professor Mushtaq Ahmad of the International Islamic University Islamabad quoting from the Quran and other Islamic literature to assert that 'only the state could wage jihad and no private individual or organization could take on that sacred responsibility'. But where does one place the mujahideen or Pakistan's non-state actors who fight proxy wars for the Pakistan army after taking training in camps in Mansehra and Azad Kashmir? Are they also doing jihad and therefore entitled to martyrdom?

Terrorists as Martyrs

The terrorists, however, regularly produce martyrs in Pakistan. A teenaged suicide bomber who failed to explode his booby-trapped jacket, which would have killed hundreds of innocent citizens in a market in Dera Ismail Khan in Khyber Pakhtunkhwa last year, came out of his faint and asked, 'Am I in Heaven? And where are the pretty divine girls promised to the martyrs?'

A week after the bitter martyrdom debate unleashed by the top pro-Taliban clerics, Prime Minister Nawaz Sharif decided to express the opinion he was reluctant to make public—the TTP under the new leader had threatened to target him and his family in Punjab—by visiting the military martyrs' memorial together with Army Chief General Ashfaq Pervaiz Kayani who in 2012 had shocked the national political consensus against 'America's war' by saying that war against terrorism was Pakistan's war.

Yet, the army would not make the necessary tweaks in their India-centric strategy after this ownership of the war mainly because of Kayani's embrace of populism even at the cost of the country's internal security. As the martyrdom debate heated up, another shock was delivered to a world wary of Pakistan's romance with terrorism. Naseeruddin Haqqani, a son of Jalaluddin Haqqani who heads the Afghan Taliban network located in North Waziristan, was killed by two gunmen in Islamabad amid rumours that his brother Sirajuddin was also present at the scene of the murder. The media talked about Naseer as a fundraiser for the network and that the Haqqanis survived on Pakistani handouts because they targeted Americans across the Durand Line. Mike Mullen, the retiring chairman of the US Joint Chiefs of Staff, had spoken angrily against Pakistan's double game, telling the US Congress that 'the Haqqani Network was a veritable arm of Pakistan's Inter-Services Intelligence (ISI) agency'.

Pakistan is in fact martyr to a kind of 'hypernationalism' based on a hatred of America. The rulers and the army have used it to unite the nation behind the geo-strategy that the army will not amend, given its indoctrination of jihad against India and India's perceived allies in the region. In his book,[1] *Magnificent Delusions: Pakistan, the United States, and an Epic History of Misunderstanding*, former ambassador to the US Husain Haqqani observes: '[ISI chief] Ahmad Shuja Pasha and the ISI continued to propel hypernationalist sentiment. Pasha once told me that this was one of the few tools Pakistan had for leveraging itself in an asymmetric relationship. Americans often ignored the rumours and misinformation routinely circulated through Pakistan's media, though sometimes they reacted to point out the absurdity of the tactic.'

30

Monster or Milestone?

Will Asif Ali Zardari be remembered for securing the largest influx of US military and economic assistance through the Kerry Lugar-Berman bill, moving Pakistan closer to Iran and Afghanistan, progressing the Iran–Pakistan gas pipeline, and presiding over constitutional corrections; or will he be remembered for surrendering Swat to the Taliban, spending time at his chalet in France while his country suffered its worst ever floods, taking on Pakistan's media and Supreme Court and failing, threatening party mavericks with physical harm and assaulting them with verbal abuse, cowardly distancing his government from Salmaan Taseer who was facing grave danger, failing to nab his wife's assassins, promoting a culture of cronyism and corruption, and hanging on to power at any cost?

Zardari was nationally popular for a brief period in 2008, which now seems as unbelievable as the fact that his predecessor, Pervez Musharraf, was once also very popular. Unpopular, ineloquent, and rightfully fearing for his life, Zardari ruled from a bunker for most of his intensely controversial presidency (2008–13). His Pakistan People's Party was punished at the polls in May 2013, but Zardari's legacy, and future, as he himself has pointed out, cannot be written off. Those who think history will not be kind to Zardari should visit the recent words of his rival, Prime Minister Nawaz Sharif.

At the small farewell lunch Sharif hosted for Zardari on 5 September in Islamabad, the prime minister noted that Zardari had the distinction of being the first elected civilian president to complete his full term and be sent off by the incoming government. As guests tucked into their broccoli soup, Sharif got poetic in his remarks, recalling even the fragrance of the roses Zardari's daughters had presented to Sharif in meetings that culminated in his party, the Pakistan Muslim League (Nawaz), and the PPP signing 2006's live-and-let-live Charter of Democracy truce pact. The prime minister credited the President for his patience, for sticking to slain leader Benazir Bhutto's policy of political reconciliation, for being a democrat, and for rehabilitating the constitution. No one, said Sharif, could take this away from Zardari.

In his own remarks at the lunch, an uncharacteristically subdued Zardari swore loyalty to Sharif. 'Step forward Nawaz Sharif [with your national policy] and you will find us supporting you from the opposition,' he said, adding that his party would 'do politics' only when the next elections roll around, in five years. At the main table, Zardari told Sharif that it was time to end the 'dogfights' on cable talk shows. Both men signed the menu cards for each other to commemorate the peace that appears to have been restored once again between them.

As head of the PPP, Zardari ruled with unusual political dexterity from the presidency despite the odds he faced while trying to change policy. His newfound instinct for survival was attributed by many to his several years in prison—on charges that could not be proved in court.

Totemic Exclusions

Sharif, too, went through the same sort of transformation. 'I spent fourteen pernicious months of my life in jail,' he told *Newsweek* in April. 'I was rotting in that small cell, and there was a debate on the BBC about the biggest achievement of India since its independence ... After an hour and a half of debate, the consensus was that the big achievement of India is that India has upheld the sanctity of the ballot box.'

Sharif and Zardari are disabused enough of the totemic exclusion of the rival in Pakistan's primitive political culture to turn over a new leaf. No longer shielded by constitutional immunity, could Zardari face old or new charges that lead him to jail again? His party and Sharif's had objected, in the Charter of Democracy, to 'the vilification campaign against ... political leaders under a draconian law in the name of accountability in order to divide and eliminate the representative political parties'. Sharif's graceful gestures of feting Zardari and keeping him alongside at Mamnoon Hussain's swearing-in, on 9 September, promise a less hostile relationship.

Things didn't go as well after the 2008 elections. PMLN's mid-level leaders thought the party's performance had been damaged by the unfamiliar sweetness spread by the Charter of Democracy. Still, the PPP and PMLN formed a short-lived coalition government in Islamabad but soon fell out over the restoration of judges sacked by then president Musharraf. Zardari had reportedly sworn on the Quran to abide by his word to Sharif, but he squirmed out of this commitment by saying that the agreement with Sharif's party, the Bhurban Declaration, was not the word of God. Zardari's first serious mistake—refusing to reinstate the sacked judges—triggered a revival of the vendetta. Zardari alienated both the PMLN and the judges, who roared back to office and pre-eminence through Sharif's street power, dooming an easier ride for the PPP.

Middle-class Indignation

Among many self-damaging populisms haunting Pakistan today is the lingering bile towards the National Reconciliation Ordinance, the US-lobbied law Musharraf enacted to quash criminal cases against opposition leaders like former prime minister Benazir Bhutto, Zardari's assassinated wife, and pave the way for the restoration of democracy, which had been delegitimized by Bhutto's and Sharif's long exile.

The NRO should have been endorsed by Parliament to convert the time-limited ordinance into long-term law and compel the restored but smarting Supreme Court to leave Zardari alone. But Parliament balked and the ordinance lay in a bloodied stink on the floor of the house. The court then swooped in, declared the ordinance void from the word go, and revived money-laundering charges against Zardari. What followed was a long-drawn-out battle between the Zardari-led government and the court, in which the former lost political prestige through reported corruption and the latter faced a growing chorus of complaints about its 'revengeful activism'.

Zardari's trail of glory is much besmirched by the exhaust left hanging in the air by the abysmal performance of two prime ministers appointed by him, Yousaf Raza Gilani and Raja Pervaiz Ashraf. The first could not avoid being fired by the Supreme Court for contempt; the second survived by the skin of his teeth after a grovelling apology to the court. Zardari did not make Gilani's job easy by taking on the Sharifs in the Punjab, even once briefly placing the province under governor's rule, ignoring the media and judicial bias against him. Shahbaz Sharif, Punjab's chief minister, let loose bilious repartee on Zardari, calling him and his comrades Ali Baba and the Forty Thieves, among other names. In the National Assembly, PMLN's Chaudhry Nisar Ali Khan excoriated the clearly inefficient government on a daily basis, unobtrusively aligning himself with two other forces that despised the 'secular' PPP: the media and the Taliban.

Zardari survived against all odds. He and his federal government completed their respective terms through 'unprincipled' flexibility and serial capitulation. In this five-year period, there was a universal middle-class dislike of him in Pakistan's most populous province, Sharif's stronghold of the Punjab. Zardari was considered the wrong man for the party, and the wrong man for the presidency. It was said he had no principles and would cut deals instead of standing up for the country's honour. It was feared that he would sell out to India, the US, and to his coalition partners the Muttahida Qaumi Movement (a terrorist organization, in most Punjabi minds) and the Awami National Party (which 'never accepted Pakistan').

Tragically, these prejudices were buttressed by the reality of corruption through the gouging of the state exchequer by unworthy officeholders deliberately appointed by the government. And the risible activism of Rehman Malik, Zardari's hammy interior minister, quickly began to symbolize the PPP's inimitably ineffectual brand of governance.

Principles or Options?

Whether you extrapolate from Machiavelli or Castiglione, a kind of unworthy wisdom has stood the test of time in statecraft: you should have principles to make your conduct predictable, but at the same time know that you are limiting your options. It works if you are strong because you can force others to conform; but if you are weak, then having no principles means you have limitless options for action and can adjust through flexibility to acts dictated by others. Today, as Pakistan slouches from one All Parties Conference to another under the diktat of the 'principles' of populism, it is becoming internationally isolated, endangering its economy, and remains internally vulnerable in the face of al-Qaeda, the Taliban, and its own non-state actors.

Did Zardari know, early or late, that he was weak vis-à-vis the army dictating foreign policy, which it saw as pegged to national security in a foreshortened way, affecting other sectors of life for which it took no responsibility? There are two domains where there are virtually no rules: politics and foreign policy. No real international law exists to compel states to behave predictably; despite laws like that against floor-crossing in Parliament to freeze political conduct, politicians always find enough space to be flexible in their loyalties. No state passes the test of completely predictable behaviour. The dictum that reigns supreme today is that there are no permanent friends and enemies in international politics. Foreign policy must remain endlessly tactile (read: transactional) so that there are endless options available for the conduct of diplomacy. Zardari sought to secure foreign policy against damage, but ran up against the fixity of the army's geopolitical thinking.

If populism in the post-Zardari period is about to hamstring Pakistan's options, what he set out to achieve after his swearing-in was a shift of the state paradigm. What he did looks like nemesis today: at his inauguration ceremony on 9 September 2008, Afghan President Hamid Karzai was the guest of honour. Then, speaking to the *Wall Street Journal*, Zardari referred to the militants active in India-administered Kashmir as terrorists; he also stated that India did not pose a threat to Pakistan, which was quickly denounced by Hafiz Saeed of Jamat-ud-Dawah. In his book,[1] *Deadly Embrace: Pakistan, America, and the Future of the Global Jihad,* Bruce Riedel observes: 'In the summer of 2008, Zardari declared India was not Pakistan's inevitable enemy and proposed, in a striking reversal of Islamabad's strategy, that Pakistan should adopt a policy of "no first use" of nuclear weapons. At the same time, his administration took some small but important steps to open trade across the [Line of Control] in Kashmir . . . Many in Pakistan, particularly in the army and the jihadist camp, were appalled at Zardari's statements and decried these small but important confidence-building steps.'

Beware the Rejoicing Third Party

For most of Zardari's term, Pakistan was internally united against the elected government in Islamabad and against the US and the international community, which were worried about Afghanistan. The country was united in favour of the army, gratefully, because of the latter's resolve to oppose the world, the US and India; and it eulogized the Supreme Court because it would somehow get rid of the PPP-led government before its time. This national consensus flew on the wings of the overwhelmingly uniform media opinion which refused to decide what to do about terrorism in Pakistan.

After the 2008 Mumbai attacks by terrorists allegedly from Pakistan, Zardari tried to be cooperative by proposing to send the chief of the military's Inter-Services Intelligence directorate to India to assist investigations. This backfired. Then came WikiLeaks. Zardari was quoted in leaked US State Department cables as supporting US drone attacks inside Pakistan while talking to the Americans. In May 2011, after the Americans killed Osama bin Laden in Abbottabad, and Zardari had welcomed the commando operation in a column for the *Washington Post,* the feud with the army exploded into the open. The situation denounced by the Charter of Democracy—an elected government clashing with the army while the opposition aligns itself against the incumbent as the 'rejoicing third party'—was re-gelling.

The lowest point for Zardari, and likely not Pakistan's finest hour, was 2011's Memogate. This scandal erupted after US businessman Mansoor Ijaz made startling allegations, first in the *Financial Times,* claiming he was operating at the behest of Zardari as relayed to him by Islamabad's then ambassador in Washington, Husain Haqqani, imploring the Pentagon to castrate the Pakistan army following the Abbottabad embarrassment. The media and the army cried treason, the ISI contacted Ijaz for evidence; and Sharif took the matter to the Supreme Court—knowing full well that he was playing the part of the 'rejoicing third party' condemned in the Charter of Democracy—charging Zardari's government of acting against Pakistan's interests. Haqqani was fired and eventually and unreasonably declared a traitor by a judicial panel.

The suspenseful unfolding of Memogate actually broke Zardari, who had endured prison with nerves of steel. He was hospitalized in Dubai as opposition politicians and talking heads dilated upon his actual and alleged ailments ranging from dyslexia to dementia. Zardari's young son, Bilawal, was given an office at the presidency and rolled out before the cameras sombrely meeting with coalition partners to give an all's-well appearance. But all was far from well. At the time, even Prime Minister Yousaf Raza Gilani and the Punjab governor, Latif Khosa, were privately declaring that the end of the government from a military takeover of sorts was nigh. Nursed back to health, Zardari returned to the helm a far more chastened man.

Slippery Sindhi?

As Prime Minister Sharif has generously noted, Zardari's singular achievement in the constitutional history of the country is restoring the original content of the 1973 Constitution—which had been disfigured by Punjab-supported military dictators—through 2010's devolutionary 18th Amendment. Greater powers were restored to the provinces and the President's power to dismiss elected governments was removed. But for the unanimity he needed for constitutional correction, compromises had to be made. So some of the so-called 'Islamic' provisions of the constitution were retained and these will continue to hamper the culture of honesty and tolerance in Pakistan.

Was Zardari a 'cunning Sindhi' who got Parliament to pass devolutionary laws to revenge his province of Sindh, where his party still rules, against the mighty Punjab? Zardari dented the Punjab's resistance to change in the status quo by renaming the North West Frontier Province as Khyber Pakhtunkhwa. The first right to use new discoveries of natural resources now rests with the provinces, something that will benefit gas-rich Sindh at energy-poor Punjab's expense. The 18th Amendment also reconstituted the Council of Common Interests, with the prime minister as its chairperson, mandated to convene at least once every ninety days. Outside the legislature, he created the administrative entity of Gilgit-Baltistan in response to the demand of the population of the Northern Areas for self-rule.

The 18th Amendment also sought to make the induction of judges in the higher judiciary a bipartisan affair. Athar Minallah, one of Chief Justice Iftikhar Chaudhry's strongest supporters, hailed the new process for judicial appointments as an 'an immaculate method'. But the Supreme Court decried the new law and forced Parliament into the 19th Amendment, which can only be viewed as masochistic given the court's interventionist overdrive against Zardari.

When recently asked what he would like to be remembered for, Zardari put the Benazir Income Support Programme on top of the list. Political vitriol and bad luck—from Pakistan's worst ever floods in 2010 and 2011—had ambushed the programme. But after initial false starts, BISP was reformed in order to win the approval of the World Bank and now provides unconditional cash assistance to 5.5 million families, covering nearly 40 per cent of the Pakistani population surviving below the poverty line. The Sharif government has decided to continue the handout programme, which its finance minister says he helped conceive, without changing its name.

Zardari's trail of glory is much besmirched by the exhaust left hanging in the air by the abysmal work of the two prime ministers appointed by him. BISP helped the PPP post electoral gains in Sindh. The party did not do well otherwise in the May polls because of bad governance and because the Taliban were clearly targeting its leaders during the election campaign. Zardari has left Islamabad to lick his wounds and nurture his party in Sindh. It is moot whether he will ever make a comeback as a ruling leader of the country. Sharif is in the saddle now and is trying to cope with the residual state no longer responding to normal governance. Compounding the gradual collapse is the misdiagnosis of what has really happened to Pakistan after years of involvement in the region's proxy wars. The latest verdict expressed through an all-parties conference presided over by Sharif says that the US is to blame for Pakistan's misfortunes, and what is needed for 'normalization' is peace with the Taliban.

What the Taliban think about Pakistan was graphically portrayed by al-Qaeda chief Ayman-al-Zawahiri in his 2009 essay, 'The Morning and the Lamp: A Treatise Regarding the Claim that the Pakistani Constitution Is Islamic'. This essay attacks Jinnah's vision of Pakistan and its non-Islamic character. Bin Laden had also weighed in on Pakistan under Zardari's rule. 'In a June 2009 audio message, bin Laden accused Zardari of being no better than or different from Musharraf, and of being rewarded with more than his usual 10 per cent for helping America, a clever reference to Zardari's nickname for corruption, Mr. Ten Per cent,' writes author Riedel. One of al-Qaeda's common themes had been that Zardari, Gilani and Kayani must be killed, and that the army must revolt and set up a proper jihadist state. Al-Zawahiri's treatise was distributed in Lahore by the city's madrasas, and some elements in the army tried to do what he had prescribed: there were at least three attempts on Kayani's life.

Still Failing

Pakistan is still on the brink of becoming a failed state as a consequence of the decades-old practice of using proxy warriors in the region. Because of the weakening of the writ of the state, neither governance nor the economy can function normally. After the decline of the state, there are only two strong entities left in Pakistan: the Taliban and the army.

Zardari tried to get out of the security trap of the irredentist state through change of policy and failed; thereafter, he sought survival in office by cleaving close to the military's worldview without winning the hearts and minds of the army. Sharif faces the same kind of dilemma: he wants to shift the security paradigm to save the state, but is doing the opposite: seeking peace, not with India, but with the Taliban.

Bilawal Bhutto Zardari thinks his father's legacy 'will be written in golden words' and fumblingly compared his presidency to that of accidental US President Lyndon B. Johnson for the *Huffington Post*. But it is Mansoor Ijaz, the man who nearly got Zardari hanged in Memogate, who has the last word about the Pakistan which Zardari, and now Sharif, must really want. In an article in October 2011, Ijaz wrote: 'Pakistan's military men may not allow civilian supremacy just yet, but a serious transition seems to be underway to at least make civilian institutions strong enough to coexist on an even footing with the army in the intermediate term. One day, those civilian institutions may indeed be strong enough to protect Pakistan's truest national interests: not Kashmir, Afghanistan, and nuclear bombs, but the availability of education, the expansion of trade ties, and the provision of energy to a frustrated nation eager to find prosperity.'

31

Political Outage

She knew she was beautiful but subordinated her ego to a charismatic father, made no mistakes of the heart that most beautiful women are prone to, became a hardnosed critic not only of the politics of others but her own too, and leaned on a well-kept diary to use the brains her parents had helped polish through good education. Her memoir *Power Failure: The Political Odyssey of a Pakistani Woman* by Syeda Abida Hussain rivets with its honesty of frank detail.

'I am a year older than Pakistan, one of midnight's children, born to privilege and a contingent sense of entitlement,' she begins with a pledge of cold realism that doesn't abandon the 700-page narrative to follow. She had just done her 'O Levels' when President Ayub Khan's son, Tahir Ayub Khan, met her in 1962 and fell in love with her.

The proposal came but was shot down by her father, Syed Abid Hussain Shah, honourary colonel during the Second World War, a feudal landowner of Jhang who was a member of the Legislative Assembly of India in 1946, and Constituent Assembly of Pakistan when it was installed after Partition in Karachi, becoming a minister in the 1954 cabinet. This was when his family met and idealized Miss Jinnah and went politically wrong when General Ayub Khan 'defeated' her in elections. The author recalls Miss Jinnah complaining afterwards that her half-sister Shirin Bai was being paid more attention as an alternative icon of the Pakistan Movement.

Ayub Khan was in top gear and the power match was irresistible in many ways, including personal security, so Syeda Abida Hussain 'Chandi' was sent off to Switzerland to do her 'A Levels' followed by a stint in Italy where she painted, till Tahir Ayub Khan probably forgot about her among his other dalliances incidental to power. She returned in 1965 when Ayub Khan had met his comeuppance after the 'teach-nothing' national blunder of a covert war that went overt, and another general, Yahya Khan, was about to kick him out, paving the way for the rise of Zulfikar Ali Bhutto, whom Chandi promptly fell for as democracy's charismatic young harbinger.

Family First

But adjustment was survival in a Pakistan where institutions refused to take root in the face of 'great leaders'. Shah Jewna in Jhang was Col Abid Hussain Shah's estate where he bred horses, grew cotton and looked after the people who lived on his land. While idealistic in politics, he was pragmatic when it came to grassroots politics, which meant that his family fell in line when military dictators ousted parliaments and rode to acceptance on the back of local governments.

Much vigour was lent to this trait by the brothers of her mother, Kishwar, who counted among them the universally admired Syed Babar Ali. Disenchantment, which should have descended on Chandi during the Bhutto era, couldn't completely obliterate her admiration for the man who gave Pakistan its only durable constitution. But it strengthened the pragmatic strain in her, nonetheless, which makes for the survival of many honourable men on whose work the country ultimately depends in our day. A generosity of assessment of rivals however remains the hallmark of her odyssey.

Chandi's dream of going to Cambridge was interrupted by her father's decision to match her with Fakhar Imam, the son of her mother's elder sister, from oddly named Qatalpur in Kabirwala, today the biggest snake pit of Shia-killing clerics in Pakistan. Deeply Shia, Chandi's family in Shah Jewna lived near Jhang, the fatal alembic in which Pakistan mixed its fate with sectarian violence under General Zia much before the Middle East woke up to it. Later, Chandi was to fight the murderous leader of Sipah-e-Sahaba, Haq Nawaz Jhangvi, at the polls while hoping Fakhar would win his local seat in Kabirwala from where Jhangvi had done his graduation in a 'mother' seminary.

Her comment on the match after protesting about her missed Cambridge stint: 'Except, I did secretly find Fakhar devastatingly attractive.' Fakhar's reaction when they first met sums up his personality, 'You look great.' A scholarly, book-reading Fakhar thought she was 'spoilt and demanding' and might be a handful, after which Chandi used the weapon she was to employ selectively in the future too: she started crying, and clinched the marriage. He confessed he had loved her since he was nine but was bugged by Shah Jewna where he felt his separate identity would be threatened. They easily resolved that crisis of identities and decided to manage two separate homes, coming together in Lahore, the city they used as a base. In 1970, on Khan Wali Khan's advice, Chandi joined the Pakistan People's Party, and became a nominated member of the Punjab Assembly. In the ripeness of time, she was to clash with Bhutto.

Bhutto Betrayal

Col Abid Hussain Shah had inherited 5300 acres of land, but after Ayub Khan was done with his land reform and the Colonel had sold bits of it, Chandi got only '2000 acres of well-developed prime and productive land'. Bhutto's land reform forced her to surrender 600 acres out of it, which rankled, because 'the capital value of this land today would exceed a couple of billion rupees!' Add to this the dystopia Bhutto created of nationalization of industries and banks, and the fallout from Sheikh Rashid's 'generic drugs', which were meant to make medicine cheap, but which failed to launch. and the cup was full to the brim.

She recalls the slight offered to her by Bhutto visiting Shah Jewna, sniffing at her father's farming efforts in comparison to his farms in Larkana. She offered to resign, which perhaps—perhaps not—made him realize how small he had shown himself to be. While 'ballooning' repeatedly in this period to add children to her family, she began losing faith in Bhutto: 'While Mother focused on his arrogance and Fakhar on his economic mismanagement, I would stand up for him, but some of the criticism made would impress the point home even with me, and sometimes while mounting counter arguments I would sound somewhat garbled, even to myself.'

She was developing the hard shell of minimalist realism politicians acquire during their apprenticeship. Soon General Zia toppled the autocrat, had him hanged through a flawed trial by scared judges—scared of Bhutto more than Zia—today remembered as 'judicial murder'. In the new setup that followed Fakhar decided to join as minister of local government and rural development, falling into the pattern fashioned by Ayub and then helplessly repeated by Zia and Musharraf. Fakhar was pragmatic and hands-on at the grassroots; Chandi was idealistic in addition to being hands-on. The pattern proves Fakhar right, alas!

Zia Zeal

General Zia eased politicians into loyalty by giving them plots in Islamabad. Fakhar was offered one which he refused to take, but which Ilahi Bux Soomro managed to transfer to himself while giving the one allotted him to his brother. Rich politicians like Mahmood Haroon did not abstain like Fakhar which provoked Chandi into challenging a friend of Haroon's who replied: 'I will agree that it would not be nice to ask for a plot as a favour, but if it is being offered then not to take it is stupid, because a refusal of this type does not come into any record.' Chandi deserved the epithet of stupid like the rare species subsisting among us who still live on the basis of ethics. Chandi sold some land—this occurs about five times in the book—bought a plot and built her own house in Islamabad.

Zia announced 'non-party' elections in 1984. Fakhar won from Kabirwala, Chandi from Jhang, and not on the women's quota. Governor Jilani promoted young Nawaz Sharif as chief minister of Punjab but soon got his male ego tangled with an already bristling Chandi who was to be wounded again by being given a seat in the National Assembly among 'nominated' women MNAs. After she was re-allotted a seat among the elected, a Sindhi next to her didn't want to sit 'next to a woman' and got himself removed. She could have killed him. Gentle Fakhar advised a cool-down but soon locked horns himself with the Zia lobby by refusing to give up his candidacy as speaker of the Assembly. ISI's infamous Brigadier Imtiaz 'Billa' failed to attract him to finance ministership; he beat Khwaja Safdar to the speakership by fifteen votes.

Needless to say, she shouted unsuccessfully her objections to MNAs' 'development fund' and lobbied with equal futility against the 8th Amendment that hounded Pakistan for the entire decade of the 1990s, with presidents developing an experimental monkey's conditioned reflex of dismissing governments they didn't like. Her consolation: she absented herself from the signature to the amendment.

Benazir In

Fakhar and Chandi landed in the 'rebel' group and soon realized they were isolated when Fakhar was actually voted out of speakership through a no-confidence vote which said he was biased against Prime Minister Junejo heading the King's Party. Later of course Junejo rebelled against Zia and founded the Junejo League, but Fakhar now leader of the opposition in the house, began asking the government to make public funds being doled out to the intelligence agencies, only to discover that Zia had revenged himself by creating the Shia-killing Sipah-e-Sahaba in Jhang. There was more humiliation coming her way: boarding a Fokker in Rawalpindi, she got rudely pushed aside to make way for Pakistan's bridegroom of jihad, Gulbuddin Hekmatyar.

At Shah Jewna, the new graffiti said 'Shia kafir' and her stud farm stood attached because its lease had miraculously lapsed!

In 1986, Benazir arrived in Lahore and overwhelmed the Zia junta. Fakhar hosted a dinner at Islamabad and Chandi heard Benazir say, 'I am sorry you may not have an Assembly to go back to tomorrow. Because of this evening, Zia and his generals would be shivering in their shoes. The report of this huge dinner must have reached them already and they are likely to dissolve the Assembly tonight.' She had to wait two more years, after Zia died in a plane crash in 1988, to come to power, but not before an epoch-making marriage to Asif Ali Zardari in 1987. The Ojhi camp blast happened the same year, further loosening the plaster of Zia's edifice of Islamic dictatorship, forcing Zia to dissolve the National Assembly.

Canny Fakhar declined to join his new cabinet, and after Zia's death, Chandi returned to Shah Jewna to ready herself to fight her next election against the dreaded Sipah chief, Haq Nawaz Jhangvi, whose minions had already announced that 'in voting for Maulana Haq Nawaz the voters of Jhang would not only ensure for themselves a key to heaven, but would also set aside the profligate woman from Shah Jewna who was a heretic and did not deserve to live, and casting a vote for her would be tantamount to inviting the wrath of Allah and burning in the fires of hell.'

Sectarian Snake Pit

She beat Haq Nawaz Jhangvi by 8000 votes as an independent candidate. The PPP won at the Centre but lost Punjab; and Hakim Ali Zardari rang to say he would like Fakhar to be governor in Punjab which of course Fakhar wisely declined. His wife's verdict: 'Fakhar has always been deeply principled, so his answer did not surprise me.' Benazir offered Chandi a ministry which she declined, and Punjab-ruling Nawaz Sharif thought she could lead the opposition in the National Assembly. She refused this too but not before tangling with another arrogant general, Fazle Haq of Peshawar ill-fame, who was plugging for Sharif. But there was a modus vivendi developing with him as 1990 rolled around and Haq Nawaz Jhangvi was killed right in front of his house in Jhang.

Chandi rushed to Shah Jewna knowing she would be named among the killers and decided she would call on the widow to condole with her. The widow's answer to her request to meet was: 'No need for you to come. You can recite Sura Fateha on the phone; I do not need your assistance. My brother Osama bin Laden looks after all my needs. You must have heard of him. He is a very famous and rich Saudi, much richer than all of you kafirs put together.' Nobody knew bin Laden then. Later it was revealed he was ensconced in Peshawar as the darling of everyone fighting to defeat the Soviet Union in Afghanistan.

Years later, when she was Pakistan's ambassador to Washington (1991–93), Under Secretary at the State Department Arnold Kantor complained to her that Pakistan was harbouring 'terrorist' Osama bin Laden. She recalls: 'A shiver went down my spine as I recalled the words of Maulana Haq Nawaz's widow . . . my response to Arnold Kantor was that this was an unfair accusation, given the reality that we were victims of terrorism ourselves because of our cooperation with the US-sponsored resistance to the Soviets in Afghanistan.' A forgivable piece of professional mendacity that has doomed Pakistan; the Americans killed bin Laden, still in Pakistan, in 2011.

Benazir Out

President Ghulam Ishaq Khan got rid of a callow Benazir and welcomed Nawaz Sharif as the next prime minister leading a broad alliance put together by a running-at-the-mouth ISI chief Hamid Gul. Since hostile next-door cousin Faisal Saleh Hayat was in with the PPP, her bramble path was more or less predetermined. The President wanted her as ambassador in Washington and Sharif was okay with it. But it was a tenure of less than two years in an increasingly hostile capital owing to Pakistan's shady nuclear programme, no matter who was in power in Washington, the Republicans or the Democrats. She fought gamely and defended Pakistan's interests knowing the future relations with America might get tougher.

Benazir was ousted after she got on the wrong side of the army. Nawaz Sharif too got into trouble with Army Chief Asif Nawaz who died exercising after, as Chandi recalled, having warned Fakhar in a private meeting that he had become flabby and had better take to the treadmill. With General Asif Nawaz gone, Nawaz Sharif tangled with an increasingly crotchety President who had his palsied finger constantly on the 58/2/B button by this time. President Khan fired Nawaz Sharif but this time the Article 58/2/B reflex was a bit of a swansong as the Supreme Court went against it. Later, Nawaz and Khan both had to leave. The abortion of the 1991 Parliament after two years was midwifed by the new army chief, the good General Waheed Kakar.

After the October 1993 elections, it was PPP redux. Benazir had Asif Ali Zardari in tow and all was to go smoothly since she got her party loyalist secretary-general Farooq Ahmad Khan Leghari to be the next president, a fellow south Punjabi feudal who had followed Fakhar's route to politics after a stint in the civil service. Now begins Chandi's frankly cloak-and-dagger anti-government conspiracy in tandem with Chaudhry Nisar Ali Khan and Leghari's strategizing lawyer Shahid Hamid. Fakhar had 'bonded' with them at Aitchison College where the feudal families of Pakistan usually sent their children for schooling.

She soon learned that Benazir and '58/2/B-hating' Leghari were at odds, in no small measure pushed along by the Nawaz Sharif group working out of her Islamabad house. Nawaz Sharif's father 'Abbaji' also got into the act, tactfully working on Chandi's weak point, her father Col Abid Hussain Shah, narrating how he had dug the first tube well at Shah Jewna and grown to admire the great man.

Meanwhile, Benazir was digging the next grave of her government taking on too many powerful people including President Leghari and her own brother Murtaza Bhutto whose wife Ghinwa she didn't get along with. In September 1996, he was killed in Karachi; in November 1996, President Leghari killed the National Assembly with Article 58/2/B. The political revolving doors brought the Muslim League back and Chandi was in the cabinet; but things couldn't remain the same with Nawaz Sharif.

Hazards of Heavy Mandate

There were policy disagreements and any other politician would have kept his peace but not her. She didn't agree with Sharif's selection of Pervez Musharraf as the next army chief in place of General Ali Kuli Khan whose family background she could vouch for as he was Fakhar's contemporary at the Aitchison. She quite correctly disagreed, in a cabinet meeting, with Sharif's decision to take down the new chief justice of the Supreme Court, Sajjad Ali Shah. Tales were carried from dinner parties and she lost her leader's confidence. An admired fellow-feudal, Nawaz Akbar Khan Bugti, had uncannily predicted Nawaz Sharif's ouster once again because of 'Punjabi hubris'. She is forced to define her class at this point:

'Feudal, in the context of rural Pakistan, only means flowing from a tradition, often upholding values of courtesy and kindliness, caring for those less privileged, sharing your bread, and nurturing relationships that are not always transactional.'

The last straw came when Sharif took on Leghari too. She reacted by offering to resign from the cabinet because 'her mother was unwell'. But in December 1997, the prime minister forced President Leghari to resign instead, the latter not using the weapon of 58/2/B that he had used on Benazir. Bugti's prediction was sailing to its fulfilment and a non-feudal leader appeared to have more personality flaws than a feudal was supposed to suffer from. Her mother died in March 1998.

Nawaz Sharif rode high with his 'heavy mandate' in Parliament when he approved the nuclear test at Chaghai; but the glory was short-lived. It developed that he had chosen the wrong man for his army chief, whose 'proxy' adventure at Kargil was exposed to a world shuddering at this gross violation of 'nuclear parity' with India. Sharif had also got the wrong kind of people to surround him. When he invited Indian prime minister Vajpayee to Lahore and had him 'accept' the birth of Pakistan at the venue of the Lahore Resolution of 1940 amid claps, two 'tense' men refused to cheer: Major General Khalid Maqbool, whom Chandi didn't like when he was defence attaché at Washington, and ISI chief General Ziauddin Butt, whom Sharif was to appoint army chief after cashiering— unsuccessfully—his chosen General Musharraf.

Army Chief Musharraf's war, started by 'mountain shepherds' at Kargil, was a disaster. Pakistan was roundly defeated by India, costing its treasury $2 billion, while Musharraf's body-language signalled a possible coup d'état to Fakhar. Chaudhry Nisar Ali Khan with his finger on the army's pulse came calling, asking for intercession with Sharif who 'was no longer listening to anyone'. Chandi tried, but Sharif was enveloped in the personal bubble powerful people can't resist.

Unable to stomach another coup, she escaped to Washington, thinking Sharif would tide over the crisis, but she was wrong. General Butt, not the most brilliant of officers ever to rise to the rank of a general, failed to take command. That meant Sharif had to go, but this time he landed in jail, the judiciary he had maltreated handing him a life sentence for trying to kill Musharraf.

Meanwhile, Back in Shah Jewna

Chandi had started on the wrong foot with Musharraf when he was army chief. She had taken WAPDA chief General Zulfiqar—once of the ISI, when the Dawood Ibrahim scandal broke, to the shame of Pakistan—to court for sending a wrong electricity bill to Shah Jewna. Wanting to duck the trial, he later called to apologize; she relented. Then Musharraf too met her and wouldn't listen to her saying terrorism was at the root of everything going wrong in Pakistan. Her verdict on him: 'Musharraf struck me as being opinionated, insecure, and dangerous. This was not a forthright soldier in the style of an Ayub or a Yahya, nor was he flinty yet unctuous like Zia. This one would more readily destruct than construct, since he had absolute power.'

For Fakhar and Chandi once again it was back to local government, stalked by Shia-killers. Sipah-e-Sahaba chief Azam Tariq who had killed numberless Shias was unaccountably released from jail, which meant Chandi's daughter Sughra would lose to a Sunni contestant in Jhang, which she did, true to a holding pattern since the days of General Zia. Then in 2002, the election under Musharraf's new 'legal framework order' saw both Chandi and Fakhar defeated, while Sughra won a seat in the Punjab Assembly and landed in Chaudhry Pervaiz Elahi's cabinet.

Predictably, all generals with drilled arrested growth come to a bad end, which in Pakistan is always unhappy and deflating for the proud army that produces them. Musharraf tried to muscle his way out of the mess he had created defending nuclear weapons and playing a double game on terrorism and ended up killing Nawab Akbar Khan Bugti, firing Chief Justice Iftikhar Chaudhry and bestowing on him the public halo he scarcely deserved. In 2007, as the blunders accumulated, Chandi was courted by Benazir and became a part of the next movement to restore democracy.

Principles, Anyone?

Are there any principles in politics? Chandi clearly had her own: don't rub me the wrong way, keep your inevitable male chauvinism under wraps, show noblesse oblige, be patriotic, and I can walk with you. When the generals took over she fell back on local government and adopted the survival mode; when democracy returned she did the politics her 'independent group' of feudal puritans collectively recommended.

She became firmly committed to Benazir's return to Pakistan after years of exile. She had a hand in the political project of Benazir and Nawaz Sharif signing the Charter of Democracy in 2006. She shuttled between Pakistan and the UAE, meeting Benazir and getting to know her personally till a kind of family allegiance gelled, like the one she had with Aitchisonian Nawab Akbar Bugti. When Benazir decided to land in Karachi she passed on to her TV anchor Dr Shahid Masood's warning that plans were afoot to assassinate her. Then when Benazir nearly got killed in the Karsaz massacre, Chandi was in her armoured truck and got injured after the second bomb blast.

By the time her odyssey comes to an end, she has sustained the deep wound of her parents' death, but is compensated by two gifted well-educated daughters, Sughra and Umme Kulsum, and a bright lawyer son, Abid, who partnered with Benazir to write her political analyses. Her writing style is the way she speaks, and when you talk to her, her Urdu is extraordinarily good, to say nothing of the Jhangochi she speaks in her Shah Jewna constituency.

32

Three Game-changing Deaths

In 2015, three deaths, one announced two years late, posted a final comment on Pakistan as a state deeply enmeshed in the causes of the disease it suffered from: terrorism. In May, Mullah Omar, the 'caliph' of the Afghan Taliban, was declared dead by Kabul saying he had in fact died two years earlier in 2013. Because of the 'special relationship' Pakistan enjoyed with the 'good' Afghan Taliban, rumours that he had lived in Balochistan or Karachi and had died in a Karachi hospital, were unleashed. The Afghan Taliban typically fell apart as an organization amid news of more internecine bloodshed as the Kabul–Islamabad 'peace talks' with the Taliban leadership made shipwrecks in Murree, Pakistan.

The second death the same month was that of Malik Ishaq, head of the banned terrorist group Lashkar-e-Jhangvi (LeJ), massacring the Shia of Quetta since the so-called Quetta Shura of Mullah Omar shifted from Kandahar after 2001. He died together with his sons and LeJ high command in a police 'encounter' in south

Punjab, the snake pit of terror radiating its venom down to Sindh and Karachi. Long thought to be in cahoots with state institutions with the judiciary consistently blinking its name-changing, the LeJ leader was counted among half a dozen killers that Pakistan couldn't convict and, if convicted, couldn't execute. LeJ's Taliban and al-Qaeda nexus was revealed when Malik Ishaq's death was avenged on 16 August through the suicide-bombing of the Punjab home minister, Colonel Shuja Khanzada (retd), formerly of Pakistan's Military Intelligence, at his home in Attock.

On 16 August, General Hamid Gul (retd), a former chief of the Inter-Services Intelligence (ISI) died a natural death, highlighting Pakistan's steady collusion with Pakistan's tormentors by fielding them against India. Outspoken to the point of betrayal, he not only challenged India and by extension the United States, but the state of Pakistan itself for its dubious romance with democracy which he thought was a Western ruse to harm Muslims. After being passed over for incompetence and spying on high offices of the state, he refused to actually 'retire' and said so, taking part in the Afghan war without the state of Pakistan taking note of it. Since his influence in the officers' class in the Pakistan army has outlasted him, it is doubtful if Pakistan will be weaned from its intoxication with jihad.

Special Guest: Mullah Omar

On 29 July 2015 the presidential office in Kabul announced that Mullah Muhammad Omar, on whose advice the Taliban had had held peace talks with Afghanistan on 7 July, was not alive and had in fact been dead since 2013. That was two days before the next round was to take place on 31 July. Mullah Muhammad Akhtar Mansur, who was the frontman for a habitually no-show Omar, denied the Kabul claim but soon had to admit that his leader was indeed dead and that he was acting on the advice of the Taliban shura (council) of religious leaders to pre-empt the splintering of the Taliban movement. He also claimed that Omar had named him the next Taliban leader before his death.

Summoned and Scuttled

Why did Kabul scuttle the peace process it had set afoot with the backing of Pakistan, China and the United States? Was President Ashraf Ghani finally convinced by his National Directorate of Security that the 7 July session was again manipulated by Pakistan and would go against the interests of the Kabul government? Was Kabul not aware that agreeing to peace talks in Pakistan signalled its acceptance of Pakistan's capacity to intervene in the affairs of Afghanistan? Now there is talk of President Ghani doing a volte-face and embarking on a strategy of dividing the Taliban before bending its fractured leadership to Kabul's stance. The tentative Murree session had gone without disagreement but its participants on the Taliban side could have put off the Afghan negotiator and his unnamed advisers.

Barnet Rubin wrote in the *New Yorker* on 29 July: 'The Afghan delegation was led by Haji Din Muhammad, a senior member of the High Peace Council. The Taliban present were Mullah Abbas Akhund, who headed the delegation, Abdul Latif Mansur, and Ibrahim Haqqani. Abbas and Latif Mansur were reputed to have belonged to the Taliban's liaison committee with the ISI, while Haqqani represented a part of the Taliban that Admiral Michael Mullen, the American chairman of the Joint Chiefs of Staff, had called "a veritable arm of Pakistan's Inter-Services Intelligence agency" in Congressional testimony on 22 September 2011. No member of the Taliban political office attended.'

The Taliban couldn't put a lid on the confusion set off by the Kabul statement, leading to the postponement of the second round of talks that Kabul may not have wanted in Pakistan in the first place. When the mists cleared, the death of Mullah Omar in 2013 was owned on all sides, triggering predictable splits within the Taliban movement already half-inclined to join the more radical, peace-opposing Islamic State (IS) in Afghanistan. Given that the Taliban is a Pashtun movement, the tendency of the Pashtun man to emphasize his individuality through disagreement rather than agreement will come to the fore after the disappearance of the already 'loose' authority of Mullah Omar. The Islamic State will suit the Pashtun temperament more than the new Taliban leader, Mullah Mansur.

Retreating into Mistrust

Kabul returned to its posture of not trusting Islamabad and its Inter-Services Intelligence (ISI), helped not a little by the brawling inside the post-Mullah-Omar Taliban. It also retreated from a recognition of the strategic overhaul in Pakistan's thinking brought about by Pakistan's new army chief General Raheel Sharif, whose policy of taking on all Taliban including the 'friendly' ones earlier given refuge inside Pakistan—from where they attacked inside Afghanistan—had triggered changes in the thinking of Beijing and Kabul, both endangered by terrorism fanning out from Pakistan. In short the change in Pakistan that had persuaded China to invest in the infrastructure linking Pakistan to Afghanistan and convince Kabul to engage in peace talks with Islamabad.

Pakistani observers, led by reporting ace RahimullahYusufzai, accepted that Omar was indeed dead and that he may have died of tuberculosis or a heart attack. When the media carried the news that Omar had in fact been treated in Karachi at the Aga Khan Hospital, the Hospital immediately denied it. Yusufzai, prefacing his comment on TV with the observation that 'it is not always safe to state facts in Pakistan', revealed more details, indirectly damaging the already murky reputation of the ISI. Mullah Omar's son Muhammad Yaqub had studied in Karachi, which fact some sources in Pakistan made more precise by naming the Taliban's favourite seminary, Jamia Banuria—which the Jamia did not deny.

The Taliban, led by Mansur, had actually split: Omar's son Yaqub had challenged Mansur and was inclined to believe with other rivals that Mansur had actually shot Omar before burying him in the Zabul province of Afghanistan. The Taliban commanders, ever ready to scramble and disagree on reports of peace talks, bristled with accusations of treachery. Mansur they thought was no caliph—as opposed to the leader of the Islamic State, Al Baghdadi, who was—and didn't deserve *bayat* (formal oath of allegiance).Then on 4 August, newspapers in Pakistan carried two items: President Ashraf Ghani saying that 'there will be no talks with divided Afghan factions' and that 'Omar's son Yaqub had been killed by opponents in Quetta'. The denials that followed made no impact.

Kabul seemed to settle back into the comfortable stance of challenging interference and manipulation from Pakistan and its spy agency, the ISI. India helped by declaring, through an ex-RAW officer, that the new Taliban leader Mullah Mansur was none else but the terrorist who 'embraced Maulana Masood Azhar on the Kandahar airport tarmac as the hijacking of IC-814 ended with the release of the Jaish-e-Mohammed leader and two others, and was the man who drove him out of the airport in his white Land Cruiser'. The reference was to the December 1991 hijack of an Indian airliner which was taken to Taliban-ruled Afghanistan to force the release of three terrorists from an Indian prison: Masood Azhar leader of Jaish-e-Mohammad accused of attacking the Indian parliament, Mushtaq Ahmed Zargar of Kashmir, and Ahmed Omar Saeed Sheikh, a Pakistani now in a death-cell in Pakistan for the murder of American journalist, Daniel Pearl.

Romancing the Taliban

Pakistan has a history with the Taliban that will obstruct any peace move supported by Islamabad. Fated to host the Afghan warriors in Peshawar when it was fighting the Soviet invasion of Afghanistan in 1979, it literally midwifed the Taliban in 1994.[1] After the Soviet withdrawal, the various mujahideen factions it hosted squared off in a civil war. By 1994, the mujahideen degenerated into pillaging-raping groups that the Afghan nation could do nothing about. Two mujahideen commanders in Kandahar, fighting over a boy they wanted to sodomize, gave a lowly, semi-literate preacher Mullah Omar and his friends a chance to take over. At this point, Pakistan's PPP government, trying to break the monopoly of the ISI over the mujahideen, backed the new militia called the Taliban. Ex-ISI boss General Hamid Gul (retd) who had earlier backed the Peshawar-based warlord Hekmatyar—today aligned with Islamic State—opposed the new entity till his successors in the ISI accepted the Taliban as their new card in Afghanistan and warned him off.

Thus a Ghilzai came to lead a predominantly Durrani shura in Kandahar, backed by a clerical consensus dubbing him amirul-momineen (caliph of the believers) after he disingenuously took out the cloak of Prophet Muhammad (PBUH) from a Kandahar shrine and wore it in front of a crowd. The PPP interior minister who master-minded the Taliban option, fell in with the transporters of Quetta who wanted the Taliban to reopen the road to Herat. Pakistan wanted a route through to Central Asia, especially with Turkmenistan with whom Islamabad had signed an agreement for a gas pipeline. Pakistan recognized the Taliban regime in Kabul together with Saudi Arabia and the UAE, while the world retreated in the face of the new government's savage treatment of opponents, Shia Afghans and women.

Revealing the Shura

The 'special relationship' Pakistan developed with the Taliban was actually a nexus exclusively controlled by the Islamist officers of the ISI, as was proved in 2001 when the army chief General Pervez Musharraf tried to disembarrass Pakistan of its fixation with the Taliban and was not supported in this new policy by the ISI commanders. Evidence of this is provided by three Western women reporters who offended Islamabad with their findings: Kathy Gannon (seriously wounded), Christina Lamb (twice deported), and Carlotta Gall (roughed up).

Associated Press journalist Kathy Gannon tells us how a Taliban official revealed ISI chief General Mahmood Ahmad's encounter with Mullah Omar negated the instructions of General Musharraf:

'The general was a religious zealot very much like Mullah Omar. He had been central to the military takeover of Pakistan in 1999 by Musharraf. A hawk with pan-Islamic visions, he had been a staunch supporter of jihadists both from Pakistan and elsewhere. This was the man Musharraf sent to negotiate with Mullah Omar. People present at the meeting and within the ISI revealed that Ahmad had a message for Mullah Omar quite different from the one that Washington had pressed his government to convey. He took the slow-talking leader aside and urged him to resist the United States. He told Mullah Omar not to give up bin Laden. Ahmad travelled several times to Kandahar, and on each visit he gave Mullah Omar information about the likely next move by the United States.'[2] Gannon was seriously wounded in Spin Boldak after being shot by her own guard near the Pakistani border of Chaman in 2014.

Christina Lamb reveals yet another side of the ISI chief Mahmood during the same meeting: 'According to Mullah Abdus Salam Zaeef, the Taliban ambassador who accompanied the Pakistan delegation to Kandahar, General Moeen Haider warned Mullah Omar about the risks of continuing to shelter bin Laden. "I am up to 80 per cent certain that the Americans will attack you," he said. As Haider talked, Zaeef said, "Mahmood leaned towards me and whispered, 'What is this silly donkey talking about?'"'[3]

Loyalty Higher than State

Lamb reports another meeting between some ISI officers and Ambassador Mullah Zaeef, who was eventually surrendered to the Americans to serve many years at Guantanamo Bay: 'Before the bombing campaign started three top ISI officers came to Zaeef's house in Islamabad to pledge their support—General Mahmood, his deputy General Jailani [sic], and Brigadier Farooq who ran the agency's Afghan desk. "We want to assure you that you will not be alone in this jihad against America," they told him. "We will be with you." Zaeef was enraged. "You speak of jihad while the Americans are stationed in your airbases and flying through your airspace, even attacking Afghanistan based on your intelligence reports!" he shouted. "You should be ashamed to even utter the word jihad!" When he looked at General Mahmood, "tears were running down his face". As for Jailani, "He was crying out loud with his arms around my neck like a woman."[4]

This 'special relationship' was extended to the Quetta shura which Mullah Omar led after his escape on a motorbike from Kandahar under heavy shelling. General Musharraf was attacked by offended air-force officers and the non-state actor organization Jaish-e-Mohammad while travelling from Rawalpindi to Islamabad. The Afghan government accused Musharraf of using the Taliban to attack Indian and American embassies in Kabul but Musharraf, probably scared of what might happen to him next 'from the inside', denied it.

The ISI kept maltreating foreign journalists who stepped too close to the Quetta Shura, as happened in the case of Carlotta Gall who 'lived in Kabul, with a foothold in Islamabad, from 2001 to 2011' and reported for the *New York Times*. She tells how an ISI officer in a Quetta hotel 'punched me twice, hard, in the face and temple, knocking me over. I fell back onto the coffee table, smashing the cups there, grabbing at the officer to break my fall and nearly pulling him down on top of me'. She was getting too close to the quarter of the city which housed the Shura.

Jihad above Loyalty

Interviewing Col Imam (Tarar) of the ISI, she got the following nugget: 'General Mahmood's support for the Taliban became so obstructive that the Bush administration demanded his removal from the top Intelligence post. Musharraf replaced him on 7 October 2001, the day the bombing campaign began. Colonel Imam remained at Mullah Omar's side even after the bombing began, until an exasperated Musharraf sent orders: What are you doing there?'[5] The Pakistani state's own journey of moving from mild to harsh Islam across its history had set off this trend of 'converting to the enemy' among its officers.

There are increasing grounds for not crediting any version of events given out officially by Pakistan. After the 'discovery' of Osama bin Laden in Abbottabad in 2011, Pakistanis routinely offer denials they don't believe themselves. Bin Laden's successor Ayman-al-Zawahiri is also said to be 'somewhere on the Pakistan–Afghan border' but could be located inside Pakistan writing letters to Islamabad's Red Mosque, as discovered in 2007. Journalist Rahimullah Yusufzai, who interviewed Mullah Omar over a dozen times, doesn't toe the official line when he says Mullah Omar was in Balochistan after his escape from Kandahar and lived in Quetta, Pishin and Chaman at different times. He however doesn't cross the line about Karachi, abstaining from confirming that Omar also lived in Karachi, where one of his sons certainly went to school and his three wives and children were probably ensconced in a 'safe house'. Another journalist and author, Ahmed Rashid says Omar was in Karachi.

Steve Coll, author of *Ghost Wars: The Secret History of the CIA, Afghanistan, and Bin Laden, from the Soviet Invasion to September 10, 2001,* investigated the rumours about Mullah Omar's location in Karachi from where Pakistan had arrested one of his deputies, Mullah Dadullah. His long article, 'Looking for Mullah Omar' in the *New Yorker* (23 January 2012) remains the most comprehensive dossier on what might have happened to Mullah Omar during his stay in Pakistan.

Karachi: Malignant Magnet

Coll quoted a Dutch scholar who lived in Kandahar and thought, on the basis of what some insiders told him, that Mullah Omar was 'in a safe house in Karachi', that Omar's movements and activities were closely monitored by the ISI; and that he was 'essentially a prisoner', all access to him controlled by the ISI.

Because of the Abbottabad affair, senior Indian officials were quoted in WikiLeaks as saying that Mullah Omar was 'under Pakistani protection'.

Coll wrote: 'One interlocutor for Omar who has attracted considerable attention from the Karzai government and the Obama Administration is Abdul Ghani Baradar. Baradar was deputy chief of the armed forces when the Taliban controlled Afghanistan, and was regarded as one of the movement's more competent leaders. Baradar has long been inside the circles of personal trust that have characterized the Taliban's leadership. Baradar engaged in sporadic reconciliation talks with Karzai's government until 2010. Early that year, Pakistan's security services arrested Baradar outside Karachi. Since then, he has been held in a Pakistani prison, reportedly near the capital of Islamabad.'[6] Islamabad of course denies this.

Given this backdrop, why did President Ashraf Ghani agree to let Pakistan convene the peace talks in Murree? One can say that China's persuasion worked because 'it can get Pakistan to deliver on anything it wants'—and it wants peace in Afghanistan and has the capacity to finance the Kabul government after America and its allies turn off the faucet. Who among those involved in Afghanistan and possessing the advantage of being persuasive with Ghani would suspect any peace talks organized by Pakistan? Most probably the United States, which has been 'double-dealt' by Pakistan consistently under Generals Musharraf and Kayani; and more forthrightly, India, currently involved in proxy hostilities with Pakistan. The advice, if it came, would require President Ghani to secure more elaborate guarantees of non-interference from Islamabad during and after the peace talks.

Flawed Policy in Control

The truth is that Pakistan's Afghan policy, as linked to its either/ or competition with India in the region, doesn't allow an Afghan policy that would reassure the world. Ahmed Rashid in his book, *Descent into Chaos: How the War against Islamic Extremism Is Being*

Lost in Pakistan, Afghanistan and Central Asia, is fair when he says Musharraf didn't let go of his policy of backing the Taliban and through them domination of Afghanistan because he thought the Americans would cut and run soon enough, leaving Pakistan holding the bag. Today, Pakistan stands isolated in Afghanistan and doesn't realize it. The nationalities in the north of Afghanistan are alienated because they think Pakistan sides with the Pashtuns in the south and ignores their rights. The way Pakistan has handled its Afghan policy one is not sure if the Pashtuns too will return the favour.

Will the next round take place after the fiasco of Murree? Most probably Kabul will test the waters and join the next round away from Islamabad in China and see if the 'fractured' Taliban are more pliable and less controlled by Islamabad than the Quetta Shura predecessors headed by Mullah Mansur. It will all depend on how well Kabul is able to alter the list of participants. Pakistan with its unchallenged capacity to manipulate the peace talks is open to influence from Beijing, which gives the driving seat to China to some extent. But Pakistan's position remains strong—anti-India and pro-Pashtun—as explained by the famous Kennedy School of Government, Harvard University 'discussion paper': 'The Sun in the Sky: The Relationship between Pakistan's ISI and Afghan Insurgents':

'It means that without a change in Pakistani behaviour it will be difficult if not impossible for international forces and the Afghan government to make progress against the insurgency. It also means that, as one southern commander put it, "if the ISI doesn't support negotiations [with the Afghan government], then they won't succeed".'

Malik Ishaq and the Vanishing State

On 28 May 2015, Malik Muhammad Ishaq, leader of the banned jihadi organization Laskhar-e-Jhangvi, was killed in

Muzaffargarh district in southern Punjab in what looked like an 'extra-judicial' encounter. The police said they had picked him up for 'identification of a weapons cache' when on the way his armed thugs tried to snatch him from custody; they attacked the police guard and were killed by answering fire. Also killed were the prisoners Malik Ishaq and his two sons. In all, sixteen men were killed, presumably accounting for the core of the terrorist organization operating out of Rahimyar Khan district. Malik Ishaq himself had completed almost a dozen years in jail for killing scores of Shia Muslims before being let out on bail in 2011 after he openly threatened the judges. And the police couldn't prevent their witnesses from absconding from the case.

The *News* on 30 July stated the following details about Malik Ishaq: 'Officially charged with seventy murders and forty-four other cases of terrorism, including the March 2009 attack on the Sri Lankan cricket team near the Qaddafi Stadium in Lahore [which took Pakistan off the cricketing map of the world], Malik Ishaq had admitted in an interview with an Urdu daily in October 1997 that he was involved in the killing of 102 people. He was arrested the same year, charged with seventy murders and tried for them for the next twelve years, only to be released on bail by the Supreme Court in December 2014 after his acquittal in sixty-four murder cases due to lack of evidence or withdrawn witness testimonies. During Ishaq's twelve years in confinement, seventy-two judges and prosecution lawyers expressed their inability to hear or pursue cases against him and his sons, most of them either going on leave or refusing to continue hearing them "on personal grounds".'

'Encounter' and the Writ of the State

Purists came on TV crying foul and condemning the police for its 'encounters' undermining the sovereignty of the state and supremacy of law. Lawyers gave erudite arguments against the police, forgetting they themselves are called *wukla* pejoratively because of their hooliganism against lower-court judges and the police. The citizens at large, however, were relieved that Malik Ishaq was finally gotten rid of, unconsciously welcoming the return of the writ of the state. Some argued that the state, led by the new army chief General Raheel Sharif, was finally completing its job of getting rid of the terrorists in south Punjab from where the state had earlier recruited them to fight its proxy wars.

Perhaps the rationale for 'encounters' was embedded in efforts to counteract the rapidly disappearing attributes of the normal state in Pakistan. Perhaps the Supreme Court while allowing military courts on 5 August to tackle the likes of Malik Ishaq was subliminally comparing Pakistan—not to India where similar laws have hunted down terrorists—but to Afghanistan, Somalia and Libya where the state has either vanished or is in the process of doing so. One must recall the classical theory of the state which says it was created to preserve the sanctity of life and property. Both attributes are exposed to elements that the state can no longer control in Pakistan. Violence increasingly commands human conduct, not law. Is it time the state recaptured its 'monopoly of violence'? Malik Ishaq's fellow-commander of LeJ, Riaz Basra, too couldn't be punished under normal legal procedure and was killed by the police in an 'encounter'.

However, it is largely believed that the 4 February 2014 decision of the US State Department to tag Ishaq as a Specially Designated Global Terrorist due to his al-Qaeda links was the beginning of his end. Malik Ishaq was in and out of Pakistani custody over the past three decades. He had dodged numerous convictions by murdering and intimidating witnesses, and even once told a judge, 'Dead men can't talk.'

A Well-oiled Killing Machine

Lashkar-e-Jhangvi was formed in 1996 by three Sipah-e-Sahaba Pakistan (SSP) terrorists: Malik Ishaq, Riaz Basra and Akram Lahori. Earlier, terrorism against the Shia and Iran was orchestrated by the same trio. When the Iranian consul in Lahore, Sadeq Ganji, was assassinated by Riaz Basra in 1990, the strong presence of SSP in politics prevented due process of law. At the Lahore High Court, where the killers faced trial, many judges retired or were elevated before the court was able to pass the obvious death sentence. The SSP wanted to pay *diyat* (blood money) for the killer it wanted spared, and even approached Iran in this respect. The power of apostatizing sectarian elements redoubled in 2011 and 'legal' political parties like Muslim League–Nawaz had to align with them to survive in certain regions. This meant: rename the banned organization and carry on. The irreducible factor in this erosion of political normalcy was the backing the state establishment extended to the terrorists in south Punjab.

Malik Ishaq's LeJ killed the Shia of Quetta in Balochistan and across the rest of Pakistan, riding under the banner of its mother organization, SSP, created in the 1980s by the state to do its dirty work: today it operates under the new name of Ahle Sunnatwal Jamaat (ASWJ) facilitated by a scared judiciary. After the killing of Malik Ishaq, ASWJ protested in Quetta but soon simmered down 'on advice' and has not protested in the rest of the country. Its leader Ahmad Ludhianvi who declared the Shia non-Muslim earlier this year, realized that this time General Raheel meant business and wouldn't tolerate any show of street power the state had earlier kowtowed to. Surprisingly, Pakistan didn't suffer any violent 'outing' of SSP, from Jhang in Punjab to Shikarpur in Sindh where the state had actually retreated earlier to give the sectarian terrorists a free hand.

Because of the 'paradigm shift' sensed in the new 'Zarb-e-Azb' (Sword of the Prophet) actions of General Sharif, Pakistan might actually dispose of the following killers it can't arrest or kill. Lakhvi of Mumbai terror fame in Adiala jail where his orders were followed by jail staff in prison till his release; so does Ahmad Saeed Sheikh in Hyderabad jail, involved in the Daniel Pearl case but actually sprung from an Indian jail; Abdur Rehman in Karachi jail, leader of Jandullah; Dawood Ibrahim of D-Company who lives in Karachi; Captain Haroon Ashiq killer of Major General Naqvi finally released after years in jail; Hafiz Saeed with UN bounty of $10 million who threatens India on a daily basis; Masood Azhar, leader of another SSP offshoot, Jaish Muhammad, sprung from an Indian jail through a hijack, now living in Bahawalpur in south Punjab; Fazlur Rehman Khalil the 'post office' of Osama bin Laden with $5 million UN head money, used in anti-India 'long marches'; Akram Lahori who is under death sentence but can't be hanged just like Mumtaz Qadri, the killer of Governor Salmaan Taseer.

Well-regarded Pakistani lawyer Babar Sattar wrote in the *News* on 1 August: 'It is confusion over what one part of the state might consider anti-state or illegal and another doesn't that creates confusion and [allows] sanctuaries for our Malik Ishaqs to prosper and overawe the writ of the state (or at least that of its civilian arm). The Ishaq encounter has now shown that the Lashkar-e-Jhangvi is fair game for law-enforcement agencies across Pakistan. But what about Lashkar-e-Taiba or Jaish-e-Mohammad? Are they still [off-limits]? When Zakiur Rehman Lakhv [of Mumbai attacks] is presented in courts, should the judges see him as an asset or liability?'

Mother of all Terrorists

The SSP had murky origins, starting with Arab money and ending up in the lap of al-Qaeda. It was based in the Punjab city of Jhang and its 'Khomeini-dog'-chanting founder Haq Nawaz was murdered in 1990, as noted by Syeda Abida Hussain in her memoir. Haq Nawaz's widow let it be known in 1990 that Sipah was funded by Osama bin Laden. The SSP even joined politics in the early 1990s despite its terrorism and was in the Punjab government, which forced it to 'clean up' its act a little. Several offshoots sprang up to replace the mother party. Jhangvi Tigers, Al Haq Tigers, Al Farooq, Al Badr and Allah Akbar, were formed to spread terror in Karachi in Sindh, and Jhang, Chiniot, Samundari and Faisalabad in Punjab. All of them later merged in LeJ in 1996 under the dual leadership of Riaz Basra and Malik Ishaq, Basra being a former central information secretary of SSP.

Because of SSP's old contacts with the Arab hunters in south Punjab, the organization was among the first to send recruits to al-Qaeda when it established its training camps in Afghanistan in the late 1990s. LeJ thus came to operate the best trained killers of the parent party. As time passed and it became a major player in the killing of Shias in Pakistan, there developed a division between the Riaz Basra/Malik Ishaq faction and the boys led by one Qari Abdul Hai associated with the training camps in Afghanistan. Later, the Basra/Malik Ishaq group became active in Punjab while the Hai group was confined to violence in Karachi.

Hai was more in favour of carrying out missions for al-Qaeda against American and pro-American targets while Malik Ishaq was determined to advance the cause of Jhangvi by killing Shias. For a time there was a blending of the two positions in the killings that took place in Pakistan. Hundreds of innocent citizens died at the hands of the Malik Ishaq/Basra faction while Hai targeted Christians and Americans. LeJ remained a Deobandi organization and Basra was often seen attending the annual congregation of the Tablighi Jamaat in Lahore along with terrorists from other jihadi outfits but was never confronted by the police because of the large number of guards around himself. He scared Nawaz Sharif once by sending him a photo of him standing next to Sharif during a party gathering in Lahore. The message: I can kill you any time I want. He had earlier nearly killed him by exploding a bomb under a bridge that Sharif's car passed and narrowly escaped being blown up.

LeJ went on killing without much obstruction till General Musharraf was forced to heed the public protest against the organization; he banned it in 2001. The following year when he got the police to kill him in an 'encounter' in Vihari, Riaz Basra had 300 cases of murder against him, including Iranian diplomats, a commissioner of Jhang and a number of prominent Shias from

Punjab. Also against his name was the massacre of twenty-five innocent Shias in Lahore's Mominpura.

A Paradigm Shift?

After 2001, LeJ became a part of al-Qaeda's Brigade 313 to avenge America's invasion of Afghanistan, and was involved in a lot of al-Qaeda work, including the abduction and death of the American journalist Daniel Pearl in Karachi. It was close to Ramzi Yusuf, the man who used to do sectarian killings before he attacked the American Trade Center in New York in 1993, and to Khalid Sheikh Muhammad, his uncle, who planned the final assault on it in 2001. Muhammad was in charge of training the Brigade 313 and LeJ was a part of this Delta Force. Muhammad had assigned targets to the Delta Force, which included Musharraf himself and the corps commander in Karachi in 2004. LeJ was involved in both attempts in tandem with agents directly commissioned by al-Qaeda. At this point the intelligence agencies noted that Jordanian salafist Abu Musab al-Zarqawi was seen in association with LeJ, thus earmarking him as a sectarian killer before he went to Iraq and began his anti-Shia terror there, laying the foundation of Islamic State of our day.

Malik Ishaq was the symbol of the state's surrender to terrorists. He realigned with SSP because it represented one of the centres of power spawned by the state policy of proxy jihad. Provincial governments vied with one another to reach a modus vivendi with these power centres to save their politicians from being assassinated.

The end of Malik Ishaq signals a radical shift in the security paradigm of Pakistan, noted by Sameer Lalwani in his paper, 'Pakistan's Shocking Strategic Shift': 'Pakistan's officer corps and national security experts have engaged in significant self-examination in their strategic literature over the past fifteen years . . . a vibrant debate is being waged over Pakistan's fluid security environment, the foundations of national security . . .

and the relative priority of its internal threats. New thinking expressed by officers in leading Pakistani military publications like the *Citadel*, *NDU Journal*, *Pakistan Defence Review*, and *Pakistan Army Green Book* have endorsed austerity measures; emphasized economic growth, technology, education, and management of water and energy resources as prerequisites for national power; and warned against an "economically destructive" conventional competition with India.

'Evidence of shifting priorities is found in the biennial *Pakistan army Green Book*, [in the writings of] Pakistani Colonels and Brigadiers, some of whom have ascended to the highest ranks of Corps Commanders. [They] have concentrated on unconventional, internal threats as much or more than the traditional rivalry with India. The 2006 issue on "Terrorism" unsurprisingly concentrated on these issues, but over 70 per cent of articles from the 2008 issue on the "Future Conflict Environment" and the 2010 issue on "Information Warfare" also reflected on internal security threats. One 2008 article openly acknowledges that the Taliban insurgency "is likely to be the most formidable threat faced by Pakistan in the near future". In a 2006 article in The Citadel, published by the Command and Staff College, Quetta, one Colonel suggested that "Pakistan does not face external threat as much as it does from within".'[7]

〜

Soldier of Misfortune: Hamid Gul

Pakistan's top spy, General Hamid Gul (retd) died of a brain haemorrhage on 15 August 2015, aged seventy-nine. Eulogies went out from the prime minister of Pakistan Nawaz Sharif and from the army chief, General Raheel Sharif, who also attended his funeral. The head of the Defence of Pakistan Council where Gul frequently protested Pakistan's ill-advised friendly gestures towards India, Maulana Sami ul-Haq compared him to the great Muslim conquerors like Salahuddin, Sultan Mehmud Ghaznavi and Shahabuddin Ghauri. Also present was Jamaatud Dawa's Hafiz Saeed whose deep purse made the 'long marches' of the council successful, handing out cash to bystanders on the Grand Trunk Road from Lahore to Islamabad. Another Osama bin Laden 'contact'—FazlurRehman Khalil—too graced the procession. Both he and Saeed had head-money on them for terrorism.

The *Hindustan Times*'s comment was less glowing: 'Originally from Sargodha in Pakistan's Punjab, Gul was General Zia-ulHaq's personal favourite. He is considered the brain behind Pakistan's proxy wars with India, first in the Punjab, and then in Kashmir, and is referred to as godfather of the terrorist group Lashkar-e-Taiba, which India says carried out the 26/11 Mumbai attack and numerous other terror strikes in the country.'

Gul was a star soldier who got to command two of Pakistan's top strike formations besides heading the Military Intelligence (MI) and the Inter-Services Intelligence (ISI). General Zia-ul-Haq who staged his coup in 1977 and hanged the elected prime minister, got him, as his ISI chief, to 'Islamize' a secular army and win the Afghan war for the Americans, who earlier wrongly grew to love Gul as a canny spook. He was host to the Afghan warlords resting in Peshawar till he picked Hekmatyar as his favourite and caused mujahideen to split about him. He later switched to the Afghan Taliban and postured as mentor to the Pakistani Taliban, getting cosy with the Haqqani group in North Waziristan and making contact with Baitullah Mehsud through his friend Maulana Sami ul-Haq whose seminary near Peshawar allowed the assassins of Benazir Bhutto to rest for the night before going for their kill in Rawalpindi.

His acolytes in the army were myriad, including ex-MI Punjab home minister, Colonel Shuja Khanzada (retd), killed by the Taliban a day after Gul expired. Khanzada had paid immediate tribute to the 'master strategist' of Pakistan, saying his death would create a vacuum in the country's 'strategic thought process'. After Khanzada's death, it appears ironic that the Taliban took to killing people he had patronized. Two ex-ISI officers, Khalid Khwaja and Col Imam went to North Waziristan with his blessings, thinking a word from him would open doors, but were cruelly put to death in 2011 by their host, Hakimullah Mehsud. Gul was hounded by failures but he remained unfazed, confident that the army and the Pakistani public at large would ignore his lack of success for the fantasies he had planted in their minds. He condemned democracy as a pagan institution and remained popular; he said 9/11 was staged by Mossad and most Pakistanis agreed with him. He admitted he had 'stage-managed' the 1990 election—in fact he began his efforts in 1988[8]—to oust the Pakistan People's Party (PPP) from government, which was taken as normal; and when Benazir Bhutto named him among her possible killers in 2007, nobody believed her.

The secret of Gul's success lay in his mining the India-centric nationalism of Pakistani textbooks for clinching arguments. One sample goes somewhat like this: 'Indian secularism is a ruse as Babri Mosque proved it. This is my reason for dislike of India. The rift with India has a solid basis and that is why the Muslims living in the subcontinent—whether in Pakistan, Bangladesh or India—are one nation. The 1965 war was an interrupted victory because finance minister Shoaib sabotaged it. Foreign minister Zafrullah Khan sabotaged the 1948 war. I strongly believe that the sole purpose of the Pakistani army is to liberate Kashmir from Indian occupation. I assure you that India is in a miserable state. Deep down, Indians are afraid of Pakistan.'[9]

The Prophet of Nihilism

This is nothing compared to how Gul got himself in knots when he was in his prognostic mood. Making two contradictory predictions that would destroy the strategic intent of the statement didn't bother him. He would say India was in a cleft stick because it needed energy to survive, but energy from Central Asia was available only if Pakistan allowed the pipelines to cross its territory. India therefore would be forced to agree to Pakistan's demands, only if Pakistan were to play its cards well. If India gave Kashmir to Pakistan it would go to pieces and if it did not then there would be a nuclear war in South Asia in which both countries would perish. Could this be called strategy?

He maintained that Indian prime minister Atal Behari Vajpayee was trying to get Pakistan to drop its visa system [through free trade] and join India in a single currency. That would make sure, according to him, that there was no Pakistan. Anybody exposed to this kind of strategic scenario-building would come away completely confused. In many ways Gul was a nihilist, someone intent upon destroying the whole regional equation because it didn't yield to his expectations. Perhaps he was too prepared at all times to serve as the oracle of the Pakistani mind with its complex mixture of paranoia and pessimism to care about appearing as a self-contradictory prophet.

How did Gul end up creating this strangely schizophrenic picture of himself? His intellectual foundation squared with Pakistani nationalism. His 'full picture' was Islamic, anti-American even when he was handling America's richly funded Afghan war; honour-based because that is what Muslims prize above all else; and inflexible because all principled (*usuli*) positions never change. The truth may be that as a strategic thinker he finally ended up being unpragmatic, determined to twist circumstance to suit imagination. He forgot the basic principle of first aligning policy to resource-base, then rejecting the other principle of keeping the policy options as flexible as possible. His strategy could be explained in one word—one that he has often used: *dattjanachahiyay* (give no ground).

The official India policy in the Pakistan army therefore was that a set-piece battle instead of an all-out war should be pursued. When the policy did not bring success it was abandoned with great reluctance in 2001, but not without offending a majority of

Pakistani opinion linking national honour to the pursuit of old policy. Hamid Gul's rationale was that while it was true that India was unconquerable, the fact was it was breaking up from within—in consequence of the failure of its secular experiment—and that Pakistan only had to give it a nudge to bring about a self-generated collapse. This too was falsified by the events of the following decades—the decade of low-intensity jihad in which Pakistan lost its internal sovereignty to al-Qaeda; and India arose as a powerful market with the potential of becoming a world leader.

Low-intensity War of Low IQ

When Hafiz Saeed and his Lashkar-e-Taiba were the darlings of the irredentist state, he attended the annual sessions of its mother organization Dawatwal Irshad in Lahore, basking in the admiration of the Punjabi youth made cannon fodder on payment from Osama bin Laden. Olivier Roy and Mariam Abou Zahab disclosed in their book, *Islamist Networks: The Afghan-Pakistan Connection,* that Hafiz Saeed was funded by an Arab who was a frontman for Osama bin Laden.

When in the mid-1990s Gul started charging that the Americans were trying to secularize the army under General Jehangir Karamat, it was repeated by the army journal *Hilal* in 1996. His line on Kashmir was also obeyed by *Hilal* in 1997, which alerted the press against changing their policy in light of Mian Nawaz Sharif's latest initiative on relations with India. General Zaheerul Islam Abbasi, doing time in jail after being convicted by a court martial general for trying to stage a military coup, confirmed through interviews leaked to the press that the army was being run as an inferior adjunct of the American army, and that the Americans were planning to occupy the Northern Areas and Kashmir.

This kind of thinking spilled over regularly into the civilian discourse. Almost everyone in Pakistan believed that the Americans would take Kashmir after making it independent so that they could spy on China. America was also supposed to be taking over Central Asia to get hold of its natural resources and encircle Iran. Gul refused to look at the evidence that the World Trade Center in New York was destroyed by al-Qaeda—with money sent from Lahore by Omar Sheikh, the killer of Daniel Pearl, while in the 'safe custody' of the home secretary—and refused equally to believe that Osama bin Laden was killed by the Americans in Abbottabad in 2011. Surprisingly, most Pakistanis agreed with him, including a judge of the Supreme Court!

Midnight Monkeys

Gul was heading the ISI when General Zia was killed by someone in Bahawalpur, his C-130 sabotaged in mid-air. The general was warned against flying to Bahawalpur in south Punjab which he ignored and Gul at the ISI was unable to decipher what was happening. After the air-crash, Gul coyly announced that the general had been killed by the CIA. Since Pakistan habitually failed to diagnose its accidents, Pakistanis still believe 'the Americans did it'. What followed was the failure on the part of the new army chief, General Aslam Beg, to enslave the PPP government to his 'strategic defiance' and keep Gul as ISI chief but got President Ghulam Ishaq Khan to use Article 58/2/B of the constitution to dismiss it for 'corruption and deviation from ideology'.

Two 'rogue' officers were caught trying to deprive the PPP of its parliamentary majority through Operation Midnight Jackals in 1989 targeting some PPP members of Parliament with bribery. The 'operation' was scuttled by a video recording that caused the subsequent dismissal from the army of Brigadier Imtiaz Ahmad and Major Amir Khan.

Journalist Aoun Sahi interviewed former Brigadier Imtiaz Ahmad in the *News* (2 August 2009) and had him saying this on record: 'In this incident my involvement revolved round the blind trust and one-sided loyalty that I accorded to my two senior-most superiors, General Aslam Beg and Hamid Gul. I was called by Aslam Beg, the then COAS, and told that the policies of this government regarding the nuclear programme, Afghan policy, and interference in the matters of army, were creating problems for the country and sought my help in the matter. These two gentlemen, Beg and Gul, controlled the Operation Midnight Jackals while federal defence secretary Ijlal Haider Zaidi assisted them. Hamid Gul was serving as corps commander Multan at the time but he used to visit Rawalpindi every week without GHQ permission. There he used to see Ijlal Haider Zaidi regularly while Major Amir and I were also asked to often meet.'

Acres of Arrogance

A report 'General Hamid Gul *nay sainkro naikararazi kaisay banayi*' (How did General Hamid Gul acquire hundreds of acres of land?) in the Urdu daily *Pakistan* (21 January 2005) revealed that Gul had acquired 15 squares of land (approximately 375 acres) along the Indian border at a time when he was serving as a major in 1966. He ousted a number of farmers from their land, who then moved the High Court. When the court decided the matter in his favour in 1986 he had become corps commander and was well on his way to becoming the ISI chief. Many plaintiffs therefore stood down. The land was in Shakargarh in three villages called Adha, Auliya and Bhopa.

As retired officers, Aslam Beg and Hamid Gul had come into big money. Beg floated FRIENDS, a discussion forum that talked about his favourite subject, strategy, before he bravely established a shady political party named Qiadat. Gul followed with his own Tehreek Ittehad Party but it too didn't get off the ground, typically failing to convince him that he had a personality disorder preventing him from grasping why things kept going wrong for him. The Americans facilitated his megalomania as General Zia's top-gun, indirectly allowing him the luxury of making mistakes without being punished for them.

War of Bribes

Barnett R. Rubin in his book, *The Search for Peace in Afghanistan*, writes, 'The 519-strong Afghan shura in Peshawar received 25,000 dollars per member as bribe from the Saudi intelligence agency, which spent 26 million dollars per week during the session. The "deal" was facilitated, according to Rubin, by the ISI chief General Hamid Gul. Sayyaf was active in helping the Moros (Muslims) in the Philippines and had connections with Ramzi Yusuf, later convicted for bombing the Trade Center. Ramzi [who later tried to blow up Benazir Bhutto's house in Karachi and carried out the first attack on the World Trade Center in 1993] had resided in the Laden-funded Bayt al-Shuhada hostel in Peshawar during most of the three years before his arrest.'[10]

Gul's mistakes were ignored by his admirers in the army and among the civilians. His hero-worshipping support to Hekmatyar produced no dividends for Pakistan or General Zia whose instructions the Afghan warlord frequently ignored. The Jalalabad offensive that Gul as ISI chief planned and executed in 1989, relying on Hekmatyar taking on Afghan President Najibullah's army, ended in a massacre of the mujahideen because Hekmatyar never joined the battle.[11] (In 2015, Hekmatyar is with the Islamic State in Afghanistan.) Gul bet on the wrong horse in 1989; in 1995 he didn't back the winning horse when he condemned the Taliban—mainly because it was midwifed by the Bhutto government. He later backtracked and became a champion of the terrorist organization, unfairly enjoying the epithet 'Father of the Taliban' with his usual panache.

The Americans gave Pakistan money and weapons to defeat the Soviet Union and happily agreed that they would not deal directly with the mujahideen. This was the bonanza that created the 'great soldiers' of Pakistan with the freedom to make mistakes of long-term strategy without anyone calling them to account. The diplomatic mails, revealed in WikiLeaks, tells us that Hamid Gul was the most commented on individual in dispatches. A typical item: 'A hawk-like man with laser-black eyes, Gul's animosity toward the United States is well known. But the audacity of his plotting with the Taliban and even al-Qaeda, as represented in the documents, has the ability to shock. If the documents are to be believed, Gul has taken a direct hand in quarterbacking attacks against US-led forces in Afghanistan. Gul calls the reports fiction and nothing else.'

Then there is the more recent record: 'In January 2008 Gul also directed the Taliban to kidnap high-level United Nations personnel in Afghanistan to trade for captured Pakistani soldiers, according to another report. The [Taliban] group led by [Qari] Naqibullah is working with the coordination of retired Pakistani General Hamid Gul. This group is targeting UN vehicles marked with black lettering, which Naqibullah believes is an indicator that the vehicle is carrying high level UN officials or members of the UN intelligence service.'

In 2008, the Bush administration forwarded a two-page unsigned document to Pakistan highlighting Gul's involvement with the Taliban and al-Qaeda networks, saying: 'Hamid Gul was a regular contact for Sirajuddin Haqqani and regularly apprised Sirajuddin of Pakistan government activity in the Federally Administered Tribal Areas (FATA). As of early 2007, Gul was involved in spotting, assessing, and recruiting young men from various Pakistani madrasas for training in eventual attacks against the US-led coalition in Afghanistan.'

In a 2009 interview given to a London-based Arab journal *Asharq Al-Awsat*, Gul boasted that when 'he sent his two sons to jihad' against the Soviet forces 'along with the Afghan jihadi leader Jalaluddin Haqqani' it was on the general pattern of ISI officers pursuing state policy without letting their personal friendships with the Taliban get in the way: 'I am a retired official but the al-Qaeda Afghan elements—Abdul Rasul Sayyaf, Karzai and others—are against Pakistan, but they are my friends.'

Gul followed one policy without contradiction: that of being on the right side of whoever is army chief. He ran afoul of General Musharraf, however; but it was less on the point of Musharraf's betrayal of jihad after 2001 and more because Gul's big-time bus-service enterprise in Rawalpindi—set up with money borrowed from Askari Bank—faced a financial shipwreck and Musharraf didn't bail him out. Before his death, as Musharraf faced a treason trial, Gul called him 'a man I never liked'.

Copyright Acknowledgements

Ahmed, Khaled. 'Can't Talk Peace to the Terrorist'. 20 September 2013. *The Indian Express.* http://archive.indianexpress.com/news/cant-talk-peace-to-the-terrorist/1171482/0.

Ahmed, Khaled. 'At the Table, with Taliban'. 5 February 2014. *The Indian Express.* http://indianexpress.com/article/opinion/columns/at-the-table-with-taliban/.

Ahmed, Khaled. 'The Pipe Dream of Peace'. 12 February 2014. *The Indian Express.* http://indianexpress.com/article/opinion/columns/the-pipe-dream-of-peace/.

Ahmed, Khaled. 'Rise of the Mob'. 4 September 2014. *The Indian Express.* http://indianexpress.com/article/opinion/columns/rise-of-the-mob/.

Ahmed, Khaled. 'Talking in Vain'. 22 September 2014. *The Indian Express.* http://indianexpress.com/article/opinion/columns/talking-in-vain/.

Ahmed, Khaled. 'Can the Taliban Be Far Behind?' 21 March 2014. *The Indian Express.* http://indianexpress.com/article/opinion/columns/can-the-taliban-be-far-behind/.

Ahmed, Khaled. 'It Made China See Red'. 6 February 2016. *The Indian Express.* http://indianexpress.com/article/opinion/columns/it-made-china-see-red-lal-masjid/.

Ahmed, Khaled. 'Touching Foot in Pakistan'. 9 August 2014. *The Indian Express.* http://indianexpress.com/article/opinion/columns/touching-foot-in-pakistan/.

Ahmed, Khaled. 'Modi-watching in Pakistan'. 22 May 2014. *The Indian Express.* http://indianexpress.com/article/opinion/columns/modi-watching-in-pakistan/).

Ahmed, Khaled. 'When Reality Outruns Strategy'. 3 May 2014. *The Indian Express.* http://indianexpress.com/article/opinion/columns/when-reality-outruns-strategy/.

~

AG Publications (Private) Limited, which produces *Newsweek* Pakistan under license from *Newsweek*, LLC, New York, has no objections whatsoever to Mr Ahmed's work for *Newsweek* Pakistan being reproduced in the book. Grateful acknowledgement is made to *Newsweek* Pakistan for permission to reprint the articles appearing on the following dates:

2013: 18 January, 22 January, 15 February, 4 June, 8 June, 10 June, 2 August, 21 September, 2 November, 15 November and 16 December.

2014: 1 January, 13 January, 2 February, 13 March, 16 March, 20 March, 6 April, 14 April, 8 May, 10 May, 21 May, 30 June and 15 September.

2015: 7 January, 10 January, 5 April, 2 August and 21 October.

Notes

Chapter 1: Terrorism, Ideology and the Crumbling State

1. Roy, Olivier. *Secularism confronts Islam*. Columbia University Press, 2007, p.43.
2. al-Ḥadith, Dar. 'Urdu Translation of Ayman al-Zawahiri's "The Morning and the Lantern"'. *Views from the Occident*. 22 December 2009. http://occident2.blogspot.com/2009/12/urdu-translation-of-ayman-al-zawahiris.html.
3. Khan wrote the book after his retirement from the Foreign Office; see, Khan, Riaz Muhammad. *Afghanistan and Pakistan: Conflict, Extremism and Resistance to Modernity*. Oxford, UK: Oxford University Press, 2013.
4. Khan, Riaz Muhammad. *Afghanistan and Pakistan: Conflict, Extremism and Resistance to Modernity*. Oxford, UK: Oxford University Press, 2013, p.278.

Chapter 2: A War Waiting to Be Waged

1. Brown, Vahid and Don Rassler. *Fountainhead of Jihad: The Haqqani Nexus, 1973–2012*. Oxford University Press, 2013, p.9.

2. *Ibid.*, p.9.
3. Waldman, Matt. *The Sun in the Sky: The Relationship between Pakistan's ISI and Afghan Insurgents.* Discussion Paper 18. Carr Center for Human Rights Policy, Kennedy School of Government, Harvard University, June 2010.
4. Lieven, Anatol. *Pakistan: A Hard Country.* London: Allen Lane, 2011, p. 185.
5. Buchanan, Patrick J. 'The American Way of Abandonment'. 2 November 2009. Patrick J. Buchanan Official Website. http://buchanan.org/blog/the-american-way-of-abandonment-2816.
6. Nabi, Ijaz. 'Most Disfavored Nation'. 2 April 2014. *Newsweek* Pakistan. http://newsweekpakistan.com/most-disfavored-nation/.

Chapter 3: Owning the War against Terrorism

1. Khan, Riaz Muhammad. *Afghanistan and Pakistan: Conflict, Extremism and Resistance to Modernity.* Karachi: Oxford University Press, 2013, p.54.
2. The same month the author was mysteriously asked by the military Command and Staff College, Islamabad, to lecture on extremism, probably on the basis of the following observation made in a column: 'But intolerance springs from other sources as well. One source is the traditional society where conservatism, as opposed to modernism, is the natural instinct. A traditional society seeks to interpret the present as an extension of the past; a modern society will connect the present with the future. The conservative person, dwelling on the past, will cultivate certitude as his basis of argument; the modern man, uncertain about the future and accepting social change, will cultivate uncertainty or doubt as the basis of his argument. It is self-doubt and questioning that causes one to accept someone who is different.' (For the full article, see: Ahmed, Khaled. 'Roots of Our Intolerance'. 22 May 2011. *Express Tribune.*)

Chapter 4: A Revolution against Democracy

1. Lal, Deepak. *In Praise of Empires: Globalization and Order.* New York: Palgrave Macmillan, 2004.

2. Khan, Imran. *Pakistan: A Personal History*. Ealing, United Kingdom: Bantam Press, 2011.
3. *Ibid.*, p.89.
4. *Ibid.*, p.93.
5. *Ibid.*, p.189.
6. *Ibid.*, p.120.
7. Committee to Protect Journalists. http://cpj.org/tags/Hamid%20 Mir.

Chapter 5: Ground Zero Karachi

1. Shahzad, Saleem. Pakistan's Military under Al-Qaeda Attack. 24 May 2011. Asia Times Online. http://www.atimes.com/atimes/ South_Asia/ME24Df02.html.
2. Abbasi was convicted of attempting a coup in 1995, which would have arguably killed the incumbent prime minister, Benazir Bhutto, and her cabinet and imposed Islamic sharia. Abbasi was a typical Islamic fanatic in the army who, after a 'cover' posting at the High Commission of Pakistan in New Delhi, was caught in a sting operation, beaten up and deported by the Indian government to Pakistan. After an undeserved promotion and a bungled operation, Abbasi was posted to the strategic northern areas to the army headquarters in Rawalpindi. It was the GHQ from where he tried ultimately to mount his quixotic coup. Given a mild, seven-year sentence by a court martial, he got out of jail in 1999 instead of 2002, after being pardoned by the new army chief cum president, General Pervez Musharraf.

Chapter 7: Penetrated by Al-Qaeda

1. Shahzad, Syed Saleem. *Inside Al-Qaeda and the Taliban: Beyond 9/11*. London: Pluto Press, 2011, p.9.
2. Hussain, Zahid. *The Scorpion's Tail: The Relentless Rise of Islamic Militants in Pakistan—And How It Threatens America*. New York: Free Press, 2010, p.71.
3. See, Schofield, Carey. *Inside the Pakistan Army: A Woman's Experience on the Frontline of the War on Terror*. London:

Biteback Publishing, 2011. The last chapter of this book had an insider view of the army and was used by Major General Feisal Alavi to publish his letter in the *London Times* predicting his own death. The *Herald* of April 2009 reported how involved officers serving in the army were with terrorism. Major Haroon Ashiq, who killed Alvi Major Haroon Ashiq, hailing from the Punjari village in Pakistan-administered Kashmir, retired from the army in 2001. He became a supporter of Lashkar-e-Taiba (LT) after he met its chief, Hafiz Saeed, in 2000 in Lahore and had later also met LT commander, Abdul Rehman Lakhvi. Immediately after his retirement, Ashiq formally joined LT as an adviser and moved to Muzaffarabad. In December 2003, he developed differences with Lakhvi and moved to Karachi to set up a garment business and begin a normal life. But old habits die hard, and Ashiq was back in Lahore by 2007. 'This is when I once again revived my contacts with the Taliban militia,' his statement says. 'I had 150 to 200 mortar guns that I had gotten manufactured during my days with LT. I sent these to [Taliban's South Waziristan leader] Maulvi Nazir in Wana.'

4.   A gist extracted from the Introduction of the book. See, Nawaz, Shuja. *Crossed Swords: Pakistan, its Army, and Wars Within*. Karachi: Oxford University Press, 2008.

Chapter 9: The Dacoits of Lyari

1.   Gayer, Laurent. *Karachi: Ordered Disorder and the Struggle for the City*. London: Oxford University Press, 2014, p.160.
2.   *Ibid.*, p.128.
3.   *Ibid.*, p.149.

Chapter 10: The Lal Masjid Secret

1.   7 July 2013. *News*.
2.   Small, Andrew. *The China-Pakistan Axis: Asia's New Geopolitics*. New York: Oxford University Press, 2015; see, Introduction.

3. Hussain, Zahid. *The Scorpion's Tail: The Relentless Rise of Islamic Militants in Pakistan—And How It Threatens America.* New York: Free Press, 2010, p.112.
4. Small, Andrew. *The China-Pakistan Axis: Asia's New Geopolitics.* New York: Oxford University Press, 2015; see, Introduction.
5. *Ibid.*
6. *Ibid.*
7. Hussain, Zahid. *The Scorpion's Tail: The Relentless Rise of Islamic Militants in Pakistan—And How It Threatens America.* New York: Free Press, 2010, p.170.
8. Small, Andrew. *The China-Pakistan Axis: Asia's New Geopolitics.* New York: Oxford University Press, 2015; see, Introduction.
9. Small, Andrew. *The China-Pakistan Axis: Asia's New Geopolitics.* New York: Oxford University Press, 2015, p.91.
10. 23 May 2012. *Dawn.*
11. Burke, Jason. *On the Road to Kandahar: Travels through Conflict in the Islamic World.* London: Macmillan, Thomas Dunne Books, 2006, p.276.

Chapter 11: Side-stepping the Yemen Trap

1. See, Ahmed, Akbar. *The Thistle and the Drone: How America's War on Terror Became a Global War on Tribal Islam.* Washington DC: Brookings Institution Press, 2013, p.107. Apart from Egyptian Atta, who became the poster child for the nineteen hijackers, the group was essentially Yemeni—ten were from the tribes of Asir, whose role in the 9/11 operation was acknowledged by bin Laden himself. Asir's tribes formed the lion's share of the 9/11 perpetrators, including those from Ghamed, Zahran and from the Jani Shahr—all Asir tribes of Yemeni origin. The largest single tribe represented in the group was the Ghamdi tribe of Asir, with four members: brothers Ahmed and Hamza al-Ghamdi, Saeed al-Ghamdi and Ahmad al-Haznawi. Other tribe members from Asir included Abdul Aziz al-Omari and al-Zahrani of the Zahran tribe, the brothers Wail and Waleed al-Shehri, Mohand al-Shehri of the Shahran tribe and Hani Hanjur, who can be identified

with the village of Hanjur, in the Abidah tribal area in Asir, which is a sub-clan of Asir's Qahtan tribe, named after the Yemenis' common ancestor. Ahmed al-Nami was described by the 9/11 Commission Report as being from Asir, and as from Abha, the capital of Asir, by bin Laden. The al-Nami tribe is a sub-clan of the Qahtani Harb tribe. In addition, Fayez Banihammad, who was born in the UAE, may have had family ties to Asir as he attended university there and was also commonly identified as Fayez Ahmed al-Shehri, which would indicate an affiliation with the Shahran tribe of Asir. By providing their full names, they gave a clue to their tribal identity and lineage.

2. See, Davidson, Christopher M. *The United Arab Emirates: A Study in Survival*. Boulder, CO: Lynne Rienner Publishers, 2005, p. 206, p. 244. The author footnoted that his information had come from 'personal interviews, undisclosed locations, 2003': 'Until September 11, 2001, many of the strongly anti-Iranian emirates had favoured a "Sunni axis" comprising the UAE, Saudi Arabia, Pakistan, and the Afghan Taliban, in an effort to curb potential Shia expansion.'

3. Haider, Syed Afzal. *Islami Nazriati Konsal: Irtaqai Safar aur Karkardagi*. Islamabad: Dost Publications, Council of Islamic Ideology—Evolution and Activity, 2006. The book records: 'Dr Maruf Dualibi visited the offices of the council' (p.961). However, the council's own report to the government in December 1981 observed that Hudood laws were discussed by the council and the law ministry 'under the guidance of Dr Maruf Dualibi who was specially detailed by the Government of Saudi Arabia for this purpose'. It seems as if Dr Dualibi sat in on discussions merely as a senior jurist and did not actually frame the laws. In fact, just the opposite happened. The CII report states that the recommendations on Hudood laws made by it were set aside 'at the government level', before their promulgation as an ordinance on 10 February 1979.

Chapter 12: Who Needs 'Big' Leaders?

1. Greenspan, Alan. *The Age of Turbulence: Adventures in a New World*. New York: Penguin Press, 2008, p.336.

2. Singh, Jaswant. *India at Risk: Misconceptions and Misadventures of Security Policy*. New Delhi: Rupa & Company, 2013, p.46.

Chapter 13: Seven Furies that Torment Pakistan

1. Gall, Carlotta. 'What Pakistan Knew About Bin Laden'. 19 March 2014. *New York Times.*
2. Barker, Kim. *The Taliban Shuffle: Strange Days in Afghanistan and Pakistan.* New York: Anchor, 2011, p.144.

Chapter 14: The Afghan National Army

1. 'Kayani Spells Out Threat Posed by Indian Doctrine'. 4 February 2010. *Dawn*: 'In a presentation to Pakistani media, Gen Kayani reiterated his widely reported comments on the Pakistan army's view of the situation in Afghanistan and the way forward there. But the army chief also made it clear that his institution's "frame of reference" for addressing the problems in that country included certain concerns that are India specific. History, unresolved issues, India's military capability and its 'Cold Start' doctrine meant that Pakistan could not afford to let its guard down. Repeating a well-known formulation, Gen Kayani said: "We plan on adversaries' capabilities, not intentions."'
2. Rashid, Ahmed. *Pakistan on the Brink: The Future of Pakistan, Afghanistan, and the West.* London: Penguin UK, 2012, p.121.
3. 16 September 2014. *Wall Street Journal.*

Chapter 15: Jaish Rides Again?

1. Wilson, John. '*The New Face of al-Qaeda in Pakistan*'. 7 October 2004. *Terrorist Monitor*, in *Unmasking Terror: A Global Review of Terrorist Activities.* Washington DC: The Jamestown Foundation, 2006, p.305.

Chapter 16: A Council of Runaway Ideology

1. 11 March 2014. *News.*
2. See, Bhutto, Benazir. *Reconciliation: Islam, Democracy, and the West.* New York: Harper Perennial, Harper Collins, 2008, p.164. Ironically,

the Islamic scholars mentioned by her were condemned in their own countries and, in the case of Arkoun, had to flee to the West. India's Wahiduddin Khan was condemned in Pakistan as a 'BJP mullah' because, sitting in India, he opposed Pakistan's Blasphemy Law, and Khalid Masud was not accepted, on record, by the Pakistani clergy, including Qazi Hussain Ahmad of Jamaat-e-Islami.

Chapter 17: Judiciary Acts Up in South Asia

1. Godbole, Madhav. *The Judiciary and Governance in India*. New Delhi: Rupa & Company, 2009; Introduction.
2. *Ibid.*, Introduction.
3. *Ibid.*, p.23.
4. *Ibid.*, p.121.
5. Noorani, A.G. 'Judicial Activism Run Riot'. 21 August 2010. *Dawn*. http://www.dawn.com/news/843460/judicial-activism-run-riot.
6. Raja, Salman Akram. 'Constitutional Conundrum'. 25 May 2010. *Dawn*. http://www.dawn.com/news/537688/constitutional-conundrum.
7. Ali, Ashtar Ausaf. 'The Exercise of Suo Motu'. 30 March 2010. *Dawn*.
8. 8 March 2013. *Friday Times*.

Chapter 18: Saint Qazi (1938–2013)

1. Khan, Riaz Muhammad. *Afghanistan and Pakistan: Conflict, Extremism and Resistance to Modernity*. Oxford, UK: Oxford University Press, 2013, p.44.

Chapter 19: Grasping Many Thistles

1. Ahmed, Akbar. *The Thistle and the Drone: How America's War on Terror Became a Global War on Tribal Islam*. Washington DC: Brookings Institution Press, 2013, p.334.

2. *Ibid.*, p.107.
3. *Ibid.*, p.107.
4. *Ibid.*, p.107.
5. *Ibid.*, p.334.
6. Markey, Daniel S. *No Exit from Pakistan: America's Tortured Relationship with Islamabad.* New York: Cambridge University Press, 2013, p.73.
7. 24 January 2014. *Friday Times.*

Chapter 20: Lambs to the Slaughter

1. 25 October 2012. *Reuters.*
2. Mousavi, S.A. *The Hazaras of Afghanistan: An Historical, Cultural, Economic and Political Study.* London: Curzon Press, 1998, p.190.

Chapter 23: Dealing in Delusions

1. Haqqani, Husain. *Pakistan: Between Mosque and Military.* Carnegie Endowment for International Peace, 2010, p.4.
2. *Ibid.*, p.4.
3. *Ibid.*, p.272.
4. *Ibid.*, p.273.
5. *Ibid.*, p.274.
6. *Ibid.*, p.276.
7. *Ibid.*, p.288.
8. Malik was also close to Imran Khan, who perhaps sincerely sought advice from him on Khan's next project in the education sector.
9. Talbott, Strobe. *Engaging India: Diplomacy, Democracy, and the Bomb.* Washington DC: Brookings Institution Press, 2004, p.294.
10. *Ibid.*, p.71.
11. *Ibid.*, p.331.
12. *Ibid.*, p. 336.
13. *Ibid.*, p.350.

Chapter 24: NS in DC

1. Shahid, Aziz. *Yeh Khamoshi Kahan Tak*: *Ek Sipahi ki Dastan-e-Ishq-o-Junoon*. 2013, p.271.
2. October 2013. *Newsline*.
3. Goldberg, Jeffrey. 'Ex-Pakistani Ambassador: My Country Supports Terrorism'. 22 October 2013. *Bloomberg*.

Chapter 25: Breaking through in Balochistan?

1. 29 March 2011. *Guardian*.
2. Grare, Frederic. 'Balochistan: The State versus the Nation'. 11 April 2013. Carnegie Endowment for International Peace.

Chapter 29: Terrorists as Martyrs

1. Haqqani, Husain. *Magnificent Delusions: Pakistan, the United States, and an Epic History of Misunderstanding*. New York City: PublicAffairs, Perseus Books, 2013.

Chapter 30: Monster or Milestone?

1. Riedel, Bruce. *Deadly Embrace: Pakistan, America, and the Future of Global Jihad*. Washington DC: Brookings Institution Press, 2011.

Chapter 32: Three Game-changing Deaths

1. See, Saikal, Amin. *Modern Afghanistan: A History of Struggle and Survival*. London: I. B. Tauris, 2004, p. 223: 'The "godfather" of the Taliban was essentially Pakistan's Minister of the Interior, Naseerullah Babar. In late 1994, he recruited, trained and armed a number of madrasa students to join a few former Pashtun Mujahideen fighters from southern Afghanistan to provide protection for a Pakistani convoy en route to Central Asia through

Afghanistan. The initial success of the group, which assumed the name "Taliban" (Islamic students) immediately received approbation of Pakistan's military/ISI leadership as well as Mawlana Fazlur Rahman, the leader of the Jamiat-e Ulema Islam party, who was a coalition partner of Benazir Bhutto and also headed the foreign affairs committee of the Pakistani parliament.'

2. Gannon, Kathy. *I is for Infidel: From Holy War to Holy Terror, 18 Years in Afghanistan*. New York City: PublicAffairs, Perseus Books, 2005, p.93.

3. Lamb, Christina. *Farewell Kabul: From Afghanistan to a More Dangerous World*. London: Harper Collins, 2015, p.109.

4. *Ibid.*, p.109.

5. Gall, Carlotta. *The Wrong Enemy: America in Afghanistan 2001– 2014*. Boston: Houghton Mifflin, 2015, p.35.

6. Coll, Steve. 'Looking for Mullah Omar'. 23 January 2012. *New Yorker*.   http://www.newyorker.com/magazine/2012/01/23/ looking-for-mullah-omar.

7. 4 August 2015. *National Interest*.

8. See, Tomsen, Peter. 'US Envoy to Afghanistan from 1989–1992'. In *The Wars of Afghanistan: Messianic Terrorism, Tribal Conflicts, and the Failures of Great Powers*. New York City: PublicAffairs, Perseus Books, 2011, p.256: 'Hamid Gul brazenly rigged the 1988 1989-1992 election, denying Bhutto's PPP a clear majority. His ISI pieced together an anti-PPP coalition, the Islami Jamhuri Ittehad (IJI), that gave a leading role to Qazi Hussain Ahmad's Jamaat-e-Islami Party. Nawaz Sharif attached his Muslim League Party, the second largest after Bhutto's PPP, to the ISI-manufactured coalition. Military Intelligence Director Durrani later admitted in a public affidavit to Pakistan's Supreme Court that Beg ordered him to provide "logistical support" to the IJI.'

9. Malik, Tahir, Bonney, Richard and Tridev Singh Maini (eds.). *Warriors after War: Indian and Pakistani Retired Military Leaders Reflect on Relations between the Two Countries, Past, Present and Future*. Pieterlen: Peter Lang AG, 2011, p.144.

10. Rubin, Barnett R. *The Search for Peace in Afghanistan: From Buffer State to Failed State.* Connecticut: Yale University Press, 1995, p.95.

11. See, Riedel, Bruce. *Deadly Embrace: Pakistan, America, and the Future of Global Jihad.* Washington DC: Brookings Institution Press, 2011, p. 39: 'This turn of events was due in part to a strategic miscalculation by the new ISI director, Hamid Gul. Now that the Soviet forces were gone, Gul decided the mujahedin should move from guerrilla tactics to conventional warfare. The first target would be the city of Jalalabad, on the road from the Khyber Pass to Kabul. The siege that followed would be a terrible mistake. The Afghan communist army held off the mujahedin, and the stalemate led to bitter recriminations within the mujahedin factions. After the debacle, Bhutto engineered Gul's removal from the ISI leadership, whereupon he became a public advocate for the Taliban, the Kashmiri insurgency, and Osama bin Laden, later blaming 9/11 on Israel's Mossad and calling it an excuse for US intervention in Afghanistan. Just before her assassination in 2007, Benazir claimed he was plotting her murder.'

Index